PUBLIC BROADCASTING
FOR THE
21st CENTURY

Edited By

Marc Raboy

Acamedia Monograph 17

UNIVERSITY
UP of
LUTON PRESS

British Library Cataloguing in Publication Data
A catalogue record for this book is available from the British Library

ISBN: 1 86020 006 0
ISSN: 0956-9057

Series Editor: Manuel Alvarado

Published by
John Libbey Media
Faculty of Humanities
University of Luton
75 Castle Street
Luton, Bedfordshire LU1 3AJ
England

PUBLIC BROADCASTING
FOR THE
21st CENTURY

CONTENTS

PART ONE

Shifting Paradigms in the Heartlands of Public Broadcasting

PART TWO

Emerging Models for Development and Democracy

FOREWORD

Pierre Juneau
World Radio and Television Council

When broadcasting was invented in the 1920s, the leaders of our societies marvelled at its promises and at what this extraordinary instrument could do for culture, education, and information. Prime ministers, presidents, and many political leaders were immensely excited by the potential of this new media for the betterment of society. For instance, the Secretary of Commerce of the United States, Herbert Hoover, who later became a Republican president, expressed the view that radio communication was not to be considered as merely a business carried on for private gain; it was a public concern impressed with the public trust, and public interest had to be paramount.

Nowadays, the rhetoric remains, and it includes television; however, the will to make proper use of these technologies has weakened. Policy makers in all countries have allowed radio and television to become overwhelmingly trivial and shallow, and, more and more, it has become a marketing vehicle. Having started in North America, this development has spread quickly to European broadcasting and is reaching the rest of the world. Developing countries will not be spared, despite their evident need for a kind of television that pays careful attention to the cultural, social, educational, and economic needs of people. In these countries, as elsewhere in the world, television viewers are naturally entitled to some distraction on the small screen, and the role that can be played by comedy or drama in expressing culture and identity, together with people's hopes and sorrows, is well known. Nevertheless, should we not be concerned about the possibility that such extraordinary instruments of communication might be completely dominated by industries catering to audiences not as citizens but as mere consumers to be delivered to the business of advertising?

The communications landscape has undergone obvious changes that can only continue. More and more television services are becoming available – another trend that is certain to continue. In liberal democracies, governments and regulatory bodies find they have little room to manoeuvre. They are faced with a host of socio-economic pressures militating in favour of a greater number of channels; demand from audiences for access to the wonders of new technologies; competitive pressures from neighbouring countries that have been faster off the mark with new services; and pressures from business interests that want to develop these new services and from advertisers who are always on the lookout for new ways of delivering their messages.

A further factor to consider is the great fascination audiovisual activities have held for young people over the last several decades, which has also played a part in the proliferation of television services around the world. All these social pressures are making their effects felt.

The multichannel television universe is made possible by the increased number of delivery vehicles available – Hertzian waves, co-axial cable, fibre optics, satellites, digitalization, and the compression of signals. This increase in the number of channels will inevitably lead to even greater competition among broadcasters for the attention of television viewers. Notwithstanding the effervescent eloquence about the electronic highways, an overwhelming proportion of people will continue to remain attentive to radio and television as we know them.

In North America and in countries of western Europe, people spend on average three hours every day watching television or listening to radio. Since many don't watch at all, this means that others watch or listen a lot more. Business organizations spend billions of dollars to reach these audiences with their commercial messages, and politicians, rightly or wrongly, often think that radio and television are the key to their success or the cause of their failure.

So why is it that we have not used these media more often, more actively, more imaginatively for educational, cultural, and social development? Certainly, we should not condemn all of contemporary broadcasting, but there is no doubt that the fear that commercial advertising might drag broadcasting in the direction of shallow amusement and triviality, rather than in the direction of social and cultural development, was well founded.

As years went by, the development of broadcasting in North America, western Europe, and Japan was indeed driven – with very few exceptions – by the logic of the advertising business and the entertainment industry – the "fun industry." In the ratings game that brutally controls the industry, success and failure have been measured not in days, weeks, or months, but in terms of minutes and even seconds. These successes and failures have translated into revenues amounting to millions, if not billions, of dollars.

In a strictly commercial, competitive system, programming that lowers ratings is out. What sticks are entertainment formulas with a proven ability to draw large audiences. An integral part of this approach is the systematic use of violence, along with the ruthless suppression of programs which might demand too much concentration from the viewer, or whose subtleties might have a dampening effect on the pace of the action or the viewer's emotional state.

A further trend is the extent to which even public television networks often feel obliged – or are, in fact, compelled by financial constraints – to compete with private sector television. Public broadcasters, both large and small, are faced with a difficult quandary. They make use of a medium that has traditionally addressed mass audiences, which means competing with commercial broadcasters, who, by each quarter of an hour, have to deliver the largest possible audiences to their advertisers. If, on one hand, the audience for a public broadcaster is too small, its political and bureaucratic masters may consider it to be an elitist luxury. If, on the other hand, a public broadcaster tries to expand its audience by resorting to more "light-weight" programmes like those offered by private competition, then the purpose served by the public broadcaster is questioned. Therefore, when one looks at the nature of television in so called Western countries, or one listens to most of radio, it is normal to wonder, for instance, whether these media can really serve development in countries of the South. It is not surprising that people who, by their occupation, have to deal with very concrete issues of society like housing, unemployment, poverty, health, migrations, violence, and the development of poorer countries do not put broadcasting at the top of public priorities.

However, the consequence of this chain of circumstances is that countries in the South or in the East, developing countries, or countries that are emerging from totalitarian regimes may not benefit from media systems dedicated to imparting knowledge and to understanding themselves, their society, their problems, and their future. Very often, through a sort of dumping process, they are most likely to inherit the by-products of our Western fun industry.

We are facing a problem here that obviously applies not only to the role of broadcasting as an instrument of development for poorer countries but to its role in richer societies as well. In a speech to the World Economic Forum in Davos, Switzerland, in February 1992, Vaclav Havel, President of the Czech Republic, described what he considered to be some of the greater problems of civilization. After referring to some of the key contemporary environmental issues, he went on to list "the dramatically widening gap between the rich North and the poor South, the danger of famine, the depletion of the biosphere and the mineral resources of the planet" and "the expansion of commercial television culture" as part of what he called "the general threat to mankind."

If this appears to be a too pessimistic or exaggerated perception, it may be because the communications environment that has developed around us is so overwhelming that we have become accustomed to it, and we find it difficult even to imagine any other set of circumstances. Perhaps we have lost the capacity to react, and, therefore, we need philosophers and dramatists like Havel to alert us to the drama of our world.

The misgivings concerning the perception of frivolity or triviality that our radio and television programming often projects may well be founded, but why must we accept this state of affairs as a basis for national or world policy? Why can't we now react like those who marvelled at the potential of broadcasting technology at the outset, and why can't we try to imagine how it could be used? Why not use the media much more imaginatively so that the media in developing countries can help people to understand the problems and possibilities of their own societies?

Isn't democracy the constant and progressive improvement in the level of participation by all citizens in the decisions affecting their lives? Democracy is not just the greater ability of professionals – politicians, professors, accountants, engineers, officials, artists, or thinkers – to run, manage, or debate the affairs of the community. This is why those media which are accessible to ordinary people and which can address society as a whole can be so strategic, provided they are used for the benefit of citizens and not only as a vehicle to reach potential consumers.

There is a great deal of talk and excitement about the accelerating pace of technological development in electronic communications. The constant reference to the information highway has become a somewhat fastidious cliche carried by a ubiquitous bandwagon. At the same time as so many are waving their hands on that bandwagon, can anyone seriously claim that there is a great improvement in the content of the media that most people watch and listen to – these ordinary people who are the basis of democracy? Yes, there is – and there will continue to be – a remarkable improvement in the communication technology that serves business, industry, government, and academia; however, there is hardly any improvement in the way we use the "community media" – that is, radio and television. Will we in fact have a sophisticated information highway for business, government, and academia, as well as fun and games for the majority of people – " for the masses," as the phrase used to go?

Northern-owned satellites – mostly American – are now beaming the output of our fun industries to all countries of the South, to India and South East Asia, to the Arab world, to China, and to Central Asia, while many of those countries, endeavouring to cope with underdevelopment, lack simple transmitters dedicated to the information and participation of the public, and while artisans lack simple sound recorders, modern typewriters or word processors, and other resources to produce information and knowledge content.

There is hardly any task more important in the broad area of culture than rethinking the role that radio and television could play in education, citizenship, democratic values, and the enlightenment of our societies and their people. To paraphrase Sir Arthur Clarke, who first proposed the concept of the geostationary satellite, technological development will not be the problem. The immense financial interests involved in both technology and commercial entertainment will take care of that. Where both imagination and statesmanship are needed is in the area where profits cannot be the motivation; that is, in providing all people, in developed as well as in developing parts of the world, with the material for the mind and the imagination needed to help make them free citizens and inspired human beings.

ACKNOWLEDGEMENTS

*T*his book began as a project of the World Radio and Television Council, whose president, Pierre Juneau, enthusiastically embraced the idea and was instrumental in generating the necessary institutional support.

The Communication Division of UNESCO, the Canadian International Development Agency (CIDA), and the University of Montreal each provided important moral and financial assistance. The planned publication of a condensed version of the book in UNESCO's *Reports and Papers on Mass Communication* series will provide additional circulation of the material.

A number of individuals were crucial to moving the project through its various stages: Alain Modoux, Carlos Arnaldo, Kwame Boafo, and Tarja Virtanen of the UNESCO secretariat in Paris; Gabrielle Mathieu of CIDA in Ottawa; Myriam Amzallag, Jean-Louis Fortin, and Roxanne Welters of the University of Montreal; Paul-Emile Lany and Catherine Ailleri of the World Radio and Television Council; Manuel Alvarado of John Libbey and Co. Ltd.; and free-lance editor Tessa McWatt.

Normally, in a project of this kind, the final result is its own reward, but I would be remiss not to underscore the generosity of the contributors, who responded to all our insistent demands with grace and professionalism.

Marc Raboy
University of Montreal
August 1995

PREFACE

*T*he essays collected in this book provide a general portrait of the situation of public broadcasting in different parts of the world. The overall purpose in commissioning them was neither to achieve geographic balance nor representation of particular types of countries, but rather to identify the strengths and weaknesses of existing public broadcasting systems, the challenges they face, and the possibilities of establishing new broadcasting institutions based on public service ideals. Such an exercise is necessarily fraught with pitfalls and will require some indulgence on the part of the reader. The selection presented here is meant to be inclusive rather than exhaustive, insofar as it aims to provide an accurate portrayal of existing types, without pretending to cover every particular situation.

Despite the rapid movement toward globalization, broadcasting is still legally constituted within the confines of national borders. Despite the great variety in degree of attention by the world's 200-odd national states, every state must at some point make fundamental decisions about broadcasting, if only to consider the allocation of frequencies to which it is entitled by international conventions. The immediate result of these decisions is a national broadcasting system in every country, made up of one or more component parts.

Within this basic structural framework, one finds a rather wide array of different systemic and institutional broadcast models. Some of these are well-known, well-established, and provide the basis for most conventional notions about public service broadcasting. Others are in more of a state of flux, or emergence, and are rapidly developing with a close eye on the changes taking place within the established systems. The material in this book consists of an equal number of contributions from each of these broad, general categories. Every one of them focusses on one or more specific aspects of what is becoming increasingly a world system. An introductory chapter attempts to elaborate on this by situating public service broadcasting in the global context.

Each of the individual contributions is an author's highly personal view of the problems of public broadcasting as seen from a particular geopolitical perspective. In this respect, the individual chapters should not be read as a collection of national reports. While clearly informative of the situations prevailing in each of the countries or regions the authors describe, these are largely critical perspectives, sometimes highly critical of the various institutional entanglements they scrutinize, while supportive of the ideals that the institutional arrangements are presumably designed to meet. The result is a series of ways of seeing the actual and potential role of public service broadcasting on the eve of the twenty-first century.

Introduction

Public Service Broadcasting in the Context of Globalization[1]

Marc Raboy

*T*he changing environment of broadcasting is on various agendas, from the Council of Europe to the numerous national states grappling with the challenges to their national communications systems; and from the G7 and its grand design for a global information highway to the burgeoning number of non-governmental organizations active in the field of mass communication. At the heart of these debates is the question of the present and future status of public service broadcasting.

Meeting in Prague in December 1994, the Council of Europe's Fourth European Ministerial Conference on Mass Media Policy identified the safeguarding of independent, appropriately funded public service broadcasting institutions as essential to the functioning of the media in a democratic society. The council's draft resolution on the future of public service broadcasting included a nine-point mission statement reiterating, from a particularly European perspective, the traditional objectives of public service broadcasting.[2]

Such statements, for all their worth, also point to the obstacles faced by conventional public service broadcasting in the current global context. In the contemporary debates on the changing environment of mass communication, there is no shortage of earnest outlines of goals and objectives for media with aims other than business or propaganda. There is no shortage of goodwill or good ideas, but the realization of the ideals of public service broadcasting is rendered problematic by a series of political, economic, technological, ideological, and developmental constraints.

In many parts of the world, the problem is still totalitarianism and the equation of the public interest with the particular interests of the national state. Where totalitarianism has been overcome, the problems facing media in the transition to democracy are often the best example of the problems of democratization generally. In eastern Europe, in most of Africa, and in much of the rest of the "transitional" world, public service broadcasting is a distant ideal, not a working reality. In those countries where the leadership has embraced that ideal, the lack of a receptive political and professional culture is often the next hurdle. Where neo-totalitarian or neo-colonial governments seek to retain power at all cost, the lack of autonomy of national media is also a problem of political will.

In the heartland of traditional public service broadcasting, western Europe (and in countries with similar systems such as Canada, Australia, and Japan) the trend toward liberalization and market reform mixed with a lack of official faith in the continued importance of public service broadcasting leads to a syndrome where precious experience is being washed away. Problems of financing, mandate, and interpretations of purpose are all indications of a more fundamental problem of political will.

National peculiarities apart, questions concerning the structures of broadcasting are increasingly global ones. In the new broadcasting environment, the issue of public service broadcasting can be reduced to this: What social and cultural goals attributed to broadcasting require a specially mandated, non-commercially driven organization, publicly owned, publicly funded to the extent necessary, and publicly accountable?

Broadcasters, politicians, media professionals and creative people, community activists, and scholars worldwide are wrestling with this question today. While the diagnosis is global, the prescriptions are necessarily context-specific. When we put them together, however, we find in the range of models, examples, and ways of framing the issues the basis for a global portrait of the issues and a sketch of a solution.

Fifteen years ago, when the International Commission on the Study of Communication Problems chaired by the late Sean MacBride reported to UNESCO, the structure of the world's broadcasting systems was a relatively unproblematic affair. The subject occupied a mere two pages in the MacBride Report, where public service broadcasting did not even require a separate index entry (UNESCO1980).

In 1980, national broadcasting systems could be typed according to the prevailing political systems in each of the countries concerned. Most European countries had a single monopoly broadcaster – although operating according to very different sets of principles in the west and in the east. In Africa, too, national broadcasting was strictly government – owned and – operated. At the other extreme, the American free enterprise model of broadcasting was operational in most of Asia and the Americas (with notable exceptions). The number of countries with "mixed" systems was small (the MacBride report mentioned the United Kingdom (UK), Japan, Australia, Canada, and Finland). Where it existed, community broadcasting was a strictly local, marginalized phenomenon with few links to the mainstream. In 1980, the letters CNN did not have the evocative authority they do today. [3]

Since that time – need we say it? – the world has changed. The evolution of broadcasting has been marked by three sets of parallel developments: (1) the explosion in channel capacity and disappearance of audiovisual borders made possible by new technology; (2) the disintegration of the state broadcasting model with the collapse of the socialist bloc and the move toward democratization in various parts of the world; and (3) the upsurge in market broadcasting and the introduction of mixed broadcasting systems in the countries with former public service monopolies.

Far from distinct from one another, these phenomena are in complex interrelationship with respect to the emergence of new forms of broadcasting, locally, nationally, and internationally. The consolidation of a world broadcasting market has been abetted by the collapse of the iron curtain, just as that process was accelerated by the technological obsolescence of attempts to control access to information and the means of communication.

At the same time, the re-evaluation of welfare capitalism – spurred on by an uneasy marriage of ideological and economic considerations – coinciding with the arrival of the new generation of broadcasting technologies has further strengthened the market model and undermined the view that broadcasting is a sphere of activity analogous to education or health care – that is to say, a primarily social and cultural rather than an economic or political activity (see Servaes 1993: 327).[4]

Until the 1980s, television was widespread mainly in the OECD and Soviet bloc countries.[5] Since then, the number of sets has tripled, although it is still unevenly distributed, and the number of satellite stations has gone from zero to 300 (although there are still only two really global channels: Turner's CNN and Viacom's MTV).[6] In 1980, there were 40 channels in Europe; today there are 150.

In 1993, every American home paid $30 per month for its "free" television, via the cost of advertising passed on to consumers; the new broadcasting industry economics will be a dog's breakfast of advertising, subscription, and pay-per-view. However, people watch only around seven channels, so the more choice there is, the less likely it is that any particular one will be among them, which is not heartening news for broadcasters.

One of the characteristics of the current context which easily leads to confusion is the blurring of distinctions between formerly distinct activities: broadcasting and narrowcasting; broadcasting and telecommunication; and public and private broadcasting. The recent policy debates surrounding the information highway have seen a flurry of new alliances and repositioning of broadcasting industry players nationally and internationally, private and public. Broadcasting will henceforth be evolving in a more complex multimedia environment, and its previous subdivisions into distinct "domains" such as terrestrial, cable, and satellite broadcasting are quickly becoming obsolete. Questions concerning the future of public service broadcasting will be played out and resolved in a broader policy framework. This framework consists of both greater constraints as well as new possibilities, but the principal normative question will remain: What should be the public function of broadcasting in a democracy? (van Cuilenburg and Slaa 1993).

The context of technological convergence and the accompanying policy debates can help to clarify the concept of public service with respect to media generally and, hence, to develop a more appropriate conception of public service broadcasting. In telecommunication, the concept of universal public service has been much more clear and straightforward than in broadcasting. The principle of universality has been tied to the operational provision of affordable access (not an issue in broadcasting as long as the main means of transmission was over-the-air, but increasingly so with the addition of various tiers of chargeable services).

The displacement of universal service by subscriber-based and pay-per view services is the strongest factor favouring a shift toward the consumer model in broadcasting and needs to be countered by policy measures and institutional mechanisms to promote the democratic function of broadcasting. This can only come about through a rethinking of what we mean by public service broadcasting.

Broadcasting may be the quintessential cultural industry (Sinclair 1994); it is increasingly the closest thing we have to a universal cultural form (Collins 1990). Until recently, "national" broadcasting systems were seen to be the main vehicles through which the national culture was sure to be reflected and, with the obvious exception of the United States, success in this respect was tied to a national *public* broadcasting system. National broadcasting systems are now, for the most part, more broadly constituted and, at the same time, national broadcasters control a decreasing share of every country's audiovisual space (Caron and Juneau 1992). But are their messages any less prominent in national consciousness? This question is an extremely difficult one to answer with any degree of certainty.

One important aspect of this question is to recognize the problematic nature of national identity itself. Identity today is increasingly multifaceted, and national identity is a particularly contested issue in many countries, even among some of the most politically stable. This poses another challenge to broadcasting, which has traditionally been organized at the national level. Where public broadcasting has been well-established, it has almost invariably been through the presence of a strong, often highly centralized national public broadcaster. It is not only the external pressures of globalization that challenge this model today, but also the internal pressures brought about by the fragmentation of traditional notions of nationhood (see Pietersee 1994). If public service broadcasting is to speak to the real concerns of its public, it has to rethink its approach to one of its most cherished objectives: the cementing of national unity. This task may be especially difficult for politicians to accept.

Traditionally, public service broadcasting has been expected to represent the national as opposed to the foreign. It may be time to refocus these conceptual categories in terms of the local and the global. There is a certain universal appeal to the products of Hollywood-based mass culture – that is, ultimately, the only possible explanation for their success. At the same time, specific publics will be interested in specific types of broadcasting programming. The global cultural industry recognizes this by developing products targeted to "niche markets." Public broadcasting has a different role, principally by conceiving its audience as a public rather than a market. Some programmes may speak to a particular national public, but on any given national territory there will be less-than-national broadcasting needs to be fulfilled. National networks, publicly or privately owned, can no longer be expected to be forces of cohesion; they can, however, be highly effective distribution systems for programmes of importance to the communities they serve. For this to occur, we need a new definition of public service broadcasting suitable to a new public culture, global in scope and experienced locally.

The idea of public service broadcasting is not intrinsically tied to that of nationhood over that of the public, nor is broadcasting, as a form of communication, tied necessarily to community (see Carey 1989). Therefore, we need to take a fresh look at public service broadcasting in the context of a changing role for the still present, still formidable (for lack of a structure to replace it) nation state. As the alternative to the state becomes the market, the alternative to public service broadcasting is constructed as private sector broadcasting; this parallel is logically flawed as well as politically short-sighted. The globalization of markets is both global and local (global products are usually produced in a single place, distributed worldwide and consumed locally, everywhere). As the nation state is left marooned between the global and the particular (Ellis 1994), so is public service broadcasting, which might explain the success of specialty services and the economies of scale justified by global products in search of small local markets. It is false to assume, however, that there is no longer a social need for public service broadcasting; it rather demands redefinition, for as John Ellis (1994) has stated, only public service broadcasting "puts a social agenda before a market agenda."

What is Public Service Broadcasting?

In this context, the idea of public service broadcasting stands out more boldly than any of the existing structures set up to manage broadcasting in its name.

It is rooted in the enlightenment notion of the public and of a public space in which social and political life democratically unfolds (Habermas 1989), as well as in the tradition of independent, publicly organized broadcasting organizations created to deliver radio programmes to audiences in the period between the two world wars.

In some cases, public service broadcasting refers to one or more institutions, while in others it is an ideal (Syvertsen 1992). Thus, in some countries, public service broadcasting refers to a particular organization or sector of the broadcasting system, while in others the entire system may be viewed as a public service. In some cases, public service broadcasting is seen as a developmental goal to be achieved. While in many cases public service broadcasting may indeed be in "crisis" (see Rowland and Tracey 1990), the ideal that it represents is certainly very much alive.

It is unnecessary here to review the origins of public service broadcasting, except to recall that both the institution and the ideal (or a certain conception of it) originated in the experience of the BBC and its founder Sir John Reith (see McDonnell 1991). The BBC still stands as the quintessential model of public service broadcasting worldwide, particularly in the view of national governments seeking to establish or to revitalize their broadcasting systems. It is indeed often impossible to separate the idea from the practical example of the institution, but do that we must. While the BBC is probably still the most successful example of a national public service broadcaster, and the UK among the most successful at anticipating and adapting to the new context of broadcasting, it is not necessarily an appropriate or easily transportable model for many situations. The ideal, on the other hand, is a universal one – to the extent that democratic values can be said to be universal.

There is no easy answer to the question of what public service broadcasting is, but a reasonably thorough attempt was made by the UK's now defunct Broadcasting Research Unit (BRU), in a pamphlet first published in 1985 (BRU 1985/1988. See also Barnett and Docherty 1991). The BRU document presented those elements of public service broadcasting which "should be retained within whatever systems are devised to provide broadcasting as new communications technologies come into use. It is not therefore a defence of the existing public-service (broadcasting) institutions as they are today or as they may become; it is concerned with *the whole landscape*" (p.i, emphasis added).

The BRU approach supported the view that broadcasting should be seen as a comprehensive environment. Its main principles can be summarized as follows:

(1) universal accessibility (geographic);
(2) universal appeal (general tastes and interests);
(3) particular attention to minorities;
(4) contribution to sense of national identity and community;
(5) distance from vested interests;
(6) direct funding and universality of payment;
(7) competition in good programming rather than for numbers; and
(8) guidelines that liberate rather than restrict programme makers.

As public service characteristics, this list also points to the inherent pitfalls of such an exercise. While some of the characteristics (eg., accessibility) are straightforward enough, certain others (eg., contribution to a sense of national identity) are highly problematic, insofar as in many states (including the British) the question of nationhood itself is not fully resolved. Distance from vested interests implies an ideal situation where the broadcasting institutions do not have their own vested interests. A notion such as good programming begs the question of taste: Good, according to whom?

The real problem, however, is not how to improve the list but rather how to apply any such set of principles. Indeed, the exercise points to a need to return to even more fundamental values regarding broadcasting and its role in society (see Blumler 1992). It also points to the need to associate the public to the various aspects of broadcasting activity. Robin Foster, reporting to the David Hume Institute in 1992, suggested that viewers and listeners be consulted regarding the level of resources to be put into particular types of programmes – a proposal not likely to be endearing to broadcasters or policy makers, although logical and coherent with respect to both public policy objectives for broadcasting and the prevailing discourse of consumer sovereignty. "As an input into determining the public broadcasting contract, ways should be found of establishing what the *public* wants public broadcasting to be; giving the public involvement in deciding what is provided" (Foster 1992: 31). However, what do we mean by "the public"?

Many authors have endeavoured to reproblematize and redefine our conception of the public in light of the changing nature of late twentieth century mass media (See eg., Curran 1991; Garnham 1992; Dahlgren 1994; Venturelli 1994). If these changes are relatively straightforward for certain actors in the sphere of broadcasting – advertisers, for example, who conceive of their target as a market, or ratings-driven broadcasters who quantify it as an audience – it is not so evident for public service broadcasters and the makers of public policy. "Broadcasting takes place in the public sphere and we come to it both as consumers and as citizens," writes Anthony Smith (1991): "Where commercial broadcasting is linked to the social world by means of markets, public service derives its legitimacy from the role its viewers play as citizens."

The notion of citizenship has severe implications for broadcasting. Citizenship can not be passive. Citizenship is political. Citizenship evokes the image of Tom Paine and the unfinished struggle for "liberty, equality, fraternity" (Keane 1991 1994). When public service broadcasting is linked to the idea of citizenship, it must logically be decoupled from the authoritarian power of the state. At the same time, it can not be commodified. It is not a question of principle but of purpose. The main point of distinction between public service and private sector broadcasting is that the latter is *only* commercially driven, while the former, despite the various shapes and forms it assumes from time to time and place to place, is necessarily propelled by a different logic.

It is critical to understand the subtleties inherent in this distinction. Within the realm of conventional public broadcasting there are two schools of thought regarding commercial activity. One has it that commercial and public service objectives are wholly incompatible and cannot be combined within a single service. The other view is that they can coexist, and public and private broadcasting can compete in the advertising marketplace to the mutual benefit of both. I would like to suggest that there is a third conceptual and structural approach to this question: Assuming that certain activities of broadcasting can be financed commercially and others can not, why not redistribute the benefits of the commercial sector to finance the non-commercial sector? This systemic approach is partially recognized in some countries which legally define their national broadcasting systems as public services, thus legitimating the regulatory intervention of the state; however, it is rarely operationalized through the appropriation of the fruit of lucrative activity to subsidize the rest. It is just assumed – with no basis in logic, only in ideology – that commercially viable broadcasting should be left in the private sector and unprofitable broadcasting activity should be subsidized some other way. On the other hand, one could just as logically argue that, insofar as the social basis of broadcasting is public service, the profits of the lucrative sector should be redistributed within the system. If this is an unlikely formula, it is not because of any conceptual flaw, but because of broadcasting's capture by private industry.

Indeed, the leaders of the global broadcasting industry have turned this idea on its head by claiming that the product they are selling is a public service. As early as 1960, CBS executive Frank Stanton proclaimed that "a program in which a large part of the audience is interested is by that very fact... in the public interest" (quoted in Friendly 1967: 291). More recently, Rupert Murdoch has stated: "Anybody who, within the law of the land, provides a service which the public wants at a price it can afford is providing a public service" (quoted in Ellis 1994: 1). To the extent that "the public" is just another way of describing the aggregate consumer market for broadcasting, they are of course correct, which is why, once again, it is important to get the terminology straight. Meanwhile, the idea of public service broadcasting has been undermined by the erosion of the public commitment to the service that has been provided by existing public broadcasting institutions. In many cases, this erosion has been egged on by the abuse of the term by national governments seeking to use broadcasting for a higher national purpose, claiming that this is in the public interest.

To the contrary, the role of public service broadcasting, as Ellis points out, is to provide a space in which "the emerging culture of multiple identities can negotiate its antagonisms" (Ellis 1994: 14), not cater to accentuating difference, as commercial multichannel broadcasting has a tendency to do. Exploring new possibilities for consensus rather than imposing it is the opposite of the former role of public service broadcasting – which goes quite a way to explaining why the traditional strategies of the major national public service broadcasters no longer work and why they are in trouble as they seek to accommodate a new *raison d'étre*. "We have been so preoccupied by the challenges to Public Service Broadcasting from within broadcasting that we have failed to notice the profound changes that have taken place in the public whom broadcasting is supposed to serve" (Ellis 1994: 16).

Public broadcasting is a public good,[7] but what makes it so is not immediately self-evident, which is what Yves Achille (1994) means when he writes that public service broadcasting is suffering from a crisis of identity. Achille refers to a triple crisis of public service broadcasting: identity, financing, and functioning. If the identity crisis could be resolved, the financial problem – essentially a question of political will – could then be addressed. As to the functional question, in countries with an established public service broadcasting tradition, nothing less than a zero-based review of existing institutional structures can bring public service broadcasting into the twenty-first century with a hope of building public and political support for its new role (see also Atkinson 1993; Paracuellos 1993; Achille and Miège 1994). On the other hand, to many analysts, a public broadcasting system with a mixed ownership structure is still a far preferable guarantee of broadcasting pluralism and diversity than the private enterprise model that is held up as its alternative (Syvertsen 1994).

In a broadcasting environment that treats the public as a body of clients or consumers, the role of public broadcasting is to address people as citizens. Public broadcasting can do this only if it is seen as an instrument of social and cultural development, rather than as a marginal alternative service on the periphery of a vast cultural industry (see Raboy, Bernier, Sauvageau, and Atkinson 1994).[8] This change implies a freshly conceived role for the state, which must see itself more as architect than as engineer; that is to say, the role of the state is to design and facilitate the functioning of a multifaceted national broadcasting system, rather than as the directive patron of a dedicated national broadcaster.

"The crucial choice," as Graham Murdock has written, "is not, as many commentators suppose, between state licensing and control on the one side and minimally regulated market mechanisms on the other. It is between policies designed to reinvigorate public communications systems which are relatively independent of both the state and the market, and policies which aim to marginalise or eradicate them" (Murdock 1992: 18). The object is to create "a new kind of public communicative space, rooted in a constructive engagement with emerging patterns of political and cultural diversity" (Murdock 1992: 40).[9]

One of the most difficult conceptual new fields to open is that which seeks to look beyond the exclusivity of traditional institutions to imagine new vehicles for meeting public service objectives. Here, a progressive approach to strategic intervention in public broadcasting could take a page from experiences with sustainable development. Development theory, once built around the idea that the introduction of full-blown communication systems to traditional societies would hasten "modernization" and hence economic, social, and political development, has gradually adjusted to the notion that small-scale horizontal communication operating at the grassroots level can be more beneficial in fostering autonomy and endogenous development (see O Siochru 1992). At the same time, however, this does not mean abandoning the demand for communication equality between rich and poor (Raboy and Bruck 1989).

In this context, small scale media technologies, opportunities for indigenous cultural expression through such means as theatre, puppetry, and video, exchanges between communities via computer, telecommunication, and broadcasting, can often be more appropriate for meeting the objectives of democratic communication than conventional broadcasting institutions centrally organized at the national level. In countries where these institutions do not even exist, it can be more politically fruitful to conceive of meeting public service broadcasting objectives at the community level, which does not obviate the need for national broadcasting, but as with so many development issues, the choices to be made involve strategic priorities (see Thede and Ambrosi 1991; Girard 1992; Lewis 1993). The social demand for local and regional broadcasting is pronounced even in the most developed countries (Garitaonandia 1993; Jankowski, Prehn, and Stappers 1993; Rushton 1993), and one of the most bitterly expressed criticisms of the dominant national public service broadcasters is their tendency to abandon local and regional needs as they retrench around high-profile prestigious national services.

Prospectives for Public Service Broadcasting

By linking the idea of public broadcasting to the notion of citizenship, we saw that it was necessary to guarantee its delinking from both the political authority of the state and the economic arbitrage of the market. The key to this is not so much a particular structure or funding formula, but a set of objectives and practices based on democratic principles and the view that broadcasting can be a means of social and cultural development.

The history of broadcasting everywhere up to and including the present has shown that only through sustained public policy action can the medium begin to fulfil its potential. Historically, a combination of public pressure, enlightened self-interest, and a favourable socio-political moment led governments in a number of mainly European countries to create public broadcasting institutions, placing them at arm's length from politics and sheltering them from the effects of commerce. Wherever this model was followed, public broadcasting became the central institution of the democratic public sphere, taking on increasing importance as broadcasting came to occupy more and more public space and time, and playing an important role in the democratization of public life (Scannell 1989).

Independence from politics and autonomy from the market have become the leading criteria for the definition of public space, but these have become relative values as broadcasting has spread and developed worldwide. No broadcasting organization today can function obliviously to market pressure, and if politics is more acutely present in some situations than others, it is never far from the centre. More significantly, public broadcasting has had to face a rising tide of scepticism and political will, and its recent evolution has been characterized by a "struggle over decline, change and renewal" (Tracey 1994).

At the same time, however, the limitations of market broadcasting, wonderful as a delivery vehicle for popular mass entertainment, have become strikingly evident (Garnham 1994). The multichannel environment provides a double-barrelled challenge for public broadcasting, obliging conventional broadcasters to adapt and open the way to new possibilities (Avery 1993). In the emerging democracies, particularly, the balancing act is to juggle the structural difficulty of creating new public broadcasting institutions and the pressures for integration to the global broadcasting market (see eg. Kleinwachter 1995). Broadcasting was conceived for commercial purposes, but public broadcasting was introduced for purposes of cultural development and democratization. By creating appropriate institutions and developing public policy accordingly, various state authorities placed broadcasting in the public interest. There is no reason why this can not continue to be done today.

For this to occur, every jurisdiction first of all needs to have clear public policy objectives for broadcasting. These can best be realized by placing responsibility for the regulation and supervision of broadcasting in the hands of an independent public agency (Raboy 1994). Next, authorities need to recognize that independence is necessary for broadcasting organizations.[11] Broadcasters, in exchange, need to accept accountability mechanisms which ensure the responsible exercise of their mandates (Blumler and Hoffmann-Riem 1992). Finally, the broadcasting environment needs to be organized and structured in such a way as to maximize the use that can be made of all the resources flowing through the system.

This reorganization would require something akin to the socialization of the broadcasting sector. There is no justification for the removal of surplus value from the lucrative branches of broadcasting activity as long as public interest broadcasting objectives can not be met without public subsidy. Private sector broadcasting should have statutory obligations to contribute to overall systemic objectives, and public broadcasters should be allowed to engage in commercially lucrative activities – without being obliged to compete with their own programmes in order to make ends meet.

Especially given the new technological context of the multichannel environment, it is possible to organize broadcasting to encompass both market activities and public service, to maximize both consumer choice and citizenship programming. People watch programmes, not channels, and consequently the appropriate point for competition in broadcasting is the point of programme supply, with independent production companies vying for programme contracts from public service broadcasters. Construction and maintenance of the technical infrastructure can remain in the market sector, but delivery service should be subject to regulated tariffs.

On the other hand, programming should be done by public corporations, in consultation with representative users councils. Supposing that in a given jurisdiction there were two public broadcasting corporations, Corporation A would have a mandate to provide generalist public interest programming, while Corporation B's mandate would be to seek large audiences. Corporation

A's work could be subsidized by the profits generated by Corporation B. Thanks to the availability of multiple channels, video recording, and playback technology, the public interest objectives of both citizenship and consumer sovereignty could be met without the information and resource loss brought on by public-private competition. Yet there would be room in such a system for a private sector of regulated carriers and competitive content providers. There would also be room for a variety of public services from the national to the local levels.

Since the early 1980s, broadcasting has been a site of ideological conflict between opposing models of society and a clash of concepts of democracy as well as notions of culture and economics (Rowland and Tracey 1990). According to one side in this conflict, the general interest demands that there be public institutions mandated to intervene strategically to guarantee quality, diversity, and independence in broadcasting that other institutional arrangements can not ensure; the other view holds that regulation and public policy regarding media are neither necessary nor legitimate.

Advocates of the public service approach to broadcasting must demonstrate concretely what institutional arrangements can be expected to meet their objectives and why these are possible only through regulation and public policy (see Hoffmann-Riem 1992). First of all, they must demonstrate what public service broadcasting should do in the new broadcasting environment and, especially, what distinguishes public from private sector broadcasting (see eg., Wolton 1992; Chaniac and Jézéquel 1993).

Private broadcasting, it may be argued, can also fulfil public service goals. However, it is unlikely that it would bother to try if not pushed in that direction by the competition and example of public broadcasters. This likelihood points to one of the most subtle arguments in favour of public broadcasting: public broadcasting sets the overall tone of the market, acts as a catalyst and serves as an example to all broadcasting services (Hultén 1995). It also points to the need to conceptualize broadcasting as an ecological environment, requiring a healthy diet of balanced offerings as well as nurturing and protection (Raboy 1993). Balance has until recently been guaranteed by the distinction between public and private services, but it is now threatened by two phenomena: the systemic disequilibrium shifting strongly toward private commercial services and the effects of commercialization on public services.

This shift can only be counter balanced by an opposite one: creation of more public service mandated organizations and removal of the pressure to meet commercial criteria. Overriding this is the legitimation of legally framing broadcasting as a public service and, consequently, considering the overall broadcasting framework as a public service environment. It is at this level that one should look at political developments such as the Council of Europe resolution referred to at the start of this essay. One has to go further than foresee a specific role for public service institutions; however, it is private sector broadcasting that should be conceptualized as the complementary form, providing services that public institutions can afford to abandon, not vice versa as at present. We need a world declaration situating broadcasting as a public service comprised of different elements each with specific structural arrangements and purposes, but all dedicated to the improvement of humankind. On the basis of such a global position, individual political units could legitimately set public policy for broadcasting on their territory.

All broadcasting, to be successful, must be programme-driven. Public broadcasting, however, is policy-motivated, while private broadcasting is profit-motivated. Public broadcasting is broadcasting with a purpose: to enhance the quality of public life, empowering individuals and social groups to participate more fully and equitably. Profit-motivated broadcasting is only interested in large audiences. Policy-motivated broadcasting is interested in reaching the largest possible audience the most effectively, in light of the specific objective of the programme concerned.

Broadcasters have their own technical language for measuring effectiveness: private broadcasters, they say, are concerned with audience share, the number of people watching or listening at any point in time, while public broadcasters are concerned with reach, the number of people who tune in over a period of time. There is another characteristic to consider, but it is difficult to measure: the intensity of the experience and its impact on one's life. Public broadcasting aims to touch people, to move them, to change them. Private broadcasting, by nature, aims to put them in the mood to consume and, above all, to consume more of what private broadcasting has to offer.

This set of distinctions may appear to be crude, but more important to consider is the extent to which existing public broadcasting has integrated the objectives of private broadcasting. Indeed, a common lament in countries where broadcasting is the most developed is that it is increasingly difficult to distinguish the programmes of public from those of private broadcasting, especially where both sectors provide advertising. Legislators and policy makers are more to blame than broadcasters for this state of affairs. By obliging public broadcasters to compete with private broadcasters on their terrain – the quest for the mass audience – we have flattened the difference. To the contrary, where private broadcasting has been obliged to compete with public broadcasting on the terrain of quality programming, the overall quality of broadcasting service has been raised.

A fundamental aspect of broadcasting as public service is universality of access. This is increasingly problematic as broadcasting evolves toward a pick-and-choose model analogous to the newsstand, where a variety of services are offered and the consumer selects and pays for his or her choice. In this context, it is essential that public broadcasting provide, first of all, a generalist programme service available to all and, ideally, free of charge to the user. As we move toward newer and more elaborate signal delivery systems, public authorities will have to ensure that everyone has access to the systems where public service is provided. At the same time, systems will have to be organized so as to avoid creating situations where better, more interesting, more rewarding, and, ultimately, more empowering services are on "higher" broadcast tiers at prices which exclude users on the basis of ability to pay.

This is the basis of the arguments for a public lane on the information highway that public interest groups and non-government organizations are putting forth in national and international debates on the new information infrastructures. The issue is larger than broadcasting, but broadcasting is at the cutting edge. Technological convergence is going to require new conceptual and operational models for content-based electronic communication, but regardless of the future of conventional broadcasting in this context, the promotion of the public interest can only come through regulation guaranteeing system access for all those with something to communicate, as well as for receivers.

Where is the money to come from? First of all, to the extent that political authorities, with public support, are prepared to make broadcasting a priority, it can come from the collective resources of society itself. In Canada, one recent proposal estimated that the shortfall in projected budget cuts to public broadcasting could be met by reducing a projected increase in military spending by 1 percent. As stated at the outset of this essay, it is a question of political will. There is no escaping the necessity of public subsidy for public service, but, even so, a major portion of the required funding can come from within the system itself. If broadcasting is recognized as a public service, the redistribution of benefits from commercial activity to subsidize the rest is a legitimate measure.

In the context of globalization and the development of a global infrastructure for information and communication, the question of public broadcasting takes on a new international dimension as well According to the head of the International Telecommunications Union, in the area of information infrastructures, "the gap between the information rich and the information poor is several orders of magnitude wider than in the area of basic service" (Tarjanne 1995). In the context of the information highway, all the more reason to emphasize public services as an equalizer, a leveller of the playing field, and an essential component of communication policies for development (see eg., L'Afrique face aux autoroutes de l'information 1995). Alongside the calls for national and global infrastructures emanating from the centre of the world media and economic system, we are starting to hear calls for a "public information infrastructure" geared to the democratic rights of citizens, as well as for a "global sustainable development infrastructure" (Schreibman, Priest, and Moore 1995).

The question of public service broadcasting is at the heart of contemporary media politics (Siune and Truetzschler 1992). It preoccupies those who would still ascribe a social purpose to mass communication but fear that such a mission has been bypassed in the new world order dominated by unrelenting technological and market forces. But this is the short view. The question of public service broadcasting cries out for new approaches that look beyond the obvious and do not shrink from challenging received wisdom (Gustaffson 1992). The challenge is not to defend any particular institutional territory, as it is often framed. It is rather how to invent something new, remembering that broadcasting service is first of all a public good.

Notes

1. An earlier version of this essay, including a detailed typology of the various existing models one encounters in the contemporary broadcasting environment, was presented to the UNESCO International Roundtable on the Cultural and Educational Functions of Public Service Broadcasting, Paris, 3-5 July 1995, in a paper entitled *"The World Situation of Public Service Broadcasting: Overview and Analysis."*

2. Summarized, the nine points state that public broadcasting should provide

    (1) a common reference point for all members of the public;
    (2) a forum for broad public discussion;
    (3) impartial news coverage;
    (4) pluralistic, innovative and varied programming;
    (5) programming which is both of wide public interest and attentive to the needs of minorities;
    (6) reflection of the different ideas and beliefs in pluriethnic and multicultural societies;
    (7) a diversity of national and European cultural heritage;
    (8) original productions by independent producers; and
    (9) extended viewer and listener choice by offering programs not provided by the commercial sector (Council of Europe 1994).

3. The Cable News Network was founded in Atlanta, in 1980, and launched its international satellite channel five years later.

4. In Scandinavia particularly, the broadcasting debate has been tied to the general critique of the welfare state. See Hultén 1992; Prehn and Jensen 1993; Sepstrup 1993.

5. Writing and critical concern about broadcasting tends to focus on television, and that is reflected here. When we speak about broadcasting in this book, however, we are referring to both radio and television.

6. The one billion television sets in the world in 1992 were distributed roughly as follows: 35 percent Europe (including former USSR); 32 percent Asia; 20 percent North America (and Caribbean); 8 percent Latin America; 4 percent Middle East; 1 percent Africa. Set ownership was rising at a rate of 5 percent a year, and world spending on television programs was $80 billion (*The Economist* 1994, based on UNESCO figures).

7. "Public goods are goods which cannot be appropriated privately. If such a good is supplied, no member of the collectivity can be excluded from its consumption. Therefore public goods must be produced by institutions other than a market economy and distributed by a mechanism different from markets" (Berger 1990: 128).

8. By cultural development, I mean "the process by which human beings acquire the individual and collective resources necessary to participate in

public life" (Raboy, Bernier, Sauvageau, and Atkinson 1994: 292).

9. Conceptualizing the public as citizen also requires a less paternalistic attitude toward the citizen as consumer. John Reith would no doubt recoil at the suggestion of his countryman Alan Peacock that public funding be used "in ways which encourage consumers to widen their experience of cultural activities and which promote freedom of entry into the 'culture market' so that cultural innovators can challenge well-established institutions" (Peacock 1991: 11). In other words, invest public money at the point of consumption as well as production, in the hope of stimulating demand and letting the market mechanism replace bureaucratic choice. This is not likely to enamour the public broadcasters, but it could have a salutary effect on public broadcasting.

10. According to Kleinwachter, the evolution of broadcasting in central and eastern Europe since 1989 can be broken into four stages: (1) awakening to the new media freedoms; (2) disillusionment over the failure to implement an ideal model; (3) political struggles over control of media, especially national television; and, finally, (4) the building of new institutions, public and private, based on law, independent of government control, competing under market conditions, and seeking to integrate into transnational broadcasting frameworks and structures. Varying from one country to the next, the basic thrust is toward the replacement of monopolistic state-owned, party-controlled systems with independent pluralistic ones but, in general, "the new broadcasting systems in the former East bloc, confronted with the realities of daily life, now have the choice between domestic governmental control and foreign commercialcontrol" (Kleinwachter 1995: 44).

11. See for example the German Constitutional Court decision of February 1994, ruling that the funding of public broadcasting should be constitutionally guaranteed and insulated from the variable humour of political decision making (Eberle 1994).

References

Achille, Y. 1994. *Les télévisions publiques en quête d'avenir*. Grenoble: Presses universitaires de Grenoble.

Achille, Y. and B. Miège. 1994. The Limits to the Adaptation Strategies of European Public Service Television. *Media, Culture and Society* 16(1): 31-46.

Atkinson, D. 1993. *La crise des télévisions publiques européennes: Ou la propagation du syndrome canadien*. Quebec City: Institut québécois de recherche sur la culture.

Avery, R. K. 1993. *Public Service Broadcasting in a Multichannel Environment*. New York: Longman.

Barnett, S. and D. Docherty. 1991. Purity or Pragmatism: Principles of Public-Service Broadcasting. In *Broadcasting Finance in Transition*, edited by J. G. Blumler and T. J. Nossiter. New York: Oxford University Press.

Berger, J. 1990. Market and State in Advanced Capitalist Societies. In *Economy and Society: Overviews in Economic Sociology*, edited by A. Martinelli and N. J. Smelser. London: Sage.

Blumler, J. G. 1992. *Television and the Public Interest: Vulnerable Values in West European Broadcasting.* London: Sage.

Blumler, J. G. and W. Hoffmann-Riem. 1992. Toward Renewed Accountability in Broadcasting. In *Television and the Public Interest: Vulnerable Values in West European Broadcasting*, edited by J. G. Blumler. London: Sage.

Broadcasting Research Unit. 1985/1988. *The Public Service Idea in British Broadcasting: Main Principles.* London: BRU.

Carey, J. W. 1989. *Communication as Culture: Essays on Media and Society.* Boston: Unwin and Hyman.

Caron, A. H. and P. Juneau. 1992. *Le défi des télévisions nationales à l'ére de la mondialisation.* Montréal: Presses de l'Université de Montréal.

Chaniac, R. and J-P. Jézéquel. 1993. Une chaîne culturelle: pourquoi? *Dossiers de l'audiovisuel* 48: 7-9.

Collins, R. 1990. *Television: Policy and Culture.* London: Unwin and Hyman.

Council of Europe. 1994. *The Media in a Democratic Society.* Draft Resolutions and Draft Political Declaration, 4th European Ministerial Conference on Mass Media Policy, Prague, 7-8 December. Strasbourg: Council of Europe, MCM-CDMM (94) 3 prov 1.

Curran, J. 1991. Rethinking the Media as a Public Sphere. In *Communication and Citizenship: Journalism and the Public Sphere in the New Media Age*, edited by P. Dahlgren and C. Sparks. New York: Routledge.

Dahlgren, P. 1994. The Media, the Public Sphere and the Horizon of Civil Society. European Film and Television Studies Conference, London.

Eberle, C-E. 1994. *Judgment on the Licence Fee by the German Federal Constitutional Court: Media Policy Prospects.* [n.p.]: ZDF.

The Economist. 1994. Feeling for the Future. A survey of television, 12 February.

Ellis, J. 1994. Public Service Broadcasting: Beyond Consensus. European Film and Television Studies Conference, London.

Foster, R. 1992. *Public Broadcasters: Accountability and Efficiency.* Edinburgh: Edinburgh University Press.

Friendly, F. W. 1967. *Due to Circumstances Beyond our Control....* New York: Vintage Books.

Garitaonandia, C. 1993. Regional Television in Europe. *European Journal of Communication* 8(3): 277-294.

Garnham, N. 1992. The Media and the Public Sphere. In *Habermas and the Public Sphere*, edited by C. Calhoun. Cambridge: MIT Press.

Garnham, N. 1994. The Broadcasting Market and the Future of the BBC. *The Political Quarterly* 65(1): 11-19.

Girard, B. 1992. *A Passion for Radio: Radio Waves and Community.* Montreal: Black Rose Books.

Gustafsson, K. E. 1992. Five Second Thoughts. *The Nordicom Review of Nordic Mass Communication Research* 1: 73-76.

Habermas, J. 1989. *Structural Transformation of the Public Sphere.* Cambridge: MIT Press.

Hoffmann-Riem, W. 1992. *Protection of the Communications Order through Broadcasting Supervision: Objectives, Instruments, Experiences.* Policy Research Paper no. 21. Melbourne: CIRCIT.

Hultén, O. 1992. The Nordic Model of Broadcasting Liberalization. *Irish Communication Review* 2: 46-54.

Hultén, O. 1995. Diversity or conformity? Television programming in competitive situations. *Nordicom Review of Nordic Mass Communication Research*, 1: 7-22.

Jankowski, N., O. Prehn and J. Stappers. 1992. *The People's Voice: Local Radio and Television in Europe.* London: John Libbey.

Keane, J. 1991. *The Media and Democracy*. London: Polity Press.

Keane, J. 1994. *Tom Paine: A Political Life*. Boston: Little, Brown.

Kleinwachter, W. 1995. From the Mountains of Visions to the Valleys of Reality: New Legal Frameworks for Broadcasting in Eastern and Central Europe. *Canadian Journal of Communication* 20(1): 25-44.

L'Afrique face aux autoroutes de l'information. 1995. Appel des participants, 16-18 March, Tunis.

Lewis, P. 1993. *Alternative Media: Linking Global and Local*. Paris: UNESCO Publishing.

McDonnell, J. 1991. *Public Service Broadcasting: A Reader*. London: Routledge.

Murdock, G. 1992. Citizens, Consumers and Public Culture. In *Media Cultures: Reappraising Transnational Media*, edited by M. Skovmand and K. Schroder. London: Routledge.

O Siochru, S. 1992. *Global Sustainability: Telecommunications and Science and Technology Policy*. Report to the EC's FAST Programme. Dublin: Nexus.

Paracuellos, J-C. 1993. Quel avenir pour la télévision publique? *Communication et langages* 98: 21-42.

Peacock, A. 1991. Economics, Cultural Values and Cultural Policies. *Journal of Cultural Economics* 15(2): 1-18.

Pietersee, J. N. 1994. Globalisation as Hybridisation. *International Sociology* 9(2): 161-184.

Prehn, O. and E. F. Jensen. 1993. Public Service and the Television Marketplace: The Case of the Nordic Countries in a Changing European Television Landscape. In *Small Nations: Big Neighbour*, edited by R. de la Garde, W. Gilsdorf and I. Wechselmann. London: John Libbey.

Raboy, M. 1993. Towards a New Ethical Environment for Public Service Broadcasting. *Studies of Broadcasting* 29: 7-35.

Raboy, M. 1994. The Role of the Public in Broadcasting Policymaking and Regulation: Lesson for Europe from Canada. *European Journal of Communication* 9, 1: 5-23.

Raboy, M. and P. Bruck, 1989. *Communication For and Against Democracy*. Montreal: Black Rose Books.

Raboy, M., I. Bernier, F. Sauvageau and D. Atkinson. 1994. Cultural Development and the Open Economy: A Democratic Issue and a Challenge to Public Policy. *Canadian Journal of Communication* 19(3/4): 291-315.

Rowland, W. D., Jr. and M. Tracey. 1990. Worldwide Challenges to Public Service Broadcasting. *Journal of Communication* 40(2): 8-27.

Rushton, D. 1993. *Citizen Television: A Local Dimension to Public Service Broadcasting*. London: John Libbey.

Schreibman, V., W. C. Priest and R. K. Moore. 1995. A Call for Establishment of "The Cyberspace Society". *Federal Information News Syndicate*, 17 April. Available from fins@access.digex.net.

Sepstrup, P. 1993. Scandinavian Public Broadcasting: The Case of Denmark. In *Public Service Broadcasting in a Multichannel Environment*, edited by R. K. Avery. New York: Longman.

Servaes, J. 1993. Beyond "Europe 1992": Communication and Cultural Identity in Small Nation States. *Telematics and Informatics* 10(4): 321-343.

Sinclair, J. 1994. Culture and Trade: Some Theoretical and Practical Considerations on "Cultural Industries". International Association for Mass Communication Research, Seoul.

Siune, K., and W. Truetzschler. 1992. *Dynamics of Media Politics*. London: Sage.

Smith, A. 1991. Public Service Broadcasting: Legacy or Prophecy? International Television Studies Conference, London.

Syvertsen, T. 1992. *Public Television in Transition*. Oslo: Norges allmennvitenskapelige forskningsrad.

Syvertsen, T. 1994. The Transformation of European Television: A Goodbye to Pluralism? International Association for Mass Communication Research, Seoul.

Tarjanne, P. 1995. Africa and the Information Superhighway. Conference paper for *L'Afrique face aux autoroutes de l'information*. 18 March, Tunis.

Thede, N. and A. Ambrosi. 1991. *Video the Changing World*. Montreal: Black Rose Books.

Tracey, M. 1994. The Future of Public Service Broadcasting: Bye, Adios, Vaya Con Dios, Au revoir, Ciao, You're Outta Here – Maybe. INPUT Conference, Montreal.

UNESCO. International Commission for the Study of Communication Problems. 1980. *Many Voices, One World*. Paris: UNESCO.

van Cuilenburg, J. and P. Slaa. 1993. From Media Policy Towards a National Communications Policy: Broadening the Scope. *European Journal of Communication* 8(2): 149-176.

Venturelli, S. S. 1994. The Imagined Transnational Public Sphere in the European Community's Broadcast Philosophy: Implications for Democracy. *European Journal of Communication* 8: 491-518.

Wolton, D. 1992. La télévision privée est-elle la solution à tous les maux? *Le Devoir*, 5 February.

PART ONE

Shifting paradigms in the
heartlands of public broadcasting

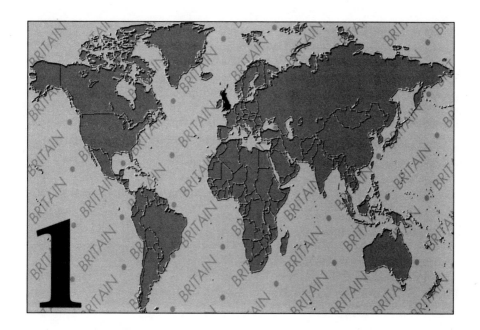

Britain: Public Service Broadcasting, from National Culture to Multiculturalism

Paddy Scannell

Introduction

*T*he question of public service broadcasting (PSB) has been back on the agenda for the last 15 years.[1] New technologies and a new political climate in the 1980s seemed to put a question mark against its contemporary relevance. Critics claimed that its original rationale had disappeared; that PSB had been merely a pragmatic response in the early twentieth century to the problems of spectrum scarcity and of financing broadcast services (which came down to the difficulties of finding an appropriate payment mechanism that correlated with use). State regulated monopolies had, at that time, appeared as the best (that is, the least worst) solution. The endemic difficulties of financing broadcasting were solved either by a licence fee or by sponsorship and/or spot advertising. PSB in this analysis amounted to no more than a necessary state intervention to regulate an industry in its infancy and to help with its teething troubles.

At the end of the century (the argument goes), the industry has grown into a giant and no longer needs any form of regulation by the political authorities of nation-states. New information technologies have solved the problem of channel scarcity and the payment mechanism. Fibre-optic cabling and geo-stationary satellites can, between them, deliver a range of services hitherto unimaginable. Channel subscription services are the gross solution to the payment problem, while pay-per-view is its refined solution. The need for regulation simply withers away as the market takes over.

Such arguments are, and have been, market-led. They start from the assumption that broadcasting is a business like any other – that its business is the profit-driven production of programme commodities and that these are produced for consumption like any other commodities. The defenders of PSB, however, take a different view of broadcasting. Broadcasting is a large scale business, certainly; however, its business is not the production of programme commodities but of a communicative relationship (Garnham 1994). Programmes mediate a relationship between broadcasters and listeners and viewers. Listeners and viewers do not consume programmes, and they are not engaged in a process of consumption but, rather, a process of interacting with and interpreting the programme output of broadcast institutions.

What is PSB? If it were simply a series of pragmatic, instrumental solutions to problems as they arose initially, it should, indeed have disappeared as those problems were overcome. However, PSB has shown no signs of vanishing in Britain or elsewhere in Europe. In December 1994, a new definition of PSB was agreed upon by the Committee of Ministers of the Council of Europe. Most member states of the European Union have PSB systems which were the foundational form upon which broadcasting in their nation-state was established and developed. The object of the resolution was to secure the future of public service broadcasting, whose objectives were re-specified in nine mission statements. Central to all was a concern "to support the values underlying the political, legal and social structures of democratic societies, and in particular the respect for human rights, culture and pluralism" (Porter 1995: 30). In Great Britain, the future of the British Broadcasting Corporation (BBC) is secure, if not indefinitely at least well into the next century. Its current position is neither static nor in decline. Within the organization there is an eagerness to extend the BBC's role as a global broadcaster of television services. Channel 4 is alive and well; indeed, it has become so profitable that its surplus (38.2 million in 1993) is currently redistributed to the other companies in the ITV network (Peak 1994: 133).

Thus, in Britain, PSB has not simply held its ground through the flurry of parliamentary enquiries, reports, green and white papers, and Broadcasting Acts of the last ten years, it has emerged from this process stronger and more secure, in some respects, than it was before the process began. PSB is not, however, the same thing at the end of the century as it was in the beginning. This chapter will briefly review the changing character of PSB in Britain, from its beginnings to the present, and then consider some of the dilemmas that it faces today, as it looks to the future. First, the attitude that characterizes PSB will be examined.

The question of whether a market- led approach to broadcasting is better or worse than a public service- led view of broadcasting can not be settled definitively one way or another. The approaches are complementary, for each adds something to the other that it does not have and, in so doing, modifies the excesses to which the other would tend if left in sole possession of the field. Both are ways of making and distributing programmes. Both produce the same kind of thing (news, entertainment, and sports), but each has a different attitude toward the task in hand. For commercial broadcasting systems, the task was, at first and it remains so, to find a profitable way of programme making and distribution, and, for PSB, it has always been to find a way of providing broadcasting as a public service. What shows up, in a profit-led system or a PSB system, are not intrinsically different things, but similar things done differently, organized differently, with different styles, and in a different ethos. Both were journeys of discovery. Both had to find solutions to certain problems endemic in the new (broadcasting). Both were impelled in the same direction (for different reasons) – namely the formation of large- scale organizations to provide nationally networked services.[2]

National Service: 1927 – 1954

The BBC was established as a state- regulated monopoly in 1927. Its original mandate, set out in its founding constitutional documents, was to provide "a national service in the public interest." This task was most fundamentally interpreted by the BBC as a duty to provide a service that was universally accessible to everyone living within the boundaries of the United Kingdom. No matter where one lived, one ought to be able to receive a good quality signal of the BBC's programme service(s). But what kind of service? The principle of mixed programmes on national channels was soon established and has remained the way that the BBC defines its mission. Between them, these two principles – programme diversity within nationally distributed channels – are ways of addressing the delegated representative role which PSB must seek to fulfil. Since the state was now representative of the whole population by virtue of universal suffrage (established by the Representation of the People Act, 1918), PSB was mandated to provide a service that was, in its own way, representative of the people-as-nation.[3] Its task was to discover how to do this. To begin to do it, it had to establish on whose behalf (for whom) it was in the business of producing and distributing a programme service.

In the era of the BBC's monopoly, its definition of its purpose was always primarily as a national service. To this end, the National Programme was introduced in 1930 and, in the years following, a complementary Regional Programme was added bit by bit. This two-channel service presumed a "national community," whose general interests the BBC had a duty to serve. Moreover, "the general needs of the community [came] before the sectional" (BBC 1933:37). As for those sectional needs (whether political, regional, or cultural), the BBC regarded itself as an impartial arbiter for their various claims, assessing their relative importance and catering for them accordingly. These policies were based on the basic principle "that broadcasting should be operated on a national scale, for national service and by a single national authority" (BBC 1933: 14).

Thus, in the era of its monopoly, the service was organized for and on behalf of an audience whose "public interest" in broadcasting was conceived in this way. The audience-as-nation was a radically new kind of public, one commensurate with the whole of society – all members of the newly extended, now fully representative, nation-state. This was the way in which the BBC interpreted its representative mandate, as providing a service that was available to each and all, no matter where they lived; a non-exclusive service that could be enjoyed by people of different social classes, living in different parts of the country, women and men, young and old. What cultural institution before broadcasting had ever been delegated such a task? It was, essentially, a task of democratic representation on the terrain of culture rather than politics. The task was to create a common culture that speaks to the whole society and that can be shared by people of widely different backgrounds, with different tastes and interests.

While Scannell and Cardiff (1991) have traced in detail this formation, here it only needs to be pointed out that the most visible way in which this task was accomplished was in the presentation of those events and ceremonies that had the effect, as John Reith (first director general of the BBC) put it, of "making the nation as one man."Two kinds of events stand out in this respect: sporting events and royal occasions. Over the years, things like the Football Association Cup Final, the Boat Race, Wimbledon, the Derby, test cricket, and rugby internationals have become punctuating moments in a new kind of national calendar created by broadcasting (Cardiff and Scannell 1987; Scannell 1988). Royal occasions – weddings, funerals, and coronations – have been consistently the most important "great occasions" on British radio and television – outstanding moments in a corporate national life (Scannell 1996).

The projection of Britishness on radio and television is well understood by the broadcasters as, precisely, ideological. Sir Michael Swann, chairman of the BBC board of governors, declared in evidence to the 1977 Committee on the Future of Broadcasting (the Annan Committee) that,

> An enormous amount of the BBC's work [is] in fact social cement of one sort or another. Royal occasions, religious services, sports coverage and police series, all reinforce the sense of belonging to our country, being involved in its celebrations, and accepting what it stands for (HMSO 1977: 263).

The ideological work of social cement presupposes a divided society bound together in a momentary unity on such occasions. The cracks and fissures have always been there. Some have remained constant; others have emerged more recently. From the start, two fault lines showed up and continue to run through the activities of the BBC to this day: namely, region and class. The unity of the United Kingdom has always been problematic. The BBC was established as, and remains, a London-based institution that claims to be able to represent the whole of the United Kingdom in its unity and diversity. As seen from other parts of the United Kingdom, the BBC is persistently biased toward the south-east of England, has a metropolitan attitude that regards the rest of the country as culturally inferior to the culture of the metropolis, and systematically misunderstands and marginalizes the cultural interests of Scotland, Wales, and Northern Ireland. Complaints along these lines arose at the start of the National Programme and have persisted to the present. In one of its most recent mission statements, the BBC has felt obliged to declare that "The British Broadcasting Corporation is not the London Broadcasting Corporation" (BBC 1992). The issue of adequate regional representation in the activities of the BBC is as sensitive an issue today as it ever was (Harvey and Robins 1993).

Class also remains a sensitive issue. The BBC has always been colonized by highly educated, white, middle-class (middle-aged) men. Finding the right tone of voice – a voice that could speak to people of all classes – has always been difficult. Also difficult has been the task of allowing other voices – of marginalized social groups – to be heard. Before the war, the working class was absent from the National Programme except as "victims" in social concern documentaries and occasional facetious portrayals as "the-man-in-the-street." Only in the output of North Region, with its vast working class audience, was there a real and successful effort to make programmes about and for that audience. The sense that the BBC is part of the world of "them" rather than "us" (Hoggart 1956) – a world that is somewhere other than where listeners and viewers are – has persisted to this day. "I always think of the BBC as down south, whereas Tyne Tees is up here." "I imagine a lot of ageing men sat in a big boardroom with grey suits" (marginal comments of licence fee payers, BBC 1995: 30).

The equation of the public interest with national service has remained the cornerstone of the BBC's corporate mission. It has been affirmed by successive parliamentary reports and white papers in the post-war era, most notably by the Annan Report, which defined the BBC as "arguably the most important cultural organisation in the nation" (HMSO 1977: 79). Some members of the committee had considered splitting the BBC in two (separating radio from television), but the report concluded that to do so "would maim an institution which the nation at large on some great national occasion regards as the natural interpreter of that event to the nation as a whole" (114). It remains the case that on such occasions – or in moments of national crisis – it is natural for the country to turn to the BBC. The most recent white paper, *Broadcasting in the Nineties*, reaffirmed that the BBC "is still, and will remain for the foreseeable future, the cornerstone of British broadcasting" (HMSO 1988: 7, 3.2).

Competition: 1954 – 1977

The BBC, in the era of its monopoly, made itself a national institution. That does not mean that it was popular. Indeed, within the BBC, there were real tensions from the beginning – that, again, run right through to the present – about the extent to which its public service mission included the provision of popular programmes. What does popular mean here? Entertainment: that is, undemanding, relaxing, "light" programme fare with a wide- spread "mass"

appeal. There is no doubt that the BBC could and did produce hugely successful, popular, entertaining programmes, from "Bandwagon" (1938), to "It's
That Man Again!" (1940), to a glorious profusion of brilliant comedy on radio
and television in the 1950s – of which "The Goon Show" and "Hancock's
Half Hour" remain, in social memory and in frequent repeats, the most mem-
orable. Although the BBC could produce these programmes, its attitude was
seldom wholehearted in this respect, and it showed. It was not obvious that
the BBC valued the provision of popular programmes or saw it as central to
its task. It was on precisely this matter, however, that it was challenged by the
arrival of commercial television in the mid-1950s.

Two things were important about the way that commercial television was
set up by the government. First, and crucially, it was not set up outside
the PSB framework already in place. On the contrary, commercial television
was set up within the PSB system and was, and remains, a state-regulated
network with a public service remit. The remit of ITV (Independent
Television as it cunningly called itself) was not basically different from that
of the BBC. It had to provide the same range of services. It had to observe
due balance and impartiality and avoid editorial comment in its news
services. It was subject to a regulatory authority, the Independent Television

Authority (ITA), whose initial task was to define the structure of the new
system and then to act as its watchdog, ensuring that the public service remit
was adequately met.[4] The second thing to note is that ITV was not internally
competitive. It was set up as a single network in competition with the
BBC. In effect, ITV was another monopoly. It had the monopoly of advertising revenue in the United Kingdom, a fact that enabled it to maintain high
advertising rates, to the intense irritation of the advertising agencies. In
effect, from the mid-1950s, there were two PSBs in competition for audiences.
ITV staked out the ground upon which the battle for audiences was to be
fought as popular programming.

The story of how the BBC initially ignored what it called "the competitor," as
if it were an impertinent johnny-come-lately, is a familiar one. Within two
years, its audience share was dipping well below 30 percent. Hugh Carleton
Greene was drafted in as the new director general of the BBC to win back the
vanishing audiences, which was accomplished by a systematic destruction of
"aunty" – the BBC's maiden aunt image. A whole raft of programmes not
only won back audiences but cocked an irreverent snook at authority,
religion, and traditional values in general. "That Was The Week That
Was" (TW3) and "Till Death Us Do Part" were the most iconoclastic (and
popular) programmes in the destruction of the BBC's "stuffed shirt" image
(Briggs, vol. V 1995: 350- 76).

By the mid-1960s, a balance had been achieved. The new techniques
of scheduling primetime to win and keep a large audience share – first
developed by ITV – were now practised by both sides. In all areas of production – from news to "serious" drama – new styles and techniques were
implemented to make the "feel" of television output more professional, more
friendly, and more for the viewers. Television became popular and has
remained so. Commercial television – within a PSB remit – made it so and

compelled the BBC to do so too. By the mid-1960s, the total available television viewing audience was shared between the BBC and ITV on a more or less equal basis, to the satisfaction of both parties. Even as that balance was achieved, however, voices began to be raised about this cosy relationship in which a monopoly had simply been replaced by a duopoly. The centre ground of popular programming with widespread appeal blocked out, it was said, the possibility of providing programmes for minority tastes and interests.

Cultural Pluralism: Channel 4 (1977 – 95)

By the mid-1960s, the task of "holding the middle ground" was becoming noticeably more difficult (Kumar 1977), and by the end of the 1960s, the strain was showing. A revealing document called The BBC and the Public Mood, written by Oliver Whitley in 1968, shows how problematic things were becoming for the BBC:

> The BBC operates today within a society which is uncertain, contradictory and divided. There has been a series of financial crises. Unemployment and redeployment are painful social phenomena; events in Vietnam and the USA have caused dilemmas of sentiment and principle; immigration on our own doorstop has proved the latest development with unwelcome realities. Nationalism, separatism and factionalism could be added to the list. So could the sharpness of domestic political divisions... A country divided and disturbed inevitably has the BBC on the rack. [...]

> There are no great remedies to the discomforts of the BBC's role as national scapegoat. A cool nerve is needed alike by its Governors and staff. The BBC has at once to be alert and deaf, to listen to silence as well as to clamour, to have a skin thick and sensitive, to step boldly and delicately (Whitley 1968: 1-2, 13)

It would be an exercise in itself to analyze the uncertain tone of this document – including the "unwelcome reality" of immigration, an extraordinary statement which reveals the extent to which "Britishness" was thought by the BBC at that time to exclude British Caribbean and Asian citizens, who were the unwelcome "they" who have landed on "our" doorstep. For all its internal confusions and uncertainties, however, and despite its whingeing tone, this paper, prepared by the secretary of the BBC for the board of governors, responds to an authentic sea change in the climate of social, cultural, and political opinion – a shift in attitude that was analyzed more thoughtfully by the Annan Committee, set up a few years later in 1974.

The committee's remit was to enquire into the state of broadcasting in Britain and to make recommendations for the future in light of its findings. It compared its findings with those of its predecessor, the Pilkington Report, which had surveyed broadcasting in Britain some 15 years earlier (HMSO 1962). It noted profound changes in social attitudes since then:

> The ideals of middle-class culture ... found it ever more difficult to accommodate to life in the sixties. The new vision of life reflected divisions within society, divisions between classes, the generations and the sexes, between north and south, between the provinces and London, between pragmatists and ideologues ... It was a rhetoric of anxiety and indignation simultaneously utopian and sardonic. It was often hostile to authority as such; not merely authority as expressed in the traditional organs of State but towards those in any institution charged with its governance ... Now people of all political persuasions began to object that many programmes were biased or obnoxious. But some, with equal fervour, maintained that broadcasters were not challenging enough and were cowed by Government and vested interests to produce programmes that bolstered up the *status quo* and concealed how a better society could evolve (HMSO 1962: 14- 15).

Faced with a barrage of conflicting opinion on the actual state of broadcasting and its future, the committee opted for "pluralism." "Pluralism has been the *leitmotiv* of all of us in this Report" (108). It wanted to create a wider range of programmes that spoke not just to the mass audience of what it labelled "the duopoly," but to those minorities and social groups whose needs, interests, and tastes were not adequately served under the existing arrangements. It therefore recommended that the available fourth television channel should go to neither of the existing authorities but to an independent Open Broadcasting Authority charged with the responsibility of developing a service that catered to all those interests currently underrepresented or excluded in the output of the BBC and ITV. The new authority should not produce any of its own programmes but, like a publishing house, would commission its programmes from a wide range of sources, including independent programme makers. In short, "We do not want more of the same. There are enough programmes for the majority ... What is needed now is programmes for the different minorities which add up to make the majority" (471-72).

In 1980, the new Conservative government brought in a Broadcasting Act, which created what was called Channel 4. It was in all essential respects as envisioned by the Annan Report, except in the matter of its institutional and financial basis. Whereas Annan had wanted the fourth channel to be under the aegis of a new broadcasting authority and to be financed from a range of different sources, the government placed the new channel under the administrative care of the IBA, as part of commercial television. Channel 4 is, thus, both a fully commercial channel, funded by spot advertising in the same way as ITV (now called Channel 3), and a fully defined PSB channel. It was created along publishing lines, as proposed by Annan, with a remit to commission a significant proportion of programmes from independent sources. It should be innovative and experimental, appealing to interests and tastes not catered for by ITV:

> Its difficult task, with the liberal encouragement of the new
> Broadcasting Act behind it, was to give a voice to the new
> pluralism of the 1980s: that explosive mixture of racial hatred with
> new multi- racial and multicultural tolerance, of the quest for
> sex equality with the consolidation of new forms of male
> supremacism, of a new tolerance in matters of sexual orientation
> with outbursts of homophobic hysteria, of a commitment to a
> welfare state with the argument that its existence was
> incompatible with the principle of a free market (Harvey 1994:
> 117- 18)

Channel 4 has been broadcasting now for about 12 years and has been
a remarkable success: its share of the total television audience is now just
under 11 percent, slightly higher than BBC 2, which has been on air since the
late 1960s. It has accomplished the difficult trick of having a distinctive
identity without catering for the mainstream audience. It has a younger audience profile than the BBC's television channels. It does cater for tastes
and interests that lie outside the mainstream; however, it has avoided the
"ghetto trap" of always reaching the same small number of people. Thus, its
programming, though eclectic, has an interest and appeal that reaches well
beyond the target groups for particular programmes. It is a new model of PSB
that has been taken up in other countries, in Australia and Denmark, for
instance.

Public Service Broadcasting Today

The development of PSB in Britain has been sketched in three broad periods,
each of which was shown to have a core characteristic: first as national,
then as popular, and finally as pluralistic. Neither the periodization nor the
characteristics of each period is peculiar to Britain. The same pattern (though
with different time-spans) is found in other countries in Europe, whose radio
and television services began as PSB systems: in Denmark (Bondebjerg 1994)
or Sweden (Kleberg 1994), for instance. All three characteristics are present
today in the make-up of the mix of services currently available to British
listeners and viewers. Each has modified and been modified by the others.
They stand out as distinctive strands woven into the fabric of broadcasting
today. They colour attitudes within the industry, in politics, and in public
attitudes. The situation today, in relation to these three thematized characteristics of the British system, will be examined as we look toward the future.

Public Service Broadcasting and National Culture

The BBC will continue to be, as the 1989 white paper put it, "the cornerstone
of British broadcasting." It has ambitions to be a key player in global television. In this respect, it hopes to catch up with its unmatched position in
radio, where the BBC World Service currently has a global audience of 125

million for its English language services, the largest of any international broadcaster (Peak 1993: 88; see Mytton 1993). On the home front, it will continue as *the* national broadcasting system on both radio and television. In this respect, the problems it confronts now are the same as they ever were. The pressures of regional radio and television remain strong, particularly from Scotland, a "stateless nation," whose demands for political and cultural independence from England have grown in significance over the years. Still, the London- based BBC gets it wrong (as it always did) about Scotland.

On 6 April 1995, the BBC's flagship weekly current affairs programme, "Panorama," was scheduled to be wholly given over to a forty-minute interview (in London) with Prime Minister John Major. Coming three days before local elections in Scotland, this decision created immediate outrage in the opposition parties north of the border. Labour and the Liberal Democrats joined forces with the Scottish Nationalists in an appeal to the Scottish law courts (entirely independent of England) for an immediate injunction against the broadcasting of the programme in Scotland on the grounds that it might give the Conservatives an unfair advantage in the imminent local elections. The Scottish courts banned the broadcasting of the programme in Scotland before the elections. The BBC appealed the decision and lost, and the programme was broadcast in Scotland a week after it was transmitted in England.

The issues at stake in this debacle can be interpreted in various ways, but there can be no doubt that if there had been local elections in England three days after the date proposed for the broadcast, it would never have been aired on that date. Indeed, at around the same time the previous year (25 April 1994), a "Panorama" programme on corruption in the Conservative-dominated London borough of Westminster was shelved precisely because it came just before local elections in England, due on 6 May 1994. The susceptibilities of political parties in England are always taken into account; in Scotland, they are not. The BBC Board of Governors subsequently apologized to Scotland and declared that the decision to go ahead with the programme was "an error of judgment." The issues that it raises are endemic to the historic, always problematic, unity of the so-called United Kingdom. However, as long as the British nation-state persists in its present form, the BBC will continue with its always tricky mandate of being representative of the whole of Britain.

Public Service Broadcasting and Popular Culture

Popular television continues to be at the heart of debates about broadcasting today and, in particular, the strategies of the BBC and ITV toward the national television audiences. The 1990 Broadcasting Act, while keeping in place a regulatory body – the Independent Television Commission (ITC) which replaced the Independent Broadcasting Authority (IBA) – was widely interpreted as an intention by the Conservative government to increase competition within the commercial sector and to root out "the old guard" in ITV. The sword of this intent was the renewal of franchises in late 1992. However, the old guard fought a successful campaign in the run-up to the passing of the act, intended to maintain the (public service) values and standards in the commercial sector. The mark of their success was the "quality threshold" requirement built into the act, which required companies bidding for franchises to show that they would maintain high standards in their programme services. The act, in its modified form, required the ITC to award franchises taking this criterion into account, rather than simply awarding them (as originally intended by the Conservative government) to the highest bidder.

The question of "quality," and what it means in respect to broadcasting, has been periodically debated since the introduction of commercial broadcasting, but it recurred with a new vigour in the early 1990s. In the late 1940s, the BBC had fought against the introduction of any system of competitive broadcasting, invoking Gresham's Law to argue that the good (that is, quality) in the long run would be driven out in the remorseless fight for the greatest number of listeners (HMSO 1950: para 163). Similar worries resurfaced 40 years later at the prospects of a multichannel television market (see Mulgan 1990). On the one hand, the commercial companies in the ITV network were anxious to prove that they could and did produce "popular quality television," as they jockeyed for position in the run-up to the franchise renewals. The hugely successful "Inspector Morse" series was often cited as an outstanding example of "quality" popular television. On the other hand, the BBC, unsure how to play its cards in the period of debate and discussion about its own future in the run-up to the renewal of its charter and licence in 1996, appeared to contemplate a strategy of vacating the centre and withdrawing to the cultural high ground, leaving popular programming to the commercial sector (BBC 1992). This would have been a folly indeed, and it was soon modified. Even so, in its most recent mission statement, the BBC acknowledges the difficulties in the "quality versus popularity" debate (BBC 1995: 25).

The BBC publication, *People and Programmes,* affirms the BBC's core purpose as making "programmes of quality" for British audiences (BBC 1995: 172). High quality, original entertainment has always been at the heart of its schedules, and a current priority is to "re-establish" (a tacit admission of lost ground) BBC Television as a major force in the area of mainstream, highly accessible, people, family, and variety shows appealing to a wide range of audiences (BBC 1995: 62-63). At the same time, however, the BBC declares that it will not organize its programme mix and schedules in such ways as to compete head-on with a more aggressively profit-driven ITV, intent on winning the mainstream, primetime television audiences by scheduling non-stop entertainment. "It is at the level of overall channel mix and scheduling that many of the hardest decisions have to be taken. Everywhere we must strive to offer audiences the widest possible editorial range, even though the consequences may be a less competitive schedule" (BBC 1995: 26).

The struggle for the centre ground – an inevitable consequence of any competitive system – will continue. It is right and proper that nationally networked television services should have, as a core concern, the production of popular, entertaining programmes. Equally, it is proper for a public service broadcaster to have to balance this commitment against other commitments to the national audience – especially the preservation of a genuinely diverse, wide-ranging mix of programme material in channel output. National, popular broadcasting: these two things go together. They have been at the heart of radio and television services in Britain for many years and continue to be so. It is the third core characteristic which is not only more recent but which puts in question some key assumptions underpinning the national, popular culture.

Public Service Broadcasting and Multiculturalism

Pluralism was the word used by the Annan Committee in the mid-1970s to catch and respond to the changing nature of the times. Today, it is more accurately caught by "multiculturalism." What is now called multiculturalism can be traced back to the 1960s, when new social movements in the United States – civil rights and feminism, especially – began to assert a new kind of political resistance. Foucault has usefully distinguished between three kinds of resistance to exploitation, domination, and subjection (Foucault 1982: 212). The first is to economic exploitation and asserts the right to the material means of life; the second is to religious and political oppression and asserts civil rights to freedom of conscience, speech, and so forth; the third is to forms of subjection that deny one's identity and asserts the right to be publicly as one wishes to be. It is this third arena of struggle that has emerged with increasing urgency in the last quarter of this century. It is a new kind of "identity" politics whose struggle is not so much against the market or the state as against prevailing social attitudes that marginalize particular groups by denying, refusing, or failing to recognize their claims as women, as non-white, as gay, etc. Charles Taylor has called it "the politics of recognition" (Taylor 1994). The struggle thus shifts from "hard" economic and political issues to a "softer" politics – an assertion of an identity (gender, ethnic, sexual) and a demand to be recognized and accepted not in terms of the dominant way of life but in terms of one's own. In such struggles, cultural issues of definition and representation assume a central importance for those who perceive themselves as routinely misrepresented or under-represented (or, characteristically, both) in mainstream culture. It is natural that such struggles should focus on the media as the daily embodiment of the culture of the mainstream. In Britain, Channel 4 was conceived of and remains a major redefinition of PSB in the light of the politics of representation in late twentieth century culture.

Channel 4, very much a child of its time, was a recognition of and a response to the growing significance of identity politics. Its institutional form and its programme policy were both, in certain respects, well adapted to responding to the demand for programmes which – in their form and content – spoke to tastes, interests, and social groups outside the mainstream. Channel 4 produces none of its programmes, except for continuity links, the famous channel logo, and a weekly feedback programme. Hence, a cottage industry of independent production companies came into existence almost overnight, at the start of the 1980s, to provide programmes for the channel. Tiny companies clustered around Charlotte Street (Channel 4's headquarters) to win commissions to make programmes that addressed black, feminist, and gay interests, among others. Often they were disappointed. Those that were successful sometimes found the tensions between their wish to find new and different forms of expression came up against Channel 4's demands for professional production standards (Arthurs 1994). It was not so easy to escape the mainstream. "The burden of representation" for black programme makers was such that whatever they did and however they did it, they were liable to criticism from some sections of the communities they represented (Daniels 1994).

Multiculturalism highlights some difficult problems in the politics of cultural representation today (see Dines and Humez 1995, which is set to be the classic American textbook on the media and multiculturalism). National services must, if they are to be that, have programme values which in some ways speak to the whole society. The BBC has always been white, male, and middle class, and this is now apparent both to its audiences and to itself in ways that are far more troubling today than in the past. *Programmes and People* admits that the BBC has a special duty to represent and serve Britain's ethnic minorities, but that in many ways it has failed. "Either you get badly represented or you don't get represented at all" was one comment (BBC 1995: 163- 68). Part of the problem is the way that mainstream cultural institutions (Channel 4 included) lump together non-white people of entirely different cultures. British Asians and Caribbeans have often been arbitrarily yoked together in "ethnic minority" programmes in attempts to satisfy both. In fact, neither party's very different cultural interests or tastes were met.

An intrinsic difficulty for mainstream broadcasting is that, however it might try to discharge its task of representing the whole society, it is hard to avoid the ghetto effect – of bracketing out the minorities in special "minority" programmes that are ignored by the majority and do not always appeal to the minority. On the other hand, it is often unclear what kind of representation is being demanded. The conflict between representative and participatory forms of democratic politics shows up in multiculturalism's often confused and confusing calls for recognition. There has been a growing concern about how, say, non-whites or gays are represented in mainstream television. Soap operas are a classic locus for this debate. Since their form, in Britain, is predominantly one of "social realism" (see Dyer et al. 1981), there has been increasing discussion about both the under-representation of, for instance, British Asian and Caribbean people in these never-ending narratives of everyday life, coupled with a concern that, when they are brought into the story-line, they should be presented in a sympathetic, non-stereotypical way. "Brookside" (Channel 4) and "EastEnders" (BBC 1) are, appropriately enough, the focus of attention in this respect, since both narratives began in the 1980s and speak to the contemporary moment (Geraghty 1995).

Here, the demand for recognition is to be an accepted, acceptable part of mainstream culture, to appear in it as ordinarily and unremarkably as the white, straight culture appears to itself in its own self-representations. Yet there is a demand for forums in which cultural difference can be flamboyantly expressed for its own sake, for the pleasure of being oneself in public. It would be crass to interpret this as cultural separatism. Rather, the desire is to be able to give expression to one's own sexual or ethnic way of being not primarily for the mainstream, but as something within and for one's own cultural community. It is, however, difficult for mainstream broadcasting, even Channel 4, to accommodate such demands, though there have been occasionally notable successes.

An alternative might be for "interest communities" to produce their own broadcasting services. This was part of the misunderstanding between some minority groups and Channel 4, when it was started in the early 1980s (Daniels 1994). The newly formed independent production companies representing various minorities thought that the new channel was to be a forum in which they could "do their own thing." Of course it was not. As a national channel operating in competition with three other mainstream national services, Channel 4 had constantly to bear that in mind as it sought to let a hundred flowers bloom. Its greatest accomplishment has been to become a genuinely national television service that accesses minority interests in ways that appeal not only to those audiences but to mainstream audiences as well. What it cannot do, however, is provide direct access for minority groups to produce their own services.

Direct access has begun to be available on radio in Britain in the 1990s. The Broadcasting Act of 1990 put an end to the regulatory role of the IBA, which was responsible, since the early 1970s, for commercial radio as well as television. It placed responsibility for television in the hands of the ITC and created a new Radio Authority with a mandate to accelerate the development of commercial radio at every level (national, regional, and local). The Radio Authority has been advancing cautiously in the direction of community radio stations. There was considerable opposition to this idea – long canvassed by advocates of hands-on, local, participatory radio – from Conservative politicians throughout the 1980s, who feared that such stations might fall into the hands of "loony-left" local councils. Now the idea of (non-political) "community of interest" radio stations is accepted, and the handful of existing stations that serve linguistic/ethnic communities (Turkish, Jewish, and Greek, for instance) is set to increase in 1996. Meanwhile, a talk-radio channel for women, with an all-female production team, has just won a franchise in London. Asian families subscribe to TV-Asia, a popular satellite subscription service that delivers a constant supply of "Bollywood" films from India, and the most popular programmes from Doordarshan. Young black Londoners listen (along with many white kids) to Choice and Kiss FM, both popular black music stations. Pirate radio still continues its time-honoured battle with the law. The pirates play the latest styles in dance music (such as Jungle), or those that are still too wild for the "legitimate" stations – Gangsta Rap, for instance.

Thus, in various ways, the tastes of today's particular interest communities can be met outside the mainstream. The media landscape is becoming increasingly diverse. For most of this century, it has been true to say that radio and television were both too centralized in the south- east (London) and too concentrated in large- scale monopolies (the BBC's monopoly of radio ended only in 1973). Only in the last decade or so have radio and television begun to operate effectively in regional and local contexts alongside the historically established, dominant "national" context.

Multiculturalism poses the question as to whether the notion of a shared national culture is any longer meaningful. Can the BBC, for instance, continue to summon up notions of the British people and a British way of life in any meaningful way? "In the past the BBC has been seen to portray a nation with clear-cut cultural values. However there is now a recognition of the multicultural, multifaceted nature of the country and public broadcasting should acknowledge and reflect this diversity: cultural, regional and social" (John Ellis, quoted in BBC 1995: 7). It is certain that the old idols of the tribe no longer have the resonance they once possessed for the majority. The British monarchy, for instance, is clearly going through one of its bad patches. A society characterized by increasing cultural diversity, however, does not necessarily fragment into many different cultures. It remains a key function of modern media, and national PSBs especially, to create and maintain new forms of common life. Entertainment – soap operas, for instance – is central to this. Also central is the projection of public events that draw in everyone. Increasingly, these events are major sports competitions. The threat, in this case, comes not from cultural fragmentation or loss of traditional values, but from the increasingly competitive television market, which has enormously raised the commercial value of the rights to premium sports events.

For many years, there were a small number of "listed events" – such as the Football Association Cup Final – which were preserved in the public domain by successive Broadcasting Acts. Listed events could not be bought out by one side or the other; both ITV and the BBC had the option (they did not have to take it) of covering the Cup Final and a handful or so of sporting occasions of comparable significance. The 1990 Act abandoned such protectionism. Since then, Rupert Murdoch's BSkyB Network on the Astra satellite has been aggressively buying up rights to soccer, cricket, and golf. Premier league soccer, the Ryder Cup, and overseas test matches are now only available to those who have rented BSkyB's satellite dishes. Moreover, while the BSkyB Sports Channel was free to begin with, this groundbait has now been withdrawn, and it has become a subscription service on two channels (Sky Sports 1 and 2). Furthermore, key sporting events will be encrypted on a pay-per-view basis with a correspondingly high charge for premium events. The net effect of these changes is to undermine an important role of national PSBs, as sporting events are taken out of the public domain and, in effect, privatized. The BBC has held on to some cherished hardy annuals, such as Wimbledon, until the end of the century. However, the cost of rights in sporting events is ever-increasing, because sport, albeit in contradictory ways, is now a key element in global television culture (Rowe et al. 1994).

Today, all of us inhabit many different cultures, some we share with many others, some with a few. We are all embedded in global, national, regional, and local cultures (Giddens 1990). Cultural differentiation is marked not simply by class and economic power, but by age, gender, sexuality, religion, ethnicity, and so on. The complexities of contemporary cultural tastes, in all their polymorphous diversity (some would say perversity), are reflected unevenly and, at times, awkwardly in increasingly diversified media landscapes at the end of the century. In the landscapes of today, the role of PSBs is still central. The measure of their success is not to be found in gross percentages of audience share but in terms of "reach." Reach measures the percentage of an audience that watches or listens to a channel in the course of a week or month. The BBC currently estimates its share of the total television audience will be around 30 percent, at the end of the century, but its reach is at least 90 percent per week. Channel 4's current audience share is just under 11 percent, but its audience reach, in the early nineties, was 79 percent of the viewing population per week, and 93 percent per month.

Public service broadcasting in Britain is often thought of, especially overseas, as peculiar to the BBC, but it is not. The BBC laid the foundations of broadcasting in the United Kingdom and still remains its cornerstone. However, commercial television in Britain operated for many years with a tight public service remit and still does so today, albeit in a weaker form. Channel 4 is remarkable proof of the continuing adaptability and relevance of public service values in contemporary society. It is both fully commercial and fully committed to public service goals. The future of commercial radio is planned by the Radio Authority with an eye both to commercial and public interest requirements. Only cable and satellite services have no statutory public service requirement. Ten years ago, there were worries that these highly commercial new technologies would seriously threaten existing PSB, but the evidence to date hardly bears this out. There are about one million cabled homes in Britain today receiving around 40 channels. In spite of a diversity ten times greater than the four available terrestrial channels (BBC 1 and 2, ITV, and Channel 4), the latest survey of viewing patterns in cabled households shows a significant increase in the audience share of terrestrial television: up from 57.9 percent in October 1993, to 65.1 percent in October 1994. All four terrestrial channels increased their share in 1994, with BBC 1 showing the greatest rise (ITC news release: 16 December 1994).Anxieties were, and continue to be, most sharply focused on the restless aspirations and activities of Rupert Murdoch. BSkyB currently reaches, by its own estimates, 4.3 million households taking satellite or cable services. In September 1993, BSkyB switched to subscription payments for most of its services, which had initially been "free." In the following year, it suffered a fall of 18 percent in average viewing per customer. This has been attributed to higher costs for subscribers and/or a less varied programme menu than the four national terrestrial channels. The latest viewing figures for cabled households show a continuing decline, over the last three years, of audience share for each of BSkyB's main channels, in contrast to the gain in audience share by each of the four terrestrial channels.

The current state of play in Britain is finely balanced. Those who forecast the demise of PSB have proved to be false prophets. Both the BBC and Channel 4 are in good shape, but not quite the shape they were in a decade ago. At the same time, the market has become sharply competitive, and both ITV and

Channel 4 are now more driven by commercial factors than they were before the 1990 Broadcasting Act. Cable and satellite services will continue to expand into more and more households, but not at the rate predicted in the late 1980s, when it was estimated that half of British households would be taking their services by the end of the millennium. Continuing political interventions, or attempts to move broadcasting out of the public sector, over the last ten years, from Conservative governments dedicated to non-intervention in British industry, show that deregulation has, in effect, meant re-regulation. In spite of Margaret Thatcher's famous remark that "there is no such thing as society," it has proved difficult to implement policies in relation to broadcasting based on such an assumption.[5] PSB has proved durable, because it regards broadcasting as a public, social good. On the evidence to date, so too does the British public.

Notes

1. I am grateful to my colleagues, Peter Goodwin and Stephen Barnett, for their helpful comments on this chapter, which I have taken into account in revising it for publication.

2. The classic account of the development of the British system is Asa Briggs's magnificent five volume history (Briggs 1960-1995). In contrast, a good account of how broadcasting in the United States moved in its early years can be found in Susan Smulyan (1994).

3. The 1918 Act gave the vote to all men aged 21 and over and all women aged 30 and over. This absurdity was removed in 1928, when women were given equal voting rights with men.

4. The Independent Television Authority (ITA), created by the Television Act of 1954, became the Independent Broadcasting Authority (IBA) in the early 1970s, when it became responsible for commercial radio as well. The IBA was dissolved by the 1990 Broadcasting Act and replaced by the Independent Television Commission (ITC), whose responsibilities for commercial radio were allocated to a new "light touch" regulatory body, the Radio Authority.

5. "There is no such thing as society. There are individual men and women, and there are families." (Margaret Thatcher, interviewed in *Women's Own*, 31 October 1987).

References

Arthurs, J. 1994. Women in Television. In *Behind the Screens: Structures of British Television in the 1990s* edited by S. Hood. London: Lawrence and Wishart.

BBC. 1992. *Extending Choice*. London: BBC Publications.

BBC. 1933. *BBC Year Book*. London: BBC Publications.

BBC. 1995. *People and Programmes*. London: BBC Publications.

Bondebjerg, I. 1994. Modern Danish Television – After the Monopoly Era. In *Nordic Television: History, Politics and Aesthetics*, edited by F. Bono and I. Bondebjerg. Copenhagen: Sekvens.

Briggs, A. 1960-1995. *The History of Broadcasting in the United Kingdom*. 5 vols. Oxford: Oxford University Press.

Cardiff, D. and P. Scannell. 1987. Broadcasting and National Unity. In *Impact and Influences* edited by J. Curran et al. London: Methuen.

Daniels, T. 1994. Programmes for Black Audiences. In *Behind the Screens: Structures of British Television in the 1990s*, edited by S. Hood. London: Lawrence and Wishart.

Dines, G. and J. Humez. 1995. *Gender, Race and Class in Media*. Thousand Oaks, CA: Sage Publications.

Dyer. R. et al. 1981. *Coronation Street*. London: British Film Institute.

Foucault, M. 1982. The Subject and Power. Afterword to *Michel Foucault: Beyond Structuralism and Hermeneutics*, by H. Dreyfus and P. Rabinow. Brighton: Harvester Press.

Garnham, N. 1994. The Broadcasting Market. *The Political Quarterly* 65(1): 11- 19.

Geraghty, C. 1995. Social Issues and Realist Soaps: A Study of British Soaps in the 1980s/1990s. In *To Be Continued... Soap Operas Round the World*, edited by R. Allen. London: Routledge.

Giddens, A. 1990. *Modernity and its Consequences*. Cambridge: Polity Press.

Harvey, S. and K. Robins. 1993. *The Regions, the Nations and the BBC*. London: British Film Institute.

Harvey, S. 1994. *Channel 4 Television: From Annan to Grade*. In *Behind the Screens: Structures of British Television in the 1990s* edited by S. Hood. London: Lawrence and Wishart.

His Majesty's Stationery Office. 1950. *Report of the Broadcasting Committee* (Beveridge Report). Cmnd. 8116. London: HMSO.

Her Majesty's Stationery Office. 1962. *Report of the Broadcasting Committee* (Pilkington Report). Cmnd. 9284. London: HMSO.

Her Majesty's Stationery Office. 1977. *Report of the Committee on the Future of Broadcasting* (Annan Report). Cmnd. 6753. London: HMSO.

Her Majesty's Stationery Office. 1988. *Broadcasting in the '90s: Competition, Choice and Quality*. Cmnd. 517. London: HMSO.

Hoggart, R. 1956. *The Uses of Literacy*. Harmondsworth: Penguin Books.

Kleberg, M. 1994. The History of Swedish Telvision. Three Stages. In *Nordic Television: History, Politics and Aesthetics*, edited by F. Bono and I. Bondebjerg. Copenhagen: Sekvens.

Kumar, K. 1977. Holding the Middle Ground: The BBC, the Public and the Professional Broadcasters. In *Mass Communication and Society*, edited by J. Curran et al. London: Edward Arnold.

Mulgan, G. 1990. *The Question of Quality*. London: British Film Institute.

Mytton, G. 1993. *Global Audiences: Research for Worldwide Broadcasting*. London: John Libbey.

Peak, S. 1993. *The Media Guide, 1994*. London: Guardian Books.

Peak, S. 1994. *The Media Guide, 1995*. London: Guardian Books.

Porter, V. 1995. Public Service Broadcasting and European Regulation. *Mediaforum* 7(3): 30- 34.

Rowe, D., G. Lawrence, T. Miller and J. McKay. 1994. Global Sport? Core Concern and Peripheral Vision. *Media Culture and Society* 16(4): 661- 676.

Scannell, P. 1988. Radio Times: The Temporal Arrangements of Broadcasting in the Modern World. In *Television and its Audiences*, edited by P. Drummond and R. Paterson. London: British Film Institute.

Scannell, P. 1993. The Origins of BBC Regional Policy. In *The Regions, the Nations and the BBC*, edited by S. Harvey and K. Robins. London: British Film Institute.

Scannell, P. 1996. *The Care-Structures of Radio and Television*. Oxford: Blackwell.

Scannell, P. and D. Cardiff. 1991. *A Social History of British Broadcasting, 1922-1939*. Oxford: Blackwell.

Smulyan, S. 1994. *Selling Radio: The Commercialization of American Broadcasting, 1920-1934*. Washington, DC: Smithsonian Institution Press.

Taylor, C. 1994. *Multiculturalism*. Princeton, NJ: Princeton University Press.

Whitley, O. 1968. *The BBC and the Public Mood*. London: BBC.

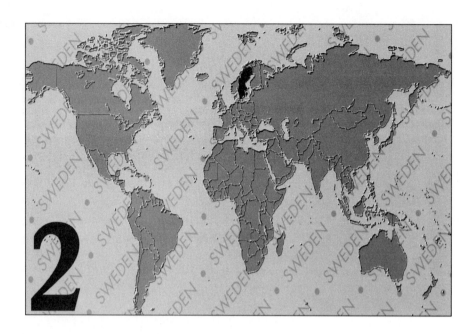

Sweden: Broadcasting and the Social Project

Olof Hultén

Mass Media and Freedom of Expression

A description of the Swedish model of broadcasting needs to take into account a number of historical and socio-political factors other than those determining the more immediate financial and structural conditions of mass media. The observation by French historian Fernand Braudel about the role of the *longue durée* is relevant (Braudel 1980). There is a strong element of permanence in Swedish socio-cultural affairs, including broadcasting policy over the decades. Visions of the future and interpretations of past experiences are influenced by such longer historical waves as the balance/ rivalry between the centre and the rest of the country. Another particularity is a Lutheran tradition of frugality, seriousness, and self-improvement.

One of the fundamental ideas in support of the national state monopoly in radio, and later television, has been the universal distribution of information, culture, and enlightenment to all sectors and corners of the country. This is not something that was or is to be a privilege of urban dwellers or elite groups. The Swedish concept of *folkbildning* has been central to public service politics. The concept implies an underdog perspective of self-improvement and conquering of knowledge among ordinary people, as well as a paternalistic perspective – the trickling down of elite culture and raising the level of taste among the masses. The idea of *folkbildning* preceded radio by a hundred years. Labour unions, temperance groups, and farmers' cooperatives used it, in the late nineteenth century, to further their interests. The same organizations (now serving as pillars of established society) were made, by Parliament, the majority (60 percent) shareholders of the modernized Sveriges Radio in 1956. They remained as dominant shareholders until 1992, when the old monolith was broken up into three public broadcasters owned by a state foundation.

Another long wave factor is a strong scepticism of commercial forces and influences in the cultural sphere, including in radio when it was introduced in 1925. Advertising was seen as in vulgar taste, and the dissemination of culture and knowledge was not to be influenced by sellers of commodities. Newspaper publishers were quick to exploit this sentiment in their effort to protect their advertising revenues. The press emphasized, instead, the educational and cultural role of radio. It was not until the late 1980s that the Publishers Association gave up its resistance toward commercial broadcasting.

From Print to Broadcasting

An authoritarian perspective dominated all aspects of Swedish print media until the middle of the nineteenth century. The monarchy set up the office of the censor in 1688 to control an increasing number of books, pamphlets, journals, and other publications. After a brief period of press freedom enjoyed between 1766-74, the first constitutional protection of freedom of expression was achieved in 1810.

The year 1766 is remarkable, however, because it marks the passing into law of the first (albeit temporary) protection of freedom of expression. The Parliament of the time was dominated by two groups (or parties), while the power of the monarchy was weak. The law introduced in 1766 abolished censorship, guaranteed freedom of expression (with the exception of heresy), and it introduced citizens' right to access to all public documents. The last principle has since then uninterruptedly remained a part of the Swedish constitution, unique in the world. The more than 200 years of legal right to public documents will probably be affected by the very different European tradition, now that, since 1 January 1995, Sweden is a part of the European Union (EU).

From 1810, protection of a free press and uncensored journalism have been upheld, continuously amended, and improved. This process has, of course, not been smooth and easy, but at times bumpy and controversial, at least until the mid-nineteenth century, when freedom from censorship was reintroduced (the first law had been established in 1766 but soon after revoked). Since then, content can only be contested through the courts after publication. The legal responsibility lies with only one person: in newspapers, the editor-in-chief. The Swedish constitution engages a jury only in cases of freedom of expression. Authorities are prohibited from tracing the sources of information, and journalists, as well as their sources, are guaranteed anonymity.

Between 1812 and 1844, a licence was required to publish newspapers and other periodicals. The licence was defended with arguments similar to those used when radio was introduced in the 1920s, including the argument that the power of newspapers is great, and it is necessary to have some control over who supplies citizens with news and other kinds of information.

The first modern newspaper in Sweden, *Aftonbladet*, was launched in 1830 by a wealthy nobleman, Lars Johan Hierta, who was interested in free trade and voting rights. He had to fight a long battle with the government, and many times had the licence confiscated, until the authorities gave up. It was only after World War II that Parliament decided to take a fresh look at the Freedom of the Press Act, 130 years after its conception. This overhaul was made in light of the experiences of the recent war, during which some newspapers were stopped, not by the Freedom of the Press Act, but by administrative decisions denying them railroad transport. Protection of the press was further strengthened in the revised act of 1949, which has since been amended again, as freedom of the press remains an important issue even today. Further developments include the introduction of the Fundamental Law on Freedom of Expression, in 1992, which gives broadcasting the same constitutional protection as print media. In most respects, the protection is the same regardless of how and where the information is published.

Critics observe that there is very strong protection given to media, while the individual's position remains relatively weak, resulting in few cases being taken to the courts. In these cases, the jury is instructed to favour freedom of expression if it has any doubts. To defend their privileges, publishers introduced, as early as 1900, a Code of Ethics and, in 1969, the Office of the Press Ombudsman. These voluntary measures have, so far, persuaded Parliament not to introduce legislation on the individual's right to privacy, as now exists in other countries.

When the new mass medium, broadcast radio, was first discussed in Sweden in the early 1920s, the daily press had already developed into a relatively mature industry. Its freedom was constitutionally protected, but its economic base was vulnerable. The newly formed Publishers Association worked hard to reduce the threats posed by radio (Hultén 1980). Protection of advertising revenues was one apparent reason; news was another. The publishers had just managed (in 1921) to create a cooperative wire service, jointly owned across political affiliations, which the government encouraged. Sweden needed a nationally controlled news service.

To these problems of the press industry and national political interests were added the experiences from the war, the revolution and civil war in Russia, as well as widespread hunger, poverty, and social unrest in Sweden (as elsewhere in western Europe). When a number of applications for broadcast licences came to the government in 1922, a broad political consensus was soon reached for a state-controlled radio monopoly.

This background is necessary to understand and appreciate the deliberations behind the monopoly model chosen for broadcasting and the arguments used in its defence. It explains why the national monopoly, later dubbed a "public service," has endured so long and strong in Sweden. The elements of the *longue durée* change only slowly.

The Broadcasting Heritage from 1925

There were more newspaper titles published in Sweden in the early 1920s than ever before or since. Anyone had the constitutional right to start a newspaper, print any news in it, and finance the operation in any way possible. One might have expected, therefore, some influence from the liberal press ideology at that time on the new mass medium. However, as a consequence of the political situation and the strong political position of the press, only a few voices in Parliament defended commercially operated radio broadcasting in private hands. There was even less support for competition between different stations.

Supporters of a monopoly argued that the state must have full control over this potentially powerful mass medium. In the wrong hands, radio could be used for political propaganda and the creation of unrest. The privacy of the home must be protected from unsolicited political quarrels and tastelessness, and the authority of parents over children must not be weakened. As the economic viability of the service was far from certain, threats to the quality of its programmes had to be avoided.

However, it was considered improper for the state to actually produce the content itself. A national monopoly, operated by a private organization under strict government control, seemed to solve most of the snags. The service was obliged to cover the whole country. The press, demanding protection of its news, offered to supply radio with "correct and impartial" news in exchange for the monopoly licence. The government, recognizing the need for a viable and dependable national news service, found the arrangement proposed by the press to be mutually beneficial, and, as a result, press institutions held the exclusive rights to produce and supply news bulletins until 1956.

The company created and licensed to operate the national radio service, Radiotjänst AB, was owned by a consortium of publishers and businesses. An industrial lobby of set manufacturers had also applied for an exclusive licence. The two rivals were asked to share the responsibility for broadcasting. The national Telecommunications Administration (Televerket) was given full control of the network and all technical facilities, including studio microphones. It was also asked to collect the compulsory receiver fee introduced to finance the programmes, a role it retained until 1989.

Programmes were to be a mix of correct and impartial news (broadcast in the evening after newspapers had been published), culture and entertainment of "good taste," and educational content. Parliament decided that only those families which wanted to listen to the programmes would have to pay. Eventually, Swedish families became very interested in the new medium, and the number of licence fees rose faster than expected. Between 1925 and 1951, governments regularly kept part of the fee income. During this period, almost 30 percent of the revenues paid was diverted to the state budget. Advertising was not explicitly forbidden at the start, but was never used – not surprising given the involvement of the newspaper publishers. Advertising was also considered culturally out of taste, if not vulgar.

An operating agreement, renewable annually, was signed between Televerket and the government, specifying the obligations of the service. A Broadcasting Commission was appointed to make sure that Radiotjänst fulfilled its obligations.[1]

Televerket had a number of reasons for wanting to control broadcasting. The wireless was a natural extension of its established wired network, and it was already planning wireless telephone service between Sweden and North America, which began in 1925. Its engineers had studied long distance telephony in the United States and no doubt had taken notice of the broadcasting activities of AT&T. The transmitters needed to broadcast radio programmes across Sweden were clearly seen as a back-up addition to the existing infrastructure, and Televerket's main interest was to use the licence fees from the households, interest-free, for investment in its other activities.

Radio was assigned a paternalistic educational and cultural role and, as such, it no doubt served well in a country where most people lacked good education, had little access to national cultural institutions and, in general, had few means of entertainment. Consequently, the government and Parliament were keen on having the widest possible diffusion of radio, and therefore set the licence fee low (US$3.25/year) to ensure that it would be within reasonable reach of the average working-class household.

The Basic Structure of Swedish Public Broadcasting

From the start, in 1925, public service broadcasting in Sweden was closely linked to the state, in particular to the government (the ministry of transport and communication) and Televerket. With the approval of Parliament needed for the use of the frequency spectrum and the introduction of a licence fee for owning a radio set, special laws for the collection of licence fees and for the liability of the responsible publisher were introduced. The basic structure is still in place after 70 years.

Culturally, most Swedes of the 1920s were undersupplied. Libraries, in cinemas, magazines, and theatres were amenities for the towns and cities, but the majority of the population lived in the countryside, in villages and small towns, and were to a large extent dependent on farming and forestry. Radio was seen as a way to spread adult education, schooling for children, and cultural enlightenment to everybody, and was to be used for *folkbildning*, for improving the minds of the Swedish population. Although the publishers had emphasized this function for self-interested reasons, the ambition rested on a longer tradition from the nineteenth century: The Church of Sweden, the political establishment, as well as the expanding industrial society all had a utilitarian interest in raising the educational level of the population. In this sense, it can be said that Swedish public service broadcasting was a legacy of the Enlightenment (Sorbom 1971).

Radio and, later, television were met with suspicion from many quarters. The new media, it was feared, would divert people from reading books, going to meetings, or being active in voluntary associations or labour unions. In fact, educational, serious, and anti-commercial attitudes have always characterized the position of official, established Swedish society toward broadcasting. Only reluctantly and gradually has this frame of mind changed, and these attitudes still constitute an important, if now not dominant, influence on broadcasting policy. In 1974, a national policy on culture was adopted by Parliament. One of the dominant goals of the policy was to stimulate local initiatives and more grassroots participation in cultural production as well as consumption. The same perspective was subsequently reflected in the laws on community access radio (1978) and local cable television (1986).

In 1940, Sweden had a larger share of households with radio than any other country in Europe. Only after 1951, however, did Parliament establish a separate Broadcast Fund, where all revenue from licence fees was earmarked for exclusive use of broadcasting.

The original Broadcasting Commission, created by the government in 1927, was to ensure that Radiotjänst fulfilled the operating conditions of its agreement with the government. Since 1935, however, its function has been to review programmes that have already been broadcast, either in response to complaints from the audience or on its own initiative.

Early Development: The Pioneer Years Until 1957

Radiotjänst served the Swedish audience with one national network until the mid-1950s. With increased experience and growing self-confidence, the company began to demand more autonomy and greater freedom in its programming. Clearly, listeners wanted more programmes and better transmitters. They began to complain about bad reception in many places around the country, and some also complained about limited output and too much serious content. Until FM networks were installed, large segments of the population had weak or no reception, and Televerket started to build a cable radio network to supplement its transmitters.

Following from the developments in the exp.'nsion of radio, a second national radio network was started, in 1955, and devoted especially to serious music. A few years later, two pirate radio stations operating off the coasts of Sweden caused Parliament to forbid advertising on these stations and instruct the national radio service to start a third network, exclusively for light music. This network opened in 1964.

Meanwhile, a report to Parliament in 1946 had introduced the idea of television, but the government did not take the initiative to bring television to the public agenda. A research and development project on television was soon established by Televerket, the Royal School of Engineering in Stockholm, and L.M. Ericsson, the telecom equipment manufacturer. Subsequently, Radiotjänst quickly decided to set up its own project group. Both bodies wanted to start experimental broadcasts with television, and a jealous rivalry developed between them.

Neither the government nor Parliament was particularly keen on television. The country needed its resources for industrial development, not entertainment. But, in 1951, the government appointed a parliamentary commission to review the options and the technical possibilities. Two years later, a consortium of industrial companies applied for a television broadcast licence. This brought to the open the question of whether to keep the public monopoly or accept private commercial television (Wirén 1986).

In 1952, the so-called Stockholm VHF Plan was accepted by the International Telecommunications Union (ITU), meeting in Stockholm on the invitation of Televerket. The frequency plan allowed for national television networks to be built in Europe. Televerket wanted a quick decision to invest in new networks for VHF and FM to replace the old incomplete AM and cable radio distribution networks.

Advertisers and the business sector wanted a private company responsible for television. As with radio in 1925, the publishers again fought hard to avoid advertisements on television. In May 1954, Televerket issued a temporary television licence to a film company called Sandrew, and, during one week, the new medium's potential was demonstrated, providing all the attention Televerket had hoped for. The government did not approve, however, and withdrew Televerket's licensing power.

Later the same year, the Television Commission published its report. The majority favoured a public monopoly, free of commercial interests in the service of "society, culture, education, and family life." This time, Radiotjänst and the publishers worked together to stop the commercial lobby initiative. The broadcaster had the support of the Social Democrat government, and in 1956, Parliament extended the operating agreement with Radiotjänst to television as well, now for a ten-year period. Televerket was to build and maintain all transmission networks, as well as continue to collect the fees for radio and new television licences. In 1956, television was officially inaugurated.

Radiotjänst was reorganized in 1957 and renamed Sveriges Radio. The press and business communities now had to share power on the board of governors with a group of new owners: the popular movements of Sweden, including labour unions, churches, adult education associations, and consumers' and women's organizations. As a reaction against earlier criticism of the state's control of both broadcast media, Parliament made room for the new owners as a way to increase the accountability of Sveriges Radio, by opening broadcasting to the people. These groups were allocated 40 percent (later increased to 60 percent) of the company's shares; the press kept 40 percent, and business organizations kept 20 percent. All these share holders, however, were only the symbolic owners of Sveriges Radio. The government appointed half of the governors, as well as the chairman.

Most of the structure of broadcasting was kept as before: Parliament was responsible for legislation, annual approval of the licence fee level, and the budget allocation. The government appointed the majority on Sveriges Radio's board of governors, all members of the Broadcasting Commission, and negotiated and signed the operating agreements with Sveriges Radio. Since 1966, the content of the Radio Act and the agreements have changed only minimally. The policy process and the power structure around broadcasting remained intact for another 25 years, which were marked by a whole range of controversies.

Expansion and Modernization: 1956-1991

The rapid growth of television alongside the three national radio networks led to increased revenues and accumulated power and influence in Sveriges Radio. In its new agreement from 1956, the broadcaster was obliged to serve the audience with unbiased information and a diversity of quality programmes, to serve the whole country as well as various minority and interest groups. As a servant of freedom of expression (a concept then used in relation to radio and television) Sveriges Radio was to be accountable, pluralistic, and respectful of its unique position in society.

For many, the monopoly itself, vested with all these obligations, was the guardian of freedom of expression. Critics of advertising and commercial influences argued that commercial services would always have to give priority to other masters than the people. A mission statement for Swedish broadcasting was coined by the parliamentary report of 1965: "a radio and television in the service of the public." The emphasis would thereafter be placed on the quality of this servant, Sveriges Radio, its independence, and its professional organization.

Television quickly captured the leisure time of Swedes. Within four years, 50 percent of households had bought a television set. The new medium caught the attention of the press and other media, as well as all other social institutions affected by it – such as the conventional mass organizations, represented on the board of governors of Sveriges Radio. They claimed that television enticed people to stay home rather than go to meetings, night classes, theatres, and public events. Television was associated with this kind of socio-cultural scepticism and ambivalence for many decades, just as radio had been.

As late as in 1977, the Broadcasting Commission summarized its views in this way: "A more important goal than striving for vast audiences for programming in our opinion is the stimulation and activation of viewers and listeners ... Thus we do not consider efforts to increase the amount of time viewers and listeners devote to radio and television proper for the broadcasting entity" (Sweden 1977: 38).

Although entertainment was cherished by the viewers, culture and information achieved extraordinarily high ratings (on the single channel). The medium conveniently brought many new experiences to a broad public: entertainment shows, classical drama, American sitcoms and westerns, British thrillers, documentaries and nature programmes, and, not least of all, sports. In 1957, Sweden hosted the World Soccer Championship tournament, a midwife as good as any to deliver television to the whole country (especially as the national team was only beaten by Brazil in the final).

Soon after completion of the first national television network, demands began to be heard in favour of viewers' choice. The second network became an issue on the political agenda after the 1961 European frequency planning conference on UHF, which allotted Sweden frequencies for three UHF networks. A commercial lobby, this time under the leadership of the Dutch conglomerate, Philips, started its preparations for a private television broadcaster to compete with the monopoly.

In 1962, the parliamentary commission already at work on revising the broadcasting legislation as a consequence of the activities of pirate radio, was asked also to propose alternatives for the second television channel. As in the 1950s' campaign for commercial television, the split between advertisers and other business interests soon became apparent in the private lobby. Advertisers' primary goal was to open the established national network for commercials in order to reach as many viewers as possible. The majority of the lobby, however, was more concerned with liberalizing broadcasting and giving independent Swedish television (after the British model), a chance to compete with the monopoly (Wirén 1986).

Two models, two principles, were competing for political legitimization. The commercial lobby pointed at audience ratings and public opinion polls as the most democratic method. This way, the viewers could decide for themselves, and there was no need for a *förmyndare* a guardian, to decide for them. The other model, recommended by the parliamentary commission, extended the existing socially responsible, representative system, with its emphasis on programme quality and cultural values.

In 1965, the commission proposed that the two television channels be coordinated within Sveriges Radio, financed by licence fees as before. In the evenings, one channel was to broadcast regional productions, the other programmes from the capital. The day-time schedules were also to be specialized: one channel for foreign programmes, the other one for programmes aimed at schools and special target groups (Sweden 1965). Olof Palme, then minister for culture and education, convinced the government of the merits of a different model. The two more or less identical channels would be operated by Sveriges Radio, but in competition with each other. A "stimulating race" for the best producers, writers, journalists, and programmes was hoped for, rather than a chase for the biggest audiences, which would follow from commercial competition. To open up the monopoly, Sveriges Radio was to be divided into six operating divisions under one board of governors and one director general, with each of the divisions responsible for its own budget.

Palme's vision persuaded Parliament in 1966. He had diffused the acute issue of advertising by promising a separate parliamentary commission on advertising in general. Clever strategy from the government saved the established public broadcasting model. The commercial lobby had failed, and the press was divided.

From an ideological point of view, most newspapers did not like the monopoly; however, in their own interests, they wanted to keep advertising off television. The press defended its position by pointing out the very special role of a diverse and viable press in a democratic society. This function was not to be jeopardized. The arguments were to be heard often from the 1970s, as Parliament introduced a press support system to counteract the market forces that were creating local press monopolies in every town and city.

The second national television channel, TV2, opened in 1969. Large numbers of young producers and journalists had to be recruited. Encouraged by the radicalism of the time, and of the obligations specified in the Radio Act and Sveriges Radio's licence agreement, TV2 – nicknamed "the red channel" – soon faced severe criticism for its programmes (Cederberg and Elgemyr 1984).

Already during the 1960s, a number of controversies had erupted as a result of increased professionalization of television news and current affairs programmes. Journalists took seriously their task to scrutinize what was happening in society, and negative reactions were only to be expected. Traditionally, public broadcasting had kept a low profile – its role was meant to serve established interests. From the late 1950s, its autonomy was made explicit in the agreement. Public broadcasting's job was to serve the listeners and viewers, first and foremost. The challenge was accepted by Sveriges Radio and defended by the whole organization, if not always by its board of governors.

Of all the controversial programmes during these years, probably the strongest reactions were caused by a number of programmes about various historical and contemporary aspects of the Social Democratic and labour union establishments. During 1971-72, the board of governors, with a majority representing those groups, discussed and criticized these programmes several times. Against the background of a number of criticized programmes during the previous 10 years, many in the Swedish political and business establishments felt that Sveriges Radio now had gone too far.

The public broadcaster rode out all these storms with its integrity and autonomy unscathed, however. Sveriges Radio developed into an active and independent institution with a professional ethos, later endorsed in the Radio Act, as well as in licensing agreements by governments of different political persuasions. The current agreement, from 1 January 1993, uses strong words: public broadcasting "shall" offer a diversity of opinion and cater to differing interests, which "implies an obligation" to "scrutinize authorities, organizations and private firms which exert influence over policy affecting the public" and "shall stimulate public discussion of important socio-economic and cultural issues" (Sveriges Television 1994: 14-15).

In retrospect, it was natural that as Sveriges Radio evolved into a much bigger professional broadcasting organization, doing away with old inhibitions and its traditional respect for established interest groups, those groups would also react. The integrity and respect public broadcasting has achieved, however, has become an indispensable part of contemporary public service in Sweden.

Decentralization of the National Monolith

During the 1960s and 1970s, accusations were frequently directed at Sveriges Radio for being overly centralized and bureaucratic, for not reflecting the diversity of the whole country, and for not creating enough jobs outside Stockholm. The broadcasting organization had established a system of regional offices, but they were totally dependent on Stockholm for putting programmes on the air. Very limited regional news was broadcast on only one of the radio networks.

There was a growing demand for more local output on both radio and television. A parliamentary report recommended, in 1973, that a system of local (regional) radio stations be established (Sweden 1973). Some wanted the system to be totally outside the old monopoly, because of Sveriges Radio's past record and lukewarm interest in decentralized broadcasting. The company itself wanted to integrate the new service into its existing operations.

A compromise was struck in Parliament in 1975: the 25 new regional stations were organized in a semi-independent subsidiary to Sveriges Radio. This was the start of an expansion which culminated in the creation of a fourth radio network, fully established in 1987, for the exclusive use by the regional stations. A sudden burst of initiatives, engagement, and vitality renewed radio journalism, as well as the organization of Sveriges Radio. It did not happen, however, without some bitter rivalry between national and local services.

The compromise did not satisfy all those demanding even more local and non-monopoly radio. Many people in Sweden had ideas about the future that did not square with those reflected in the monopoly model adopted by Parliament. Public access radio was seen by some as a potential stepping stone toward deregulated and commercial radio. Parliament supported licensing of very local, non-profit community stations in 1978. For the first time since 1925, someone outside the monopoly could get a broadcast licence. One factor influencing the introduction of public access radio was the general shift in the role of the state, which took place during the 1970s (Hultén 1988). The urge to decentralize state power affected the school system, the health system, and other national administrative services as well. The state and its broadcasting had to come closer to the people. Another element behind the introduction of local access radio was the long-standing criticism of public broadcasting by churches for not transmitting enough religious programmes.

A number of community radio associations were given temporary licences to broadcast. Non-profit organizations, churches, and student associations, among others, were able to broadcast their own programmes (at their own expense). Networking was not, and still is not, allowed. All programmes had to be produced specifically for each group. Despite these limitations, the experiment was defined as a success, encouraging Parliament to make non-commercial community local radio a permanent feature of the Swedish media system in 1982.

Some of these local groups were part of an effort to introduce "free radio" (private commercial radio). Three stations sponsored by the Swedish Employers Federation (whose local chapters were defined as non-profit organizations) in the three biggest cities acted and sounded like any commercial station, except for the lack of spot advertising. Instead, jingles with pro-business messages were inserted.

By the time Parliament allowed commercial local radio, in 1993, around 2,500 licensed groups and associations were broadcasting on 165 transmitters all over the country. Broadcast time could fill more than 40 round-the-clock stations. Relatively few groups broke the law by selling advertising, but one licensee was taken off the air after being charged with inciting racism.

Transformation in the 1990s: The Dual Structure

As an important prelude to the changes to the Swedish broadcasting structure in the early 1990s, cable television was introduced in 1986. Its introduction was not in reaction to issues related to the public broadcaster, but, moreover, a direct consequence of satellite developments in Europe. Sweden was well aware of this technology and its potential usefulness. A thorough government study of a Nordic direct broadcast satellite (DBS) project, called Nordsat, had been carried out with the neighbouring countries (Nordic Radio and Television 1980). Nordsat was designed and intended as a cultural project, to stimulate integration in the Nordic region through exchange of television programmes by DBS. The idea was turned down in 1981 by the four Nordic governments (Denmark, Finland, Norway, and Sweden) because of the high costs and unclear cultural effects of the project (Hultén 1981).

The European Space Agency (ESA) had launched and deployed, in 1983, a joint European low-powered communication satellite called Eutelsat, intended for telephony. As demand for long-distance telecommunication by satellite was low, the operating consortium (owned by the national telecommunications monopolies, or PTTs) decided to lease Eutelsat's idle transponders for television transmission. The pioneer television channel, Sky Channel, formally linked from Britain for use in Malta. Eutelsat never tried to enforce the rules for point-to-point satellites, and demands for downlink and retransmission rights of Sky and other channels grew. The Swedish government, receiving such applications in 1982-83, was now in the same situation as the government had been in 1923: What were they to do?

A parliamentary commission, appointed a few years earlier to prepare policy on new information technologies, was asked to look into satellite and cable as well (Sweden 1994a). The commission concentrated on how to regulate cable systems for mass media use, but its perspective was clearly one of industrial policy. New jobs would be created, and cable was the beginning of a universal broadband communication system. The commission saw few consequences for established national cultural policies or for broadcasting if some foreign satellite channels were to be retransmitted by cable systems. In 1986, Parliament accepted one of the most liberal cable laws anywhere. The dominant lobbyist was Televerket, again protecting its interests. This time, monopoly was considered neither politically correct nor economically efficient (Hultén 1986).

The building and operating of cable systems was left, unregulated, to the market. Domestic cable channels had to respect the restrictions against advertising on Swedish television. Cable could carry no advertising intended directly and exclusively for Swedish viewers. However, local access television, foreign channels, as well as Pay-TV could be offered to cable subscribers.

On New Year's Eve, 1987, a commercial channel intended for Swedish (and Scandinavian) viewers, TV3, was launched from London by a Swedish steel and forest company called Kinnevik. Cable operators finally had something unique to sell and interest in cable increased. In a few years, most of the areas suitable for cable were connected. In February 1989, the first European satellite suitable for direct reception, Astra, was introduced, and it became obvious that the Swedish defence against commercial broadcasting was obsolete. TV3 moved from Eutelsat to Astra (in which Kinnevik was one of the principal investors).

The Swedish Cable Authority advised the government to change the law, since it was no longer possible to enforce it. Astra viewers with their own receivers could now watch anything they wanted, regardless of Parliament's approval. According to the law, however, Astra viewers connected to cable systems were denied access to TV3. In 1992, the law was changed.

Today, both cable networks and their content are part of a deregulated market. A cable network is defined as a system with more than 100 homes connected, and the rules applying to cable are similar to those for the press. Cable television, however, has to meet three basic obligations: (1) all nationally licensed terrestrial channels and a local access channel must be transmitted free of charge; and (2) the volume of advertising on cable-originated channels must not exceed 10 percent of broadcast hours, the same rule as for other domestic channels.[2]

* The Swedish Parliament was simultaneously forced to review its policy for terrestrial broadcasting. The majority in Parliament realized that if nothing were done, advertising revenues would flow abroad and, thus, not necessarily benefit domestic programme production. In 1989, a study ordered by the Social Democratic government presented three alternative options: accept advertising on public channels, reserve commercial revenues for a new private national broadcaster licensed by the government, or allow advertising on both private and public channels.

Although a substantial minority in Parliament still did not want any change at all, the dominant attitude in the Social Democratic party and its government was to open the public channels to advertising and, hopefully, reduce the licence fee. The political opposition, as well as a minority among Social Democrats, wanted to break the monopoly.

The minister of culture, Bengt Göransson, was definitely against commercialization of public broadcasting. In September 1990, he gave permission to a private satellite channel, called TV4 (dominated by the Wallenberg industrial group), to use a transponder on the Swedish high-power satellite Tele-X, which had been launched earlier that year. Göransson's ad hoc decision, in practice, short-circuited the parliamentary vote to follow in 1991 (Hultén 1992).

* After 30 years of discussion about commercial television, Parliament finally resolved what had become an unavoidable dilemma (Sweden 1991). Since satellite and cable distribution had already been liberalized – satellites by the EU's directives and the cable market by Parliament's own cable legislation – the only arena where Parliament still had exclusive power in relation to broadcasting was the control of terrestrial and DBS frequencies. In June 1991, the DBS frequencies allocated to Sweden by the World Administrative Radio Conference in 1988 were put under the management of the state-owned Swedish Space Corporation, which now operated two high-powered satellites, Tele-X and Sirius.

* Parliament's decision to create a new, private national terrestrial channel in 1991 meant the public television broadcaster was denied advertising. The board of governors of Sveriges Radio had, for the first time, determined it wanted advertising to increase its budget in the wake of increased competition, but the terms creating TV4 called for maximizing the new channel's available financial resources. In exchange for its advertising monopoly, TV4 accepted a number of public service obligations and began broadcasting in March 1992.

The licence agreement between TV4 and the state specifies, among other things, high quality news reflecting the whole country, domestic and Nordic drama, as well as a certain volume of children's programming. Policy regarding news and information is the same as for public television: It should be unbiased, diverse, and show respect for the ideas of democratic government. Advertising is allowed for up to 10 percent of total broadcast time (in an individual hour, 13 percent), in principle inserted only between programmes and not directed toward children under 12 years of age. The Broadcasting Commission reviews the performance of the new broadcaster.

After the 1991 parliamentary decision on commercial terrestrial television, legislation on private radio followed in the spring of 1993. The government was now a conservative-led coalition, and the minister in charge of media policy, Birgit Friggebo from the small Liberal party, was a convinced radio deregulator. As a result, the Swedish law on private radio is very liberal in comparison to other countries in Europe.

Parliament accepted Friggebo's view that coming technological changes in the near future meant there would soon be no frequency bottlenecks for radio (Sweden 1992). According to this logic, there are no reasons for the state to make demands on the private stations, which should have the same privileges as newspaper publishers. However, frequencies need to be allocated and their use protected from intruders. The newly created Radio and Television Authority (1994) is responsible for the allocation of licences.

The greatest innovation in the radio law of 1993 was the licensee selection process: by auction to the highest bidders. As of December 1994, 82 licences had been sold, bringing in substantial annual revenues to the state budget.

All licences are given on a local basis, each holder limited to only one – in the name of freedom of expression. Owners of newspapers cannot dominate a station; that is, they cannot have control of more than half the shares. The only obligation regarding content is that a third of transmission time must be filled by programming "specially made for the station." Licences expire at the end of the year 2000. They will be automatically extended, unless the frequencies are needed for the introduction of digital radio. New licences will be allocated as demand arises. Licences can be freely bought and sold.

The gap between the goals of the law and reality is a good lesson for students of media policy. Of the 82 stations licensed between October 1993 and November 1994, less than a handful are independent and local. Four national chains dominate, the biggest one being owned by France's NRJ, Europe's largest commercial radio company. Two networks are controlled by newspapers, and half of the stations in Stockholm are foreign-owned. Almost all programmes, including news, are centrally produced and networked.

The non-profit access stations are guaranteed frequencies (at no costs) for local transmitters. Since 1993, local access licensees have been allowed to supplement their budgets with advertising. There are 160 access radio stations in service, with 1,300 licensed organizations transmitting programs.

Sveriges Radio and Sveriges Television were formally split into two separate organizations in 1993. Today, public radio and television face increasing competition, although it has not yet reached a really aggressive state.

Advertising revenues of commercial broadcasters are still rising. Sveriges Radio operates four segmented networks and 25 regional stations. Private, local radio is a euphemism for highly integrated, transnationally syndicated and formatted music outlets.

Sveriges Television's two networks are challenged by three major commercial general entertainment channels, of which only one, TV4, is terrestrial (reaching 98 percent of the population). The cable and satellite channels, TV3 and TV5 (Femman[3]) still have a more limited reach (currently about 60 percent of the population). In addition to these general channels, a growing number of Swedish Pay-TV and specialty channels, as well as the gamut of European-wide thematic channels, are offered Swedish viewers.

The main rival to Sveriges Television today is TV4. After less than two years "on the ground," it has surpassed the two public channels and now attracts the biggest share of the audience. Together, the three terrestrial channels are watched by more than 80 percent of all viewers (in satellite/cable homes 70 percent), the two satellite-only channels have a little more than a 10 percent share, and all other channels split the remaining audience.

The Policy Process

The brief historical review of Swedish broadcasting reveals a very strict parliamentary control of terrestrial stations. This national political control is now much weakened. First of all, the Fundamental Law on the Freedom of Expression (a part of the Swedish constitution since 1992) situated cable in the tradition of the print media. There are few constraints, but the most significant one is the obligation to carry Sveriges Radio and Television and TV4. Second, satellite television has been declared by the EU a free market. No country is allowed to prevent uplink and reception of transborder satellite channels, as long as the obligations specified in the EU's Television Directive are fulfilled.[4]

Broadcasting policy in Sweden still reflects a cultural perspective in the old tradition, subordinating market forces to a cultural political agenda (Hultén 1984). The protection of such values is becoming more futile as broadcasting by satellite and cable gain ground. Terrestrial television, because of its enormous impact and influence, is still seen as the primary source of information, values, and entertainment; therefore, a social and cultural dimension is still very strong, and TV4, for example, is obliged to meet a number of conditions. Private local radio, on the other hand, was introduced very much in the tradition of the print media. No content obligations are enforced, licences (still necessary for frequency allocations) are considered private property, and there is no mechanism for challenging an established station.

The policy-making clout of the Swedish Parliament on broadcasting hinges on the trade-off between the audience reach of conventional terrestrial channels and channels distributed by satellites or cable. When the latter are able to reach a greater percentage of the audience, it might be attractive for TV4 to leave the terrestrial network. Transmission costs would be significantly reduced, and the levy TV4 now pays to the Radio Fund (the account into which all licence fee revenues are deposited and through which public broadcasters are supported) could disappear, as well as the programme obligations in its agreement with the state.

Aside from the legislative role of Parliament, the government has always played a significant role through the licence agreements vis-a-vis public broadcasting and, now, TV4. The agreements contain a number of conditions, some of which have a long tradition and some of which are new. The review of these agreements (more frequent now than before the 1970s – every four years for Sveriges Radio and Television and seven years for TV4) is a political matter and the outcome of a negotiating struggle between political, corporate, and market forces, where the latter have gained.[5]

Commercial radio, access radio, and cable and satellite broadcasting are the responsibility of the Radio and Television Authority. This government agency was created in 1994 by joining three smaller offices. It allocates licences for private radio. In relation to cable, its duties are limited to scrutiny of must-carry and local-access channel obligations. In relation to satellite broadcasting, the role is to check that the EU Directive is followed by channels uplinked from Sweden.

The government appoints all members of the board of a new state foundation, which since 1993 has owned the public service organizations. Many among the previous share holders of Sveriges Radio are currently competitors. The government also appoints the members of the Broadcasting Commission, which reviews programmes and advertising practices. Commercial radio, access radio, and cable and satellite broadcasting are only examined on the latter account; they have no content obligations to meet. Criminal liability is a matter for the courts.

The broadcasters themselves are naturally important actors in the policy process. The increasing market orientation of broadcast media give them a growing role. All aspects of broadcasting are influenced by this role, including the activities of public channels and all others making up the input side of the media. As a consequence, legal matters and court disputes have begun to take up a considerable amount of time.

Among legislators, the government, and public broadcasting, there is a long tradition of interaction and interpretation of laws and agreements (Ortmark 1979; Hadenius 1992). In time of licence renewals and during the work of parliamentary commissions, these relations are especially crucial. The autonomy of programmes has been respected, although proposals to set up formal audience advisory councils have been shelved by Parliament.

The value of the users' licence fee has been tied, since 1978, to an index related to cost increases. Today, the licence fee is approximately US$7.50, which is paid by over 3 million households. Of this sum, Sveriges Television receives 60 percent; Sveriges Radio receives 35 percent; and UR (Educational Radio and TV) receives 5 percent. In return for financial security, public broadcasting has been required to organize, operate, and produce in a gradually more regionalized mode since the 1970s. Parliament expects 40 percent of all domestic production on radio and television to originate in the regions. In 1992, the government refused to allow public television to reorganize its two separate news departments into one.

The experience of relations between TV4 and the Broadcasting Commission show how difficult it is to enforce rules on commercial practices. Scores of programmes were found to break the law: by being too generous in displaying products in programmes; by putting advertising breaks within programmes; by advertising to children under 12 years old; and by not clearly identifying sponsored programmes. Only after the government publicly stated that no changes to the Radio Act in relation to advertising rules was to be expected until the renewal of the licence in 1998 did TV4 seem determined to respect the law. The head of the Broadcasting Commission was furthermore recruited by TV4 in the summer of 1994.

TV4 argues that the rules governing its commercial activities are more severe than those applying to its competitors, TV3 and TV5, which, as satellite channels, come under the EU Directive. Those two channels claim foreign status – TV3 as a British and TV5 as a Luxembourg station. The biggest bone of contention is that EU, not Swedish, rules permit programmes to be interrupted by commercials and also to be directed toward small children, during and around children's programmes.

This example illustrates the complexities of the new commercial broadcasting industry in Sweden. Commercial networks and stations, together with advertisers, do have common interests on many matters in Sweden as well as on the European level. Cable operators have organized a common platform to protect their interests in relation to Swedish rules, demands of satellite channels, and copyright holders. On the whole, however, the industry is still too young and turbulent to have evolved into a unified lobby.

Public Broadcasting and the Competition

As revealed by this brief historical account of broadcasting developments in Sweden, competition to public broadcasting came late. Demands to abolish the monopoly and to introduce private ownership and advertising on television and radio were repeatedly turned down until 1991 and 1993, respectively. With comparatively liberal laws on commercial radio and cable television, Sweden can be characterized as a three-tiered broadcasting market: public channels financed by licence fees, privately owned terrestrial channels, and satellite channels competing for commercial revenues in a more and more aggressive rivalry.

The nature of the commercial rivalry influences the public channels in many ways. Some viewers and listeners think it unnecessary to finance public channels offering the same programmes as commercial stations. This is not yet a public issue in Sweden. Audience support, through licence fees and through watching and listening, is considerable. Criticism of bad programmes, of managerial mismanagement and disregard for audiences, has not been an issue in Sweden, as it has been for other European public broadcasters, since the 1970s (Nowak 1991; Hultén and Ivre 1978). Demands to privatize some of the public channels have been made, and they will no doubt become louder in the future. The timing of such demands will depend on the levelling off of advertising revenues, expected around 1996-97. Continued support of a public service, attracting maybe as much as half of all viewers and listeners, reducing commercial revenues correspondingly, cannot be an attractive scenario for the private sector.

Studies in Sweden reveal a big difference in programme profiles between public broadcasters and the private sector (Hultén and Nilsson 1994). Sveriges Television has significantly more drama, domestic productions, and diverse children's programmes. TV4 is not meeting its formal programming obligations; for example, in 1992, the company closed its children's department. When it does, costs will go up. TV3 and TV5 show no Swedish drama or other high-cost productions. Less than 20 percent of the broadcast time on TV3 is produced in Sweden, and TV5 has a low percentage in this respect. Talk shows and reality shows are the only primetime fare of Swedish origin on TV3.

One of the most important current and future issues is the content profile and programme quality of the public and private broadcasting sectors. Systematic studies of the output are too rare and irregular for good policy making (Hultén 1994). Issues of quality on public channels are also muddled by confrontations between traditionalists and modernists. What is quality television in the 1990s? That is a question which demands an answer in a manner and shape which is useful to policy making.

Public Broadcasting as a Social Project of the Future

(Support for the idea of public service is still strong in Sweden) The audience seems to appreciate the quality, integrity, and variety of what public broadcasting offers, although many in the audience, especially among the youngest generation, also enjoy (and prefer) what the expanding commercial sector brings. Public broadcasting is still financed by licence fees, and, today, almost 85 percent of television-viewing households pay the fee without reminder; 92 percent pay thereafter; and, according to recent polls, 60 percent of the population think they get good value for their money.

There has also been continued political support for public service, although the reasons for it have shifted since 1925. Radio was then made primarily to serve a number of actors in the public sphere: the state, the established political system, the press, and cultural and educational institutions. Focus has gradually changed from paternalism to a democratic model of public service: to serve people's needs and rights to know and to speak.

This is not to say that there is one unambiguous vision of public service. Many still emphasize high culture and education, as in 1925. Others regard critical journalism as the hallmark of public broadcasting, as in the 1960s and 1970s. Still others give priority to local and regional interests in this age of globalization. The mental framework of the *longue durée* contains different forces.

Parliamentary commissions reporting in 1965 and 1977 marked the most important shift of priorities from the old to the new. The notions of public broadcasting as independent and professional (1965) and as pluralistic and decentralized (1977) were supported by changes in consecutive updated versions of the Broadcasting Acts and licence agreements. But public broadcasters have had to fight for their right to push the limits of freedom of expression. Viewers and listeners have, directly and via the political system, demanded their right to be properly served by public broadcasting.

There are now two main issues facing Swedish public broadcasting and European public broadcasting generally: (1) its own role in the mass media system; and (2) the structure and control of private media conglomerates. The two are, of course, interrelated. The first issue is dependent on public broadcasting itself to prove its value, through diversity, quality, accountability, and distinctiveness from commercially sponsored services (see Sweden 1994b). The commercial sector, meanwhile, has entered a phase of large-scale transnational synergy and integration on a scale never seen before in the history of the mass media. This creates growing political concern, even fear, in different countries and on the EU level. It raises the very difficult political problem of how to balance pluralism and economy, structural diversity and private ownership and control (see Le Duc 1987).

New distribution technologies, from the Internet to video-on-demand, have been heralded as the solution to the problems of pluralism where established media have become monoliths centralized in a few hands. But this is not enough, if we consider that the democratic process is as much about expression and creating content as it is about distribution.

Public service broadcasting will continue to be a vital factor in this effort. If it did not exist, it would have to be invented, but not in the culturally paternalistic fashion of the past. In the future, it will not serve as a vehicle for social engineering, but as a source of independent journalism and diverse cultural expression.

Notes

1. The contract period was increased to three years following a parliamentary review in 1934, and, after 1943, the licence agreement with the government was signed by Radiotjänst, now placed on an equal footing with Televerket.

2. The European Union Television Directive allows 15 percent on satellite channels from EU member states.

3. Femman is a U.S.-owned satellite station, operated in Sweden and distributed by Tele-X, the Swedish DBS. The company claims, however, that it is a Luxembourg station and, thus, outside the reach of Swedish Law.

4. An interesting case here is the recent decision by the EU Court that a country can stop a satellite channel exclusively intended for it if the only reason for such a channel to originate in another country is to dodge the laws of the receiving country.

5. The latest renewal process for public broadcasting started in early 1995, to be finalized in a new agreement on 1 January 1997. The review of TV4's licence agreement is due a year later.'

References

Braudel, F. 1980. *On History*. London: Weidenfeld and Nicholson.

Cederberg, J. and G. Elgemyr, eds. 1984. *Tala till och tala med: Perspektiv pö den svenska radion och televisionen* (Speak to and talk with: Perspectives on Swedish radio and television). Stockholm: Legenda.

Council of Europe. 1994. *The Media in a Democratic Society*. Draft resolutions and draft political declaration, 4th European Ministerial Conference on Mass Media Policy, 7-8 December, Prague. Council of Europe, MCM-CDMM (94) 3 prov 1.

Gilder, G. 1994. *Life After Television: The Coming Transformation of Media and American Life*. Rev. ed. New York: W.W. Norton.

Hadenius, S. 1992. Vulnerable Values in a Changing Political and Media System: The Case of Sweden. In *Television and the Public Interest*, edited by J. G. Blumer. London: Sage.

Hultén, O. 1980. Rundradions organisering in Sverige 1922-24: Argument för och emot monopolet (Organization of broadcasting in Sweden 1922-24: Arguments for and against monopoly). *Statsvetenskaplig Tidskrift* (3): 121-34.

Hultén, O. 1981. Why Nordsat-Why Not? *Media, Culture and Society* (3): 315-25.

Hultén, O. 1984. *Mass Media and State Support in Sweden*. 2d. ed.Stockholm: The Swedish Institute.

Hultén, O. 1986. Current Development in the Electronic Media in Sweden. In *Media in Transition*, edited by U. Carlsson. Göteborg: Nordicom Sweden

Hultén, O. 1988. "Citizens" Community Radio: Public Access in Sweden. A Case of "Old Technology" and New Ideology. Paper presented at the 16th IAMCR General Conference. Working session on Democratization of Communication, 24-28 July, Barcelona, Spain.

Hultén, O. 1992. Sverige inför dualt nationellt rundradiosystem (Sweden introduces a dual broadcast system). Copenhagen: Pressens örbog 1991.

Hultén, O. 1994. Möngfald eller likriktning? (Diversity or homogenization? Studies of TV output). In *Nordicom-Information* 4: 9-22.

Hultén, O. and I. Ivre. 1978. Sweden: Small But Foreboding Changes. *Journal of Communication* 28(3): 96-105.

Hultén, O. and C. Nilsson. 1994. *Det svenska TV-utbudet 1987 och 1993. Undersökning av sändningstid och programkategorier* (Swedish TV programme output 1987 and 1993. Study of broadcast hours and programme categories). Working report 41, Department of Journalism and Mass Communication, Göteborg University.

Le Duc, D. R. 1987. *Beyond Broadcasting: Patterns in Policy and Law*. New York: Longman.

Nordic Radio and Television via Satellite. 1980. Final Report. NU A1979: 4E (English Version), Stockholm.

Nowak, K. 1991. Television in Sweden 1986: Position and Prospects. In *Handbook of Comparative Broadcasting*, edited by J. Blumler and J. Nossiter. London: Sage.

Ortmark, Å. 1979. Sweden: Freedom's Boundaries. In *Television and Political Life: Studies in Six European Countries*, edited by A. Smith. London: MacMillan.

Siune, K. and W. Truetzschler, eds. 1992. *Dynamics of Media Politics: Broadcast and Electronic Media in Western Europe*. Euromedia Research Group. London: Sage.

Sörbom, P. 1971. *Läsning för folket* (Reading-matter for the people: A study in the early history of popular education in Sweden). Stockholm: P. A. Norstedt and Söner.

Sveriges Television. Information Department. 1994. *The Laws and Agreements 1994*. The Basic Rules Applying to Sveriges Television. Stockholm: Sveriges Television.

Sweden. Broadcasting Commision. 1965. *Radio och Televisionens framtid i Sverige* (The future of radio and TV in Sweden). Report of the Broadcasting Commission. Public document SOU 1965:20.

Sweden. Radio Commision. 1973. *Radio i utveckling* (Development of Radio. On local radio, etc). Report of 1969 Radio Commission. Public doc. SOU 1973:8.

Sweden. Ministry of Education and Cultural Affairs. 1977. *Radio and TV 1978-85*. Proposals of the Swedish Broadcasting Commission. Abridged English version of the Final Report.

Sweden. 1991. *Om Radio och TV-frögor* (On radio and TV issues). Governmental Bill to Parliament.

Sweden. 1992. *Den avgiftsfinansierade radio-och TV-verksamheten 1993-96 m.m.* (The licence fee financed radio and television 1993-96). Governmental Bill to Parliament, 1991/92:140.

Sweden. Ministry of Culture. 1992. *Regler och villkor för privatradio* (Rules and conditions for private radio). Public doc. Ds 1992:22.

Sweden. Advertising Commission. 1993. *TV-reklam-frögan* (TV advertising). 3rd report from Advertising Commission. Public doc. SOU 1973:10

Sweden. Mass Media Commission. 1994a. *Via satellit och kabel* (Via satellite and cable). Report by the Mass Media Commission. Public doc. SOU 1984:65.

Sweden. 1994b. Green Paper on Public Broadcasting issued by the Swedish government. *En radio och TV i allmänhetens tjänst!* (A radio and TV in the service of the public!). Public doc. Ds 1994:76.

Swedish Press Commision (SPC). 1994. *Dagspressen i 1990-talets medielandskap* (The daily press in the media landscape of the 1990's). Report from the 1994 SPC, Stockholm.

TV10 SA vs Commissariaat voor de Media. 1994. Judgement of the EU Court (5th chamber), Case C-23/93, Netherlands.

Weibull, L. and B. Börjesson. 1991. *The Swedish Media Accountability System*. Department of Journalism and Mass Communication, University of Göteborg.

Wirén, K-H. 1986. *Kampen om TV. Svensk TV-politik 1946-66* (The struggle over television. Swedish television policy 1946-66). Stockholm: Gidlunds.

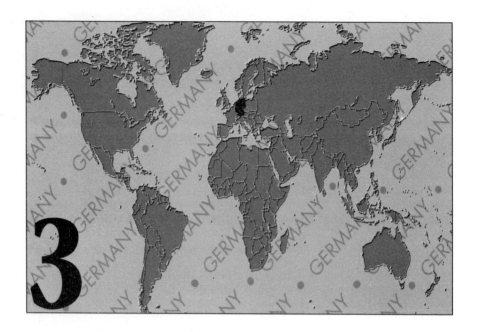

Germany: The Regulation of Broadcasting

Wolfgang Hoffmann-Riem

Historical Background and Current issues

On 29 October 1923, regular radio first began in the German Reich (see Lerg 1980). Under the influence of the electrical equipment industry and the Reichspost (PTT), the medium was primarily entertainment oriented. The government permitted news and public affairs programming to only a limited extent, and it strictly controlled both. This structure enabled the National Socialists to increasingly wield broadcasting as a tool of propaganda after 1933 (see Diller 1980).

In the period after World War II, broadcasting was created as a public service institution obligated to provide programming that was independent and pluralistic (Bausch 1980a, b). Broadcasting was modelled on the British Broadcasting Corporation (BBC), especially in northern Germany, and broadcasters were obligated to the commitments inherent in that model. Since this did not correspond to the German broadcasting tradition, special guarantees for independence and pluralism had to be developed. The individual state legislatures sought to set down such guarantees in law. In the process, two types of norms were provided for (see Hoffmann-Riem 1990).

First, there are commitments with respect to conduct: public broadcasters are obligated to observe the duties of care and truth in their reporting and to air balanced programming; they are prohibited from giving one-sided preference to individual interests. As institutions, public broadcasters have been created as independent corporations whose revenues are mainly secured from broadcasting fees. Advertising has long been permitted, subject to restrictions as to time and content, but broadcasters may not pursue profit-making interests. Second, the internal organization of broadcast stations is regulated in such a way that representatives of relevant societal interests – churches, sports associations, trade unions, employer groups, and representatives from cultural organizations and political parties – form internal organs that influence budgeting, personnel, and certain decisions on the structure of programming. This organization is based on the idea that the various pluralistic interest groups balance each other out and, if need be, can block attempts to gain unilateral control of programming. Balanced programming is thus assured, satisfying all interests.

In 1950, broadcast stations, originally founded in certain regions, joined together to form a network, the *Arbeitsgemeinschaft der öffentlich-rechtlichen Rundfunkanstalten der Bundesrepublik Deutschland*(ARD), which provides regional programming distributed nationwide. The network's activities were initially limited to radio. Television broadcasting, which was launched in Germany in 1935 but banned by the allies immediately after the war, began again in 1952. The second nationwide TV broadcaster, the *Zweites Deutsches Fernsehen* (ZDF), was established via treaties between the states in 1963 in order to build up a centralized television broadcaster, and it has a legal framework similar to that of the state public broadcasters joined in the ARD.

Private enterprises, in particular press publishers, repeatedly called for a change in the existing laws and tried to be licensed as broadcasters. There were vivid discussions and political controversies around this subject in the 1970s and 1980s. Until 1984, attempts to establish commercial broadcasters failed. Since then, however, a number of private organizations have been licensed. Special state laws, as well as an Interstate Treaty on Broadcasting, established the legal framework and provided for state supervisory institutions, the *Landesmedienanstalten*. Since 1984, public broadcasters have had to compete with commercial broadcasting companies who are mainly dependent on advertising revenues. Advertising and sponsorship is allowed on public television, but it is restricted to 20 minutes each weekday and is not allowed on holidays. Pay-TV is still in the process of development.

This situation has remained almost unchanged since the re-unification of Germany. The former German Democratic Republic (GDR) broadcasting authority, which was responsible for the government-controlled broadcasting in the East (Riedel 1977), was dissolved on 31 December 1991. All of the eastern states have created new broadcasting norms and, thus, adopted the system of dual broadcasting set up in the West. New public broadcasting authorities have been established, and the legal obligations of private broadcasters have often been formulated more weakly than those in the western states.

Private broadcasters have consolidated to a large extent. RTL Plus, the private German-based private television company with the largest transmission range, was able to make a profit for the first time in 1990. Today, it attracts more viewers than either of the two public systems, ARD and ZDF. Competition between the broadcasters of the two systems, and within each system, has become the striking feature of the broadcasting order (see Kiefer 1994).

This development puts public television in the difficult position of having to compete for a viewing audience in order to politically justify its service and also because it is partly financed by advertising. Moreover, the price of programmes has risen to an exorbitant level, due to economic competition in the market. When choosing programmes, therefore, concessions have to be made to economic feasibility and resale value. On the other hand, public television faces the accusation that it "allows itself to become increasingly commercialized" and that it "converges" with the choice of programmes of private broadcasting companies, thus violating its own programme commitments (Schatz *et al.* 1989; see also Kröger 1991).

There are further problems for public television in the influence held by governments and political parties and because of a general insistence on proportional representation in the internal organs of the services. Furthermore, stagnation at the personnel and organizational level has, so far, prevented substantial self-reform, or, at the very least, suggestions for future-oriented reforms with respect to the new competitive situation.

Due to new technological developments – especially the prospect of digital compression – and the success of commercial broadcasters, public broadcasters are under heavy pressure. A discussion on their future has started (see, e.g., Weiß 1991; Vesting 1992; Plog 1994; Langenbucher 1994). Although the existence of public broadcasting itself is not in jeopardy, there are expectations on the part of its competitors, as well as influential politicians, that public broadcasting get rid of advertising and rely solely on revenues from broadcasting fees.

The objection raised against such demands is that fee revenue would not suffice to finance the public system. Furthermore, mixed financing from advertisements and fees provides protection against one-sided dependence on a single financial source and, thus, on those who determine the extent of that source. In addition, minimal financing via advertisements is a meaningful incentive for public broadcasters, bearing in mind that they too have to be oriented to a large audience and should not focus only on niches. In the meantime, the Federal Constitutional Court has declared the hitherto existing mixed financing of public broadcasting to be constitutional. However, the excessive influence of the state on the fee-setting procedure was criticized. The procedure must now be shaped in such a way that, on the one hand, an efficient financing system is guaranteed and, on the other hand, the programming autonomy of the broadcasters is respected. For example, politicians should not view decisions on the amount of the licence fees as an opportunity to exert influence on the programming conduct of public broadcasters.

Legal Framework

The development of the media sector has always been dependent on economic, technological, political, social, as well as cultural conditions of the respective society. The influence of Germany's legal system deserves special mention, because for years it has resisted the privatization of broadcasting but has now been aligned with the worldwide trend of liberalization and, thus, of deregulation and reregulation.

The Constitutional Guarantee of Freedom of Broadcasting

Communications policy in Germany has, above all, been heavily influenced by the Federal Constitutional Court. The basic right of freedom of communication and media (Article 5 of the Basic Law) was the starting point, and it created a framework for formulating detailed requirements for the structure of the media system and the conduct of journalists and media companies. Over time, the Court has interpreted the law to mean that freedom of opinion in the media is not merely a subjective right of the individual to ward off state interference, but also an objective guarantee to ensure the ability of the media system to function. In the interest of citizens' free formation of opinion, the state – acting through the legislature – must create positive assurances for the media to function. This requires commitments with regard to conduct and structural guarantees of pluralism, and, in this regard, the court considers the state as the guarantor of freedom. As a justification for the regulation of broadcasting, the court has thus referred not only to scarcity of frequencies and to broadcasting's special status as a financial undertaking, but also to broadcasting's power to influence citizens.[1] Competition among broadcasters cannot alone ensure that a significant number of social groups and intellectual movements truly have their say. This situation could result in the risk of concentration of power over opinion and abuse of such power for the purposes of one-sided influence on public opinion. Broadcasting – in contrast to print media – must not, therefore, be entrusted to the free play of the powers of the market.

Two elements are, thus, united: Broadcasting itself is conceived as a trustee of society, and the state has the task of ensuring through positive precautions that it actually assumes this trustee role. However, the state may not intervene in the content of communication, although it must create the structural guarantees of independence and plurality.

With this concept, the court is closely aligned with European public service broadcasting, in particular with that in Britain, as well as with U.S. case law.[2] Nevertheless, such a concept does not fit in with the philosophy of deregulation and privatization and of trust in the economic market, which has increasingly gained influence in the United States and Great Britain, and for which acceptance is growing worldwide, including in Germany.

Broadcasting today is no longer a national affair; it is not possible to maintain national or regional public service broadcasting at a time characterized by large, international media markets, commercialization of the broadcasting system, and widely deployable communications technology and software. In particular, representatives of economic and political interests – in Germany, these were initially large publishing companies, but they have now been joined by other, internationally active, multimedia organizations – are insisting that public service broadcasting either be dismantled or forced into a niche. Such forces have found some support within the European Union (EU) (see, for example, EU 1984) and from politicians who favour deregulation.

The Federal Constitutional Court still tries to protect public broadcasting, as the previously mentioned decision on the constitutionality of licence fees demonstrates. The court has always taken pains to maintain as much of public service broadcasting as possible. For this reason, it has clung to its concept of freedom of broadcasting and has rejected the deregulation philosophy, repeatedly emphasizing that market opportunities are an issue of economic freedom and not freedom of opinion. The state continues to be obligated as the guarantor of the media order, while it may allow private broadcasting alongside internally diverse, independent public broadcasting. Moreover, private broadcasters must also be committed to public service ideas, though their commitments may be less stringent than those of public broadcasters. The court sees in private broadcasting the economically unstoppable drive toward mass appeal and the disregard for minority interests. However, it believes that it is able to accept this as long as public broadcasting remains functional and basic provision is ensured: The entire spectrum of the population must be offered programming by public broadcasters that provides comprehensive information to the full extent of the classic broadcasting mandate.

To sum up, the wording of Article 5 of the Basic Law[3] makes no mention of a basic provision or of the relationship between private and public broadcasting. The court has, however, interpreted this norm in such a way as to salvage as much as possible from the classic broadcasting mandate. Its hopes here do not rest with private broadcasting but, rather, with public broadcasting. For this reason, it has sought to stabilize the latter, to keep it functional in the competitive struggle as well. From the standpoint of constitutional law, public broadcasting has a "guarantee of existence and development." It must remain capable of providing comprehensive programming, and it must have access to new technological opportunities. To this end, it must also be equipped with adequate financial underpinnings.

Broadcasting Law and Competition Law

Now that the Federal Constitutional Court and the individual state legislatures have laid the groundwork for the dual broadcasting system, and since private broadcasting is on the rise, the legal conflicts have changed. Particularly important is the battle concerning whether public broadcasting is subject to the same competition rules in the dual broadcasting system as private broadcasting (Hoffmann-Riem 1991). The basic idea underlying public broadcasting is, of course, that it does not operate on a profit-making basis and does not determine its conduct according to factors governing the economic market. Although it competes with private broadcasters for journalistic quality and audiences, it is not in economic competition with them (Kiefer 1994). The refusal to accept economic competition as a regulator is, however, rejected by arch-liberal theoreticians and practitioners. They believe that economic competition is, by far, the best assurance for programming competition and, thus, for diversity. They assert that the broadcasting order is best ensured when economic competition is functioning (see Hoppmann 1988: 163; Mestmäcker 1986; for criticism of this position see Hoffmann-Riem 1991; Rahn 1990).

Although the assertion of such authors is not supported by the Federal Constitutional Court, it has support from those courts dealing with the Act on Unfair Competition and the Act against Restraints of Competition, as well as from the Federal Monopolies Office, which keeps watch on the functioning of the economic market. Support also comes from the EU, which is seeking to apply EU competition law to public broadcasting. It is usually respected that public broadcasting programmes are, in themselves, not market commodities aimed at economic exchange; however, with respect to advertising, the purchase and sale of broadcasting rights and the awarding of contracts for programme production make public broadcasters subject to the same legal rules as other market participants. Public broadcasters counter this argument, however, asserting that they need special rights in order to fulfil their obligation to provide comprehensive programming.

The new legal battlefront makes clear that the issues have changed. Previously, the main ones were political communication and the assurance of the basic right to freedom of opinion and communication in a democracy, followed by the guarantee of public service. Now, the thrust is to ensure processes of economic exchange. Broadcasting has moved increasingly away from its cultural mandate and is on the way toward being treated as an economic commodity subject to market processes (Hoffmann-Riem 1990; 1995). With the exception of the Federal Constitutional Court, most German courts have had a strong hand in reinforcing this trend. While many legal commitments enacted in line with broadcasting's older tradition of cultural policy continue to apply on paper, there are only limited possibilities for ensuring their practical relevance. Broadcasting is forced to fight for survival – not merely for viewer ratings, but also for broadcasting rights to attractive programmes and to sell its own productions. In many countries of the world, the conduct of broadcasters is predominantly economically oriented, and the power of law to oppose this trend is waning. Even public broadcasting seems unable to avoid this process. Although it may not seek to make a profit, it views itself as having been thrown into economic competition and aligns itself accordingly. In addition, in the programming of public broadcasters, one can observe substantial efforts to adapt to private commercial broadcasting – even when it is still clearly distinguishable from its competitors and still maintains its public service orientation (Kröger and Zapf 1994).

Regulation of Commercial Broadcasting

Due to its understanding that Article 5 of the Basic Law requires guarantees of law ensuring the ability of the media system to function, the Federal

Constitutional Court has asked for an effective regulation of commercial broadcasting. The main objective has to be the guarantee of diversity of information and communication, which is an indispensable element for citizens' freedom of opinion. Consequently, the German media laws provide for structural safeguards of diversity, and they contain regulations related to programming conduct. The provision of structural safeguards is an attempt to combat concentration and to favour broadcasting companies in the licensing process that are composed of different enterprises. There are also attempts to give culturally oriented groups some access and to provide for regional or local programmes by way of what are called window programmes, which private broadcasters are forced by law to insert into specified time-slots. Programming-related obligations deal with due care, fairness, and special prohibitions against one-sided influence. Advertising restrictions, as well as safeguards for the protection of minors, have been harmonized by the Interstate Treaty on Broadcasting. Some media laws contain special programme restrictions – for example, when they ask for the promotion of international understanding or of German re-unification. In addition, there are regulations that seek to protect personal integrity and to provide for other aspects of consumer protection.

From the broadcasters' standpoint, the legal precautions and, thus, the complex legal obligations are ambivalent. In some respects, they fight them as burdensome ballast and, in doing so, invoke lofty ideals of freedom. In other respects, however, they are well aware that the norms also act as a protective shield for broadcasters, once they are established. Even commercial broadcasters have learned to live with these norms, realizing that the legal restrictions also make it difficult for new competitors to receive licences and prevail in the market. For public broadcasters, the protective norms guaranteeing their existence and development are regarded as necessities for survival in the battle with purely commercially oriented competitors; however, at the same time, these norms threaten to interfere with their ability to innovate and reform. The legislatures and the courts, nevertheless, proclaim that these norms foster the attainment of the desired objectives: for example, that the broadcasters' trustee orientation helps to ensure the citizens' freedom of opinion or that well-functioning competition is a basis for informational diversity. Whether these objectives will be fully attained or are attainable at all is doubtful. It may be presumed, however, that these values would be even more strongly endangered if the norms did not exist.

Public Broadcasting – Especially Television

Organization and Programming Commitments

The main bulwarks of German public service broadcasting are the ARD and ZDF. As previously mentioned, the broadcasters are legally independent from the government and financed by licence fees as well as advertising revenues (for details see Hesse 1990; Hermann 1994). They are under an obligation to provide so-called internally pluralistic integrated programming. A given pallet of programming must be diverse. For the purpose of monitoring the legal requirements, the broadcasting laws have provided for two special internal organs, the Broadcasting Council (*Rundfunkrat*) and the Administrative Council (*Verwaltungsrat*). The Broadcasting Council's main tasks are to ensure pluralism by monitoring independence and diversity in programming; the Administrative Council is to ensure that the administration and financial management comply with the regulations. Since supervision is thus accomplished "internally" – that is, by an organ of the broadcaster itself – there is no need for an additional, "external" supervisory body. Nevertheless, each state government makes sure that its public broadcaster observes the relevant laws, even though its supervisory powers are somewhat restricted (so-called limited legal supervision). State governments are prohibited from intervening in the shaping of programming itself (for details, see Berendes 1973; Hesse 1990).

The internally pluralistic structure is the result of a unique feature of German broadcasting law. So-called socially relevant groups, which are usually enumerated by statute, delegate representatives to serve on the Broadcasting Council; some delegates are elected by Parliament. These representatives then take on responsibility for the functioning of the broadcaster. They are recruited from a variety of spheres of interest in order to facilitate a reciprocal balancing of interests and, thereby, reduce the risk of one-sided broadcasting. Legal responsibility for programming, however, rests solely with the director general. Nevertheless, the Broadcasting Council, which is responsible for programming matters, possesses advisory and supervisory powers. It may focus on both individual programmes as well as the general structure of programming. Although it normally restricts itself to criticism of programmes following broadcast, in some organizations and in exceptional cases, it passes judgment on sections of programmes prior to broadcast. The Broadcasting Council also takes part in programming-related decisions on personnel, organization, and budgetary matters and, to this end, is endowed with considerable powers of intervention (for details, see Fritz 1977; Kabbert 1987; Cromme 1985).

Political and Financial Dependencies

Although originally conceived of as a guarantor of independence from the state and other power holders, the Broadcasting and Administrative Councils have, in reality, emerged as agents of political influence (for reports by insiders, see Menningen 1981; Vogel 1983; Plog 1981; Ronneberger 1986). The members of these bodies usually form coalitions mostly along party lines, meeting in so-called cliques (*Freundeskreis*) to agree upon joint conduct. The cliques, aligned with the respective state governments, often function as transmitters of executive interests. Consequently, the right of these bodies to take part in the appointment of managing personnel has sometimes been abused for political ends. If the governing party has been in office for decades, as in Bavaria, its influence will surely have been used to the full extent. On the other hand, in regions with changing majorities in the government, as in the northern states, a proportional system has emerged.

In spite of political affinities, public broadcasting is, on the whole, marked by political balance and a relatively high degree of journalistic independence. From a comparative standpoint with respect to independence from the state, the German public broadcasters more closely resemble the BBC than, for instance, the Italian RAI or the French broadcasters France Television 2 and 3. Proponents of political interests have a relatively insignificant amount of influence on daily programming. Because the Broadcasting Council's control over programming is restricted to exceptional cases, journalists are left to orient their work according to their own professional and ethical values. At the same time, however, even control measures that are limited to exceptional cases have an effect on day-to-day work, since they help to define the zone of "permissible" activities and, thereby, prompt or even provoke anticipatory compliance.

The state government's legal power to monitor the lawfulness of broadcasting activities, in the event that internal control bodies fail to function properly, has been subject, by law, to so many limitations that in practice it has been exerted only in a few cases. However, the government's supervisory competence helps to promote informal respect for government interests. Influence generally tends to be exercised in informal interactions not easily grasped by third parties. In addition, a government representative, although unable to vote, usually takes part in the meetings of the Broadcasting Council.

Programme Strategies

Under multichannel conditions, public broadcasters are forced to develop programme strategies that help to distinguish them from their commercial competitors. On the other hand, there is a tendency for commercial programmes to include traditionally popular elements from public programmes. In this situation, public broadcasters may adopt several different strategies:

[One model] would prioritize *by program type*, presuming that if commercial television concentrates on entertainment and topical news, public television should offer documentaries, plays, education, the arts, and science. This, however, is a formula for decidedly boxing public television into a corner, offering almost nothing for those entertainment gratifications that are central (though not necessarily exclusive) in many viewers' expectations of television. More fundamentally, this model ignores the fact, that in principle all kinds of programs can be different from how private broadcasting tends to shape them.

Another model would prioritize *by audience target*, presuming that if commercial – and especially advertising supported – television concentrates on mass-appeal programs, public television should serve the neglected minorities. Such a prescription is not only open to the same objections as those raised against differentiation by program type; it also arbitrarily excludes the majority from the benefits of a public service approach. The equation between 'public' and 'universal' should not be lightly dismissed. When public broadcasting does justice to the needs it strives to meet, not selectively but as widely as possible, it enables an openness in the process through which views, insights, and preferences initially shared by a few can also be found by a majority to be interesting and worthwhile. It is through such a dynamic component that public broadcasting can serve as a meaningful 'cultural forum' (Newcomb and Hirsch 1983) and a factor in cultural development.

Only a third model would enable public broadcasting at one and the same time to be different, meet public needs, and stay attuned to all viewers. It must be guided by a sense of qualitative priorities, differing from market-driven television not so much by the areas of programming presented, as by the characteristics of functions, gratifications, standards, and quality striven for in them. It must also cultivate a reputation for accessibility to public concerns and responsiveness to public needs. Though no single policy outcome follows from this prescription, which must be applied differently in the varying cultures and conditions of diverse broadcasting systems, a number of emphases could flow from it (Blumler and Hoffmann-Riem 1992: 27).

This third model has been accepted by German public broadcasters – at least in theory. In practice, it is very difficult to implement. A special problem is the balance between programmes for the majority and for minorities. The programme director of ARD, Dietrich Schwarzkopf, cites such a concept of "balance" as the vital course that public television will have to follow in the future:

On the one hand, a balance that attracts a sufficiently large number of viewers, meets the requirement of 'broadcasts for everyone' and justifies the financing through rates to be paid by all viewer-customers. On the other hand, this balance guarantees a distinctive profile of programmes by providing a service that the private companies either do not provide in the same way or not at all. This balance cannot be achieved by limiting the programmes to the so-called strictly public fields of information, culture, and education whilst ignoring the field of entertainment, an art form supposedly presented much better by the private companies. This balance also prohibits putting too strong an emphasis on entertainment whilst disregarding the other areas of the programme instructions laid down by law; the public television service would be accused of commercializing itself by the strict critics and friends of this public service as well as by those journalists close to the private companies (Schwarzkopf 1990: 681).

Schwarzkopf lists two vital responsibilities that determine the profile of the public television service: (1) Accepting cultural responsibility – cultural programmes represent an indispensable element of public television and should be broadcast at prime viewing times too; and (2) The integrative function: public television should encourage mutual understanding, particularly in connection with the re-unification of Germany. It should demonstrate and analyze the differences and similarities existing between various parts of the country. However, the final integrative objective cannot be an all-encompassing uniformity; rather, in order to establish and preserve a sense of identity, the vital regional differences must be sufficiently presented in the reports from various parts of the country.

Public broadcasters have particular strengths in information programming (Kröger and Zapf-Schramm 1994). The presentation of background information and contexts, the analysis of problems and help, and advice concerning individual everyday problems are essential areas of responsibility for the public television service. But there is a challenge by programme strategies of commercial broadcasters:

> Commercial broadcasting will tend all the more to televise an event, the more it is capable of attracting attention. This means that sensational and extraordinary events tend to be accorded a special rank. There is also a certain arbitrariness with respect to the socio-geographic region from which the news comes, favouring parochialism. Moreover, when the whole world is used as a resource for the display of extraordinary images, reality becomes distorted, forced toward those characterizations that vividness, simplicity, and intensity tend to generate (Blumler and Hoffmann-Riem 1992: 28, quoting Cohen, Adoni, and Bantz 1990).

The commercial competitors are usually strong in the field of entertainment (see Kröger and Zapf-Schramm 1994):

> Among commercial programmers, much competition is waged over attention-holding, production values (attractive stars, glossy sets, glamorous locations, pace, etc.) and sustaining tension. Stories are built around figures that can be speedily and universally understood and appreciated. Actors' local and social ties tend to be treated as theatrical props. Personalities are simplified into near-unidimensional stereotypes, only momentarily enriched to generate a paradox or an unexpected story twist. The imagination is piqued as external stimulus, but there is little incentive for deeper reflection. The melodramatic tension that arises from scene to scene is the plot, instead of its being an outcome of some deeper development. Emotions are excited without imaginative faculties being put to work (Blumler and Hoffmann-Riem 1992: 29).

In this environment, it is very difficult for the public broadcasters to have success in rating figures without resorting to the same strategies. But the imitation of a predominant commercial style can only be successful to a certain degree. Most public broadcasters will accept the following strategy, at least in theory:

> Entertainment in public channels should aim to stimulate and quicken imagination and thought, not shut it off. Its characters, even when standing for something emblematic, should have those less resolved qualities of complexity, potential, and uncertainty that stamp real-life individuals. Its conflicts should invite reflection on interests, temperaments, taboos, and preferences that originate in the real world and

pose dilemmas that viewers can absorb as belonging to life as they know it or could imagine it. Images should tell a story about real persons, not just allegories (Blumler and Hoffmann-Riem 1992: 30).

Special problems to develop a consistent programme strategy are linked to the ARD, a network combining programmes of different public broadcasters. Programme strategies have to be coordinated. Usually it takes a major effort for the different broadcasters to represent a unified position. There is no consistent strategy on how to conceptualize communication policy – neither at the organizational level nor at the "message level." Another problem that German public broadcasters face stems from the intertwined relationships between the print media and private broadcasting companies. To a large extent, German newspapers are very critical of the public broadcasting service – at least as far as questions are concerned relevant to politics or the licence fees (see Weiß 1988; Hasebrink, Schröder and Krause 1988). There is some suspicion that the programme guides – owned mostly by publishing companies which also have economic interests in broadcasting – are not always fair when dealing with public broadcasters.

Commercial Broadcasting

Public Service Obligations

As previously mentioned, commercial broadcasters are also bound to some public service obligations (Hesse 1990). The regulations vary from one state to the next, though the Interstate Treaty on Broadcasting, as well as the decisions of the Constitutional Court, have provided for some harmonization. Broadcasters are allowed to screen one-sided programmes, provided that the total programme range of all broadcasting is varied and balanced. They are free to choose their formats, but the formats are restricted to those that have become conditions of licence. All licensed stations are required to conduct conscientious investigations, demonstrate fairness, and observe general laws. Family viewing policies provide for youth protection by banning pornographic shows or by restricting violent programmes to late-night viewing only. Several of these programme obligations are almost identical to those of the public broadcasters.

Supervision

The crucial question is whether public service commitments are heeded by commercial broadcasters, and this question leads to the issue of effective broadcasting supervision. The supervision of private broadcasting is strictly separated from that of public broadcasting. The supervisory bodies are autonomous juridical organizations endowed with independence vis-a-vis the government and financed by a portion of the fees collected from viewers and listeners to finance public broadcasting (see Hoffmann-Riem 1993).[4] They are normally composed of two organs: The chief executive position is held by a director, who is responsible for day-to-day administration. He or she is joined by a collegial board. In most states, this collegial board is a large organ – modelled on the Broadcasting Council in public broadcasting – that follows the concept of pluralistic representation and is responsible for basic policy issues (see Wagner 1990). There are smaller executive boards within some of the media authorities (Hamburg, Berlin-Brandenburg, Saxony, and Mecklenburg-Western Pomerania). On the smaller boards, unanimous decisions have been reached in many cases, and the formation of close-knit cliques according to political leanings has mostly been avoided. On the larger, pluralistic collegial boards, large voting majorities are likewise to be found, although these consistently display a more diverse voting pattern. Their size, and thus their complexity, has led to efforts to form cliques (see, e.g., Reese 1989).

The history of broadcasting supervision in Germany is far from being a success story, especially as far as public service commitments are concerned (Hoffmann-Riem 1995). Due to the undefined, value-neutral terms set forth in the state media laws, the organizational options, and the many underlying media policy controversies, there has been a considerable amount of legal uncertainty. This is confounded by operational uncertainty. For instance, the media laws require in the licensing procedure that broadcasters also be assessed for their economic, journalistic, and organizational capabilities. However, there is a dearth of sufficiently reliable data on, for example, the necessary costs of local radio or anticipated returns. There are factual uncertainties in other areas as well, as in the evaluation of the organizational structures of licence applicants or broadcasters, particularly in terms of horizontal economic integration (see Röper 1990, 1991, 1993). The ingenious methods of interlocking and creating figureheads have made it nearly impossible to gain an up-to-date overview. German broadcasting law is rather lax in combatting concentration. The degree of concentration, especially vertical integration, is rather high, thereby undermining the concept of competition in the market place as a guarantor of qualitative diversity.

Applicants for a broadcasting licence must fulfil certain minimum prerequisites, for example with respect to their economic and journalistic capabilities (see Hesse 1990). A prognosis that the statutory requirements will be fulfilled is required before the licence is granted in a comparative procedure, which enables the state media authorities to select the "best applicant" and formulate stipulations. This is the most important point of departure for the control of the broadcasting order, particularly for preventive control of diversity (Wagner 1990). Normally, the state media authority calls upon competing applicants first to reach agreement with one another – for example, to agree on the formation of a joint broadcaster association or on a split frequency (use of the same frequency by several broadcasters at different, pre-arranged times of day). If they are unable to do so, or do so only in part, a preferential decision has to be made, which has very often favoured the financially stronger applicant (see Wagner 1990; Hoffmann-Riem and Ziethen 1989). Nevertheless, the state media authority is required to take into account a variety of criteria, which vary from state to state but mainly aim at ensuring programming diversity. In this regard, the proposed pallet of programmes or the composition of the company – for example, the degree of variety among the participating interests, with the inclusion of special cultural associations – may be just as important for the decision as precautions to ensure pluralistic programming councils or guarantees that the autonomy of journalists is protected against pressure from the capital side (see Wagner 1990).

In addition to granting licences, the state media authorities are responsible for the day-to-day supervision of the conduct of broadcasters. With the exception of Bavaria's authority, they are not empowered to review programmes in advance, but they may lodge objections to them. Supervision is limited to monitoring conformity with statutory requirements. The supervisory and sanctioning tools range from a mere notice of statutory violation, to an objection, and beyond to an order to refrain from certain violations in the future (see Wagner 1990; Holgersson 1993). Statutory violations can lead to revocation of the licence – although usually only after prior, repeated objection – and, in some cases, temporary suspension of the licence or prohibition of specific programmes. Subsequent directives designed as an additional specification of the licence are also possible as a means of sanctioning.

Despite formal supervisory and sanctioning instruments, the state media authorities very often prefer to use opportunities for informal cooperation (Hoffmann-Riem 1995). The informal procedure makes it possible to clarify uncertainties interactively, to react flexibly, to maintain cooperative relationships as long as possible, and to avoid court conflicts and the associated risks. A formal set of sanctioning instruments in the form of administrative requirements and prohibitions, or even the use of compulsory tools or fines, can rapidly lose their effectiveness when over-used; moreover, they may lead to still further statutory penetration and formalization of relationships, which most participants consider to be an impediment to the fulfilment of duties. Broadcasters also prefer the "policy of raised eyebrows" and usually react to informal references. However, they are, at the same time, encouraged by the practice of informal reactions to test the limits of the state media authority's tolerance. Generally, in practice, normative requirements have often been relaxed rather than tightened by way of changed interpretation in the interest of broadcasters.

Political Dependencies

Measured against the requirements of the rule of law, informal agreements are problematic, regardless of their practical advantages. The public normally has no access to these, and it is usually impossible to engage the courts in a review of the solutions reached. This dynamic poses a certain risk that in such informal bargaining situations, the power would remain in the hands of those who are also in control elsewhere in society and the law's potential as a power corrective would go unused. Especially in the media sector, one must give serious consideration to the objection that powerful media undertakings – at the moment, particularly publishing companies and multimedia firms – have better access to political power holders. They have apparently made use of this, not only in the phase of legislation but also during important stages in the licensing procedure. It cannot be stated with certainty that – regardless of its measure of independence – a licensing and supervisory authority will be insensitive to power constellations. The close interpersonal ties among the directors, as well as the relationships between many members of supervisory bodies, representatives of state policy, and the media industry, make such fears all the more valid. Licensing and supervisory practice have, thus far, not been marked by contrary indications. Therefore, a cooperative network or even a "capture" (a close relationship between private enterprises and the government) may eventually be a model that proves helpful for developments in the Federal Republic.

In spite of such risks, the possibility of flexibility and informality has proved to be an important tool in fulfilling supervisory functions (see Grothe and Schulz 1993; Holgersson 1993). Since a market economy basically accords priority to the self-interest of private enterprises, and since the supervisory authority has only limited insight into the workings of broadcasters (see, e.g., Thaenert 1990), the supervisory authority must depend on obtaining sufficient information and cooperation from those they supervise.

As previously mentioned, there are risks associated with informal supervisory practice. These have, thus far, been reduced only to a limited extent by involving the public. External third parties have no rights of participation in the supervisory process. Some state media authorities have involved the public on their own, thereby creating an additional threat and sanctioning tool. Broadcasters normally do not appreciate it when they become the subject of public discussion, let alone when they are publicly stamped as offenders. However, state media authorities practise restraint with regard to calling in the public. As a result, press releases and notifications are usually formulated most guardedly, and the public generally does not have access to the meetings of the supervisory bodies or committees. There is no German tradition of institutionalized civil activity in the broadcasting sector, such that even from a civic perspective, there is no strong pressure to increase public access. Now that the debates on media policy have waned, broadcasting no longer belongs to the preferred objects of public criticism and corresponding activities.

The importance of political, especially party, orientations of the supervisory authorities seems to be less than in public broadcasting. This is most likely related to the fact that the powers of the supervisory bodies are restricted and less effective than in public broadcasting. Missing are, in particular, the rights of participation in decisions regarding financing, budget matters, and personnel, as well as organizational issues of the broadcasting companies. On the other hand, there is some pressure by the governments on the supervisory authorities, especially as far as decisions on the locations of broadcasting companies are concerned. The state governments have sought to exert influence in an informal fashion on broadcasters and their state media authority in order to secure the location of desired broadcasters in their state. Since Germany does not have a centre of cultural policy, a number of cities are competing to be the leading media metropolis, and smaller regional centres are taking great pains to encourage part of the prestigious, revenue-generating media industry to locate in their areas. Media policy has developed into a "locating" policy. Very often, the state supervisory bodies have adopted this policy and sacrificed the implementation of public service obligations to the achievement of this goal. Prior to granting the licence, state media authorities often demand assurances on headquarters and on the location of production centres, as well as, on occasion, promises of certain volumes of production at the place of licence. The media laws in part stipulate that such assurances are positive criteria for the selection decision under the comparative licensing procedure. Competition between states has given media companies a number of advantages. For instance, they can apply for a licence in a state where, from their point of view, broadcasting requirements are usually relaxed. If there are plans to tighten up broadcasting laws or if supervisory authorities ask for stricter implementations of laws, companies can threaten to relocate in another state. With regard to programming that is broadcast nationwide, all states are obligated under the Interstate Treaty on Broadcasting to respect the decision reached by the state media authority which has issued a first licence.

Self-Regulation of Broadcasters

Broadcasters usually prefer modes of self-regulation to state interventions. Due to the difficulties of supervision, the supervisory authorities also often seek to leave much to the responsibility of broadcasters. For example, in order to prevent stricter regulations in the field of the protection of juveniles, German broadcasters have founded the *Freiwillige Selbstkontrolle Fernsehen*. Its judgements on the suitability of programmes for children and young people and compliance with the relevant norms have to be taken into account by the state media authorities.Other current proposals designed to help ensure the social compatibility of television are also based on the involvement of "public opinion as a steering resource." These include the establishment of a Media Council, a body with no executive powers, which would seek to stimulate public discussion through an annual report on developments and risks in the field of electronic media. Another proposal deals with the establishment of a foundation for consumer protection in broadcasting matters (Groebel *et al.* 1995).

Appraisal

Despite some tendencies to rely to a greater extent on modes of self-regulation, the need for regulation has not led to mitigation of legal public service commitments. The broadcasting law and broadcasting supervision by state media authorities still provide for a safety net – although experience shows that it has some holes. As far as public broadcasters are concerned, there have been no substantial changes in the legal commitments. The main focus of concern is the degree of implementation.

Though public broadcasters have had to make some concessions in order to acquire sufficiently high rating figures, their programming is still significantly different from that of their competitors (see Kröger and Zapf-Schramm 1994). Although it is difficult to define and measure quality, many observers agree that Germany's public broadcasting has maintained its standard. Many think that it is still one of the best, if not the best, in western Europe – measured in terms of traditional public service criteria. The long tradition of public broadcasting, the proficiency and ethical values of journalists in the system, and the sound financial basis have enabled public broadcasting to keep programming standards in spite of the attempts to adjust more to mass appeal.

On the other hand, there are various criticisms of commercial broadcasting. If its regulation and supervision is measured against the traditional requirements of public service broadcasting, then the overall assessment of broadcasting regulation must be sceptical (see Hoffmann-Riem 1995). To all appearances, licensing and supervision of broadcasting has lacked the instruments to raise the standard of commercial broadcasting programming to that obtained by public broadcasting and oriented toward embedding freedom of communication in the functioning of democracy and the self-realization of all citizens. In this regard, those responsible for supervision of commercial broadcasting have their hands tied. In particular, supervision cannot establish and enforce corresponding programming duties, since that might constitute acting somewhat like a censor and, through substantive intervention, threatening the functioning of a self-regulating formation of public opinion. The accomplishments of public broadcasting have also not been attained through external supervision. These were possible because public broadcasting created room for the public service idea to grow, because of its financial and organizational structure (especially its independence) and a professional orientation tailored to this situation.

A systematic analysis of broadcasting regulation shows that the traditional objectives of public service broadcasting have been realized only to a limited extent by regulation and supervision, whether in the area of advertising restrictions, reducing violent programming, or promoting children's programming designed for the educational and informational needs of young people (see Hoffmann-Riem 1995). Very often, existing regulations have been implemented only reluctantly. Broadcasting supervision was, on the other hand, able to contribute to preventing obvious violations of some of the rules. The easiest to ensure was the observance of those rules that the broadcasting industry essentially accepted. The enforcement of rules finds particular support in the established broadcasting industry when this helps to ensure its overriding interest in maintaining the status quo or in preventing the entry of new competitors. The question is whether this type of regulation is sufficient to promote the public interest.

There have been, however, some examples of supervisory activities that have been maintained despite considerable resistance by the broadcasting industry. These include advertising restrictions and limitations on cross and multiple ownership. With these measures, broadcasting supervision could expect strong political support from the government or sections of the general public. There had been pressure to enact rules and to enforce these even against opposition, which reveals the significance of the political climate, but also the quality of public participation in the chances for successful broadcasting supervision. An active public discussion can lend additional support. Nevertheless, the broadcasting industry has consistently learned how to side-step rules in such fields or to follow only their interpretation. The success of broadcasting supervision has, therefore, remained very limited in this area as well.

Outlook

The example of Germany shows how difficult it is to realize the idea of public service broadcasting in today's context. There are no signs that this will change in the multimedia future and during the creation of a global communication structure. The German constitution clearly favoured the public broadcasting model, but in a commercially organized system, public service obligations for broadcast programmes will not be guaranteed by legal regulations alone. Legal stipulations can be supportive – especially if they tally with the basic ethical views and the interests of those in positions of responsibility. However, if they clash with economic or corporate media interests, they are, by and large, ineffective, unless they are backed by powerful opposing interests. For example, broadcasting will tend to be most strongly oriented to the public service idea if it can count on the support of critical public opinion, which is formally or informally anchored in decision-making processes, and if the corresponding creative personnel have sufficient freedom to counter the possible pressure of external interests. The interests of broadcasters in commercial success, however, are also indirectly the interests of the individual employees of the broadcasting corporations. In public broadcasting, on the other hand, the dependence on economic success is much less pronounced, which means that public service interests stand a much better chance of being addressed.

The economic pressure on broadcasters will tend to increase rather than decline in the future. The internationalization and globalization of the broadcasting market has substantially strengthened competition and turned economic calculation into a central determinant. Public broadcasters can hardly evade these realities, especially since, at least in the field of programme procurement and access to rights and talent, they must also act on the economic market. The multiplication of transmission capacities enabled by digitalization and data compression, as well as other technological innovations, will compound economic competition. It can by no means be assumed that this will trigger competition for improved journalistic quality oriented to much more than viewing ratings, dependent advertising, or Pay-TV revenue. The emergent company links and strategic alliances at the levels of programme production, the sale of rights, broadcasting, resale, programme promotion, the acquisition of advertising, and ownership in the transmission networks can lead to an accumulation of power. Bearing this in mind, it would seem more likely that the room for manoeuvring by creative personnel will diminish rather than expand. Of course, new market niches with new room for manoeuvring will always emerge; however, anyone who wants to be successful in niches must accept certain constraints. The changed market conditions will in no way alter the fact that broadcast programmes are primarily produced as industrial products (Hoffmann-Riem and Vesting 1994). The constraints of industrial production will tend to be reinforced by the new technologies – irrespective of an extension of the possibilities of limited interactivity. Above all, the technological changes will not change economic dependencies. On the contrary, economic competition for advertising revenue, which cannot be increased at will, and for the payments of recipients will become stiffer, while programme strategies will be increasingly oriented to the goal of revenue growth or even to that of the mere survival of broadcasters.

The already discernible segmentation and fragmentation of the audience and, correspondingly, of the programmes will probably continue and be accompanied by a highly differentiated special-interests orientation and new forms of narrowcasting. This does not fundamentally contradict the public service idea. Up to now, however, this idea has been oriented mainly to full-format programmes and to the goal of societal integration, and must, therefore, initially be aligned to these new programme realities and the new reception habits of viewers. There is clearly still a conceptual dearth in this respect.

New technologies enable forms of interactivity and of transition between individual and mass communication. It can be expected that the majority of recipients will only make limited use of the interactive opportunities – probably, for the most part, in the mode of access to mass-produced programmes. The decisive aspect for programme quality and, thus, for broadcasting's contributions to society's development will probably not be the technology of access to programmes but will be the quality ensured by corresponding programme production. The programme producers – not the broadcasters – are the main gatekeepers of public service orientations. They will have to increasingly orient their activities to market forces and, in doing so, incorporate the reactions of the recipients. The multitude of programmes provided and the associated growing disorientation, together with the possibilities of manipulation which will tend to increase due to segmentation and fragmentation, will, however, make it difficult for recipients to give feedback in such a way that public service orientations will predominate wherever the market could allow them to.

In future, the argument of scarcity can no longer serve as a justification for regulation in the field of broadcasting. Yet even to date, scarcity has not been the reason for broadcasting legislation, in terms of content, but has been merely a starting point and, thus, the legal anchor for a public service commitment. Even in an age of abundant frequencies, the constitutional and socio-political justification for the regulation of broadcasting will continue to exist (see Hoffmann-Riem 1995). The currently hollow nature of many programme segments may indeed prompt a growing call for content-related orientations, for substantial information and, consequently, for a more strongly perceived societal responsibility on the part of media enterprises. It will only be possible to sustain the public service idea in the future if such possibilities are supported in a variety of ways. In this respect, legal regulation will also be able to make a major contribution. In isolation, however, especially without the support of society, it will be powerless.

Notes

1. See the decisions by the Federal Constitutional Court of 28 February 1961; 27 July 1971; 16 June 1981; 4 November 1986; 24 March 1987; and 5 February 1991.

2. That is, the decision of the Supreme Court in Red Lion Broadcasting Co. v. FCC, 395 U.S. 367 (1969). See generally the articles in Blumler 1992.

3. Article 5(1): "Everyone shall have the right freely to express and disseminate his opinion by speech, writing and pictures and freely to inform himself from generally accessible sources. Freedom of the press and freedom of reporting by means of broadcasts and films are guaranteed. There shall be no censorship."

4. The names of supervisory bodies vary from state to state. The collegial board is designated as the Media Council (*Medienrat*), State Broadcasting Committee (*Landesrundfunkausschuö*), Executive Board (*Vorstand*), or Broadcasting Commission (*Rundfunkkommission*).

References

Bausch, H. 1980a. *Rundfunk in Deutschland*. Vol. 3, *Rundfunkpolitik nach 1945*. Erster Teil. Munich: dtv.

Bausch, H. 1980b. *Rundfunk in Deutschland*. Vol. 3, *Rundfunkpolitik nach 1945*, 2. Teil. Munich: dtv.

Berendes, K. 1973. *Die Staatsaufsicht über den Rundfunk*. Berlin: Dunker and Humbolt.

Bertelsmann Stiftung, ed. 1994. *Bericht zur Lage des Fernsehens för den Präsidenten der Bundesrepublik Deutschland*. Gütersloh: Verlag Bertelsmann Stiftung.

Blumler, J. G., ed. 1992. *Television and the Public Interest: Vulnerable Values in West European Broadcasting*. London: Sage.

Blumler, J. G. and W. Hoffmann-Riem. 1992. New roles for public television in Western Europe: Challenges and Prospects. *Journal of Communication* 42 (1): 20-35.

Bullinger, M. 1980. *Kommunikationsfreiheit im Strukturwandel der Telekommunikation*. Baden-Baden: Nomos Verlagsgesellschaft.

Cromme, F. 1985. Die Programmüberwachung des Rundfunkrates. *Neue Juristische Wochenschrift* 38 (7): 351-360.

Debus, M. 1994. Der Werbemarkt 1993 - Segmentierung der Zielgruppen. *Media Perspektiven* 6: 286- 296.

Diller, A. 1980. *Rundfunk in Deutschland*. Vol. 2, *Rundfunkpolitik im Dritten Reich*. Munich: dtv.

Frank, B. 1991. Informationsinteressen und Informationsnutzung Möglichkeiten und Grenzen der Politikvermittlung im Fernsehen. In *Aufgaben und Perspektiven öffentlich-rechtlichen Fernsehens*, edited by Ralph Weiß. Baden-Baden/Hamburg: Hans-Bredow-Institut.

Fritz, R. 1977. Massenmedium Rundfunk - Die rechtliche Stellung der Rundfunkrate und ihre tatsächliche Einflußnahme auf die Programmgestaltung. Diss. jur., Frankfurt am Main.

Gebel, V. 1989. Probleme der Anwendung und des Vollzugs der Werberichtlinien-eine

Quadratur des Kreises? In *BLM Rundfunkkongreß am 10./11.10.1989: Rundfunk in den 90er Jahren - zwischen Kultur, Kommerz und Internationalisierung, Dokumentation*, edited by Bayerische Landeszentrale för neue Medien (BLM). Munich: Reinhard Fischer.

Groebel, J. *et al.* 1995. *Bericht zur Lage des Fernsehens*. Gütersloh: Verlag Bertelsmann Stiftung.

Grothe, T. and W. Schulz. 1993. Reflexives Recht - ein innovatives Steuerungskonzept für den Rundfunk? In *Landesmedienanstalten -Steuerung der Rundfunkentwicklung?* edited by O. Jarren, F. Marzinkowski and H. Schatz. Mönster/Hamburg: LIT Verlag.

Hans-Bredow-Institut. 1994. *Internationales Handbuch für Rundfunk und Fernsehen 1994/95*. Baden-Baden: Nomos Verlagsgesellschaft.

Hasebrink, U., H. D. Schröder and D. Krause. 1988. *Formen der Berichterstattung über öffentlich-rechtliche und private Rundfunkveranstalter in der Tagespresse*. Hamburg: Hans-Bredow-Institut.

Hellstern, G. M. 1989. Baden-Württemberg: Landesanstalt für Kommunikation. In *Rundfunkaufsicht - Vol. 16/I Begleitforschung des Landes Nordrhein-Westfalen zum Kabelpilotprojekt Dortmund*, edited by G.M. Hellstern, W. Hoffmann-Riem and J. Reese. Dösseldorf: Presse und Informationsamt der Landesregierung Nordrhein-Westfalen

Herrmann, G. 1994. *Rundfunkrecht. Fernsehen und Hörfunk mit neuen Medien*. Munich: C.H. Beck.

Hesse, A. 1987. Werbung und Rundfunkfreiheit. *Zeitschrift Für Urheber-Und Medienrecht/Film Und Recht*31(11): 548-558.

Hesse, A. 1990. *Rundfunkrecht: die Organisation des Rundfunks in der Bundesrepublik Deutschland*. Munich: Vahlen.

Hesse, K. 1978. Bestand und Bedeutung der Grundrechte in der Bundesrepublik Deutschland. *Europäische Grundrechte Zeitschrift* 5(3): 427-437.

Hesse, K. 1992. *Grundzüge des Verfassungsrechts in der Bundesrepublik Deutschland*. 18th ed. Heidelberg: C.F. Möller.

Hoffmann-Riem, W. 1989. Kommentierung von Artikel 5 Abs. 1 und 2 (Meinungs- und Medienfreiheit). In *Alternativkommentar zum Grundgesetz*. 2d ed. Neuwied: Luchterhand.

Hoffmann-Riem, W. 1990. *Erosionen des Rundfunkrechts. Tendenzen der Rundfunkrechtsentwicklung in Westeuropa*. Munich: C.H.Beck.

Hoffmann-Riem, W. 1991. *Rundfunkrecht neben Wirtschaftsrecht*. Baden-Baden: Nomos Verlagsgesellschaft.

Hoffmann-Riem, W. 1994a. *Finanzierung und Finanzkontrolle der Landesmedienanstalten*. 2d ed. Berlin: Vistas.

Hoffmann-Riem, W. 1994b. Kommunikations- und Medienfreiheit, 7. In *Handbuch des Verfassungsrechts der Bundesrepublik Deutschland*. 2d ed. Edited by E. Benda, W. Maihofer and H. J. Vogel. Berlin: Walter de Gruyter.

Hoffmann-Riem, W. 1995. Licensing and Supervision of Broadcasting. Experiences in Six Countries. Manuscript.

Hoffmann-Riem, W. and M. P. Ziethen. 1989. Hamburgische Anstalt für Neue Medien. In *Rundfunkaufsicht - Vol. 16/I Begleitforschung des Landes Nordrhein-Westfalen zum Kabelpilotprojekt Dortmund*, edited by G.M. Hellstern, W. Hoffmann-Riem and J. Reese. Düsseldorf: Presse und Informationsamt der Landesregierung Nordrhein-Westfalen.

Hoffmann-Riem, W. and Th. Vesting. 1994. Ende der Massenkommunikation? Zum Strukturwandel der technischen Medien. *Media Perspektiven* 8: 382-391.

Holgersson, S. 1993. Programmkontrolle der Landesmedienanstalten: Anspruch und Umsetzung. In *Landesmedienanstalten - Steuerung der Rundfunkentwicklung?*edited by Otfried Jarren, Frank Marzinkowski and Heribert Schatz. Münster/Hamburg: LIT Verlag.

Holgersson, S., O. Jarren and H. Schatz, eds. 1994. *Dualer Rundfunk in Deutschland*. Münster/Hamburg: LIT.

Hoppmann, E. 1988. Meinungswettbewerb als Entdeckungsverfahren. In *Offene Rundfunkordnung*, edited by E. J. Mestmäcker. Baden-Baden: Nomos Verlagsgesellschaft.

Interdisziplinäre Berater- und Forschungsgruppe Basel AG - IBFG. 1989. *Studie zur wirtschaftlichen Tragfähigkeit von Lokalradios in Bayern*. Schlußbericht vom 28, Juni 1988. Munich: Bayerische Landeszentrale für neue Medien (BLM).

Jarass, H. D. 1978. *Die Freiheit der Massenmedien*. Baden-Baden: Nomos Verlagsgesellschaft.

Jarren, O., F. Marzinkowski and H. Schatz. eds. 1993. *Landesmedienanstalten - Steuerung der Rundfunkentwicklung?* Münster/Hamburg: LIT.

Kabbert, R. 1987. *Rundfunkkontrolle als Instrument der Rundfunkpolitik: Einfluß im Prozeß der öffentlichen Meinung*. Nürnberg: Verlag der Kommunikationswissenschaften.

Kiefer, M.L. 1991. Massenkommunikation 1990. *Media Perspektiven* 4: 244-261.

Kiefer, M.L. 1994. Wettbewerb im dualen Rundfunksystem? Betrachtungen aus wirtschaftswissenschaftlicher Sicht. *Media Perspektiven* 9: 430-438.

Krüger, U. M. 1991. Zur Konvergenz öffentlich-rechtlicher und privater Fernsehprogramme. Entstehung und empirischer Gehalt einer Hypothese. *Rundfunk und Fernsehen* 1: 83-96.

Krüger, U. M. and T. Zapf-Schramm. 1994. Programmanalyse 1993 von ARD, ZDF, SAT.1 und RTL. *Media Perspektiven* 3: 111-124.

Langenbucher, W. R. 1994. Das schleichende Gift der Quote - Der öffentlich rechtliche Rundfunk in der Sackgasse. *epd/Kirche und Rundfunk* 66 (24.8): 3-7.

Lerg, W. B. 1980. *Rundfunk in Deutschland*. Vol. 1, *Rundfunkpolitik in der Weimarer Republik*. Munich: dtv.

Menningen, W. 1981. Rundfunkarbeit als politisches Mandat? *Rundfunk und Fernsehen* 29 (2/3): 185-199.

Mestmäcker, E. J. 1986. Meinungsfreiheit und Medienwettbewerb. *Zeitschrift für Urheber- und Medien/Film und Recht* 32 (1): 63-77.

Newcomb, H. and P. M. Hirsch. 1984. Television as a Cultural Forum. In *Television-the Critical View*. 5th ed. Edited by H. Newcomb. Oxford: Oxford University Press.

Plog, J. 1981. Organisation und gesellschaftliche Kontrolle des Rundfunks. In *Fernsehen und Hörfunk för die Demokratie*. 2d ed. Edited by J. Aufermann, W. Scharf and O. Schlie. Opladen: Westdeutscher Verlag.

Plog, J. 1994. Soziale Kommunikation und Gemeinwohl. *Media Perspektiven* 6: 262-267.

Radeck, B. 1994. Werbung bei ARD und ZDF sichert die Programmfreiheit. *Media Perspektiven* 6: 278-285.

Reese, J. 1989. Nordrhein-Westfalen: Landesanstalt für Rundfunk (LfR). In *Rundfunkaufsicht - Vol. 16/I Begleitforschung des Landes Nordrhein-Westfalen zum Kabelpilotprojekt Dortmund*, edited by G.M. Hellstern, W. Hoffmann-Reim and J. Reese. Düsseldorf: Presse und Informationsamt der Landesregierung Nordrhein-Westfalen.

Riedel, H. 1977. *Hörfunk und Fernsehen in der DDR*. Köln: Literarischer Verlag Braun.

Rinke Treuhand GmbH. 1989. *Effekte von Kooperationsformen im lokalen Rundfunk in Nordrhein-Westfalen*. Vol.3, *56 Entscheidungsverfahren und Ergebnisse im Überblick, Landesanstalt für Rundfunk Nordrhein-Westfalen-Schriftenreihe*, edited by Landesanstalt für Rundfunk Nordhein-Wesfalen. Düsseldorf: Landesanstalt für Rundfunk Nordrhein-Westfalen.

Ronneberger, Franz. 1986. *Kommunikationspolitik III: Kommunikationspolitik als Medienpolitik*. Mainz: Von Hase and Koehler.

Röper, H. 1990. Formationen deutscher Medienmultis. *Media Perspektiven* 12: 755-774.

Röper, H. 1992. Formation deutscher Medienmultis 1992. *Media Perspektiven* 2: 2 -22.7

Röper, H. 1993. Formationen deutscher Medienmulties 1992. *Media Perspektiven* 2: 56-74.

Saxer, U. 1994. Das Rundfunksystem der Schweiz. In *Internationales Handbuch für Rundfunk und Fersehen 1994/95*, edited by Hans-Bredow-Institut. Baden-Baden: Nomos Verlagsgesellschaft.

Schatz, H. 1990. Die Zukunft des öffentlich-rechtlichen Rundfunks. Einführung in die Problemstellung. *Rundfunk und Fernsehen* 39 (1): 29-32.

Schatz, H., N. Immer and F. Marcinkowski. 1989. Der Vielfalt eine Chance? Empirische Befunde zu einem zentralen Argument für die "Dualisierung" des Rundfunks in der Bundesrepublik Deutschland. *Rundfunk und Fernsehen* 1: 5-24.

Schneider, H. 1971. *Verfassungsrechtliche Grenzen einer gesetzlichen Regelung des Pressewesens*. Berlin: Duncker and Humblot.

Schröder, H. D., ed. 1991. *Finanzierung lokaler Hörfunkprogramme*. Baden-Baden: Nomos Verlagsgesellschaft.

Schurig, Chr. 1988. Programmzulieferung zwischen Wirtschaftlichkeit und Vielfalt unter Berücksichtigung baden-württembergischer Verhältnissen. In *Jahrbuch 88*, edited by Direktorenkonferenz der Landesmedienanstalten (DLM). Munich: Neue Mediengesellschaft.

Schwarzkopf, D. 1990. Programmstrategien des öffentlich-rechtlichen Rundfunks im dualen System. *Media Perspektiven* 11: 681-688.

Seufert, W. 1988. *Struktur und Entwicklung des Rundfunk-Werbemarktes*. Düsseldorf: Presse- und Informationsamt der Landesregierung.

Sieben, G. 1994. *Gutachterliche Stellungnahme zu einer Substitution der Werbeeinnahmen der öffentlich-rechtlich Rundfunkanstalten durch zusätzliche Gebähren*. Bonn: Author.

Steinmaurer, T. 1994. Das Rundfunksystem der Schweiz. In *Internationales Handbuch für Rundfunk und Fernsehen 1994/95*, edited by Hans-Bredow-Institut. Baden-Baden: Nomos Verlagsgesellschaft.

Stock, M. 1980. Kommunikationsfreiheit ohne Medienfreiheit? *Rundfunk und Fernsehen* 28 (3): 336-360.

Teichert, W. and P. Steinborn. 1990. *Werbemarkt Hamburg: Gutachten zu den wirtschaftlichen und marktpsychologischen Voraussetzungen für werbefinanzierte Hörfunkprogramme im Agglomerationsraum Hamburg*. Hamburg: Schriftenreihe der HAM.

Television without Frontiers. 1984. Green Paper on the Establishment of a Common Market for Broadcasting, Especially for Satellite and Cable, 14 June, Eur. Comm. Doc. Com. (84) 300 final.

Thaenert, W. 1990. Programm- und Konzentrationskontrolle privater Rundfunkveranstalter. In *DLM Jahrbuch 89/90 - Privater Rundfunk in Deutschland*, edited by Direktorenkonferenz der Landesmedienanstalten - DLM. Munich: DLM.

Vesting, Th. 1992. Verfassungstheoretische Überlegungen zur Zukunft des öffentlich-rechtlichen Rundfunks. *Medium* 22 (1): 53-56.

Vogel, P. O. 1983. Tödliches Ende auf Parteisohlen. *Evangelischer Pressedienst / Kirche und Rundfunk* 65: 1-6.

Wagner, Chr. 1990. *Die Landesmedienanstalten*. Baden-Baden: Nomos Verlagsgesellschaft.

Weiß, H. J. 1988. Meinungsgestaltung im Interesse der Zeitungen? Eine Analyse der Zeitungspublizistik zur Erhöhung der Rundfunkgeböhr (Okober 1987 bis Januar 1988). *Media Perspektiven* 8: 469-489.

Weiß, R., ed. 1991. *Aufgaben und Perspektiven des öffentlich-rechtlichen Fernsehens*. Baden-Baden/Hamburg: Nomos Verlagsgesellschaft.

Wöste, M. 1990. Nur knapp die Hälfte für Lizensierung und Kontrolle. Die Einnahmen und Ausgaben der Landesmedienanstalten 1985-1990. *Media Perspektiven* 5: 281-304.

Wöste, M. 1991. Programmquellen privater Radios in Deutschland - Rahmenprogramm, Beitragsanbieter und PR-Audioagenturen. *Media Perspektiven* 9: 561-567.

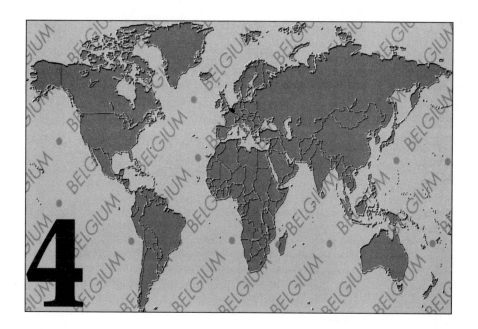

BELGIUM: THE POLITICS OF PUBLIC BROADCASTING

Jean-Claude Burgelman & Peter Perceval[1]

Introduction

A historical perspective of public service broadcasting in Belgium brings to light the constant transformation of the notion of public broadcasting, reflecting new social orientations in Belgian society. The evolution of public broadcasting is linked to society's structural modifications; hence, the nature of the obligations forced upon the management of communication services and the way in which these constraints are implemented are due to a social interplay of power relationships.

A historical approach also involves reflection on how the European Union (EU) strategies affect the broadcasting sector. Since Belgium is a small country within a large economic structure, EU strategies create specific difficulties.

Competition from new Belgian commercial networks aside (international networks have only a small audience of less than 5 percent), the history of Belgian public service broadcasting can be split up into three major periods. These periods have been delineated by the development of the cultural and linguistic (regional) division of the country as recorded in the statutory laws

–1930 to 1960, 1960 to 1979, and 1979 to 1991. To these three periods must be added the current state of affairs, which was created in 1991 with the passing of a bill that created a completely new situation for Dutch-and French-language radio and television in Belgium.

1930 to 1960

Although regional private radio networks were already operating before passage of the law of 18 June 1930, it created the public broadcasting service *Nationaal Instituut voor Radio-Omroep/Institute National de Radio-diffusion* (NIR/INR) and granted it a monopoly on national broadcasts. The monopoly was defined in purely technical terms: the NIR/INR obtained the sole broadcasting rights to the three national radio frequencies that had been attributed to Belgium at the Conference of Prague in 1929.

The ideological reasons behind this decision are embedded in the wording of the law: "Because of its unequalled power of impact ... because of the unlimited number of people to which it addresses itself, because of its extraordinary capacities in the fields of information, propaganda and culture, radio broadcasting occupies a singular position which calls for an exceptional statute, even in the most liberal country in the world" (quoted in Burgelman 1990: 529-30). The most liberal country in the world at the time (the United States), however, had chosen to let private enterprise deal with radio broadcasting.

Since this novel monopoly was grafted on that of the Belgian telephone service, they are similar in a number of respects, the most important of which is the close link between the institution and government. Public service radio broadcasting was directly and personally controlled by the minister of telecommunications and was financed by an annual endowment from the government. Since the endowment came out of the government budget, the yearly presentation of the budget never failed to cause a parliamentary debate on public service broadcasting. This mechanism of financing remained a contentious issue in all discussions of internal reform, aside from those dealing with the statutory laws.

Nevertheless, there was a flexible side to this legislation: the NIR/INR obtained a government contract that guaranteed its statute for 12 years. Hence, public service radio broadcasting had a close contractual relationship with the government (defining its so-called independent origin). Notwithstanding this contractual relationship, the minister presided over NIR/INR's board of directors.

In making such a considerable effort to establish a broad and very hierarchical structure, the legislator almost forgot that, ultimately, the service's aim was to broadcast. In this respect, the law was limited to prescribing a strict neutrality, specifying, however, that only the board of directors was responsible in matters of broadcasting.

Legal analyses reveal that this neutrality rule was intended to counter-balance the institution's unconstitutional monopoly position, guaranteeing liberty of the press and of speech. A manual for journalists, dating from 24 years later, seems to imply that neutral broadcasting especially meant not giving cause for offence.

Moreover, the legislators considered the concept of neutrality as the best guarantee to allow authorized radio stations to produce and broadcast their messages. Some researchers even considered it a democratic instrument for public participation. The bill's implementation and, especially, the creation of the monopoly indicate why the legislator chose the specific structure and legislation mentioned above.

Contrary to what its legal history might suggest, the nature of radio broadcasting was already determined well before the creation of the NIR/INR. Experiments from the beginning of the century had introduced the radio era in Belgium, and, in 1923, Radio Belgium was created as the first fully operational commercial station. Subsequently, several other radio stations were created to ensure the presence of political parties on the air. These initiatives were supported by major financial institutions. Even though the stations were closely linked to, or even established by, political parties (Socialists, Catholics, and Liberals), they produced public service broadcasts once the monopoly was installed.

The amalgamation of private and political interests therefore resulted in the legal recuperation, in 1930, of the regional chaos which had been created by the strict ideological division of broadcasting among the several national political parties. The bill proposed by the minister of telecommunications was enacted in May 1930, and licences were granted to the already existing broadcasting organizations. However, another detail suggests that the legislator and the political parties had ulterior motives: the bill creating the NIR/INR was introduced in the House of Representatives in April 1929, and initiatives in radio broadcasting supported by the political parties were implemented in the course of the following months.

The creation of a national monopoly still did not affect the legislation regarding private radio stations. The legislator left open the possibility for local private initiatives, not only to guarantee pluralism for the public but also to win the Catholic party's support. The latter opposed the monopoly, because they already had a well-functioning private radio station, Radio Belgium.

A critical analysis of the situation established by the new statute uncovers other elements that influenced the creation of a monopoly within the already existing structures. First and foremost, the monopoly gave more power to the minister of telecommunications. The Liberal party, which initiated the creation of public service radio, had found a solid power base in this ministry. The minister held a key position in the institution, since he was solely responsible for its organization and was the president of the board of directors. Therefore, the neutrality requirement appears to have been a scheme to play down any major influence by whatever parties were not in power. At least from this point of view, the monopoly seems to have been a means to increase party political influence.

An analysis of public radio personnel management at this time supports this hypothesis. All personnel appointments were primarily partisan, based on three criteria: political conviction, region, and, to a lesser extent, professional competence. Hence, a specified number of positions for each party were occupied by people from all regions, and each appointment was subjected to thorough consideration on the highest political levels. Consequently, promotions were often unexpected and illogical, bypassing those officially targeted for promotion, because they had the "wrong" party affiliation, which, ironically, they found themselves having to renounce.

A similar divide and rule strategy was enforced for broadcasts by authorized radio companies. Each political party was entitled to broadcast one day a week on only one authorized station. Moreover, the admission of authorized radio broadcast companies was supposed to avert Flemish dissatisfaction with the lack of representation in Radio Belgium's management and operation (which was to be officially represented by the NIR/INR). Finally, the required neutrality of informative broadcasts was only meant to establish a relative political peace.

This political strategy called for an arrangement in which the three main national parties – Catholics, Liberals, and Socialists – were represented on every level. The board of directors, for example, consisted of nine members and the minister-trustee or his representative. This meant that appointments were easily distributed among the three major political parties, in order to maintain an equilibrium, but it also resulted in tripled subdivisions on every level, creating a cellular division of its personnel.

NIR/INR's organization also meant that the structure of public service broadcasting was part of the compartmentalization of other public institutions, such as health services, unions, and cultural organizations, which was based on party structure and ideology (see Burgelman 1989 and 1990a). Consequently, when the NIR/INR first split up its cultural services into Flemish-and French-language divisions after the elections of 1937, it did so not only in anticipation of the country's federalization some 50 years later or because of the regional parties' electoral success. The main reason for the division lay in the creation of a new triple structure that would admit new party representatives.

As far as political influence is concerned, it is important to point out that the legislator did not stipulate that any party membership was necessarily incompatible with being a member of the board of directors. Since one of the board's tasks included appointing personnel, the results, under these conditions, were self-evident. Journalists, especially, were supposed to get support from one of the board's members, if they wanted to start the appointment procedure. This structure finally resulted in extreme control of information. The few journalists working for the NIR/INR had to content themselves, on the minister's orders, with reports coming from the Belgian press agency

BELGA. During the first days of World War II, this servile attitude toward the authorities created an incident in which journalists, still refusing to take sides, cited reports from the Nazi press agency. Belgian public service broadcasting in the period before the war can be characterized by the existence of the political will to dominate the medium. This situation was caused by the political reasoning behind the law of 1930 and resulted in the manipulation of appointments and the dependence of public broadcasting on the state. At the same time, this period demonstrates how the concept of public service broadcasting can operate without being clearly defined by the law; in this case, it was defined in a negative way by a practice of political control.

The war temporarily put an end to the division of the monopoly. After the war, the NIR/INR resumed its activity with the same statute as before, with the exception of a few details. Except for the disappearance of the contract, only two changes occurred. First, there were 16 members of the board of directors. This number, divisible by four, can be explained by the post-war power balance which saw the rise of the Communist party alongside the three traditional parties. Instead of redistributing the already available posts, new posts were created on the same level, in this case, on the level of the board of directors. Among the new members of the board, one also finds the governors general who were directly appointed by the government. The other members of the board of directors continued to be appointed both by Parliament and the government.

The second structural change was more easily noticed by the general public. The major private radio stations – which had continued to exist in spite of the national monopoly – were integrated into the NIR/INR as regional broadcasting stations. Although they were legally entitled to, the subsequent ministers of telecommunications refused to allow for the further existence of private radio stations. They continued to defend the monopoly by arguing that the citizen's personal liberty would be best guaranteed by a public service. This system would guarantee open-mindedness about all citizen's opinions, whatever ideology they adhered to. The broadcasts by authorized radio stations were dispensed with and replaced by "open forums," which were apportioned by the board of directors. Still, according to official history, regional pressures from the French-speaking part of the country complicated the existing situation, which is said to have led to the decision to reform the Belgian public service and divide it into an autonomous Flemish and Walloon section, finally resulting in the law of 1960. This division, which was made law on 16 March 1954, long before the creation of a federal Belgian state, initiated a larger independence of public service broadcasting. However, the law reinforced control of all public institutions (the official document refers to them as "institutions of public interest," which explains somewhat the nature of the measures involved). Although it is difficult to measure its impact, the law's very existence indicates that the authorities were unwilling to lose control of public service broadcasting.

Any analysis or explanation of the post-war situation in Belgium has to take into account that the preservation of pre-war structures and practices limited the influence of new political participants. Notably, the Communist party's popularity was not translated into a similar influence on the public service broadcasting system. On the contrary, the law of 1954 strengthened the traditional parties' influence on public interest institutions. Moreover, this law not only reinforced the link between government and public service radio broadcasting, it also turned NIR/INR personnel into civil servants. A civil service statute inevitably meant being subject to a hierarchy of sanctions in case of undisciplined behaviour.

The existing statute still, however, gave far-reaching power to the board of directors. They were still responsible for the appointment of high-ranking personnel, such as the administrative head of office, the choir master of the music service, and the editor-in-chief of the cultural services. The governors general also had to submit any appointments of lower-ranking officials in these categories to the board's vote. Hence, the governors general possessed only executive power. This state of affairs was justified as a kind of popular control, but actually served to enhance the minister's power, since he presided over the board of directors. In practice, the board only confirmed decisions that had already been made elsewhere in the government.

The integration of private radio stations in the guise of regionally based NIR/INR stations completed the monopoly. This development centralized not only all technical operations, but also all informative radio broadcasts in the country. Moreover, the integration of regional stations expanded the public service's structure. In this larger organization, the three appointment criteria still had to be taken into account, which inevitably complicated the political influence in broadcasting. Regionalism was more related to channelling power relations among the national parties than to bringing the NIR/INR closer to the public – an example of which is the fact that the German-speaking community (annexed to the east of Belgium after World War II) did not receive a public service contract until 1977. In short, the NIR/INR was characterized by a chaotic and hierarchical organization brought about by the political compromise that was forever trying to divide public service broadcasting in order to better control it.

By emphasizing the absence of any controversy over the monopoly, one could describe this period in the history of public service broadcasting as its golden age. Nothing could be less true, however, since state interference in public institutions by the minister-trustee was cause for heated discussions.

Post-war development and strategy did not result from the establishment of social democracy. Some theorists assert the contrary to explain the narrow links between the state and public broadcasting in several countries during this period, assuming that information played a crucial role within a social-democratic context. However, as far as Belgium is concerned, the news service was structurally and financially marginalized by the board of directors. Before 1960, radio and television, together, rarely employed more than 20 journalists in both linguistic sections. During the ideological conflicts of the 1950s, the ministers involved (trustees and others) did not hesitate to intervene and to make it very clear that the journalists were, first and foremost, supposed to serve.

In 1954, the institution made the move toward television, which upset the existing equilibrium in the radio service. New employees had to be appointed, and the political parties had to partition a new structure. Because the personnel themselves rarely protested, their attitude toward this political manipulation has not been much discussed; however, in one incident, which for years was cited as an example of how the Catholic faction manipulated the public broadcasting service, a Socialist journalist who was entitled to a promotion due to rank and years of service was overlooked in favour of a Catholic colleague, and he did not hide his frustration. Although a compromise between the Socialist representatives on the board of directors and its other members quickly put an end to the journalist's objections, the row had already been vented in the Socialist press. Notably, their argument did not question the method of appointment, only the outcome. In this first major period in Belgian public broadcasting, its organization was characterized by political opportunism, not systematic consideration of the idea of public service. Since a solid definition of a public broadcasting service was non-existent, the institution was quickly taken over by prevailing political strategies and run according to the needs of the day. In general, Belgium created a public broadcasting service with a national monopoly not in order to guarantee a democratic functioning of the new and powerful media, nor to allow expression of the country's cultural and linguistic characteristics, but mainly to develop a strategy of political hegemony that would allow for the control of political information. The political parties tried to maximize their influence by manipulating the institution's personnel.

The Statute of 1960: Independence

The new law on public service broadcasting was published in the Belgian statute book (*Le moniteur belge*) on 21 May 1960. Although Flemish and Walloon services were part of the same corporation until 1977, when they were officially split up, from 1936 onwards these services gained more and more autonomy within the overall corporation, and gained legal autonomy after 1960. While the focus of this discussion is on the Flemish service, it should be noted that the same mechanisms have influenced the Walloon institution, which has a lot in common with its Flemish counterpart. The new statute brought a radical change to the public broadcasting service's position toward the government and the public, and the way in which the concept of public broadcasting had been defined altered significantly. The dominant historiography on Belgian public service broadcasting often emphasizes that the new statute established the service's cultural autonomy and guaranteed a policy of free information, because of obligatory neutrality and less government interference. In general, and compared to the one from 1930, the new statute was well received. As far as the choice of monopoly (without private radio stations) is concerned, however, the government adopted the same strategy: the public service held a monopoly on radio frequencies. This strategy was even reinforced by a Royal Decree in 1965, when the government put all radio frequencies under the disposition of the

RTB/BRT (*Radio et télévision belge / Belgische radio en televisie*). Once again, the lack of frequencies was given as an explanation. Although the monopoly was maintained on the national level, the regional institutions were placed under control of a regional minister, notably the minister for cultural affairs, who was no longer a member of the board of directors. Instead of a minister, the government dispatched a representative who was entitled to challenge all decisions, but who did not possess the right of veto.

Another often mentioned difference with the statute of 1930 is that the board of directors was no longer appointed in part by the minister, but by Parliament only. According to legal sources, this change in procedure was intended to guarantee a more democratic functioning of the institution. From 1973 onwards, the appointment of the board was directly linked to electoral results, so as to reflect the new power balance that was created, in 1971, by the introduction of regional cultural councils. The principle of equal representation by the several parties was replaced by a system of proportional representation, first by the three major parties (from 1960 onwards) and then by all parties represented in the cultural councils (from 1973 onwards). As a result of this new system, the Flemish autonomous board of directors was first constituted by 10 members, then by 13 in 1973, and by only 12 in 1980. These changes reflect the evolving power relations after the subsequent elections.

Legal sources emphasize that the new law drew the government's attention away from structural control of the institution. In particular, the institution's position with respect to the public had been clearly defined. Apart from stating objectives of information, education, and entertainment, the law specified that all news broadcasts should be characterized by strict objectivity. The text uses the same definition of "neutrality" as the old statute did, only replacing the word "neutrality" by "objectivity." Furthermore, the open forums – which had replaced the broadcasts by authorized radio stations – were themselves replaced by a system of programmes by authorized broadcasting stations. In order to understand the public service's federal division, it is important to look at the close link between the linguistic communities' cultural problem and the battle between the parties in power. Traditionally, the Catholic party's electorate was larger in Flanders, while Wallonia chose to support the Socialist party during the major post-war ideological conflicts. Hence, the federal division of the public service corresponded to an ideological division; that is, Catholics and Socialists hoped to obtain maximum influence in the Flemish and Walloon services, respectively.

The division of the unitary structure into two autonomous parts gave rise to an attempt to split up the service's structure ideologically, in order to create a new balance. In August 1960, the political parties made a secret agreement to split up the new structure according to the three criteria that had been used in 1930. This agreement, debated in Parliament in 1961 because of a Socialist complaint, has been interpreted as a mechanism that had been forced upon the new public service's structure. However, it was only a consolidation of mechanisms that had already existed since 1930.

In contrast, the institution's evolution reveals a constant and independent tendency to take measures which, on one hand, had to steer the institution away from political interference and which, on the other hand, had to create a cellular structure easily manipulated by the internal elite's personal influence. From his first day in office in 1961, the director general, for example, appropriated all responsibility concerning the content of programming.

The statute of 1960 also put an end to the minister's direct control over the public service. The section prohibiting the enigmatic practice of "preventive censorship" was interpreted by most people as a ban on interfering with internal affairs.

A second strategy of isolation from the political world can be found in the development of management structures. Since 1960 the number of services and departments have increased. This increase was part of the Flemish parties' strategy to maximize their political influence, but the resulting number of personnel made political control rather difficult. This rampant growth was used internally to centralize power and to increase the institution's autonomy.

Although these developments removed the institution from the political world, they did nothing to lessen the influence of politics on the public service. On the contrary, political interference had been structurally built into it. Moreover, the agreement of 1960 proves that the political parties wanted to continue their approach to the NIR/INR in this manner. The institution's projects for independence would only be realized when they became politically opportune. In addition, the major parties' political strategies prevented the participation in broadcasting by the new parties which rose in the 1960s.

A final isolationist strategy was developed through management of personnel. Before 1960, the central authorities controlled all appointments, and each potential appointee had to have some form of political support. With the expansion of the organization and the increase in personnel, a very strict and complex system of entrance examinations was introduced after 1960. Under the guise of guaranteeing objective recruitment, these examinations did not, however, decrease political pressure. On the contrary, those who passed the examinations were pressured to disclose their political convictions, and the subsequent six-month training period became a means of channelling political pressure and allowing authorities time to establish an applicant's political profile.

Later, in 1976, because journalists no longer tended to be party members, and because it was increasingly difficult to have them tow party lines, the training period was increased to two years, giving the establishment more time to politically influence the trainees. The management also decided to renew its guidelines for journalists.

To the public, this evolution was presented as a consequence of the debate on the content and objectivity of news programmes, which were almost constantly discussed by the board of directors. Almost every successive board had to deal with some party's complaint in these matters. These complaints did not result in journalistic or ethical conclusions. On the contrary, they were always used to defend more radical changes. What was really at stake was revealed by the actions taken as a result of this debate. Between 1966 and 1974, three different reorganizations of the news service occurred, putting journalists under the authority of new managing directors and within a new executive framework. The result was that the tripartite structures, which distributed all available positions by party line, were gradually introduced among journalists as well. In the end, the whole news service was politically balanced.

This period in the history of Belgian public broadcasting was monopolistic *de jure* and can be summed up by saying that, from 1960 until 1979, the institution generally functioned according to the same mechanisms as before. The statute of 1960 merely made the clever move to integrate these mechanisms into the new management structure, making the board of directors' control superfluous and, hence, considerably reducing its power.

The statute of 1960 represented the consolidation of 30 years of political power struggle. In 1960, this political struggle resulted in an ideologically balanced dual structure, based on the regional communities and linked to the national level. Between 1960 and 1979, this *lottizzazione* (decentralizing movement) was reinforced by the formalization of personnel policy and programme content. In this context, some journalists called for a new statute because of "public discontent." This demand once again identifies an attempt to reflect new power balances. Indeed, since 1960, a considerable shift in the three major parties' electoral position had taken place.

The Final Regionalization: The Statutes of 1977 and 1979

The statutory reforms of 1977 and 1979 are often said to be the logical result of 20 years of experience with the statute of 1960. The federal structure and the endless debates on the objectivity of programmes were given their final form. After the announcement of a new statute as early as 1966, Parliament drew two statutory conclusions from the developments since 1960.

First, they finally installed a federal structure. After the regionalization of cultural services, the law of 18 February 1977 regionalized the remaining technical and administrative services. It also added a third institution for the German-speaking community to the already existing Flemish and Walloon services. From 1979 onwards, the institution was administered by a 12 member board, appointed by the cultural council (which led to the creation of the current Flemish Parliament). Broadcasting was largely, for non-technical matters, under regional government jurisdiction in the 1970s and became entirely a regional matter, including technical aspects, in 1991.

Second, the programming content attracted the authorities' closer attention, because objectivity was then required of all "programmes of an informative nature." However, one of the clauses in the decree, which seems to define the institution's position toward the public, specifies that it should retain its educational, informative, and entertainment function.

Nevertheless, these interventions did not prevent a lack of confidence in public broadcasting. Eleven months after the 1979 statute, a new government announced, among its policy projects, the abolition of the public service's monopoly, the official reason for which was a number of conflicts between journalists and politicians concerning exaggeratedly tough interviews during the formation of the new Cabinet.

The reforms of 1977 and 1979 appear to be logical, considering the history of Belgian public service broadcasting. They incarnate the apogee of two evolutions: regionalization and the increase of control over programming content. Actually, these two laws only validated an already existing situation. The institution had already been regionalized in 1973. Moreover, the clause that stipulated that all news broadcasts had to be objective aimed at justifying the political control exercised by the new directorate for public education, whose chief executive was a Socialist.Nevertheless, the way in which these reforms were brought about remains remarkable. A public debate on the service's objectivity and a related press campaign had already been taking place since the early 1960s. It seems that the newspapers sided with their preferred political party – a fact that is borne out by the strong parallels between the criticism of news broadcasts by the board of directors and that by the newspapers with corresponding political affiliations. Therefore, it would not be wrong to say that a real campaign was taking place in which political parties established the agenda which was carried out by the newspapers, even though parties and newspapers often reached different conclusions.

The political establishment expressed its criticism in a multiplicity of reforms, attempting to maintain their appointment policy. Notwithstanding many crises, their control over the public service remained very strict.

Newspapers, on the other hand, simply demanded the abolition of the monopoly. To understand this strategy, it is important to note that, later on, the government decided to entrust Flemish publishers with private television broadcasting enterprises. Those publishers who finally participated in this project, in 1987, pretended that they did so because the law forced them to. However, this seems unlikely, because after 1987 they launched another attack on the public service, which closely resembled that of the 1970s. Although this does not necessarily suggest a conspiracy against the public broadcasting service, two elements seem to prove a certain complicity on the publishers' part. First, at the end of the 1970s, some publishers were already involved in private radio station projects; hence, they had an obvious interest in the broadcasting market. Second, they obviously needed to expand their activities and find others, since print media were undergoing an economic crisis due to the mid-1970s oil crisis, and, thus, the previous taboo on radio and television advertising represented one of the options.

Furthermore, cable distribution companies in Wallonia (organized in inter-regional companies) were also interested in the outcome of the broadcasting debate. The interested private parties took advantage of the legal void that had been created by the European Commission's legislation in the field.

Political Disregard for Public Service Broadcasting: 1979-1992

The so-called conflicts that led to the government's decision to abolish the monopoly quickly disappeared from public debate. A political report on the public service's inadequacies was announced but never published, and, after 1979, scrutiny of the public broadcasting service became restricted to its funding.

The political establishment had found a new motive for its broadcasting policy: commercial advertising. Political interest in public broadcasting disappeared, and new interest groups openly presented themselves. In Flanders, print media publishers tried to enter the market, while in the Walloon provinces and in Brussels, the Belgian financial holding, Bruxelles-Lambert, extended its interest in Luxemburgian commercial television by participating in inter-regional cable distributors. Together with and for these interest groups, the government developed a new media regulation. In 1987, a private television monopoly was established for the Flemish region, and, in 1991, the Flemish government reformed the public service's statute twice. Central to these reforms were the regulations concerning advertising. The public broadcasting company was allowed to receive an income by advertising, and it earned over 500 million Belgian francs.

Except for some details, management structures remained unchanged. However, the service's new statute also compelled the board of directors to defend its policy in a five-year plan. The Flemish government was authorized to inspect these plans every year and to adjust the attributed budget during the course of each year. Already, this has led to important conflicts.

The debate on the content and the quality of public service broadcasts was pushed to the background. Nevertheless, the reorganization policy that was intended to create politically advantageous posts continued unabatedly, even though it seemed to stabilize between 1979 and 1987. Although there was hope that the end of reforms and reorganization had been reached, an extra impulse was needed to confront the competition from private television. At the beginning of the 1990s, this impulse led to the reintroduction of the three appointment criteria, which is why radio and television have been structurally separated on all levels. Finally, the Flemish also created an advertising department under state control, in cooperation with those newspaper publishers who did not participate in commercial television. Although this advertising agency was not a legal part of the public service, it still had to respect the three appointment criteria. Therefore, the main administrators of the advertising department, coming out of the public service, were designated by the labour unions.

The public service's budget in this period suffered from the private sector's considerable influence. The Flemish private television station was a financial success and made a considerable profit for its shareholders, the Flemish newspaper publishers. In 1992, the public broadcasting service ran its two television stations and five radio stations with a budget of BEF 8 billion, partly coming from advertising (10 percent), but mainly from the annual endowment discussed above. At the same time, commercial television earned BEF 5.5 billion in advertising. Therefore, public television stations were marginalised, even though public radio broadcasts still held 80 percent of the market. The Flemish commercial television station is of major economic importance to the regional broadcasting industry, which did not even exist before 1987. Nevertheless, its cultural relevance remains questionable, even though cultural considerations led to the granting of an advertising monopoly, which was later abolished by European authorities. All this did not prevent commercial television from buying most of its programmes from abroad.

Conclusions

The concept of public service broadcasting in Belgium has never been subjected to a rational, or even ideological, debate, but always to the shifting power relations of the day. Such a conclusion puts into context the current debate on public broadcasting within a commercial environment.

In Belgium, and in the relevant international literature, the function of public broadcasting has been defined as a means to a democratic society. The official Belgian discourse refers to this definition. Apparently, the creation of a public broadcasting service and the decision to grant it a monopoly were defended by the service's importance in creating democratic consensus. However, a closer look at the Belgian situation reveals that this function has never really taken the public into account. Democratic control over public broadcasting was first exercised by the Belgian government and then by Parliament. Although logical, this process has allowed political parties that were represented in these institutions, via Parliament, to manipulate the public broadcasting service's policy and management. In fact, Parliament even became useless when the public service started to function as a tool for party political strategies. Therefore, it has become difficult to justify the existence of public service broadcasting as a democratic institution.

The Public Television Audience Advisory Council is another example of this situation. Its creation was required by the Flemish service's statutes of 1979 and 1991, but it never functioned, simply because no members were ever appointed. Nonetheless, the law was carefully created so as not to bring the council into conflict with any political strategies, since it was to be created according to the criteria mentioned in the cultural agreement of 1973. As previously mentioned, this agreement stipulated a proportional division of all appointments between the political parties and the ideological pressure groups that were represented in the democratic institutions.

Official discourse still tries to justify the political definition of public service broadcasting by saying that, ultimately, in a democratic system, the citizen's representation is taken care of by the political parties and, therefore, no other options are available. However, an analysis of the Belgian situation and its history have proven that this negative definition of public broadcasting leads to severe malfunctions (no one has succeeded in showing what a public service finally is, but many have succeeded in manipulating it). Taking into account the real definition, the malfunctions were inevitable, especially when one considers that Belgian democracy functions by means of coalitions and that, as a result, no single party can possess a hegemony in public service broadcasting. However, the attempts by all parties to establish a hegemony within public service structures led to intense struggles within the institution after 1960. In 1980, when the institution was 50 years old, the government allowed itself to question its existence, because of its failed political strategies. Moreover, this same government focused on a private project that was to be carried out together with the publishing industry. This shift can only be explained by political strategies for the increase of power. Moreover, it also explains why the 1977 reform was more easily carried out in the French-speaking region – the Walloon institution's new statute was voted on in the same year, while the Flemish institution had to wait two years. The Socialist party had always been in the majority in the French-speaking part of the country, so that the power balance there was less complex, making it a lot easier to balance institutional structures ideologically.

The current situation also seems to be the result of political and economic convergence. On the Walloon side, as previously mentioned, the Luxemburgian commercial television's strategy ran parallel to participation in the inter-regional cable distribution companies. In Flanders, a convergence between the print publishers and party politics led to the creation of, and the legislation on, Flemish commercial television, illustrating that a similar strategy was at work. Moreover, with respect to the Flemish situation, publishers' business regulations allowed for the participation of other interested companies, like the inter-regional cable distributors. Rather than establishing their own broadcasting station (RTL4 and 5) on the Flemish market, Dutch publishing groups have recently participated in Flemish commercial television. Still, a new Flemish television station has appeared: VT4, a joint Swedish and U.S. project, which has taken advantage of the opportunities created by the lack of European Union legislation or protection. Like the public broadcasting service, the first commercial station, VTM, will be confronted with a series of problems, because its sponsors own the rights to many of the international programmes that are currently offered by the two Flemish television stations. Therefore, it is possible that the Flemish public service will be marginalized in favour of private channels financed from abroad, as is already the case in the Walloon provinces. For the moment, the public service still has an audience of 25 percent, while the private channel reaches 43 percent of the viewing audience.

In this context, it seems absurd to discuss the crisis of public service broadcasting in terms of programme quality or public perception. In the Flemish situation, it is clear that one first has to tackle the tradition of political interference in the public broadcasting company. Taking into account the current situation, that would mean starting from zero again. It is clear that the solution lies not only in the replacement of the politically involved public servants by independent employees, but, above all, in the reform of the organization itself.

It would be equally absurd to see resolution of the problem in a discussion of the funding of public service broadcasting – as if the cause of the crisis were to be found in the authorities' lack of funds. It is certainly not because of insufficient funding that the elaborately organized public service always needed more money. Of course, structural problems have been made worse by the general evolution of the broadcasting market, especially by the inflation of production costs. It would be wrong and very difficult, however, to look in this direction for a solution to the crisis in public service broadcasting. The problem is how authorities can participate in, as well as anticipate, one of the most global and, hence, least malleable markets in the world. Another problem lies in the difficulty of stressing the specific qualities of small participants in a European market, which is dominated by hardware producers and private interests.

In this context it seems paradoxical to judge the public service's legitimacy based on its commercial profitability or viewing figures, while its main objectives are of a socio-cultural nature. In a small country, the public endowment is insufficient to guarantee a smooth-running public broadcasting service. Therefore, mixed funding – that is, the use of public and private revenues – has to be considered an alternative. A potential synergy between private and public broadcasting stations is also to be considered. Unfortunately for Belgian public broadcasting, these solutions have no political value.

In the absence of a humanist vision of society and a project for cultural emancipation, Belgian public broadcasting has few guarantees for its future. Sadly enough, all elements for a thorough privatization and general marginalization of the public service are present. After all, according to advocates of liberalization, the viewer/consumer is entitled to freedom of choice.

Notes

1. To a large extent this report is based on comparative research on the history of public broadcasting and universal service in Belgium, France, and the United Kingdom. The project is destined for the Centre National d'Études en Télécommunication (CNET) and was supervised by J.P. Simon and P. Flichy. The first results of this research have been published in Burgelman, Verhoest, Perceval, and Van der Herten 1994.

References

Biltereyst, D. 1991. Resisting the American Hegemony: A Comparative Analysis of the Reception of Domestic and US Fiction. *European Journal of Communication* 6: 469-497.

Burgelman, J. C. 1989. Political Parties and their Impact on Public Service Broadcasting in Belgium: Elements from a Political-Sociological Approach. *Media, Culture and Society* 11(2):168-193.

Burgelman, J. C. 1990a. *Omroep en politiek. Het Belgisch audiovisueel omroepbestel als inzet en resultante van partijpolitieke machtsstrategieën, 1940 1960.* Brussels: BRT Uitgeverij.

Burgelman, J. C. 1990b. Der Einfluß der Parteien auf die Personalpolitik im ffentlichen Rundfunk Belgien. *Media Perspektiven* 1: 33-41.

Burgelman, J. C. 1990c. Postwar Broadcasting Developments in Belgium: Formal Discourse versus Political Reality. *Medien Journal* 14(3): 122-131.

Burgelman, J. C. and C. Pauwels. 1992. Audio-visual and Cultural Policies in the Small European Countries: The Challenge of a Unified European Television Market. *Media, Culture and Society* 14:169-183.

Burgelman, J.C., P. Verhoest, P. Perceval and B. Van der Herten. 1994. Les services publics de communication en Belgique, 1830-1994. *Réseaux 66*: 67-98.

Burgelman, J. C., D. Biltereyst and C. Pauwels, eds. 1994. *Audiovisuele media in België: Analyse en belied.*Brussels: VUB Press.

Heinsman, L. and J. Servaes. 1991. *Televisie na 1992. Perspectieven voor de Vlaamse en Nederlandse omroep in Europa.* Leuven: Acco.

Pauwels, C. 1995. Grenzen en mogelijkheden van een kwalitatief cultuur-en communicatiebeleid in een economisch geïntegreerd Europa. Een kritische analyse en prospectieve evaluatie aan de hand van het gevoerde en te voeren Europese omroepbeleid. Ph.D. diss., Free University of Brussels.

Perceval, P. 1995. Geschiedenis van een consensus. Ph.D. diss., Free University of Brussels.

Verhoest, P., Y. Punie and J. P. Vercruysse. 1994. *La politique des télécommunications en Belgique, 1830-1991.* Bruxelles: Synedi.

Witte, E. 1994. *De breedte van het scherm.* Brussel: BRT.

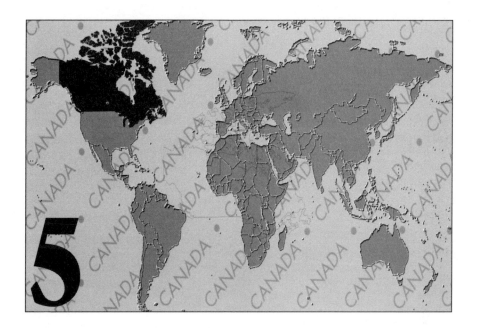

Canada: The Hybridization of Public Broadcasting

Marc Raboy

Introduction

All broadcasting in Canada, according to the Canadian Broadcasting Act, is declared to be "a public service essential to the maintenance and enhancement of national identity and cultural sovereignty" (Canada 1991: art. 3). By virtue of this legislation, Canadian broadcasting is deemed to be a single system comprising public, private and community elements. It is to be effectively owned and controlled by Canadians (foreign ownership is restricted to 20 percent in any single broadcasting undertaking), is to make maximum use of Canadian creative and other resources, and is to serve the needs and interests and reflect the circumstances and aspirations, of Canadian men, women and children. These circumstances include equal rights, linguistic duality, the multicultural and multiracial nature of Canadian society, as well as the special place of aboriginal peoples within that society. In the event of conflicting interest between public and private sector elements of the system, the objectives of the public sector are supposed to prevail. Overseeing and implementing all of this is an independent public authority for the regulation and supervision of the Canadian broadcasting system.

It would be difficult to argue substantially with these formal provisions of Canadian broadcasting policy. However, the gap between policy and practice is such that the promise of public broadcasting in Canada is more often than not a pious wish. The history of Canadian broadcasting is intimately tied to the political sociology of twentieth century Canada, and its present circumstances provide a suitable snapshot of the cultural politics of a middle-sized liberal democracy with a relatively developed economy as it faces the challenges of globalization in the third millennium.

History

Canadian broadcasting legislation dates from the early 1930s, when the Canadian state first decided to intervene in the sphere of radio. Previously, radio in Canada had evolved according to the free-market, commercial model developed in the United States, with a small number of non-commercial stations operated by educational institutions, provincial telephone companies, and, especially, the Canadian National Railway. But considerable public dissatisfaction with the unrealized potential of radio, and a well-organized campaign by a broad coalition of associations in the Canadian Radio League, pressured the government into considering a range of alternative models.

In 1929, a Royal Commission on Radio Broadcasting, headed by the president of the Canadian Bank of Commerce, concluded that radio had a cultural and educational function and proposed to the government that a national, publicly owned corporation be created to operate and oversee all radio broadcasting in Canada (Canada 1929). Its approach was motivated partly by nationalism ("The State or the United States" was one of the popular slogans of the Canadian Radio League), partly by the influence of the British model (BBC), and to a great extent by the interventionist climate of the times (when the Royal Commission went to New York to visit the studios of NBC, they met with the governor of the state, Franklin D. Roosevelt, who encouraged them to propose a strong state role in radio).

Although many sectors of Canadian business supported the proposal, it was strongly opposed by those groups with direct interests in radio – mainly set manufacturers and newspaper owners – and their opposition made the centrist (Liberal Party) government of the day hesitate. But in 1932, a newly elected Conservative Party government adopted the first Canadian Broadcasting Act, creating a Canadian Radio Broadcasting Commission (later changed to the Canadian Broadcasting Corporation, or CBC) and envisaging the eventual phasing-out of private commercial broadcasting. This background gives some indication of the vast historical consensus in favour of public service broadcasting in Canada, a country which, in spite of its unquestioning participation in the world capitalist system, has managed to recognize that certain social values can only be maintained by insulating them from the marketplace.

The full plan of the 1929 Royal Commission was never realized, however. Canadian broadcasting, from the 1930s through the 1950s, developed as a "hybrid" of the commercial and public-service-monopoly systems, as private commercial radio and national public radio evolved side by side. Television was introduced first as a public monopoly and then, after 1960, according to a similar "mixed" (public-private) model.

As the broadcasting system became more complex, and as it became clear that different types of broadcasting enterprises had to co-exist within this single system, a major change came with the introduction of an independent agency for the regulation of all broadcasting activity. First introduced in 1958, the role of the regulator became extremely important in the 1970s and 1980s, as the system had to deal with new technologies as well as a range of economic and political challenges. Today, it is known as the Canadian Radio-Television and Telecommunications Commission (CRTC), and is responsible, as the name implies, for all telecommunication as well as broadcasting activity in Canada. In 1995, its main concern was charting the new regulatory requirements indicated by the convergence of broadcasting and tele-communication technologies in the emergence of the new communication environment popularly known as the information highway (CRTC 1995).

Contrary to most conventional European examples, public broadcasting in the Canadian experience has always been an enclave within a broader industry. Its main instrument, the CBC, has never been entirely sheltered from the industrial aspects of broadcasting (although the CBC enjoyed a monopoly in television during most of the medium's first decade, and CBC radio, since 1974, has been commercial-free). On the other hand, as a regulated industry, no sector of broadcasting can claim to be entirely independent of public purpose, as the Broadcasting Act makes clear.

As a hybrid system, there are two ways to look at the developments in Canadian broadcasting over the past fifteen years. On one hand, there has been a definite shift toward privatization of conventional public broadcast-ing, as commercial and budgetary pressures on the CBC force it to adopt a posture increasingly resembling that of the private sector, as more and more of its production activities are farmed out to privately owned independent companies, and as public funding which used to go to the CBC is diverted to subsidizing private broadcasters via Telefilm Canada's broadcast development fund. On the other hand, these developments can also be seen as a "public-ization" of the private sector, insofar as that sector has become increasingly reliant on public funding and public policy measures, not only through such mechanisms as the Telefilm fund, but also various CRTC regulations and the protection afforded Canadian cultural industries under the Canada-U.S. Free Trade Accord, the North American Free Trade Agreement, and the General Agreement on Tariffs and Trade.

So, as the multichannel environment continues to expand, as the relation-ship between audiovisual product and distribution system takes on a new shape and form, and as the policy apparatus redefines its role under the guise of adapting to the so-called information highway, the question of the future of public broadcasting has to be properly repositioned. The Broadcasting Act is not naive when it describes all of Canadian broadcasting as a public service, but the system governed by the act has been inconsistent and, at times, incoherent, in operationalizing that description.

The most striking example of this inconsistency is still the chasm between Parliament's mandate to the CBC and the government's refusal to provide the resources the CBC needs in order to do its job. But there are more. Community broadcasting (in television) has as its only institutional base the obligation of cable companies to provide a community access channel. Educational broadcasting has become a viable complement to public and private broadcasting in some parts of the country, in spite of the fact that its structure has more to do with the bizarre peculiarities of the Canadian political system than the public service requirements of broadcasting. The policy discourse continues to emphasize access – the core element of any public service – but concrete developments and innovations are increasingly tied to some variant of the consumer model, where the quality of service is invariably tied to the ability to pay.

The debate on the information highway is illuminating in this respect. In the face of the new technological context, conventional television, both public and private, faces a serious challenge. The key to success in this environment will be content quality and delivery efficiency. The old formulas based on brand (channel) loyalty, which allowed conventional broadcasters to get away with packaging trash alongside of popular programmes, will no longer work. In fact, many fear that the conventional broadcasting model itself will no longer work. As a result, broadcasters have had to scramble to respond to the changes. At the CRTC's information highway hearings in March 1995, a coalition of Quebec francophone broadcasters, public and private, presented a common brief arguing that the challenges facing generalist mainstream television were common to all broadcasters. At the same hearings, the Canadian Association of Broadcasters – which has represented the interests of private broadcasters since 1926 – presented itself as the champion of Canadian content regulation, going against the grain of its historic position on this issue (see McCabe 1995).

In Canada, the crisis of public broadcasting has been felt most acutely in the angst surrounding the financial and existential crisis of the CBC, as it careens like a corporate Titanic on the verge of capsizing. Public broadcasting in Canada, however, is far more than the CBC, and if public broadcasting is to have a future, it will most likely be through new and alternative forms – including several that can still involve a revitalized and rejuvenated CBC.

In the recent intense debates on the future of Canadian broadcasting, there has been a palpable shift from the traditional idea that public broadcasting could and should refer exclusively to a national broadcasting service. The CBC remains the centrepiece and most important single institution of the Canadian broadcasting system, but the space it occupies continues to shrink. At the same time, however, the total space occupied by public service broadcasting in Canada has been enhanced by the addition of public educational broadcasting services, by the formal recognition of community broadcasting as a distinct and legitimate part of the system, and by the active involvement in the policy-making process of representative organizations from dozens of less-than-national publics. The CBC itself has moved into specialty broadcasting, and the CRTC has, in some cases (albeit rare ones), insisted on obliging private broadcasters to meet their public service obligations. Independent television production is increasingly reliant on public funds. All of these developments require a new conceptual, as well as strategic, approach to the notion of public broadcasting in Canada. Typically, this has been slow to emerge, as public debate on the question tends to focus narrowly on the CBC in the face of the diminishing political will to support public broadcasting and an increasingly hostile technological environment. The public service commitment of Canadian broadcasting faces grave challenges, in spite of the rhetorical reassurances enshrined in the legislation governing it.

This in itself is not unique. However, Canada provides a particularly interesting vantage point for observing these changes, because the types of questions they raise have been with us for such a long time – in fact, since the beginning of broadcasting: What is the appropriate mix of public and commercial broadcasting activity within a single system? What is the appropriate relationship of foreign to domestic programme origin, of national to less-than-national programme content? What is the appropriate social role for broadcasting?

Continuing Issues

To a remarkable extent, the major defining issues of Canadian broadcasting have remained unchanged since the 1930s.[1] By the time the CBC was established in 1936, the major themes that continue to characterize Canadian broadcasting had been established. These can be summarized by three sets of tensions: (a) between private capital and the state, over the economic basis of broadcasting; (b) between the state and the public, over the socio-cultural mission of broadcasting; and (c) between dominant and alternative visions of the state, over the relationship of broadcasting to the politics of Canadian nationhood. Overriding these are the constant pressures of North American continentalism against the desire for Canadian broadcasting to be *Canadian* and the tendency of each succeeding wave of technological change to re-introduce old problems that the system thought it had resolved.

In the 1940s, following the massive expansion of the CBC as one of the government's leading information instruments in the war effort (another one being the National Film Board), the system appeared to have reached a workable equilibrium. The CBC was clearly the dominant single element in the system, charged with realizing the national purpose in broadcasting. It had also achieved an important degree of success at involving community organizations in both rural and urban areas in public interest programming and organizing participatory listener groups. Its leadership in news gathering was unchallenged. Its signal was the only one available in many parts of the country, and it was moving toward full coverage of the territory, in both English and French.

In 1948, the CBC was mandated to develop and introduce television as a public service monopoly – a policy position further underwritten by the 1951 report of the Royal Commission on the Advancement of the Arts, Sciences and Culture (Canada 1951). When it began broadcasting in 1952 and for the rest of the decade, Canadian television was strictly a public affair, as the government pursued a 'single station' policy, by which no more than one station (in each language) would be licensed in any community, either to the CBC or a privately owned affiliate. But by the end of the 1950s, private industry pressure, a new Conservative government, and a slowly rising public cost combined to create a private sector in television. Privately owned second channels were awarded in most major markets in 1960, and the national CTV network began broadcasting in 1961.Soon after CBC television began broadcasting in 1952, it became clear that the service could not be supported by the license fee, even when supplemented with advertising. In fact, from the beginning the high cost of television had led to creation of the affiliate system, whereby private corporations were allowed to own and operate stations dedicated to distributing the CBC signal. During the 1950s, the license fee was abolished and an annual grant from Parliament became the norm for balancing the CBC's budget. This formula remains in effect to this day, despite repeated calls for more stable, multi-year funding. Nevertheless, the CBC in the 1950s quickly completed two national public television networks, in English and French, and established a distinctive alternative to American television from over the border.

A major shift occurred in 1958 following the election of the Conservative government headed by John Diefenbaker. In a new Broadcasting Act, the private sector finally got the independent regulatory authority it had been arguing for since the end of the war. The act created the Board of Broadcast Governors (BBG), which became the CRTC in 1968. One of the first activities of the BBG was to authorize the introduction of private commercially driven television, which began operating in major cities in 1960, and on a national network basis in English in 1961. As CBC television was dependent for an important part of its revenue from advertising, public and private competition in television has been an important factor ever since. Cognizant of the economic pressure that the new private sector was bound to face, however, the BBG also felt the need to introduce quotas for Canadian content, which it initially set at 55 percent.

The CBC and the private sector were now competitors, but the public broadcaster continued to obtain the major portion of its funds from the annual parliamentary grant. The public cost of public television rose steadily through the 1960s, at the same time as the purpose of public broadcasting moved to the centre of national political debate.

Canadian political unity was severely called into question by the emergence of radical nationalism in Quebec in the 1960s, and the federal government determined to use cultural policy and the CBC in particular as a strategic instrument. Paradoxically, the discovery of a political purpose for public broadcasting was a financial boon for the CBC, while sowing discord between the politicians and the professionals working in television. The CBC went through a series of melodramatic crises surrounding attempts to define and play out its proper role – with the net result of a serious loss of credibility, particularly in Quebec. When the broadcasting legislation was updated in 1968, the government wrote in a specific mandate obliging the CBC to "contribute to the development of national unity and Canadian identity" – a measure that was widely seen as a threat to turn the corporation into a propaganda vehicle. The act still defined the CBC as Canada's national, not public, broadcaster.

The 1968 Broadcasting Act enshrined the basic principles and structures of Canadian broadcasting as a single system comprising public and private elements, under the supervision of an independent, public regulatory authority, the CRTC. On the margins of the system, however, social pressure from the youth and oppositional movements that grew up in the 1960s led to a range of community broadcasting initiatives in radio, video, and television. Community radio stations were set up in major cities, on college campuses, in rural Quebec, and in northern native communities. Community media began to attract strategic institutional support: in Quebec, for example, the government decided to finance community radio and television as one way of occupying space in this sphere of federal jurisdiction; later, the federal secretary of state would fund minority-language community media as well as autonomous native broadcasting initiatives. At the same time, political pressure to redefine the nature of the Canadian state finally led to the first provincial incursions into public broadcasting, in the guise of educational television networks set up, first in Quebec and Ontario, later in Alberta and British Columbia, and eventually in Saskatchewan and the north. By 1992, educational television accounted for some $233 million in public spending (ATEC 1993). All of these forms can clearly be considered public broadcasting (Salter 1988).

Public dissatisfaction with the increasingly bureaucratic and centralized nature of the CBC poured out at CRTC hearings in 1974, at which the regulator rapped the knuckles of the public broadcaster and suggested that it seek a new relationship with its public as the best way to distinguish itself from the dominant North American commercial mould. One concrete upshot of the 1974 hearings was the abolition of advertising on CBC radio. Despite the exhortations of the CRTC, however, the CBC was unable to reduce its dependence on advertising in television. Advertising on CBC television reached a peak of $309 million in 1992, accounting for 22 percent of the corporation's total budget (around 31 percent of the budget for television) (CBC 1994a), which has led to the view that it should be more properly seen as a hybrid or "semi-private" broadcaster.

The government's commitment to the CBC was shaken in the late 1970s by the perception that public broadcasting had not fulfilled its role as a contributor to national unity. Following the election of a pro-sovereignty government in Quebec in 1976, Ottawa instructed the CRTC to conduct an inquiry into the CBC's news operations. The CRTC exonerated the CBC of actually exhibiting unfair bias, but in comparing its French and English operations found that they demonstrated the extent of non-communication between

Canada's "two solitudes." Nonetheless, only the CBC covered the entire territory in both official languages – one of the fundamental distinctive marks of a public broadcaster.

Canada's geographical and linguistic requirements made the CBC arguably the world's biggest and most complex television broadcaster. By the mid-1960s, the CBC was producing more in English than any of the American networks and more in French than the national system in France (Nash 1994). However, the Americanization of Canadian television continued nonetheless. As the cumulative offer of American programmes on Canadian primetime reached an estimated 80 percent in 1970, the CRTC stiffened the rules to require 60 percent Canadian content during primetime (Hardin 1985). Paradoxically, it continued to license more private stations, increasing the competitive pressure on the CBC and the tendency to move toward homogenized commercial formats across the public and private television schedules.

The implications for public broadcasting were manifest in the report of the Federal Cultural Policy Review Committee which, in 1982, endorsed the government's new economistic thrust and made concrete recommendations designed to shift the emphasis in public funding from the CBC to the private sector. Leaning on the Broadcasting Act's requirement that the system as a whole should provide a "balanced" programme offer, the committee suggested that the role of the CBC should be to serve as "an alternative to private broadcasters" (Canada 1982: 273).

Sceptics recalled that the public broadcaster was supposed to be the central agency of the Canadian system and not a kind of "PBS north," but a possibly irreversible process had begun. The committee proposed that the CBC reduce its reliance on advertising revenue (an ambiguous proposal in the sense that it could only lead to improved quality if the government increased public funding) and eliminate in-house production in favour of contracting out to private producers in all areas but information programming.

The minister of communications integrated many of the committee's proposals into an important policy document published in March 1983 (Canada 1983). The paper outlined a new strategy for broadcasting, whose central point was to promote the private sector's capacity to produce quality television that Canadians would watch and that could be marketed worldwide. To aid this, it created a new Broadcast Program Development Fund, administered by Telefilm Canada, to subsidize independent production for broadcast on both public and private sector television. The new role designated for the CBC was to be a provider of Canadian programming produced in the private sector through the assistance of Telefilm. In other words, the government shifted its support for Canadian television production and programming from a public corporation to private corporations. In real terms, this has meant the privatization of a large part of the production activity formerly accomplished by the CBC – production which is now accomplished by private production companies using public funds, and in many cases for the benefit of private broadcasters. Since the late 1980s, the Broadcast Program Development Fund has been responsible for injecting some $140 million a year into the system, and in this sense it is not stretching things to characterize Canadian private broadcasting as "semi-public."[2]

Despite the increased visibility of publicly funded Canadian programmes on private television, and the diminished role of the CBC as the principal producer of Canadian programmes, the CBC is still by far the greatest exhibitor of Canadian programmes. In 1994, Canadian content on CBC television was about 85 percent in primetime, while the total across the entire system was about 75 percent foreign (CBC 1994b).[3] The CBC's preponderant contribution to a Canadian screen presence continues to be a major aspect of its role as a public broadcaster.

However, the new environment now included not only traditional over-the air private broadcasters (generally outnumbering the CBC two-to-one in every market); it also included, for the growing number of cable subscribers,[4] the full gamut of U.S. networks, a range of Pay-TV (since 1982) and specialty services (since 1987). It also included the as-yet underdeveloped alternative public services provided by provincial educational and community broadcasters.

The Conservative government of Brian Mulroney, elected in September 1984, was committed to a general policy of public sector rollback. One of its first moves was to instruct the CBC to cut its budget by about 10 percent. In April 1985, the government set up a Task Force on Broadcasting Policy to propose "an industrial and cultural strategy to govern the future evolution of the Canadian broadcasting system through the remainder of this century." A key aspect of its mandate was to take account of "the need for fiscal restraint" (Canada 1985).

The task force took to its role in the fine tradition of Canadian broadcasting inquiries going back to the 1920s. Although the minister had asked for a quick and expeditious report, the task force held public meetings around the country and solicited public input from interested parties, while conducting an ambitious research programme. Finally, it produced an 800-page report, with more than 100 recommendations, in which the essential public service nature of Canadian broadcasting was reaffirmed, and the key role of both new and old public broadcasting institutions (not only the CBC, but the provincial, community, and native broadcasters) was reasserted (Canada 1986).

The task force proposals were referred to the parliamentary committee on communications and culture, which repeated the process with its own round of hearings and consultations, refining the proposals while maintaining the overall thrust favourable to support for public broadcasting. The government then introduced legislation to replace the outdated broadcasting act, and this was referred to yet another parliamentary committee, which conducted yet another round of public hearings (Canada 1988a, 1988b).

The result was a genuine public debate over the social purpose and possible structure of broadcasting, in which hundreds of organizations and thousands of individuals got to speak out and present visions that corresponded to their own interests. The powerful broadcasting organizations, both public and private, were compelled to take part in the process as well, in order to maintain their credibility (while obviously continuing their habitual behind-the-scenes lobbying activity) (see Raboy 1995a, 1995b). Eventually, a new Broadcasting Act was adopted, basically reaffirming the mandate of the CBC, and introducing the notion that all broadcasting in Canada was a public service.

It is important to recognize, however, that while the public debate culminating in legislation was being carried on in the essentially symbolic sphere of policy discussion, the system was evolving according to the government's broad agenda. The new broadcasting act clearly affirmed the public nature of all Canadian broadcasting, but from that declaration to the actual realization of public service objectives was a long way indeed. The fact is that public broadcasting, since the mid-1980s, has received declining material support from public funds while public funds have flowed, through independent producers, to private broadcasting; meanwhile, private broadcasters and their upstart cousins, the cable distributors, have been subjected less and less to public service obligations.

One example serves to illustrate the general problem. The CBC's mandate under the Broadcasting Act of 1991 is to

> be predominantly and distinctively Canadian... reflect Canada and its regions to national and regional audiences... strive to be of equivalent quality in English and in French... contribute to shared national consciousness and identity... (and) reflect the multicultural and multiracial nature of Canada (Canada 1991: art. 3).

An important aspect of this broad and detailed mandate is the requirement to serve the regions. The challenge of balancing national and regional programme requirements has always been a strain on CBC management. National programming has a higher and more easily identifiable profile. It is prestigious and, to a certain extent, internationally marketable. It is based in two major production centres, Toronto (English) and Montreal (French), and can be more easily attuned to the expectations of national politicians in Ottawa. Regional programming, on the other hand, is difficult to contain. Its effect is difficult to measure. Closer to the population it serves, it often reflects the potentially divisive undercurrents of regional politics and is often out of tune with national policy objectives, in a broad sense. Good, popular public broadcasting in a region is also threatening to the financial security of local private broadcasting outlets.

The CBC virtually eliminated its regional television services in December 1990, closing eleven stations in different parts of the country and reducing non-national programming to two daily newscasts in each province. These cuts provoked a massive public outcry, not only in regions with a long tradition of contesting Ottawa's centralism, like the prairie provinces and Quebec, but even in the Ontario heartland of Windsor. City councils sought injunctions to require the CBC to fulfil its legal mandate, mayors petitioned members of parliament, laid-off CBC employees and their unions prepared proposals to purchase their stations and run them as cooperatives, and users took to the streets. For many Canadians, the elimination of local and regional CBC programming has come to symbolize the hubris and, to some, the passing of the CBC (see Skene 1993).

Whither Public Broadcasting Today?

The election of a Liberal government in October 1993 was supposed to reverse this tendency, but somehow, not surprisingly, it did not. During the nine years of Tory government, cumulative cuts had reduced the CBC's base funding by $276 million (CBC 1993). Despite Liberal campaign promises, and post-election public assurances by the minister, the federal budget of February 1995 added further cuts which, according to CBC president Anthony Manera, increased the 1985-97 reduction to $350 million. In a rare display of public dignity surpassing corporate loyalty, Manera, looking all the world like Gorbachev trying too hard too late to salvage the organization to which he had dedicated his career, resigned. He had repeatedly stated that he would not manage further funding cuts but, apparently, no one had believed him.

Just how serious was the CBC's financial situation? Reduction in service has been apparent at many levels. The shutdown of local stations, trimming of staff, cancelled programmes, increased reliance on advertising, and farming out of production, have all translated into a less distinctive, less popular personality – particularly in English television – which the encroaching 500-channel universe continues to undermine.

The CBC in 1995 was still, however, a considerable enterprise. It still received close to $1.1 billion from Parliament in 1994-95 (about $950 million for operations and $140 million for capital expenses), and anticipated another $300 million in television advertising revenue. This represented one-third of all federal spending on heritage and cultural programmes and made the CBC the largest single player in the system. Eighty-nine percent of Canadians claimed to tune in CBC television at least once a week (Kiefl 1994).

Of course, another way of looking at this was to say that the CBC's total space in the system was progressively shrinking. In 1992, it accounted for 40 percent of the total spent on radio and television in Canada, 25 percent including subscription revenues flowing through the cable industry.[5] By 1989, CBC's average share of the English television audience was down to 19 percent, while Radio-Canada held a more respectable but still diminishing 29 percent. By the fall of 1993, English television's share had plunged to 13.6 percent (Kiefl 1994), while in the spring 1995 ratings, Radio-Canada had rallied to 25 percent, after sinking to an all-time low of 22 percent in the fall of 1994 (*Le Devoir*1995a, 1995b).[6]

As the CBC's ship rocked unsteadily in increasingly stormy seas, the overall environment of Canadian broadcasting was shifting as well. Here too, the CBC's place was ambivalent. As the CRTC identified and addressed the presumed threat of U.S. direct-to-home satellites by licensing new specialty services, the conventional television market continued to fragment. At the same time, however, the CBC was actively involved in developing new services, with new corporate partners, which again raised two distinct spins with regard to its mandate: should the CBC concentrate on providing a distinctive, streamlined public service on the margin of an increasingly commercial television market, or should it participate in expanding the public service horizons of broadcasting?

The problem was a combination of money and political will. These two issues were at the heart of a long round of parliamentary committee hearings held during the fall of 1994, at which the CBC's mandate and funding formula were scrutinized once again. Proposals put before the committee ranged from privatization of all or parts of the CBC's activities to simply increasing its parliamentary appropriation (see Canada 1995).

Simply stated, the main question facing Canadian public broadcasting was this: What should it be doing (mission), how (content) and with what funds (financing)? In its own submission to the parliamentary committee, the CBC presented a three-pronged strategy, aimed at programming, account-ability, and financial security:

> The commitment that we offer is to create a new CBC – a CBC that provides more service, and better service; a CBC that is more open and transparent – but a CBC that costs fewer tax dollars. The commitment we seek is the tools to do the job. We need funding that is dependable and diverse (CBC 1994b: 1).

The CBC would be more Canadian (95 percent in primetime and 80 percent throughout the day) and less commercially driven, "devoted to public service rather than to private profit"; striving to do more than just "provide a pastime, it [would] also contribute actively to the quality of Canadians' lives *as citizens*" (CBC 1994b: 5. Emphasis in original):

> The most fundamental distinction between the CBC and the private sector is that public broadcasting is driven by values of service rather than profit. Our programming must be more thoughtful. It must pro-vide the kind of text and context that empower citizens to make informed choices in a democratic society. It must move and amuse them with programs that best reflect their own values and experiences (CBC 1994b: 12).

This was as good a definition as any of public broadcasting, but, good intentions aside, the CBC was unfortunately ill-equipped to turn it into some-thing concrete.[7]

Aside from its shortfall in funding, the CBC's new strategy was also based on an anticipated incursion into the area of new services. "If public service broadcasting is going to be useful in the multi-channel universe, it will have to be a multi-channel service itself... The CBC must follow the way that audi-ences use media – there is no choice about that" (CBC 1994b: 14). This was undoubtedly the case, but convincing the CRTC and the government has been a Sisyphean uphill drive. The CBC, in 1993, was associated with no less than six specialty licence applications; it was awarded one on its own and a second in partnership with the private sector. Again, one could not have expected more given the prevailing logic of the mixed ownership system, but the overall result was not particularly edifying for broadcasting's public service objectives.

Another problem recognized by the CBC was the absence of appropriate mechanisms of accountability – not to its official masters, for there were enough of those, but to its public. "[W]e have the wrong kind of accountability," stated the CBC brief. "Institutional reporting does not satisfy the public" (CBC 1994b: 32). Instead, it proposed to enhance existing audience feedback mechanisms at the programme level, institute an on-air president's annual report, and create a "citizens' advisory council" with rotating membership and wide representation, to operate alongside the board of directors. Manera resigned before any of these proposals could get far beyond the drawing board, and the CBC was too bogged down in fighting corporate brush fires to change its basic posture in any significant way.

Meanwhile, it was put clearly before the parliamentary committee that there was essentially no way to maintain the level of public expectation of the CBC without the government biting the bullet and continuing to provide major public funding. As the CRTC stated in its 1994 decision renewing CBC network television licenses, "At issue is the extent to which the objectives for the Corporation set out in the Act are realistically achievable" (CRTC 1994). However, the issue of alternative financing was, as outgoing CBC board chairman Patrick Watson told the committee, "a red herring ... A decisive minister committed to leadership and clarity of vision would, in my judgment, say to his officials, come to me with a proposal that works and we'll do it" (Watson 1994: 7).

Indeed, regardless how one sliced it, maintaining the traditional policy objective of a strong Canadian screen presence meant finding more money, not less, for public television. Access for and to Canadian content in the overall new environment would also require public subsidy, as the CRTC recognized in its convergence report (CRTC 1995). Even assuming maintaining government funding and advertising revenue at existing levels, more money needed to be found simply to maintain the existing level of Canadian screen content. Where could this possibly come from? The answer was from distribution.

Distribution could generate revenue in various ways. The cable industry, for example, with 38 percent of total broadcasting revenue, accounted for only 6.4 percent of the amount spent on Canadian programming (essentially through its regulatory obligation to support local community television). The CBC, in comparison, with 20 percent of the total revenue – 13 percent from its parliamentary appropriation and 7 percent from advertising – accounted for 42 percent of spending (Communications Management Inc. 1994, based on Statistics Canada data). With cable penetration in Canada approaching 80 percent and steadily climbing, cable revenues appeared to be an attractive source of funding for public broadcasting.[8] The recent documents emanating from official sources have made it clear that new distribution mechanisms, such as direct broadcast satellites or video dial-tone systems, will be expected to make substantial contributions to Canadian programming as well (see Canada 1995; CRTC 1995).

Indeed, by mid-1995 it was clear that the only "solution" to the financing of public broadcasting lay in taking the Broadcasting Act at its word and adopting a holistic approach to the economics and policy expectations of the system as a whole: to stop treating a distribution franchise as a license to print money, to stop agonizing over the fiscal belly-aching of both private broadcasters and the CBC and insist they meet their respective mandate requirements, and to open up new windows of public service in the expanding media environment.

Some of this had begun gingerly with the creation of the CBC's all-news English language cable service, Newsworld, in 1987 – and, eight years later, its French-language equivalent, le *Réseau de l'information* (RDI). Fitting into the CRTC's logic of using the cable service as a locomotive for adding on new user-financed specialty services, Newsworld and RDI were vibrant, apparently meaningful, additions to the environment, at no direct public cost (the services are financed exclusively by cable fees and advertising, although they benefit from CBC infrastructures and news staff). According to research done for the CBC, Newsworld was the only Canadian specialty service for which more than 50 percent of subscribers felt they were getting what they paid for (Kiefl 1994).

One path to the future was for the CBC to continue branching into additional specialty services, while maintaining its generalist channels. The corporation was institutionally prepared to go this route, which had the advantage of "unbundling" its services and requiring separate services to seek an accommodation with a particular segment of the public (see Ellis 1994). Another route would be for the CRTC to insist more forcefully on public service objectives when awarding new licenses to all supplicants and enable new players to enter the public sector.

With all the various reports before it, the government could probably find the authoritative backing somewhere to do just about whatever it pleased. The point is, after all that had been said and learned about public broadcasting in the previous 10 years, it was time the government went beyond policy -talk and did *something*. With the exception of the largely symbolic Broadcasting Act, one had to go back to 1983 to find a major policy-driven government initiative that had left its mark on broadcasting. On the public side, broadcasting had been lurching back and forth, essentially by default, victimized by federal fiscal policy and the higher mission of industrial development. Yet, incredibly, people still believed in public broadcasting, and within the system, to the extent that the system allowed, some even tried to practise it.

Behind the rhetoric heralding the coming of the information highway and its cornucopia of audiovisual goodies, the key to repositioning public broadcasting in Canada, therefore, lay in amalgamating the following:

(1) a redefined mandate, structurally recombining national, regional, local, generalist, and specialized services, including those offered via the CBC and other institutions;

(2) funding based on a more appropriate distribution of the wealth and resources generated by the broadcasting system, supplemented by public subsidy and strategically targeted advertising;

(3) programming that met definable audience needs and interests, as opposed to mere addition of more and more entertainment; and

(4) public accountability, through mechanisms that established a two-way flow of information and communication between broadcast professionals and their audiences.

Given that broadcasting in Canada had developed as a hybrid creature – to the point where, today, it can best be described as a semi-public, semi-private system – any proposals for reforming it, to be viable, had to take these aspects into account. The hardest question to deal with in this context was this: Why continue to emphasize exclusively protecting the institutional corporate framework of the CBC rather than broadening the horizons of public broadcasting? Some broadening has occurred, to a limited extent, but real innovation awaits the imagination, political will, and tenacity of the government. As it now stands, by insisting that the CBC, as the main corporate embodiment of public broadcasting in Canada, compete with the private sector directly, for audiences, for advertisers, and now for access to cable channels and their value-added subscriber base, public broadcasting is being painted into a corner. The way out is to insist on activating the principle, recognised in law, that Canada has a public broadcasting *system*.

Notes

1. For a more extensive version of this history, see Raboy 1990.

2. According to one report, the Canadian independent production industry was a $688 million business in 1991-92 (Groupe SECOR 1994).

3. According to the CBC, 90 percent of the CBC's spending on programming went to Canadian production, as opposed to 55 percent in the private sector.

4. From a humble 20.5 percent in 1970, to 60.8 percent in 1984, cable penetration of Canadian households had reached 74.1 percent by 1994 (Statistics Canada 1994).

5. Compilation based on Statistics Canada data.

6. The 1994-95 fluctuations in the francophone markets had analysts perplexed: among other things, the spring 1995 figures showed Radio-Canada ahead of its principal rival TVA in primetime, with eight of the top-ten rated programs, while TVA's news programming was attracting more viewers than Radio-Canada's.

7.The CBC document also made a valiant attempt at defining the thorny issue of "quality," which it presented in these terms:
  – we will not exploit or titillate in order to deliver audiences to advertisers;
  – we will be devoted to the French and English duality of Canada, and also respect the reality of citizens of all origins and regions;
  – we will program for minorities across the country: the English inside Quebec, the French outside of Quebec, the North, the remote areas;
  – we will provide a forum for democratic debate, for insight, and for spiritual reflection;
  – we will not sacrifice our reality for foreign sales;
  – we will produce the best of Canadian journalism at home and abroad, maintaining balance and fairness. We will protect our reputation for the most believable radio and television news in Canada;
  – we will produce and commission the finest of Canada's arts and entertainment, and the most stirring of Canadian ceremony and sport (CBC, 1994b: 13).

8. In fact, the CRTC and the cable industry have created a production fund which was expected to generate as much as $300 million by the end of the century in "voluntary" contributions from cable companies "to facilitate the production and broadcasting, during peak viewing hours, of high-quality Canadian programs in categories currently under-represented within the broadcasting system" (such as children's programming) (Canada 1995: 58).

References

Association for Tele-Education in Canada (ATEC). 1993. *Creating Access to Tele-Education.* Burnaby: ATEC, 1993.

Canada. Royal Commission on Radio Broadcasting. 1929. *Report.* Ottawa: King's Printer.

Canada. Royal Commission on National Development in the Arts, Letters and Sciences. 1951. *Report.* Ottawa: King's Printer.

Canada. Federal Cultural Policy Review Committee. 1982. *Report.* Ottawa: Minister of Supply and Services Canada.

Canada. Department of Communications. 1983. *Towards a New National Broadcasting Policy.* Ottawa: Minister of Supply and Services Canada.

Canada. Department of Communications. 1985. *Review of the Canadian Broadcasting System: Terms of Reference for the Task Force.* Ottawa: DOC Information Services.

Canada. Task Force on Broadcasting Policy. 1986. *Report.* Ottawa: Minister of Supply and Services Canada.

Canada. House of Commons. 1988a. Standing Committee on Communications and Culture. *A Broadcasting Policy for Canada.* Ottawa: Queen's Printer.

Canada. Communications Canada. 1988b. *Canadian Voices Canadian Choices: A New Broadcasting Policy for Canada.* Ottawa: Minister of Supply and Services Canada.

Canada. Statutes of Canada. 1991. *Broadcasting Act*, 38-39 Elizabeth II, c. 11.

Canada. House of Commons. 1995. Standing Committee on Canadian Heritage. *The Future of the Canadian Broadcasting Corporation in the Multi-Channel Universe*. Ottawa: Public Works and Government Services Canada.

Canadian Broadcasting Corporation (CBC). 1993. 1985-1997 Budgetary Cuts as at April 26, 1993. Internal document. Ottawa: CBC.

CBC. 1994a. *Annual Report 1993-94*. Ottawa: CBC.

CBC. 1994b. *A New Commitment*. Submission to the Parliamentary Standing Committee on Canadian Heritage. Ottawa, 1 November.

Canadian Radio-Television and Telecommunications Commission (CRTC). 1994. Decision CRTC 94-437. Canadian Broadcasting Corporation, 27 July, Ottawa.

CRTC. 1995. *Competition and Culture on Canada's Information Highway: Managing the Realities of Transition*. 19 May, Ottawa.

Communications Management Inc. 1994. *The Changing Economic Structure of the Canadian Audio/video Industry: Implications for Public Policy*. Ottawa: CBC and Department of Canadian Heritage.

Ellis, David. 1994. *The CBC & Alternative Revenue-Generating Mechanisms: A Conceptual Analysis*. A Report for the Department of Canadian Heritage, Ottawa.

Groupe SECOR. 1994. *Canadian Government Intervention in the Film and Video Industry*. Montreal.

Hardin, Herschel. 1985. *Closed Circuits: The Sellout of Canadian Television*. Vancouver: Douglas and McIntyre.

Kiefl, Barry. 1994. Testimony to the Parliamentary Standing Committee on Canadian Heritage, 22 September, House of Commons, Ottawa.

Le Devoir. 1995. Un automne désastreux pour la SRC, 6 January.

Le Devoir. 1995. La SRC forte en soirée, mais faible en information, 5 May.

McCabe, Michael. 1995. CRTC should make sure Canadian content isn't run off info highway. *The Gazette*, 10 May.

Nash, Knowlton. 1994. *The Microphone Wars: A History of Triumph and Betrayal at the CBC*. Toronto: McClelland and Stewart.

Raboy, Marc. 1990. *Missed Opportunities: The Story of Canada's Broadcasting Policy*. Montreal: McGill-Queen's University Press.

Raboy, Marc. 1995a. The Role of Public Consultation in Shaping the Canadian Broadcasting System. *Canadian Journal of Political Science* 28(3): 455-477.

Raboy, Marc. 1995b. Influencing Public Policy on Canadian Broadcasting. *Canadian Public Administration* 38(3): 411-432.

Salter, Liora. 1988. Reconceptualizing the Public in Public Broadcasting. In *Communication Canada: Issues in Broadcasting and New Technologies*, edited by Rowland Lorimer and Donald Wilson. Toronto: Kagan & Woo.

Skene, Wayne. 1993. *Fade to Black: A Requiem for the CBC*. Vancouver: Douglas and McIntyre.

Statistics Canada. 1994. Household Facilities and Equipment 1994, cat. no. 64-202. Ottawa: Statistics Canada.

Watson, Patrick. 1994. Testimony to the Parliamentary Standing Committee on Canadian Heritage, 24 November, House of Commons, Ottawa.

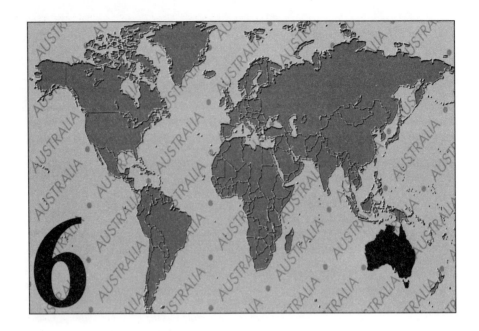

Australia: Broadcasting, Policy, and Information Technology

Marcus Breen[1]

Introduction

Rapid changes in contemporary society are inextricably linked to the introduction of new communication technologies. This environment challenges the traditional model of public service broadcasting, with its emphasis on social benefits and equitable distribution of information. Simultaneously, the new environment reinforces the need to maintain fundamental elements of the traditional. The push and pull of these configurations are necessarily dynamic, deeply influenced by new local and global exchanges that serve to recast national broadcasting, telecommunication policies, and cultural considerations into a challenging set of relations (Frith 1991). These new relations recognize the rich potential offered by new technologies applied within the contested government policy context of social democracy.

In order to highlight these new challenges, three recent examples from the long-standing "mixed" broadcasting system in Australia will be used. They illustrate the state of flux in public service broadcasting and provide substantive indicators around which this contribution will proceed: the challenge to public service-oriented regulation of commercial broadcasters in a deregulated market economy; the multiple sites of activity challenging established models of national publicly funded broadcasting, including globalization trends and issues; and the rapid, yet insufficiently funded, deployment of alternative sectoral broadcasting services. These examples support the view, maintained here, that despite the need for reconceptualization, the traditional model of public service broadcasting can be optimistically reconstituted to meet public requirements. This reconstitution demands a sense of proportion about what can be achieved in the face of the relentless rationalizing of globalized telecommunications. Effective policy occurs only in circumstances where governments recognize and acknowledge the primary challenge of democratically conceived access to information. In Australia, this has been a point for considerable political debate. Before examining the cases, a background of Australian public service broadcasting and its development will be outlined.

Public Service for Whom?

The Reithian model of broadcasting operating in the United Kingdom was introduced into Australia with the launch, in 1928, of the Australian Broadcasting Company (ABC). The founder of the BBC, Sir John Reith, insisted on middle-class standards of public proficiency, deeply embedded in the quest for a respectable use of the media, in order to produce national benefits such as coherence and quality. The Reithian model's application in Australia was a manifestation of a colonial attachment to all things British. The ABC's arrival as a national public broadcasting institution followed already inflated expectations for the new wireless technology and close government management of the media. Even before the ABC was launched – to maintain both a moral and a broadcasting standard – the commonwealth government agreed to allow the Amalgamated Wireless Company of Australia Ltd (AWA), to operate a licence system of sealed radio sets, with listeners subscribing to particular stations. Soon after, a two-tiered system of "A" and "B" class licences was introduced, with the "A" stations responsible for "providing a comprehensive service that would cater to all sectors of the community" (Miller 1993: 42). In 1928, the commonwealth government bought these licenses to create the ABC. It maintained its commitment to comprehensiveness.

This sort of involvement by the national government was to become a feature of the history of Australian public service broadcasting. Prior to the entry of the government into broadcasting, a commercial sector had operated according to the "A" and "B" class licences noted above. These licences operated as a market regulating mechanism on both the commercial and content components of radio broadcasting. Developed in the 1920s after the official commencement of broadcasting in 1923, the class licences were indicative of the strong influence of commercial interests in establishing control of Australian broadcasting. From this point, the privately owned AWA

led a system whereby listeners purchased sealed sets, which confined subscribers to the stations they had paid to hear. The limitations of this system
quickly became apparent. Arguments for public benefits prompted the introduction of the mixed system of broadcasting, arriving after a series of three
heated broadcasting policy conferences in 1923-24.

Public debate about radio oscillated between the view that it provided either a
form of liberating new insights or a public and moral nuisance. These views
circulated from within the ABC and challenged the commercial sector. The
issues were fully debated during World War II, and, in 1942 ,the parliamentary Joint Committee on Wireless Broadcasting Act (1942), which lasted, with
numerous alterations, until 1992. The act set the tone for commercial broadcasting regulation, providing an apparatus for the maintenance of
publicly agreed objectives. Some were part of the process of identifying
nation building functions in the mass media, but were inadequately articulated in the early years of reproducing the Reithian model. In particular, local
programming content and its relation to locally constructed audiences
became a key issue in the discussion. It is considered by critics and policy
makers the regulatory motif around which a national broadcasting debate can
be located (see for example, Counihan 1992, Cunningham 1992: 538).

The historical precedent for local content was set when a local music quota
for radio was introduced in 1942, to occupy 2.5 percent of music time on air,
following a recommendation from the Gibson Committee. In expressing its
opinion, the committee established the fundamental elements of the political
economy of broadcasting policy in Australia until 1992:

> Although the Commission (ABC) – and the commercial stations –
> could have done a great deal to promote Australian music and artists,
> we are not satisfied that enough is being done in this young country to
> develop native talent. The lot of the professional artist is hard in a land
> of slight population, where music publishers and the Columbia
> Gramophone Company, which has a monopoly in the making of
> records, faces a comparatively small market for their products (cited in
> *Australian Broadcasting Tribunal* 1986: 137).

In many respects, the triumvirate of issues identified in 1942 – the youth of
nationhood, a relatively small population, and monopoly corporate behaviour – are issues that local content regulation still seeks to address.

In 1949, the final regulatory mechanism was put in place with the formation
of the Australian Broadcasting Control Board (ABCB). Formed to overcome
criticisms of political interference in broadcasting in general, and national
programming concerns in particular, the ABCB existed as a statutory authority, with the minister (for posts and telecommunications) retaining the
ultimate power to award and revoke licences. As a manifestation of an authoritarian tendency in Australian political history, this "total power" over the
control of broadcasting meant that the free flow of information in Australia
relied on political affiliations and acceptability. Even the ABC was caught up
in this culture, with government-appointed boards functioning as a conduit
for political, rather than the public, interest. There is ample evidence to

support the view that the ABC, as a Reithian vehicle, was a deeply class-oriented institution whose primary responsibility was the moralizing and "middle-classing" of the entire society (Thomas 1980).

The introduction of television, in 1956, served to reinforce these concerns. During a lengthy period of conservative governments (until the Whitlam Labor Government of 1972-74), television extended the already "mixed" system operating in radio, where commercial operators competed in the market for advertisers and audiences, and the ABC offered a government-funded comprehensive and independent service. *The Broadcasting and Television Act* (1956) sought to bring the best elements of the U.S. and British systems to Australians, with a raft of television-related clauses appended to the act, which changed its name to reflect the introduction of television. However, it was flawed by its emphasis on the recognized strengths of the U.S. approach with a strong advertising base. Inevitably, television in Australia had a commercial orientation, where public interest was secondary, save only for the regulatory structures which were managed by the ABCB and, from 1977, the Australian Broadcasting Tribunal (ABT). These included regulations aimed at restricting the amount of foreign content in drama, advertising, and children's programming, with particular specifications for "quality." Who defined the quality and which "public" was unclear. Instead, demands for quality often reflected the expectation of one social group seeking to impose a taste regime on another (Jacka 1993: 3). A further feature of the Australian system was the government's agreement to allow the commercial licensees to build and own their transmitters, thereby removing them from effective control by the state (Cunningham 1993: 23).

Four phases of Australian television development have been identified: (1) 1956-1963: press proprietors move to own and control television, with two commercial stations and the ABC in Sydney and Melbourne, dependence on U.S. content on commercial stations and British content on ABC; (2) 1964-1975: structural consolidation and local programming content explosion; (3) 1975-1987: colour television and local content issues become a focus for public debate as the ABCB makes way for the ABT with transparent public interest functions; the formation of a second public broadcaster, the Special Broadcasting Service (SBS), for ethnic interests; VCRs and satellite distribution challenge the regulatory system of control; and, in 1982, the recommendation to introduce Pay-TV; and (4) 1987-present: industry maturity with networking and the introduction of cross-ownership laws, as a result of which, after 1987, it was illegal to own monopoly press and television interests in the same service area, with a maximum audience reach of 60 percent of the population by any one station/network (Cunningham 1993: 23-33).

It is the last stage that is important to this chapter. A public debate over cross-ownership laws generated considerable interest in calculations of market share and audience reach (Chadwick 1989). In particular, a new set of economic determinants were introduced that, in turn, offered a new set of conceptual considerations to the regulatory regime that managed the commercial sector. No longer was the ABT the only regulatory structure – it was abandoned, in 1992, in favour of the Australian Broadcasting Authority

(ABA) – but economy began to prevail as a means of delivering social objectives with market regulators, such as the Trade Practices Commission being asked to decide on issues which had previously been the exclusive domain of the broadcasting regulators. Indeed, following the shifts in monopoly ownership of media in general in 1986-87, broadcasting began to adopt industrial features which the existing mixed structure was ill-equipped to accommodate. Consequently, the Trade Practices Commission – a monopoly and fair trading institution – became a player in the Australian media, regulating ownership and control. The long-standing social goals to be generated by the media, prescribed by government and consensually accepted by the population for determining the form and content of broadcasting, were no longer acceptable:

> A competitive framework is assumed to be the best means to secure the policy goals of fairness, balance and provision of social good (O'Regan 1993: 38).

New communications producing technological diffusion from the 1980s onwards forced a recognition that it was no longer possible to maintain a tight network of influence over morality, class, and values. Subsequently, blatant manipulation by public figures of broadcasters for political purposes began to dissipate. It has not, of course, ceased to be an issue, with undue influence wielded since the 1980s by Rupert Murdoch's News Corporation and Kerry Packer's publishing and television network.

The policy environment adopted an otherwise unknown cultural quest, where "entrepreneurial" initiatives were assumed to generate a system of socially beneficial self-regulation. Acceptance of the market as the ultimate regulator did not overwhelm the policy environment, which has recently reasserted itself as it has become more attuned to public issues and market failure.[2]

Alongside the shift to the entrepreneurial approach came the third tier of broadcasting, following a federal government commitment to provide public access to public or community radio and television (Seneviratne 1993). This shift threw into relief the difficulties facing the ABC and regulated commercial broadcasters. They could argue that their public interest responsibilities were being met by other operators serving specific community or "niche" requirements. Commonwealth funding for the community sector, although small, confirmed the *de facto* move away from the two tiered commercial-ABC structure, and acknowledged that social needs would be met by offering communities of interest access to broadcast media.

As these changes took place, the ABC was expected to maintain the integrity of its traditional responsibility as a national and independent broadcaster. The mixed model had to change and with it the role of the ABC. Faced with these challenges, the ABC reworked its defining document which outlined "The Functions and Role of the ABC," in The ABC Act (1992).[3] The result was a confused and confusing set of responsibilities that are at the centre of unresolved contradictions about the function of publicly funded broadcasters in an expanding market economy with an open(ing) global orientation

(McFayden 1993). For its part, the mandate of the publicly funded regulator overseeing a set of public service objectives – such as local content on commercial radio and television – was unsustainable in the face of market objectives. Yet, the ABC did not, could not, due to public and government party pressure, make the transition to a full commercially based, advertising-funded institution. Most of its funding comes from money appropriated by Parliament, which oversees the ABC's activity and ultimately controls the purse strings of the organization. Other funds are generated by the sale of merchandise through an ABC retail outlet network and sponsorship of the ABC's regional Asian satellite programming. These changes were introduced by the Australian Labor Party (ALP), in government since 1983, committed in its statutes to a reformist democratic socialist set of objectives. The ALP's public policy objectives were related to its trade union and working class constituency. As such, they contained a political flavour that could not fit with market imperatives. However, the government was assisted in its reform agenda by an often misinformed and intellectually moribund bureaucracy, keen to accommodate quantitative measures of assessment in a drive toward privatization and deregulation (Cunningham 1992a; Paltridge 1990). Inevitably, policy became a poor relation of the imposing power of globally conceived economic concerns. Local communication objectives were kept as background relief to the big picture.

Privatization, Social Democracy, and Amelioration

Privatization involves "all forms of public intervention that increase the size of the market sector within the communication and information industries and give entrepreneurs operating within it increased freedom to manoeuvre" (Murdock 1990: 9). Privatization has four components: denationalization; liberalization; commercialization of the public sector; and regearing of the regulatory environment (Murdock 1990: 9-12). These characteristics of communication and information technology policy reform are similar to those applied to economic policy in a privatizing society and have operated in a virtual hand-in-glove relationship in Australia. What are often overlooked in policy studies are the political efforts taken to ameliorate the consequences of privatization on the public interest. A fundamentally optimistic social democratic model is required to generate such a perspective (see Wilson 1994).

Amelioration of privatization in the communication policy context can occur but should be seen as a second order solution to privatization – with the first solution being not to privatize. Amelioration in the market economy provides a sort of social science indicator that counteracts defeatist market analysis and critique, which frequently deny market realities rather than searching for public policy solutions. In this context, it is useful to examine political documents that set the policy objectives about communication in Australia. For example, the ALP's National Committee of Inquiry: discussion papers (1979) raised questions about "media bias" in Australian politics, where negative coverage of the ALP and its constituency was either "overtly political" or of a "social and cultural nature" (Jeansch 1979: 13). The proposed solution included the following: making better use of existing media facilities; encouraging diversity in the number of media outlets available; establishing additional media outlets sympathetic to the ALP; and making better use of party-based media (Jeansch 1979: 18). In the same inquiry, it was pointed out that the "social and economic context" of the 1980s was expected to be "the most momentous in Australian history" (ALP 1979: 4). This is the political backdrop to the social democratic model of government in Australia which is most frequently overlooked by critics of communication policy. Attempts to ameliorate the momentous changes brought about by privatization did not, however, acknowledge the enormity of the policy task and the necessity for ongoing "responses within stable and relatively predictable parameters" (Lindsay 1993: 38). The implementation of a media solution to resolve the class and communication interests of the Labor constituency required more than rhetoric to succeed. In the short term, the 1979 statement recognized the need for a change and for diversity in the media mix, in order to produce political and public benefits.

Children, Money, and Government

The complex policy web applied to the mixed broadcasting environment requires three key features: transparent public processes of the establishment of regulation and monitoring; ongoing public education; and government commitment to adequate funding. The mixed model is under pressure, with two scenarios likely. It may cease to exist or be transformed into an unwieldy structure, where the public service elements of universal service are provided in a sort of constant *post-factum* clean-up exercise, as commercial operators fail in their responsibilities. Consistently, well-organized commercial obstacles, combined with a poorly structured sense of rational policy objectives, challenge the survival of broader political objectives.

Outright antagonism to public responsibility is a feature of commercial broadcast operators, who have constructed a popular culture media increasingly defined by an anti-statist, libertarian marketplace agenda. A graphic illustration of this agenda in action came early in 1992, when the ABT withdrew a children's "C" classification for two episodes of the Nine Television Network's programme "Skippy." According to the ABT's Children's Program Committee, the programmes did not provide an adequate children's point of view and could not be said to qualify under the conditions of the Children's Television Standards. These consist of regulations which are variously set at establishing a generic child's point of view for television programmes, which are then assessed according to a score based on the relative cost of the programme type, its duration, and the Australian input. The arguments put by the commercial protagonists in this debate centred not on the kangaroo, but on the rights of the ABT and, thus the state, to exercise influence over the quality of commercial television programming. Privatizing advocates consider this a "betrayal of the deregulatory principles" enshrined in economic language (Dunlevy 1992: 13). Fundamental questions such as these have also been raised about Australian advertising content on television (Sinclair 1992).

The commercial operators' preference remains "market-driven self-regulation" (Westerway 1992: 10). This critical rupture in the agreed system of programme regulation introduced aggressive commercialism to the relatively passive commercialism of Australian broadcasting. Consequently, since the introduction of the Broadcasting Services Bill (1992), in which the ABT was replaced by the ABA and regulatory changes were made regarding children's programming, commercial television operators have to meet children's "C" drama programme standard quotas, but under flexible codes. The ABA noted that commercial broadcasters were meeting the "minimum requirement" of "C" classification, leading to a review of the standard in 1994 (*Australian Broadcasting Authority* 1994: 16). One outcome of the review may be a new regulation demanding an increase in the time allocated by commercial broadcasters to first-release Australian children's drama and Australian content generally.[4]

If the "Skippy" case indicated changing priorities mobilized through an adjusted national political economy in the 1990s, it did not represent the end of the debate about a mixed broadcasting system. Market amelioration has been operationalized at other sites in this debate. For example, in the 1980s and 1990s, state and federal government funding provided a steady and increasing stream of resources to the Australian Children's Film and Television Foundation, established in 1982 to challenge the "bottom line" priorities of commercial television operators, by providing quality children's drama (Edgar 1994: 8). It received in total more than A$17 million from 1982-1994 (Australian Children's Television Foundation 1993-94: 24). This piece of the broadcasting puzzle suggests that the public service policy environment is overwhelmingly confused. Commercial operators are reluctant to fulfil their obligations to all sectors of society and require a regulatory regime to police their contribution. Meanwhile, the government is unwilling to enforce a comprehensive regulatory regime, while taking responsibility for funding productions commercial operators are unwilling to fund. It is an indication of a government keen to assuage the commodity fetish of commercial operators, yet wanting to support broad public service goals (Breen 1994).

Another example illustrates how the ABC became ensnared in what seems sure to be both a mortal and permanent management crisis, revealing that traditional public service broadcasting priorities are mismatched with the emerging institutional structures that accompany privatization. As an institution whose primary purpose is to guarantee a comprehensive broadcasting radio and television service for all Australians, the ABC has been under pressure for the past decade. In 1994, commercially compromised programming and satellite television captured the news headlines.

In September 1994, a former presenter on ABC TV's *Great Ideas* programme appeared on commercial television, claiming that a lifestyle programme's "infotainment" segment had been funded by a large Australian company. An "extremely positive" overview of the company's operations was broadcast (Middleton 1994: 3). The admission was followed by others that included suggestions that a number of co-production arrangements had been made between ABC-TV and commercial operators. "Editorial independence" was raised as an issue, only to be further complicated by the announcement that the ABC had in place "co-production sponsorship guidelines" (Lenthall and Potter 1994; Potter and Lenthall 1994). These revelations were enough to generate concerns among ABC supporters, audience, and government ministers about the integrity of the national broadcaster as a news and information source. With a long commitment to non-commercial, public funding, ABC broadcasting has stood as a qualitative talisman for the Australian community since its creation. As with the "Skippy" scenario, issues were at stake that reflect the "new culture in the place" (Simper 1994: 23).

The issues can be itemized as follows. First is the spoiling action of a commercial operator in bringing to public attention "commercial" activities on the publicly funded national broadcaster. The lack of clarity about commercial relationships for the ABC and its operations has challenged the previously cosy differentiation between commercial operators and publicly funded ones. This is due to a new set of relationships impinging on the financial operations of a broadcaster like the ABC, in a deregulated environment, where "outsourced"[5] independent film and programme makers replace in-house labour, thereby creating the need for new economic arrangements between the broadcaster and its local suppliers. "Outsourcing" may also raise questions about the reliability of independent views free of commercial influence.

Second, the use of infotainment and lifestyle programming on publicly funded television raises questions about changing social needs. For example, consequences of a deregulated labour market include less secure employment arrangements and lower wages, prompting industries such as the travel industry to respond by creating package tours that appeal to those financial realities as well as to "lifestyle" motives in their advertisements. Lifestyle programmes could be seen to offer a service in the changing social life of the nation, and yet there are also numerous travel-holiday programmes on commercial television. Duplication by the ABC of infotainment programming of commercial television challenges traditional notions of public service broadcasting. Or does it? The real issue is that the ABC should provide infotainment, as a public service, with guarantees that appropriate journalistic criteria of fairness and accuracy apply. Alternatively, it may be that infotainment, as a genre of broadcast television, is a contradiction for public service broadcasters. A public broadcaster may be better positioned in the broadcasting market by not producing such programmes, thereby avoiding the clouds of "commercial compromise" that hang heavily over it. Yet in rejecting such programming, its mandate to provide universal programming cannot be met, and it can be seen to fail its obligation to provide a quality service. Furthermore, lifestyle programmes are suitable for broadcast to Asian nations to Australia's north, via satellite. In an expanding service economy, where tourism is significant in calculations of national economic performance, perhaps the ABC should provide such programmes to promote the tourist trade, thereby meeting an objective of its charter – to be a national "outreach" organization.

Third, co-productions have become so commonplace in the past decade, due to funding pressures, that it is no longer possible to confidently write about public funding of an organization such as the ABC. It is unlikely that public broadcasters can effectively function as a conduit for the circulation of democratically generated ideas, when funding arrangements are in place that facilitate programming which reduces the independence of the organization's editorial policy. "Independence," itself, is no longer a term that can be used with much clarity. Ideology and public service broadcasting are not separate spheres. Yet there are times when "independence" is used as a simplistic foil to debates about who public service broadcasters speak for and to in the 1990s. A source of information that serves public interests, freed of commercial constraints, is necessary. It is, however, also necessary to recognize that rhetoric alone will not magically provide funds for programme creation.

Finally, a set of guidelines – *The ABC's Code of Practice* – is in place. There has been virtually no public consultation about them. Issues in and around the guidelines of publicly funded organizations need close scrutiny. In particular, it follows from the previous issues raised about programming and co-productions that a corporatist style of management has evolved in the ABC, which is of no surprise given the developments in this direction in the rest of Australian society. A strong managing director, David Hill, oversaw the direction of the organization in the late 1980s and into 1995 (when he relinquished his position to Brian Johns, former head of SBS-TV and the ABA). Hill's hierarchical, rather than "flat," management approach produced its own authoritarian reflexes, which are antagonistic to public process. The corporatist management structure has not replaced public processes entirely. The ABC board has a strong role in maintaining the direction of the organization. Its current chair, researcher and academic broadcasting policy lawyer, Professor Mark Armstrong, is constrained by the honourary and part time nature of the position. The daily observance of guidelines for arrangements with commercial programme providers rests with departmental managers and others. At the end of 1994 and into 1995, investigations into ABC management and programming activities took place, including an internal ABC inquiry and one by the Senate committee. Evidence from these public and internal ABC inquiries suggested that the policy settings and processes in place were incapable of directing the organization as it sought to maintain its public service obligations and meet new demands.

The next ABC crisis occurred at the Parliamentary funding level, regarding a 1992 decision by federal cabinet to allocate A$5.4 million to ABC-TV to operate a satellite service, ATVI (Australian Television International, also referred to as AusTV), transmitted primarily to South-East Asia. This service grossly overspent its allocation, accepted sponsorship, and continued to lose money, while not attracting a substantial Asian audience (Lenthall 1994: 4). The introduction of satellites should have meant the arrival of new opportunities to provide improved universal services through the ABC. Instead, the organization has failed to appreciate the fragmentary nature of contemporary political economy and withdrawn from its core service obligations. Alongside other commercial operators, it is also planning moves into Pay-TV, which officially began in Australia on 26 January 1995. These moves must be seen against the backdrop of claims that innovation is a feature of the ABC, as outlined by ABC Chairman Mark Armstrong:

Pioneering is part of the Charter obligation, willingly undertaken. The ABC is the research-and-development arm of Australian broadcasting. It must remain strong as the world gets ready to dump its program output directly into Australian households (Armstrong 1993: 13).

The question must be asked whether public service obligations are met by progressive innovation or by producing "defensive" local programming content. Certainly there is an intention to align two unreconcilable objectives. More complicating, still, is the statement from the minister for communications and arts, Michael Lee, who made the following comment on the anouncement that David Hill had been replaced by Brian Johns:

The ABC's core activities are paramount and while it is important that the ABC does not get left behind in the introduction of new technology, it is the traditional free-to-air radio and television services that have always been paramount and I think they will always be paramount (Dore and Fenshaw 1995: 2).

The remarkable discontinuity between the statement of the board chair and the communications minister illustrate the policy chaos prevailing in the public service sector.

Symbolic Collisions

Despite the claw-back to tradition in the minister's statement, the debate about the ABC has changed in the 1990s toward issues of competition and efficiency, linked to funding and new technology such as satellites and Pay-TV. This has meant that although non-commercial or public broadcasting does not explicitly compete with commercial broadcasting for advertising revenue, it is operating in the same domain. Since 1992, however, the government-funded Special Broadcasting Service provides "block advertising" at the beginning and end of its programmes, as a means of self-funding. More significantly, most broadcasters compete for audiences, even those audiences that could be considered "special interest," such as users of the ABC, who expect a comprehensive news service but often receive a mirror image of commercial ones. These audiences have to be drawn and kept away from the mass market programming of commercial broadcasters and newer satellite and subscription services. Further complications follow because both commercial and non-commercial broadcasting exist in the same programme supply and labour market, and the prices paid for inputs to their services operate in the same market (Jacka 1993: 4). Commercial imperatives are, therefore, necessarily part of the total broadcasting economy and challenge a less defined feature of public service broadcasting; that is, that the provision of services to special interests with little or no consideration for quantifiable assessments of programme delivery (audience reach) has been another part of the public service tradition of the ABC – and rightly so.

The "material collision" between the marginal or special interest concerns of the ABC and SBS and commercial constraints are real. Perhaps the greater collision is between the symbolic changes taking place in the past 10 to 15 years, over the nature of publicly funded national broadcasters. A set of economic and organizational frameworks, developed in association with technological changes and constructed in a normative theoretical context, would be useful (Bauer 1994: 29-30). These frameworks should include the fundamental public interest issues that are frequently shut out of the economic, organizational, and technological framework, where they should at least be accorded a place as equal "agents" in policy discourse (Melody 1990). The original frameworks that were well established in the secure post-World War II years, have not held up in terms of their symbolic impact. Terms such as "public service," "universal service," "national," "non-commercial," and "public" all refer to publicly funded broadcasting, but do not encompass emerging broadcasting forms, such as those provided by new technology in narrowcast forms, or community broadcasters (Melody 1994). Moreover, they are linked to a concept of "the public," which, in the context of broadcasting, has been "remarkably unexamined" (Scannell 1989: 135).

An ABC of the Future

Significant claims have been made for maintaining the ABC according to the established models that predominated until the mid-1980s. Generally, it was a fully state-subsidized vehicle that would serve non-commercial interests with universal service guarantees. As the Australian policy environment meshes with global interests, such a model can only be sustained by policy blinkers. This is not to say, however, that a traditionally constructed organization should cease to exist. Rather, a reconstructed model that provides publicly beneficial, fair, and equitable services to all sectors of society needs building.

Synthesising economic and social policy theory with the practicalities of broadcasting, so its actual role as a public broadcaster can be defined, is the challenge. That challenge consists of three basic attributes (Barr 1994):

1. *Fundamental institutional change, driven by local and international privatization:* In the 1990s, discussion about the ABC must be in terms of the prevailing paradigm of the political economy – the drive for competition and efficiency. Should the principles of economics be applied to public service broadcasting? Would even a tacit agreement to accept economic imperatives render the traditional institutional structures of public service broadcasting inoperative? Such questions imply a defensive approach, rather than a normative one, responding to the societal changes constantly underway. Yet the demands to speak for and with minorities, while giving voice to dissent can be recognized as necessary features of democratic process. The ABC needs to recognize that the basic tenets of public service are not written in stone. They are consistently a site of contestation.

2. *Compromise against comprehensiveness:* An extension of the application of economic language applied to public broadcasting has seen an increase in

calls for select service, or a niche market approach. Some critics maintain that in a country of Australia's dimensions and with its wealth, the private sector should support even public service broadcasters by advertising, while others simply argue for selling off the service (Walsh 1992). Yet the task of satisfying all audience needs can only be met by an organization legally obliged to provide a comprehensive service.

As a catalyst for programming innovation, the ABC sets the agenda for key political, economic, and social debates. Whether this function is still to be demanded of public broadcasters is not a simple question, especially when an appropriate understanding of the complexity of economic processes is appreciated. If most social needs are met by the market, it could be argued that non-market services are in effect peripheral to the prevailing concerns of society. Alternatively, comprehensiveness is about ideas, which are not only derived from economy. Ideas should be what public service broadcasters value and which are offered to society as the "service."

3. *Technologies of abundance:* The ABC is confronting a diminishing funding pool and expanding broadcast outlets. Video cassette recorders, satellites, and fibre optic cable have accelerated questions about the ABC's role and purpose in the nation's life. If the ABC is recognized as a programme maker, not a system operator, it may be more appropriate for its programming to be offered on commercially operated facilities. More dramatically, the ABC may have to accept that it can offer education, training, and public interest material on the new communication systems. It may have to do this on a commercial basis, in agreement with private operators, while the government maintains its commitment to comprehensiveness by funding such programming services.

In the next section we will consider, in more detail, the relationship between the traditional mandate issues of public service broadcasting and communication and information technology policy through examining the case of indigenous media as an emergent new model for public broadcasting.

Indigenous Media: Technology and Policy

If the ABC and commercial broadcast media were the only services offered in Australia, areas of the vast continent would be totally isolated from communications technology. Since the Whitlam Labor Government of the 1970s, indigenous media have served a public purpose for Aboriginal people and others in isolated and remote areas of Australia. More recently, a variety of services have been provided in an effort to promote the following: indigenous self-determination; self management and control of indigenous affairs; and indigenous identity (Molnar 1994: 1). By 1994, with federal government funding, the following systems were in place: 30 indigenous community radio stations; five Aboriginal commercial community stations; two open narrowcast stations; 80 Broadcasting for Remote Aboriginal Communities Scheme (BRACS) television and radio stations; ABC remote radio; SBS metropolitan radio and television; two high-frequency shower short wave radio services; remote commercial television services; and a remote commercial television station. Feeding into these services were 150 media associations spread around the country, whose interests have been coordinated, since 1992, by the National Indigenous Media Association of Australia.

In a public service broadcasting context, such a range of operations can be seen to extend the mixed broadcasting system. The use and proliferation of electronic – primarily audio – media, as opposed to print, can be attributed to the fact that the oral qualities of the communications are ideally suited to cultures whose preferred form of communication is the oral circulation of highly specific language-based stories, using song and dance (Breen 1992). Consequently, radio and video technologies are user-friendly, in the indigenous context. The adaptability of the media has made it possible for Aboriginal and Torres Strait Islanders (recognized as a separate ethnic group from the far north of Australia) to create their own forms of communication.

Although the story of indigenous media is a successful one, the limitations inherent in the policy process are amply evident. In particular, a shortage of comprehensive policies for all sectors of indigenous media has been identified (Molnar 1994: 6). The impact of resource limitations for staff, equipment, and training has been detrimental to the sector in general. Incredibly, this point was made in the 1984 Willmot Task force (*Out of a Silent Land*), when a call was made for an "integrated policy of national, regional, and local elements" (Willmot 1984: 125). It still applies. Moreover, as if to reinforce the developments outlined in the section above on the ABC, a policy vacuum, combined with a funding shortage, has developed for indigenous media.

The BRACS system is an example of this problem, where an appropriate technology is underutilized and poorly administered, often without any consultation with or preparation of the people concerned. In particular, BRACS, originally intended for satellite communications, was proposed as a magical technological solution to indigenous broadcasting. Local Aboriginal communities would re-broadcast relevant radio and television programmes to remote places, using a simple technology. A BRACS system consists of a small receiver, a VCR camera and recorder, a television monitor, and power source, plus a studio. When trained, indigenous people can use the hardware to generate and transmit local programmes to their communities, thereby making use of a narrowcast medium, which provides specific communities with local content (Molnar 1993). BRACS radio and video content includes songs, stories, oral histories, music, reports on sporting events, and special information days on health and education. Unfortunately, although the opportunity exists for invigorating cultural expression, it has not always been siezed. In some cases, the BRACS system has been used to "collect" mainstream television from the Aussat satellite. This has been "essentially integrationalist" and had little to do with public service, self-determination, and self-management (Molnar 1994: 15).

By constructing a process of indigenous media empowerment that can be underutilized or misused, the policy outcome often serves to confirm the strong, often racist resistance from mainstream media to funding indigenous initiatives of any kind. In the case of BRACS, the technology offers a solution to the disintegration of indigenous culture by building bridges between members of the community and others. Along with the rest of the indigenous media in Australia, BRACS needs consistent and increasing support to fulfil the public service goals underlying its introduction. A coordinated policy is required, with well-established objectives agreed to by the users of the technology. As the indigenous media example demonstrates, the fragmentation of the traditional public service model is a challenge to public and private broadcasting policy, and this challenge needs to be faced by addressing convergence of technologies in the light of maintaining public interest principles.

Convergence and Public Interest Broadcasting

Telecommunications is a feature of contemporary society that sits like a cloud over the broadcasting sector, gradually and with greater and more determined energy, drawing public broadcasting into a technology vortex with no end in sight. The changes brought about by this shift make technological convergence the most conspicuous challenge facing public interest broadcasting in virtually all societies. This is complicated by the three domains across which convergence operates: networks, services, and corporate organization (Lindsay 1993: 36). Although we will not consider these in detail here, it is important to remember that policy in the new era must work across technical and institutional formations that are constantly moving.

The convergence of computing and telecommunication functions providing an integrated information network has been underway for two decades. Both the direction and pace of these developments have been influenced by government policies in the telecommunications sector, which have sought to keep pace with technological developments in the computing industries (Melody 1990). Previously discrete spheres of policy activity in broadcasting and telecommunications have collided, to then diffuse in a confusing array of issues. Consequently, the "leakage" of policy issues from the telecommunications sector across the previously distinct public broadcasting sector is palpable. A multichannel society, offering through a myriad of services a gross form of comprehensiveness, now exists. This "information society" is rich in options and poor in its public responsibility. It is driven by commercial operators' objectives to commodify social activities for which audiences and advertisers can be matched. The "trade paradigm" has come to dominate the information society (Reidenberg 1993: 289). From the global privatizing perspective, the result is that the trade in information objective appears to receive tacit approval from policy makers under pressure to withdraw from, yet condone, commodity relations.

Three driving forces have created the conditions under which "the industries of information" have emerged as an agglomeration of shared interests: "global corporatization," "deregulatory policies," and digitization (Smith 1990: 9-10). What is significant for public service broadcasting and the attendant policies is that national perspectives still find a space in which to manifest themselves. The fragmentation of the traditional public service model will continue to challenge the private and public broadcasting philosophies. Furthermore, as digitization offers an economy of substitutable content, communities of interest will seek to express their own concerns at a micro level, while corporations will seek to absorb them in a global arrangement (Naughton 1994). The victors may be the previously disenfranchised, who manage to put some of the digitized fragments together to suit their own interests, in a liberatory challenge from below (Goggin and Newell 1995: 39). An optimistic social democratic model will at least allow for this outcome.

Checks and Balances

This chapter has identified the examples of the continuing regulatory regime operating through the ABA to maintain local content, the ABC's unsettled attempts at sustaining its traditional public service services, and the operation of special and narrowcast technology in remote communities. New technology and the information society have led to the unravelling of the core components of the mixed broadcasting system in Australia. This does not mean the end of public service broadcasting. It does, however, mean that a new set of priorities must be established that meet the public interest in the global information system.

While it is appropriate to assert the importance of a publicly constructed process of vigilance over the changes taking place, it is more necessary to have a clear view of intended outcomes. These outcomes must include universal service obligations, which function as part of what has been termed "fair information practice rules" (Reidenberg 1993: 288). Establishing the rules is often the point at which a public discourse is either established by government and policy workers, or restricted by vested interests. In this case, the optimistic social democratic model must be operationalized as a feature of government objectives, where access and equity issues are given adequate space in which to circulate. That is, the universal service obligations will function on the basis of access and equity to information that are deemed to be publicly necessary for the health and well being of the society, where the process of arriving at the agreed objectives is fully participatory, consultative, and transparent. It must also be open to constant review.

In this respect, the objectives of policy should be of a general nature, rather than restricted to one sector of broadcasting law and policy. This has been recognized in the Australian context, in the lead up to 1997 and the introduction of a "competitive and liberal" telecommunications regime, where a new set of policies that consider the primacy of "convergence" in the communications area will be established (Australia 1994: iii).[6] A "competition policy" is now a feature of a limited, yet important, debate about the future of telecommunications, altering the previous policy obsession with privatization. Consequently explicit social policy objectives have been identified as part of the body of telecommunications policy:

The hallmark of the Government's involvement in communications has been the recognition that change is inevitable and unstoppable and that the Government's primary role is to assist the community in gaining the full benefits from that change (Australia 1994: 6).

The question that remains is, as the government has noted, "what is the appropriate definition of universal service in an open market environment, and the extent to which legislative arrangements should allow the ... definitions to be altered over time?" (Australia 1994: 54). Inevitably, the power relations between industry participants in a competitive, relatively deregulated environment will determine the policy outcome. The question for the government is whether it is capable of maintaining the public interest as an adjunct to the objectives of universal service obligations. In a broadband future, however, where information is mediated by its exchange value, and where transactions can be keenly monitored, the powerful will insist on avoiding their universal service obligations, and, thus, the fair rules that should apply to broadcasting and information. Commitments by governments to the detailed, transparent monitoring of services being provided must be a policy priority. Where regulatory authorities exist, a coordinated response to convergence issues needs to be established, which will reinforce a commitment to public service issues. In situations in which the fragmentation of communication services continues, difficult decisions will need to be made about what resources governments can commit to public service broadcasting. In particular, advocates of the mixed system will recognize that the complementary functions of the ABC, SBS, and community broadcasting should be regarded as key components in a responsible, democratic broadcasting policy. In the longer term, a new set of issues may arise which will provide a strong case for an entirely different set of propositions about the funding and formulation of public service broadcasting. Nevertheless, the issues discussed in this chapter will continue to be at the heart of the policy environment in which public service broadcasting operates.

Notes

1. The author would like to thank the following colleagues for their assistance with this contribution: William H. Melody, Helen Molnar, Dianne Northfield, Trevor Barr.

2. A "policy environment" is the larger operationalization of a set of protocols and rational rules governing public society. It is the context in which the aims and objectives of public service broadcasting are established.

3. The ABC's Charter provides evidence of the contradiction and confusion between public responsibility and commercial orientation. The basic functions and duties of the ABC which Parliament has given to the ABC are set out in the Charter of the Corporation (section 6 (1) and (2) of the ABC Act). Appearing alongside the Charter is a Code of Practice relating to programming matters.

4. Television Program Standard (TPS) 14 – Australian Content of Television Programs – includes the following programme objectives: (a) that programmes are identifiably Australian; (b) that they recognize the diversity of cultural backgrounds represented in the Australian community; (c) that they are developed for an Australian audience; and (d) that they are produced with Australian creative control (*Australian Broadcasting Authority* 1994: 55). Recently, local content has been prioritized in two public reviews: the Australian Broadcasting Authority *Australian Content: Review of programme standard for commercial television*(1994) and *Networking Australia's Future,* The Interim Report of the Broadband Services Expert Group (1994).

5. Outsourcing refers to the ABC's practice of contracting the production of programmes to independent producers.

6. *The Ministerial Review of the Post-1997 Telecommunications Policy and Regulatory Structure* gives an indication of how a mixed set of objectives could be achieved. The ten major chapters raise these issues: regulatory arrangements relating to industry structure; competition policy; powers and immunities; universal service, affordability, and content; consumer protection and privacy; national interest considerations; technical regulation; electronic addressing and directories; industry policy; and institutional arrangements. (Northfield 1994: 3).

References

Armstrong, Mark. 1993. The ABC is Integral to Australia. *Australian Financial Review*, 14 July.

Australia. 1992. *Australian Broadcasting Corporation Act.* Commonwealth of Australia.

Australia. 1994. *Beyond the Duopoly: Australian Telecommunications Policy and Regulation.* Issues Paper.

Australian Broadcasting Authority. 1994. *Australian Content: Review of the Program Standard for Commercial Television.* Discussion Paper, Sydney.

Australian Broadcasting Tribunal. 1986. *Australian Music on Radio*, Sydney.

Australian Children's Television Foundation. 1994. *Annual Report 1993-94.*

Australian Labor Party. 1979. National Committee of Inquiry. *Reports and Recommendations to the National Executive.*

Barr, Trevor, and Brenda O'Connor. 1994. Public Broadcasting: New Frontiers? *Futures Paper: Directions for the Australian Broadcasting Corporation.* A Swinburne University Research report for Friends of the ABC. Melbourne: Media and Telecommunications Centre.

Bauer, J.M. 1994. Conceptual Frameworks for the Design of Telecommunications Policy. In *Telecommunications in Transition: Policies, Services and Technologies in the European Community*, edited by C. Steinfield, J. M. Bauer and L. Caby. Thousand Oaks, CA: Sage.

Breen, Marcus. 1992. Desert Dreams Media and Interventions in Reality: Australian Aboriginal Music. In *Rockin' the Boat: Mass Music and Mass Movements*, edited by R. Garofalo. Boston: South End Press.

Breen, Marcus. 1994. One for the Money: The Commodity Logic of Contemporary Culture in Australia. *Media Information Australia* 72 (May): 62-73.

Chadwick, P. 1989. *Media Mates*. Melbourne: Sun Books.

Counihan, Mick. 1992. Radio, Records and the First Australian Music Quota. *Media Information Australia* 64 (May): 6-16.

Cunningham, Stuart. 1992a. The Cultural Policy Debate Revisited. *Meanjin* 51 (3): 533-543.

Cunningham, Stuart. 1992b. *Framing Culture: Criticism and Policy in Australia*. Sydney: Allen and Unwin.

Cunningham, Stuart. 1993. Television. In *The Media in Australia: Industries, Texts, Audiences*, edited by S. Cunningham and G. Turner. Sydney: Allen and Unwin.

Dore, Christopher and Jennifer Foreshew. 1995. ABC to Refocus on Traditional Services. *The Australian*, 10 February.

Dunlevy, Lyn. 1992. How Regulators Pulled a Switch. *The Age*, 2 December.

Edgar, Patricia. 1994. Untitled. Australian Children's Television Foundation. *Annual Report 1993-94*.

Frith, S. 1991. Anglo-America and its Discontents. *Cultural Studies* 5 (3): 264-269.

Goggin, Gerard, and Christopher Newell. December 1994 - January 1995. Citizen C'ber: Telecommunications and the Question of Equity. *Arena Magazine*: 36-39.

Harding, Richard. 1979. *Outside Interference: The Politics of Australian Broadcasting*. Melbourne: Sun Books.

Jacka, L. 1993. *Remapping the Australian Television System*. CIRCIT Working Paper, no. 2, June.

Jaensch, Dean, ed. 1979. *Australian Labor Party: National Committee of Inquiry: Discussion Papers*. Australasian Political Studies Association, monograph no. 3, Flinders University.

Lenthall, Kate, and Ben Potter. 1994. Senate Approves Inquiry into ABC. *The Age*, 22 September.

Lenthall, Kate. 1994. Push for Probe on ABC Expands. *The Age*, 21 September.

Lindsay, David. 1993. *When Cultures Collide: Regulating the Convergence of Telecommunications and Broadcasting*. CIRCIT Policy Research Paper, no. 29, August.

McFadyen, Stuart. 1993. Cultural Development in an Open Economy. *Canadian Journal of Communication* 18: 515-521.

Melody, William, H. 1990. *Telecommunication: Policy Directions for Australia in the Global Information Economy*. CIRCIT Policy Research Paper, no. 7.

Melody, William, H. 1994. The Mosaic Model of Cultural Development. In *Enhancing Cultural Value: Narrowcasting, Community Media and Cultural Development*, edited by M. Breen. CIRCIT conference proceedings, March.

Middleton, Karen. 1994. ABC Will Investigate Influence Claims. *The Age*, 19 September.

Miller, Toby. 1993. Radio. In *The Media in Australia: Industries, Texts, Audiences*, edited by S. Cunningham and G. Turner. Sydney: Allen and Unwin.

Molnar, Helen. 1993. Remote Aboriginal Community Broadcasting (Australia). In *Alternative Media: Linking Global and Local*, edited by Peter Lewis. UNESCO: Paris.

Molnar, Helen. 1994. Indigenous Media Development in Australia: Inadequate Government Response to Indigenous Broadcasting Initiatives. A paper for the International Communication Association Conference, Sydney, 11-15 July 1994, to be reprinted in *Cultural Studies*, forthcoming.

Murdock, Graham. 1990. Redrawing the Map of Communications Industries: Concentration and Ownership in the Era of Privatisation. In *Public Communication The New Imperatives: Future Directions in Media Research*, edited by Marjorie Ferguson. London: Sage.

Naughton, Tracey. 1994. To Watch is O.K. but to Air is Divine: Community T.V.-The Big Picture. In *Enhancing Cultural Value: Narrowcasting, Community Media and Cultural Development*, edited by M. Breen. CIRCIT Conference proceedings, March.

Networking Australia's Future. 1994. The Interim Report of the Broadband Services Expert Group. Canberra: Commonwealth of Australia.

Northfield, Dianne. 1994. Australian Telecommunications Industry-Preparing for 1997. *Stream 2.2 The Current Policy Development Process, Compendium of Legislative Reviews and Related Research Activities.* Melbourne, CIRCIT, November.

O'Regan, T. 1993. *Australian Television Culture.* Sydney: Allen and Unwin.

Paltridge, S. 1989. *Australian Satellites: Promise, Performance and the Next Generation.* CIRCIT Policy Research Paper, no. 1.

Potter, Ben, and Kate Lenthall. 1994. ABC Widens its Inquiry into Favourable Treatments. *The Age,* 20 September.

Reidenberg, Joel, R. 1993. Rules of the Road for Global Electronic Highways: Merging the Trade and Technical Paradigms. *Harvard Journal of Law and Technology* 6 (Spring): 287-306.

Scannell, Paddy. 1989. Public Service Broadcasting and Modern Life. In *Media, Culture and Society.* London: Sage.

Simper, E. 1994. The ABC of Sponsorship. *The Weekend Australian,* 24-25 September.

Seneviratne, K. 1993. Giving a Voice to the Voiceless: Community Radio in Australia. *Media Asia* 20 (2): 66-74.

Sinclair, J. 1992. *Globalisation and National Culture: Structure, Regulation and Content in the Advertising Industry in Australia.* CIRCIT Policy Research Paper, no. 24, June.

Smith, Anthony. 1990. Media Globalism in the Age of Consumer Sovereignty. *Gannett Centre Journal* (Fall): 1-16.

Thomas, Alan. 1980. *Broadcast and be Damned: The ABC's First Two Decades.* Melbourne: Melbourne University Press.

Walsh, Max. 1992. Column. *Sydney Morning Herald,* 9 June.

Westerway, P. 1992. *ABTEE Newsletter.* Australian Broadcasting Tribunal, 9 March.

Willmot, Eric. 1984. *Out of the Silent Land.* Report of the task force on Aboriginal and Islander Broadcasting and Communications. Canberra: Department of Aboriginal Affairs.

Wilson, Helen. 1994. *The Radio Book 1994.* Christchurch: New Zealand Broadcasting School, Christchurch Polytechnic.

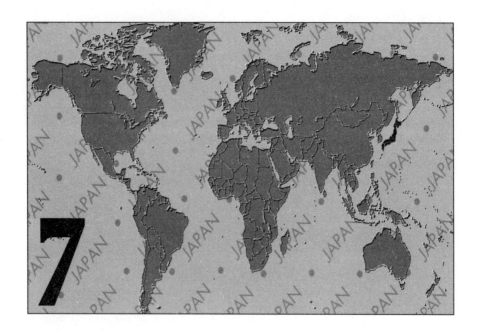

Japan: Public Broadcasting as a National Project

Shinichi Shimizu

The Current Situation

The Japanese broadcasting system after World War II is a combination of British-style public service broadcasting, financially supported by licence fees, and U.S-style commercial broadcasting, dependent on advertising revenues. The Japanese broadcasting industry is one of the largest in the world. It includes a nationwide public service and five commercial terrestrial television networks, as well as three public and one private direct broadcast satellite (DBS) stations and 11 private communication satellite Pay-TV channels. It also has three nationwide public radio (AM and FM) services and numerous commercial AM and FM radio stations broadcasting locally.

The number of households with televisions in Japan is estimated at 38.7 million, and the number of television sets is estimated to have reached over 77 million, with two sets per household. The percentage of those with VCRs is as high as 80 percent. However, dissemination of multichannel cable television is limited, with only about 5 percent of television households subscribing to the service, compared with 60 percent in the United States.

The public broadcaster, Nippon Hoso Kyokai (NHK), or Japan Broadcasting Corporation, is supported almost entirely by licence fees. Commercial broadcasters are supported by advertising, with the exception of one private DBS and the 11 satellite pay television channels, which are subscription services. As a result of growth in the advertising market, Japanese commercial broadcasters have grown, and the number of commercial broadcasters has reached 174, of which 36 broadcast both radio and television; 80 broadcast television only (one of them is the DBS satellite channel, WOWOW); and 58 broadcast radio only. Their annual income has risen to more than four times the revenue obtained by NHK from licence fees.

Before World War II

Radio broadcasting began in Japan, in 1925, with three private non-profit radio stations established in the major cities of Tokyo, Osaka, and Nagoya by local newspapers and electronics enterprises in the respective areas. The three stations, managed by local press and business executives, quickly merged into a public corporation, in August 1926, under the new government policy of establishing a nationwide radio network. The ministry of communications appointed former ministry officials to eight of the top 14 executive posts at the new broadcasting organization. No one from the press associated with the former three radio stations was appointed to this level. Executives of the Tokyo radio station protested the appointments, criticizing the ministry for "failing to understand the mission of the new organization, which should be to serve the public." However, resistance to the ministry decision soon withered, as it was generally regarded in Japan in those days that broadcasting was a service that should come under the direct control of the government (NHK 1967).

The new corporation was the predecessor of today's NHK and enjoyed a monopoly of broadcasting until after the end of World War II. Legally, the public broadcasting monopoly, which covered the entire nation, was not a government institution, but its programming and management were severely controlled by the broad and various administrative rules and ordinances enforced by the minister of communications through the Wireless Telegraph Act of 1915.

Thus, the minister of communications had virtually absolute power over the life and death of NHK, and its broadcasting activities were used to promote government policies and strengthen national unity by the successive governments in the 1930s and 1940s, prior to and during World War II. It was widely considered then that NHK was practically an extension of the ministry of communications and was executing its business in place of the government.

After World War II

The broadcasting system underwent a drastic change as a result of Japan's surrender to the allied powers in August 1945. The general headquarters for the allied forces took a series of measures to disassociate NHK's broadcasting activities from the government, under their democratization policy toward Japan. Although NHK's monopoly remained as before, the supervising power of the government over NHK's operation was greatly reduced and restricted.

At an early stage of the occupation, general headquarters did not show interest in a Japanese proposal to create private broadcasting organizations. A memorandum from the headquarters to the Japanese government, in December 1945, clarified that the allied powers would allow NHK to continue its operation as a unified and monopolistic system of broadcasting in Japan. However, it made no reference to the establishment of private broadcasting companies.

The Japanese government, therefore, withdrew its plan to assign one of NHK's two radio networks to the proposed private broadcasters. The government thus tacitly confirmed NHK's special status as the main instrument of broadcasting in Japan, even if a pluralistic, competitive system of public and commercial broadcasting would be adopted in the future.

Two years later, general headquarters changed its insistence on the monopolistic broadcasting system and suggested in an October 1947 memorandum to the Japanese government its willingness to allow private broadcasting parallel to NHK's public broadcasting. NHK's monopoly ended in June 1950, when the "Three Radio Laws," the Radio Law, the Broadcast Law, and the Radio Regulatory Commission Law, were put into effect under the new Constitution of 1946. The new laws, formulated during the allied occupation, paved the way for the establishment, for the first time, of privately owned commercial broadcasting companies.

Under the Radio Law, broadcasting stations are licensed as a type of wireless station. The Broadcast Law spells out the basic principles and requirements under which NHK operates as a public service broadcaster, and it recognizes the establishment of commercial broadcasting as a business enterprise allowed to operate parallel to NHK. The old NHK was reorganized to become a public corporation under the Broadcast and Radio Laws, both of which embody Japan's guarantee of freedom of speech as expressed in Article 21 of the 1946 Constitution: "freedom of speech, press and all other forms of expression are guaranteed. No censorship shall be maintained."

General headquarters, in spite of consistent negative responses from Japanese officials, demanded, unfailingly, the creation of the third law stipulating the establishment of an autonomous regulatory organization, the Radio Regulatory Commission, modelled after the Federal Communications Commission (FCC) of the United States. Japanese officials finally gave in and agreed to the creation of a seven-member commission to administer the air waves, which would work independently of the government authority.

On 21 April 1951, the commission issued preliminary licences to 16 private radio broadcasting companies established in major cities in Japan by local newspaper and business interests in the respective areas. Then, in February 1952, the commission established technical standards for transmission of black-and-white television broadcasting, choosing the U.S standard of a six-megacycle frequency bandwidth over NHK's provisional Japanese standard of a seven-megacycle frequency bandwidth.

A private television company, Nippon Television Network Corporation (NTV), promoted the six-megacycle U.S. standard, while NHK and Japanese electrical appliances manufacturers advocated the seven-megacycle standard. According to the director of NTV, the commission chose the U.S. standard, since it would afford better chances of introducing the well-advanced U.S. technology when shifting from monochrome television to colour.

The Radio Regulatory Commission, however, had a short life. It was abolished by the Japanese government on 31 July 1952, in the name of organizational simplification. The Japanese government decided to delegate its authority to the minister of posts and telecommunications. At midnight on the day of its abolition, the commission issued Japan's first preliminary television licence to NTV, a commercial television company established by the *Yomiuri Shimbun*, one of Japan's leading dailies. However, the commission reserved its decision on the applications from the public service broadcaster, NHK, and another commercial broadcasting company, Radio Tokyo, predecessor of the Tokyo Broadcasting System (TBS).

The abolition of the Radio Regulatory Commission, after only two years in existence, reflected the policy of the Japanese government to recover its administrative authority over the air waves, leading to the return to the traditional monopolistic radio administration set up under the minister of posts and telecommunications. The abolition came three months after the Japanese Peace Treaty came into force and the allied occupation of Japan ended.

The ministry of posts and telecommunications (MPT) then set up the five-person Radio Regulatory Council, attached to the ministry as a consultative organ for the minister. However, it has no independent authority. Its function is to examine and investigate matters related to the regulation of radio waves and broadcasting and to make recommendations to the minister.

Birth of Commercial Radio and Television Broadcasting

The first two commercial radio companies, one in Nagoya and the other in Osaka, started operation on 1 September 1951. Since then, Japanese broadcasting has continued under the dual system, with public service NHK and commercial broadcasters operating parallel to one another.

Although not the first to receive a television licence, NHK inaugurated television broadcasting in Tokyo on 1 February 1953. It was followed by commercial NTV in August of the same year. Then, in October 1957, the MPT granted 34 provisional commercial television licences and established the base for today's prosperity of commercial television in Japan. Educational television was launched by NHK in January 1959, and colour television broadcasting was started in September of the following year by NHK and four commercial television stations in Tokyo.

NHK's Current State of Affairs

Today, NHK is one of the biggest public broadcasting organizations in the world. It has a staff of 13,300 in 54 domestic broadcasting stations with production facilities, and it also has 25 overseas offices. NHK has 30 affiliate companies and organizations with some 4,400 employees. The affiliates support NHK through their business activities and enable it to carry out its duties as a public service broadcaster (see Shimizu 1988 and 1991b).[1]

NHK operates two nationwide terrestrial television networks; two DBS satellite television channels, each with independent programming; three national radio services (two medium-wave and one FM); and a nationwide teletext service and an overseas shortwave radio service in 22 languages, called Radio Japan. It is also a major programme supplier for an experimental high-definition television (HDTV) channel and TV Japan satellite services in the United States and Europe. On its two terrestrial television channels, NHK broadcasts more than 13,120 hours of programmes yearly, or 253.5 hours weekly, while on its two DBS satellite channels, it broadcasts 17,264 hours yearly, or 332 hours weekly.

The Japanese public network was established under the 1950 Broadcast Law, with the aim of promoting public welfare through nationwide broadcasting. To ensure that the public interest is served as far as possible, the law provides a specific structure for NHK, with a board of governors as its highest decision-making organ. The board consists of 12 members with wide knowledge and experience in their respective fields, such as journalism, academic research, or business. It has powers and responsibilities to decide the management policy and other important matters related to the operation and business of the public broadcaster. As representatives of the public, they are appointed by the prime minister, with the consent of both Houses of the Diet or Parliament. The board of governors appoints and dismisses the president, chief executive officer, and the auditors. It also approves the president's appointment or dismissal of the executive vice president and directors.

NHK is subject to supervision from Parliament and the government in accordance with the provisions of the Broadcast Law. The legislation covers all aspects of its organization, finance, and business. The annual financial report, budget, and operating plans for the coming year, as well as inventory, balance sheets, and surplus and deficit accounts, must be submitted for approval annually to Parliament, through the MPT and the Cabinet.

Financial independence, vital to the integrity of a public broadcaster, is made possible by NHK's licence fee system. The Broadcast Law stipulates that homes equipped to receive NHK's television service must pay a monthly licence fee to legally receive its programmes. In its budget, NHK proposes a licence fee level in line with the estimated costs of its annual operational plans. Both Houses of Parliament consider the budget and decide to accept or reject it. NHK's licence fee rate for the coming year is, thus, set by Parliament when it approves NHK's budget of revenues and expenditures.

Despite this supervision by Parliament and the government, NHK maintains quite an independent existence. It accepts no investment, advertising, or financial assistance from the government or any commercial or other organization. With the voluntary licence fee system to guarantee its financial independence, NHK is able to fully serve the public without being subject to undue influence by the current government or any other group. It is also free to operate without sacrificing the programming needs of any minority audience group.

NHK collects licence fees directly from contracted TV households – Y1,370 a month per terrestrial TV household and Y2,300 (the terrestrial licence fee plus a DBS surcharge of Y930) per DBS satellite household. The current fee rate was set in April 1990.

The number of households that had licence fee contracts with NHK was 34.6 million at the end of January 1994, nearly 90 percent of all television-owning households in Japan. The number of households with DBS satellite contracts was 5.7 million, an increase of more than 860,000 over the previous year. As much as 85 percent of the contracted households pay these fees through direct debiting of their bank or postal savings accounts, assuring a stable income for NHK.

For its fiscal 1995 (April 1995 to March 1996) draft budget, NHK estimated its total revenues from licence fees (97 percent) and others would be Y570.74 billion, or about US$5.707 billion, an increase of Y4.1 billion (0.7 percent) compared to the previous year. Total expenditures, including business expenditures of Y506.7 billion and capital expenditures, are estimated at Y573.4 billion, an increase of Y21.2 billion (3.9 percent).[2]

The total operational revenues of NHK's 28 affiliate companies in fiscal 1993 were about Y205 billion, comparable to those of a Tokyo network company. Their total operating profit was Y2.54 billion, an increase of 29 percent compared to fiscal 1992. The affiliates include NHK Enterprises, Inc., Japan Broadcast Publishing Co., NHK Integrated Technology, Inc., and NHK Joho Network, Inc. NHK's total operational revenues in 1993 being Y551.3 billion, the total operational revenues of the NHK "conglomerate" reached more than Y756 billion, and was expected to reach Y1,000 billion by the year 2000.

NHK's Advantages over Private Broadcasters

Broadcasting has developed in Japan under the bureaucratic guidance of the government. This tradition exists even today, as the MPT still holds the national policy planning and regulatory authority over matters related to broadcasting and telecommunications. A special role is reserved for NHK.

Whenever a new venture in the field of broadcasting is planned – be it DBS, HDTV, or a transborder television service – NHK is called upon by the MPT to spearhead development and to popularize it. This is seen in the successive revision of Articles related to NHK in the Broadcast Law. The Articles in Chapter II of the 1950 Broadcast Law mandated NHK to play a leading role in developing broadcasting in Japan. Article 7, Chapter II, in the original 1950 version, stated only that the purpose of NHK was to conduct its broadcasting for the public welfare in such a manner that its broadcasting would be received all over Japan.

The newest version of the law (1994), after 20 revisions, states that NHK's purpose is to conduct its domestic broadcasting with rich and good broadcast programmes for the public welfare and in such a manner that its broadcasting may be received all over Japan. It must also conduct business necessary for the development of broadcasting and reception and, at the same time, conduct international radio and television broadcasting.[3] Thus, the Broadcast Law has given NHK a broad mandate and guarantees NHK's position as one of the largest multiservice public broadcasters in the world.

In contrast to NHK, the management of privately owned commercial broadcasters is more or less left to the market economy. Neither the Radio Law nor the Broadcast Law stipulates the form of management, organization, or financing of private broadcasters. Being private business entities, their form of management and financial sources are principally placed at the owners' discretion. The Broadcast Law provides regulations only on programmes and permission of contract provisions of Pay-TV channels. Private broadcasters are not allowed to operate as a single business organization with a nationwide service area (except in shortwave radio), and multiple ownership of television or radio stations is prohibited, so as to discourage the concentration of mass media. The single ownership of all forms of media (television, radio, and newspapers) is also banned (see Shimizu 1993b). On the other hand, commercial broadcasters are protected from an excessive free competition among themselves and the intrusion into the market by big business through the regulations stipulated in the Radio and Broadcast Laws and the MPT ordinances. Commercial broadcasters in major cities had grown and prospered until the beginning of the 1990s, when Japan's booming "bubble economy" (so-called because of the sudden burst that ended the economic boom) collapsed.

Although independently run, they form *de facto* networks centred around five television stations in Tokyo, competing fiercely with NHK, as well as with each other. In the heavily populated metropolitan areas around Tokyo, Osaka, and Nagoya, five or more commercial television channels are available, in addition to the NHK's two terrestrial and two DBS channels. More than 85 percent of total TV households have access to at least four commercial television channels.

NHK's Advantages over Other Public Broadcasters

A) Independent and Autonomous

The Broadcast Law of 1950 guarantees NHK's autonomous management through a board of governors as its highest decision-making organ. The powers vested in the board are meant to ensure freedom of expression in broadcasting and independence from outside influence, including political pressure. In the past, the control of finances of the former Nippon Hoso Kyokai was in the hands of the minister of communications. The new Broadcast Law transferred the budgetary control to Parliament to ensure that NHK's management and operations accurately reflect the wishes of the general public. Unlike some public service broadcasters in other countries, which rely on government grants for their annual revenues, NHK relies almost entirely on fees it collects directly from contracted TV households.

Under the Broadcast Law, broadcasting stations are subject to abstract and minimum regulations concerning broadcasting programmes, such as non-disturbance of the public security, political impartiality, non-distortion of facts, and harmony among broadcast programmes by providing cultural or educational programmes as well as news and entertainment. Otherwise, the law guarantees, in principle, the freedom of programme compilation, and broadcasters have a responsibility to exercise self-restraint to ensure the appropriateness of their programme content.

B) Large Number of Fee-Paying Viewers

NHK operates four television channels and three radio services with a staff of 13,000, and it receives fees from 34.6 million TV households, including 5.7 million DBS-receiving homes. It is, therefore, better off than other public service broadcasters in the world. For example, the BBC, which operates two television channels and five radio services with a staff of 25,000, has about 22 million licence-fee-paying households. The annual licence fee rate of NHK and the BBC is comparable, about US$150 per household.

C) DBS-Channels Assure Revenue Increase

In addition to its four television channels, NHK operates two terrestrial channels and two DBS satellite channels, while most other public service broadcasters in the world operate only one or two terrestrial television channels. Its licence fee revenues from terrestrial TV households are not expected to increase, because of the saturation of TV-owning households, but its revenues from DBS households are expected to increase as the number of DBS dish antenna owners increases. At the end of July 1994, the number of DBS households reached more than 8 million, of which 6 million had contracts with NHK.

NHK expects that the number of DBS households will reach more than 10.4 million by the end of March 1996, and the contracted households will reach 7.5 million. In fiscal year 1995, NHK estimated an increase of 12.4 percent, or

Y7.8 billion, in DBS fee revenues, which is expected to reach Y71 billion in total, in spite of the fact that the operational revenues and profits of commercial networks recorded a setback in recent years due to the recession after the collapse of the bubble economy.[4]

Thus, under the circumstances, NHK is in a better position than commercial competitors to allocate substantial funds for producing large-scale entertainment and current affairs programmes, strengthening educational programmes for children, and reinforcing sports programmes on its terrestrial and satellite channels.

According to the fiscal 1995 budget, NHK plans to invest Y411 billion, Y15 billion more than the previous year, in programme production and broadcasting of domestic radio and television services. It will also invest Y60 billion in construction of broadcast and production facilities, including about Y8.2 billion for the expansion of DBS and HDTV facilities.

D) Research and Development Activities Pave Way for Advanced TV Services

NHK has been leading the Japanese broadcast industry, not only through its broadcasting activities but also through its research and development activities at its Science and Technical Research Laboratories established in 1930. With a staff of some 310 engineers, the laboratories are engaged in wide-ranging research and development, which anticipate the needs of an advanced information-based society. As Japan's sole integrated research institute for broadcasting technology, the laboratories have been vital to NHK's progress, while also contributing to the industry's global development.

Research at the laboratories is concentrated in three main areas – new broadcast media, improvement of conventional broadcast services, and basic technology to support future broadcasting – with a budget of more than Y12 billion annually. Within these areas, special efforts are concentrated on the research and development of new media such as HDTV and Integrated Services Digital Broadcasting (ISDB), which will be the main broadcast media in the twenty-first century.

E) 40 Years Experience of Competition with Commercial Television

NHK has been competing with aggressive commercial networks for more than 40 years. The competition has helped NHK to produce and broadcast many popular programmes with elegance, style, and depth, such as its high-rated serial dramas and quality investigative documentaries. Thus, it helped NHK to advance its position as one of the most competitive public service broadcasters in the world.

Although no longer dominant and always top-rated among the most severely competing terrestrial television channels, NHK is both the largest producer of domestic programming and the biggest buyer of foreign programming. Its income remains the highest of all Japanese broadcasting organizations, thanks to licence fee income from its terrestrial television channels and surcharge fee earnings from the satellite channels.

In normal times, NHK's premier General TV channel and five commercial networks share ratings, on average, more or less evenly. However, when something important, be it an earthquake, typhoon, or war, takes place, viewers turn to NHK, since their confidence in NHK has built up over the years.

When a ferocious earthquake hit the western Japanese commercial centre of Kobe and Osaka in the early morning of 17 January 1995, most households tuned in to NHK's radio and television broadcasts. According to a Video Research survey, the news bulletin on NHK's General TV channel at 5:51 a.m., minutes after the earthquake, secured a 31.6 percent rating. Its regular local morning newscast at 6:30 a.m. and national newscast, "Good Morning Japan," at 7 a.m. registered 41.9 and 37.3 percent ratings, respectively, in the Kansai (Kobe-Osaka) region. The earthquake claimed more than 5,000 victims. NHK continuously broadcast news and information related to the earthquake on its terrestrial television channels and radio (AM and FM) networks for more than a week. According to the survey, reported by the *Nihon Keizai Shimbun* (30 January 1995), a special news programme broadcast on Sunday, 22 January, at 7:00 p.m., featuring the aftermath of the earthquake, secured a 31.1 percent rating, a very high rating for news and information programmes.

When North Korea announced President Kim Il Sung's death on Saturday, 9 July 1994, NHK-TV's noon newscast, which was extended until 12:45 p.m., secured a 18.9 percent rating, and its 4:00 p.m. news, which usually received 5 percent, registered a 23.5 percent rating. The special newscasts by major commercial networks, TBS and NTV, covering Kim Il Sung's death, secured ratings of 8.4 and 8 percent, respectively. The same phenomena occurred when the Persian Gulf War broke out in January 1991 (see Shimizu 1991b).

According to a survey on media contact during emergencies, conducted by NHK's Research Institute for Public Opinion, 73 percent of those surveyed replied that they got information on earthquakes and typhoons from NHK, while 14.9 percent said they relied on commercial stations, and only .5 percent turned to newspapers. As for election result bulletins, 69.7 percent turned to NHK, 13 percent watched commercial television, and 7.3 percent got information from newspapers.

These figures confirmed the phrases passed on for generations among the Japanese public: "When something major happens, turn to NHK" and "NHK in times of crucial events." This viewers' faith in NHK in an emergency is reflected in the fact that as many as 90 percent of Japanese households pay viewing fees to NHK, although payment of the fee is voluntary. According to one of NHK's top executives, "this 90 percent figure is high enough to justify the receiving fee system, as it proves that it is well accepted by the Japanese public" (Kono 1993).

NHK's Current and Future Problems

In July 1994, the NHK announced that it would strengthen its news and information programmes and extend terrestrial channels' broadcasting hours further to meet the needs of its viewers and to compete with rival commercial networks. With "Challenge and Progress" as its slogan, the NHK would also make more effort to provide its audience with high quality drama and entertainment programmes that would be heart-warming and intellectually stimulating. NHK has to cope with the following major issues to meet the challenges of the forthcoming multimedia era in the twenty-first century.

A) DBS Satellite Broadcasting

NHK's DBS satellite broadcasts will, as most have forecast, become popular, creating the challenge of attracting viewers of all ages to the new channels. NHK has made a commitment to reform terrestrial educational television, not only to educate young Japanese viewers but also to serve the needs of other sectors, including the aged and the socially disadvantaged.

In a document entitled *Vision for the Twenty-first Century and its Challenges – NHK's Future Framework,* published in February 1993, NHK said it would fully integrate both terrestrial and satellite broadcasts into its network system, operating as one network with four television channels. It also said that NHK would convert all satellite broadcasts to HDTV as soon as most satellite receivers in the service area were either HDTV compatible or equipped with appropriate converters.

NHK's future depends on the growth in fee-paying DBS-receiving households and the penetration of HDTV receivers to homes, which will eventually be an important revenue resource. In its 1990-95 management plan, NHK estimated that the number of DBS-receiving households would reach 10 million, with fee-paying contracted households reaching 9 million by the end of March 1995. However, the collapse of the bubble economy has constrained the growth of the satellite broadcast sector in Japan, including HDTV receivers. The number of fee-paying DBS households reached only 6 million by the end of June 1994, with actual dish-owning households estimated at 8 million. NHK hopes that the number of DBS homes will again increase substantially, once the recession ends, as some 35 percent of all new television sets sold on the market have built-in DBS receivers. The audience for DBS is certain to expand as more people replace their old model sets.

B) Hi-Vision: NHK-developed HDTV

NHK's technical laboratories and manufacturers were cooperating to develop a flat panel type Hi-Vision (HDTV) set that can be hung on the wall, and it will be ready for practical use by 1998, when the Winter Olympics are held in Nagano, Japan. NHK has formed a consortium with 25 firms and manufactures, including Texas Instruments (Japan), to develop a 40-inch plasma display Hi-Vision television receiver, which can be put on the market by 1998, costing, initially, about $4,000. NHK started experimental, regular one-hour Hi-Vision broadcasting on one of its DBS channels in 1989. Then, for three years from November 1991, the Hi Vision Promotion Association, a consortium of NHK and commercial broadcasters, engaged in daily eight-hour Hi-Vision broadcasts on the newly launched BS-3b satellite.

Unlike the United States, which is developing a digital HDTV system for transmission on terrestrial and cable channels, NHK developed an analog HDTV transmission format called MUSE for use on the Japanese DBS satellite channels, because it was technically the only feasible method to carry the highly compressed data of HDTV on the internationally allocated bandwidth for satellite broadcasting. All other aspects of the Hi-Vision television system are digital. NHK continues to research and develop a digitally based HDTV transmission system, primarily to support the network's future multimedia services.

In February 1994, a senior official of the MPT said that the ministry might drop the NHK-developed Hi-Vision system in favour of digital technology being developed in the United States. The statement caused a considerable flurry among executives of NHK and electronics manufacturers and a sense of uncertainty about the future of Hi-Vision in the public.

Under pressure from leading Japanese electronics companies, the MPT official retracted his remarks the next day and said that the ministry would promote Hi-Vision broadcasting, using a DBS satellite, BSAT-1, set for launch in 1997. He said the broadcast would continue at least until 2007, when the satellite's life comes to an end (*International Herald Tribune*, 23 and 24 February 1994). In the wake of the flurry, the MPT granted licences to NHK and commercial broadcasters, instead of the Hi-Vision Promotion Association, to engage individually in Hi-Vision broadcasts beginning in November 1994.

To coincide with the start of the revamped Hi-Vision broadcast, manufacturers, such as the Sony Corporation and Matsushita Electric Industries Co., have begun to promote cheaper Hi-Vision production equipment and receivers. They have started marketing a Hi-Vision receiving set at less than US$5,000 – one half of the previous price, in the hope that it will stimulate the creation of a Hi-Vision market. Only 30,000 Hi-Vision sets had been sold to homes by October 1994, but Matsushita estimated that as many as 100,000 sets would be sold in 1995. NHK's Broadcast Culture Research Institute forecasts that the number of Hi-Vision receiver owners will reach four million by the year 2000 and 12 million by 2005.

NHK has produced a wide variety of Hi-Vision TV programmes since the start of experimental broadcasting in 1989. As many as 730 titles (about 700 hours) were stocked in the library. They include concerts, operas, ballets, dramas, sports, travelogues, and video arts, many of which were co-produced with foreign broadcasters and producers. NHK has broadcast these quality Hi-Vision programmes regularly, since November 1994, on its newly scheduled Hi-Vision channel, as well as in converted form on its terrestrial and DBS channels.

C) International Television: TV Japan

In 1991, NHK launched TV Japan, an independent international television service, which carried NHK news and other programmes for 15 hours a day to Japanese-speaking viewers in North America and for 11 hours in Europe. Local companies, established in New York and London with the funding by Japanese commercial enterprises, took charge of the operation, charging subscription fees from the contracted viewers. As of June 1994, the operators secured about 22,000 subscribing households in North America, including Hawaii, and 7,000 in Europe, but their operation has been in the red.

Given the mandate from Parliament to start an international television service,NHK was scheduled to start, in April 1995, a daily three- to five-hour non-scrambled broadcast using TV Japan channels in North America and Europe. NHK expects that about five million households in North America and Europe will be able to watch the free TV Japan service. NHK will cover the cost of the new service, which is estimated between Y1,000 million to Y2,000 million a year.

NHK hopes to undertake a similar service in Asia in the near future, but as many Asian countries are sensitive to direct-to-home transborder satellite television services, NHK will continue to rely on communication satellites for distribution of news and programmes to cable television operators and terrestrial broadcasters in the Asia-Pacific region. Since the audience of the Japanese language TV Japan is limited, NHK produces English news programmes for international distribution. It also dubs or subtitles in English its main daily evening newscasts and current affairs programmes on TV Japan.

The MPT announced, in April 1995, that services offered by two foreign satellite television broadcasters outside Japan – four channels in the Star TV and TNT and Cartoon network – would be allowed to be received and transmitted by Japanese cable television operators. This is one step to opening up the Japanese cable programming market to foreign satellite broadcasters beaming to Japan from outside the country; however, those who will benefit from this decision are few. The aim of the MPT decision was to allow foreign broadcasters and operators to receive and retransmit TV Japan, and many Asian broadcasters and cable operators are now receiving NHK's news and programming distribution service using communication satellites for selective re-distribution through their networks.

D) Financial Prospects

As NHK's accounts for fiscal 1993 recorded an accumulated carry-over surplus of Y60.2 billion, the corporation said it would not seek an increase in licence fees until fiscal 1996. NHK President Mikio Kawaguchi declared, however, that he would seek an increase later, because he expects extra expenditures for the international television service starting in April 1995, the full-fledged Hi-Vision broadcast starting in 1997, and the coverage of the 1998 Nagano Winter Olympics as the host broadcaster.

E) NHK in the Multimedia Era

In spite of the information super-highway fever stimulated by the MPT's major policy announcement, *Towards the Creation of a New Info-communications Industry,* in January 1994, the prospect for its realization by the target date and its practical use by the public is uncertain in the current gloomy economic situation. The future of multichannel cable television, still at the level of 5 percent penetration in 1994, is also not promising, according to media experts, because of complex government regulations and the availability of varieties of programmes on the prevailing terrestrial and satellite channels (see Schilling 1994).

Referring to how NHK would cope with the so-called multimedia era, NHK President Kawaguchi, a former entertainment programme producer, said, the 450,000 tapes of software stocked in NHK's programme library would not be enough. "We have to produce new programmes ... As software will play a decisive role in leading the media industry in the age of multimedia and the convergence of broadcasting and telecommunications, we will try our best to produce quality software to suit the taste of our audience." NHK's confidence in this regard is based on the fact that satellite channels specializing in foreign programmes are having a hard time attracting subscribers in Japan (see Shimizu 1993a).

F) NHK in the Twenty-first Century

In January 1995, NHK announced a new mid- and long-term management guideline entitled *Towards Culturally Richer Broadcasting,* in anticipation of the multimedia, multichannel era in the twenty-first century. The long-term directive was drafted in connection with the next five-year management plan beginning from fiscal 1995.

In the long-term management guideline, NHK said it would (1) bolster Hi-Vision satellite broadcasts and make its two DBS channels broadcast Hi-Vision services in the early years of the twenty-first century; (2) reinforce and improve its terrestrial television channels (general and educational services) to suit the diverse needs of its viewers; (3) strengthen international satellite television broadcasts (TV Japan); and (4) intensify research and development for early realization of a new multichannel, multimedia broadcast Integrated Services Digital Broadcasting (ISDB) system (see NHK 1994; Ohsaki et al. 1994).

In the early 1980s, European public broadcasters stood idle and saw the potential satellite broadcasting services being taken up by private operators.

NHK, on the other hand, took action and started an experimental DBS service in May 1984, following years of research and experiments in the 1970s and early 1980s. In June 1989, NHK started the full-fledged two-channel round-the-clock DBS broadcasts, charging extra DBS fees on top of regular terrestrial licence fees from 1 August the same year. After five years, the income from the DBS subscribers contributed to an increase in NHK's revenue from licence fees, with an estimated number of DBS households reaching 13 million in 1998 and with contracted fee-paying households nearing 9.5 million.

NHK started regular one-hour experimental Hi-Vision broadcasting in 1989, using one of the DBS satellite channels. Although the dissemination of Hi-Vision receivers is still limited, the NHK mid-and long-term management guideline says it will go ahead with and expand the HDTV broadcasts and turn its two-channel DBS broadcasts into Hi-Vision services in the early years of the twenty-first century.

NHK's Science and Technical Laboratories are engaged in developing the ISDB new broadcast media system. It will meet the diverse needs of viewers in the twenty-first century through high-quality, multichannel, multimedia satellite broadcasting. An advisory group to the MPT on digitization of broadcasting recommended, in April 1994, to adopt ISDB as the future broadcasting system and complete standardization of the digital broadcasting system by 1996, in order to keep pace with rapid technological developments.

The ISDB transmission system being developed by NHK's laboratories will cover the following digital services on a single satellite channel: multichannel broadcasting, digital audio, still images, facsimile, teletext, telesoftware, and telemusic. A prototype of this ISDB system was demonstrated on the occasion of the general assembly of the Asia-Pacific Broadcasting Union (ABU) held in Kyoto, Japan, in November 1994.

The multimedia transmission system will be adopted after 2007, when a new generation DBS satellite, capable of accommodating 21 GHz band transponders in addition to the current 12 GHz, is put into operation. The NHK laboratories are making concerted efforts to innovate pragmatic transmission and receiving apparatus, including a set top box, for the multimedia ISDB system, which, along with the quality software NHK produces, will be vital to the survival and prosperity of the Japanese public broadcaster in the twenty-first century.

Notes

1. NHK was permitted, by a revision of the 1950 Broadcast Law, to set up and finance profit-making subsidiaries.

2. NHK's Income and Expenditure Budgets (in billions)

	Fiscal Year		
	1993	1994	1995
Operating Income	Y553.7	Y566.7	Y570.8
License Fees	Y534.2	Y545.5	Y553.5
Other Income	Y 19.5	Y 21.2	Y 17.3
Operating Expenses	Y532.5	Y522.2	Y573.3
Budget Surplus	Y 21.2	Y 14.5	-Y 2.7
Capital Expenditure	Y 16.6	Y 13.8	Y 0.0
Balance	Y 4.6	Y 0.7	-Y 2.6
DBS Satellite Operation			
DBS Receivers' Fee Income	Y 58.7	Y 63.1	Y 71.0
DBS Operation Expenses	Y 46.5	Y 54.0	Y 65.4
Surplus	Y 12.2	Y 9.1	Y 5.6

3. Article 9 in Chapter II of the Broadcast Law adds that for the accomplishment of this purpose, NHK shall conduct AM and FM radio services, television broadcasting, as well as sound multiplex (on FM and TV channels), character multiplex (teletext) broadcasts, and international radio and television broadcasting. The Article also stipulates "researches and investigations necessary for the improvement and development of broadcasting and its reception" as NHK's main business. It also lists NHK's other business matters added in the course of deregulation and revision of the Broadcast Law since its first enactment in 1950. The latest revision of the Law, in 1994, mandated NHK to engage in an international television service, TV Japan, parallel to the short wave radio service of Radio Japan.

4. Tokyo Commercial Broadcasters – Settlement of Accounts

	Fiscal Year		
	1991	1992	1993
NTV, Nippon Television Network Corporation (Channel 4)			
Operating Income	Y296.5 billion	Y199.8	Y196.8
Operating Profit	Y 12.1	Y 7.0	Y 4.9
Current Profit	Y 15.2	Y 2.8	Y 2.7
TBS, Tokyo Broadcasting System, INC. (Channel 6)			
Operating Income	Y213.7	Y203.8	Y190.3
Operating Profit	Y 10.6	Y 5.4	Y 6.9
Current Profit	Y 15.0	Y 1.7	Y 2.3
Fuji TV, Fuji Television Network, INC (Channel 8)			
Operating Income	Y264.5	Y270.4	Y257.5
Operating Profit	Y 23.3	Y 16.2	Y 10.3
Current Profit	Y 10.0	Y 7.2	Y 3.8
TV Asahi, Asahi National Broadcasting Co. (Channel 10)			
Operating Income	Y177.8	Y166.0	Y156.5
Operating Profit	Y 21.7	Y 6.3	Y 10.3
Current Profit	Y 10.1	Y 1.9	Y 3.8
TV Tokyo, Television Tokyo (Channel 12)			
Operating Income	Y 78.8	Y 74.3	Y 71.3
Operating Profit	Y 1.7	Y 0.54	Y 0.29
Current Profit	Y 0.47	Y 0.90	Y 0.11

References

English Language References:

Communications Study Group. 1991. *Japanese Legislation of Telecommunications*. Vol.5, *Broadcast Law of Japan*. Tokyo: The Telecommunications Association.

Communications Study Group. 1994. *Japanese Legislation of Telecommunications*. Vol.4, *Radio Law - As Amended*. Tokyo: The Telecommunications Association.

History Compilation Room. Radio & TV Culture Research Institute. Nippon Hoso Kyokai (NHK). 1967. *The History of Broadcasting in Japan*. Tokyo: NHK.

The Japan Times. 1994. Nationwide Network Proposed for 2010 Completion, 1 June

Kono, Naoyuki. 1993. Public Broadcasting in the Multi-Channel Environment - from a Japanese Viewpoint. Speech delivered at the annual conference of the International Institute of Communications (IIC) in Mexico City.

Ministry of Posts and Telecommunications (MPT). *MPT News*. Biweekly newsletter edited by International Policy Division, International Affairs Department of the Ministry of Posts and Telecommunications, Tokyo, Japan.

Ministry of Posts and Telecommunications (MPT). 1994. Toward the Creation of a New Info-communications Industry. *MTP News*, 21 January.

MPT Ordinance: *The Fundamental Standards for the Establishment of Broadcasting Stations.* 1993. In *Establishment of Private TV Stations, TV and Film Industries in Japan,* by Shinichi Shimizu. London: International Institute of Communications.

National Association of Broadcasters in Japan. 1994. *Minkan Hoso* (Private Broadcasters), 16 June.

Nomura, Yoshio. 1963. System of Broadcasting in Japan and its Characteristic. *Studies of Broadcasting* 1. Tokyo: Radio and TV Culture Research Institute, NHK.

Ohsaki, Kouji, Takeshi Kimura, and Naoki Kawai. 1994. Transmission Structure of Digital Broadcasting. Paper presented at 1994 IEEE International Conference on Communications, 1-15 May.

Omori, Yukio. 1989. Broadcasting Legislation in Japan - Its Historical Process, Current Status and Future Tasks. *Studies of Broadcasting* 25. Tokyo: Radio and TV Culture Research Institute, NHK.

Pollack, Andrew. 1994. Japan Planning its Own Information Highway. *The International Herald Tribune,* 2 June.

Public Relations Bureau. NHK. 1994. *NHK Factsheet '94: No. 10 Broadcast Engineering: Toward New Broadcasting Technology.* Tokyo: NHK.

Radio Regulatory Bureau. MPT. 1973. *Radio Laws of Japan.* Tokyo: Japan International Cooperation Agency.

Radio Regulatory Bureau. MPT. 1980. *Radio Laws of Japan.* Tokyo: Japan International Cooperation Agency.

Schilling, Mark. 1994. Japan Rushes into an Interactive TV Future. *The Japan Times,* 30 May.

Shimizu, Shinichi. 1987. DBS in Japan: Saviour of the Public Network? *Intermedia* 15 (6).

Shimizu, Shinichi. 1988. Public Service Broadcasting in Japan - NHK Prepares for the Twenty-First Century. *Media Asia* 15(4). Singapore: Asian Mass Communication Research and Information Center (AMIC).

Shimizu, Shinichi. 1991a. Public Service Broadcasting in Japan: How NHK Faces the Future. In *Broadcasting Finance in Transition - A Comparative Handbook,* edited by Jay G. Blumler and T. J. Nossiter. Oxford: Oxford University Press.

Shimizu, Shinichi.1991b. The Changing Face of Japanese Broadcasting: Toward a Multi-Channel, Multi-Media Era. Paper prepared for the research project, Public Broadcasting in National and Global Life: A Comparative Analysis, by Professors Michael Tracey and Willard Rowland, Jr., Center for Mass Media Research, School of Journalism and Mass Communication, University of Colorado at Boulder.

Shimizu, Shinichi. 1993a. The Implications of Transborder Television for National Cultures and National Broadcasting: A Japanese Perspective. *Media Asia* 20(4), 1993. Singapore: Asian Mass Communication Research and Information Center (AMIC).

Shimizu, Shinichi. 1993b. *TV and Film Industries in Japan.* London: International Institute of Communications.

Uchikawa, Yoshimi. 1964. Process of Establishment of the New System of Broadcasting in Post-War Japan. *Studies of Broadcasting* 2. Tokyo: Radio and TV Culture Research Institute, NHK.

Japanese Language References:

Media Study Team. Dentsu Research Institute. 1993. *A Research for Information and Media Society.* Tokyo: Dentsu Research Institute.

NHK. 1977. *The 50 Year History of Broadcasting.* Tokyo: Nippon Hoso Publishing Company.

NHK. 1995. *Towards Culturally-Richer Broadcasting: NHK's Mid and Long-Term Management Guideline.*

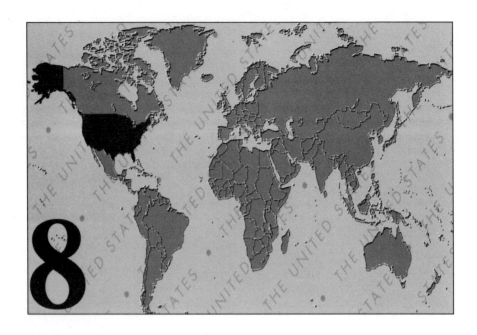

THE UNITED STATES: PBS AND THE LIMITATIONS OF A MAINSTREAM ALTERNATIVE

Michael Tracey

Introduction

*I*n the closing weeks of 1994, a special advertising section appeared in the pages of *The New Yorker*. There was something paradoxical about the location, for here was the magazine of cultivated America, a magazine which applauded itself with the unctuous ditty of "possibly the best magazine that ever was." Here was Brahmin culture, clever culture, "I'm aware of the irony in this humour" culture, sophisticated culture, correct culture, big vocabulary culture, anointed culture. This was definitely not a rag to be found next to the check-out stand of Safeway, rubbing shoulders with the *National Enquirer*. Here, in an act of extreme unction, was the special advertising section. The subject was public broadcasting. Glossy and carefully crafted, the declaration echoed the merits and quality of the output of public television, both past and future. Here were the motifs and icons of a self-belief in institutional worth: "The McNeil-Lehrer Hour," "The American Experience," "Frontline," "Tony Brown's Journal," – the great and good, the senior clerics of the established church of American public broadcasting.

Standing in front of that most ubiquitous of public television's symbols –"Sesame Street's" muppets – was Ervin Duggan, as cerebral, urbane, and decent a figure as had ever occupied the presidency of the Public Broadcasting Service (PBS). The glossy pages of the advertisement were an iconography of an institution that had become a sanctuary for a certain type of American public television. On offer was the worthy, the intense, the serious, the upright, the correct, the self-consciously caring, the curious, and the learned. It was an iconography that screamed its loathing for the shallowness and trivialities of the rest of American television, and, thus, for all those "ordinary" Americans who more readily watch commercials than public television. The pages were not just a statement of difference, they were a sanctification of the serious soul of the institution and of those who defined it and used it. The earnestness of the showcase was almost pompous, speaking of a profoundly developed sense of worth but with apparently little inkling of mirth, speaking of a concept of "civilized" but with little grasp of pleasure, and speaking of the need to inform and educate society but somehow forgetful of the importance of entertaining it as well. In other words, public television in the United States had become, perhaps always was, priggish. Where it projected a certain intelligent populism, it was more often than not borrowed, often from the "art" of British television, and, thus, not really populist at all. It was achingly obvious, for example, that nowhere in the imagination of the dispersed community of American public television was there the creative ability, focus, or traditional craft to produce shows like the British "Prime Suspect," let alone "Fawlty Towers" or "Are You Being Served?." All these years, one realized, "Masterpiece Theatre" had been not a statement of the brilliance of the system, but a metaphor to a fundamental weakness that would at some point become apparent and destructive.

None of this would have mattered very much in terms of the wider international debate about the future of public broadcasting if there had not been murmurings that the future lay in the American public television model. Some, such as Rupert Murdoch, declared it loudly, arguing that populist television should be left to commercial stations and that public television should plug the gaps, delivering programmes that the market system didn't; in short, emulating the American way of doing things. More worrying was that quite serious and powerful public broadcasters were having similar thoughts. Understanding the character of American public television, then, begins to take on an increased significance.

American public television approached 1995 with the knowledge that the Republican Party now controlled Congress and, in the shape of Representative Newt Gingrich, would be asking some difficult questions about federal support for the Corporation for Public Broadcasting (CPB) and, thus, for the whole system. It approached the coming storm in a particularly ill-prepared way. Much of its difficulties were obviously not of its own making, since the decline of the public sector was by this time a universal phenomenon. However, elsewhere the defenses were stronger, more articulated, and supported by the continuing place of the public broadcaster at the centre of the journalistic and imaginative life of the society as a whole. In the United States, almost uniquely, there was no profound guiding philosophy.

There were no figures who represented an ethos of public broadcasting's importance to society or a discourse that melded theory and practice. The chant in the United States was muted, heard in the distance from remote corners of the Commonwealth. More curious, however, was that the existing body of belief was guilty of a remarkable false consciousness that did not see its marginalized condition, its continuing lack of substantive relevance to the larger society, and its exile; instead, it saw power, influence, and captivation of the public as "audience."

The concept of false consciousness is always contestable, and in this context needs to be examined through a historical point. Localism was built into the structure of public broadcasting from its inception. It was a structural condition that was encouraged, even mandated, because the federal government in the 1960s and 1970s was determined to ensure that a government-sponsored system would not adversely affect the networks. Public television in the United States was never meant to have the significance and centrality of public broadcasting in other countries. The debate that was never undertaken was whether or not such a structure could possibly serve the larger public interest, or even that of the local community. Indeed, much of the weakness and inefficiency of the system stems from its structure – its disparate nature that fuels gross fiscal inefficiency and philosophical fragmentation. This condition was a deliberate act of political vandalism, but it was vandalism that, over the years, has been translated, particularly by the managers of the numerous stations, into something joyous and benign. In short, much of the public broadcasting community is in denial, shackled to its own ways of seeing.

The ferocity and fervour with which disciples assert the validity and importance of the local structure lies in the fact that, whatever its objective inadequacies, it touches an important piece of the mythos of American culture: the closeness of community, the American version of *gemeinschaft*. In a 1927 essay, John Dewey commented,

> American democratic polity was developed out of genuine community life, that is, association in local and small centers where industry was mainly agricultural and where production was carried on mainly with hand tools. It took form when English political habits and legal institutions worked under pioneer conditions. The forms of association were stable, even though their units were mobile and migratory. Pioneer conditions put a high premium upon personal work, skill, ingenuity, initiative and adaptability, and upon neighborly sociability. The township or some not much larger area was the political unit, the town meeting the political medium, and roads, schools, the peace of the community, were the political objectives ... The imagination of the Founders did not travel far beyond what could be accomplished and understood in our congeries of self-governing communities ... We have inherited, in short, local town-meeting practices and ideas. But we live and act and have our being in a continental national state (Dewey 1927).

One can argue whether this view of the life of the republic ever existed. There is no argument, however, that what was being vested in the nation state was a continental, integrated industrial and agrarian society with a collective sense of self, seething with a sense of ideological purpose.

It is not especially fanciful to see a certain symmetry between the larger sensibility and an intellectual and organizational architecture for public broadcasting - a hankering after the local in an irresistibly global age. Here was a profound difference to other systems which sought to speak to, represent, and bind together collectively the nation, the society rather than its particularities and constituent pieces alone. As a result, however, the institution could never seem to recognize that the only public institutions that could survive, let alone thrive, were those that welcomed, not shirked, intelligent populism, and which sought to build a truly national mandate. One of the lines of the advertising campaign in *The New Yorker* (28 November 1994) reads, "There's always something special on PBS. From historical pilgrimages and the war against poverty to a celebration of the senses and reducing youth violence, upcoming public television programmes are sure to enthral and enlighten the most demanding viewer." That is a fascinating phrase, loaded with patricianism, even paternalism, that would have satisfied John Reith. Every single example mentioned of upcoming programmes is either educational or a documentary, which, although important parts of television, in themselves have never built the audience base without which the "public" in public broadcasting becomes an empty concept.

A level of denial and falsity of consciousness in the positions adopted at all levels of the American public television system have already been suggested. Paradoxically, the consequences of critiques of and challenges to that system serve only to feed the denial and the falsity. Certainly, there is an atmosphere of siege once more surrounding public television. Robert Dole, Newt Gingrich, and their congressional colleagues, along with the Heritage Foundation, Laurence Jarvik, the Centre for the Study of Popular Culture, the columnist and television personality George Will, and numerous editorialists in conservative newspapers and magazines, are all saying that public television is biased, or unnecessary, or should be laid to rest.

The consensual view, from those who broadly define themselves as the supporters and friends of public broadcasting, appears to be that these conservative attacks demonstrate the tough times which public television faces. They also seem to be held as a kind of badge of merit, with which the significance of the institution is defined by the power of those who assault it. In fact, the attacks deflect from the discussion that should be taking place about the service offered this society by public broadcasting. Springing from such overtly partisan and, often, crudely simplistic viewpoints, the criticisms have served the institutional status quo by offering the establishment of public broadcasting the comforts provided by the quality of their enemies. If one is being attacked by the Republican leadership or right wing intellectuals paid for by conservative businessmen, then one must be doing something right. It is a sentiment which has bred an unfortunate complacency, typifying what John Kenneth Galbraith has described as a "culture of contentment." The net effect has been to inhibit the discussion which should be taking place about the fundamental problems of the organization, funding, and purpose of public television in the United States, a debate which is taking place within every other public broadcasting system around the world.

The certainty of rectitude is fed by what appears to be a deep ambivalence toward the public-as-audience. One gets a very real sense from within public television that American culture and society are viewed as something to be kept at arms' length, a dark and dangerous continent smothered in corrupted values and ethics, peopled by the "fallen" of mass culture, and beyond redemption. Public television is to be a protected zone, safe, serious and pure – a kind of televisual green-lung amidst the devastation.

Translated into programming terms, the logic is that any programme that is too popular should more properly appear on commercial television. Here, in fact, is one of the basic conceits of the American public television community: if you are attracting too many viewers, if you are too popular, then you must be doing something wrong. Not so hidden within this notion is a clear disdain for the American popular mind, which also suggests a rejection of one of the richest traditions of public broadcasting elsewhere – a belief in the ability of the creative programme maker to marry quality with popular appeal, a real faith in the potential of the "ordinary" citizen-as-audience member to grow. Indeed, one might argue that it was here, within this core thesis, that public broadcasting most profoundly connected with democratic culture and practice, addressing both the sovereignty and the potentiality of the individual. If this interpretation of those within American public broadcasting is accurate –of course, it will be denied –it must rank as the most worrying fact about the system.

Public television is available in more American homes than any other single network –more than NBC, CBS, or ABC, and more, by far, than any cable service –yet its audience share is only about 2 percent. The reason for this is not primarily to do with competition, since even when the viewing was restricted in the years before cable, public television's audience was still marginal. The reason can lie only in what has been suggested: dysfunctional organization, fiscal recklessness, and conceptual confusion, all amplified by the hubris of a cultural elite which, it seems, has a deep fear of the "mob." At 2 percent of the audience share, one has to question public television's claim to be a national broadcaster.

The rise of the multichannel society in the United States, ahead of anywhere else on earth, has brought into sharp focus aspects of public television and its place within American society which are inherent, but which had, until the new television, remained largely invisible. The problem confronted by public television, fashioned by the Public Broadcasting Act of 1967, are conceptual and structural. At the conceptual level, the act maintained public television's educational role but added a more general role, such that it now matched the definitional trinity of most public broadcasting organizations – informing, educating, and entertaining. Structurally, the two axes which constituted "the system" were local and national. This duality in both concept and structure was, and remains, an inevitable source of tension.

Existing in American public television, therefore, is a conceptual and structural confusion; a myth around the concept of "local"; a nervous ambivalence about the audience; and the withering impact of competition.

Conceptual Confusion

The Carnegie Commission Report of 1967 preferred "public television" to "educational television" as a way of suggesting "'education' in the broad sense of informational and cultural programming as well as instructional." It seemed to want to enliven and soften the dry, forbidding instructional image and to have the system become a more general, entertaining service. However, in all the years since, public broadcasting has never clarified the distinction or the exact relationship between the two models. Indeed, it appears to waffle between them according to whatever funding sources it is addressing at the moment.

For many state governments and certain entrenched federal bureaucracies, the public broadcasting community presents the view that the nation is a classroom, and public broadcasting is the teacher. To corporate sponsors, it presents itself as a popular, generally upscale, "good" entertainment vehicle, particularly capable of drawing elite, higher income and politically powerful audiences. To confused congressional leaders, it slips back and forth between these images, and few in Congress or in most prior administrations have succeeded in pinning it down.

The debates about the implications of change, of where public television and radio should go, are far from new. Today, however, they have a fresh urgency. One has to consider, for example, the argument about an enhanced or rediscovered educational role for public television. Henry Becton, president and general manager of the WGBH Educational Foundation, wrote recently that, "At the start of the 1980s, WGBH could aptly be described as a television and radio broadcaster. Today, as we head into a new decade providing a far wider range of services, WGBH can more accurately be called an 'educational telecommunications center'" (Becton 1993). He went on to describe the potentialities of developing "interactive software, home video cassettes, educational print materials and videotex columns; we address the needs of the business sector through such services as satellite teleconferencing." Ten years ago, the late Michael Rice wrote, responding to earlier versions of this argument, "This is a treacherous ambition" (Rice 1981: 22). In May 1988, *Broadcasting* quoted the former president of PBS, Bruce Christensen, as saying that PBS would "focus increasingly" on education, training, and international services. Perhaps the most futuristic description of a reconceived public broadcasting service has come from George Hall, then head of public television's Office of New Technology Initiatives, and James Fellows, president of the Central Educational Network. Hall offered the "brave new word Teleplex ... to label what was once strung out as a 'public telecommunications center complex.'" Fellows elaborated: "The invention of Teleplex makes it possible to describe public television's new institutional framework – not just a station or channel, not just a television network or a one-way video service – but a genuinely new concept with a new name" (Fellows 1993).

Whatever is meant by the "educational" remit of public broadcasting, its case is not served by the fact that the nation overwhelmingly plays hooky. There simply is not much of an audience for American public broadcasting, whether as compared to its foreign counterparts or, more pertinently, to its commercial competition in the United States. On the instructional side, public broadcasting has a minimal presence in the schools. There is no educational radio to speak of anymore, and educational television is available in only about one-fifth of the nation's classrooms, where it is little used. The private Whittle-Channel One (a satellite-delivered, advertising-funded service for schools), the CNN Newsroom, and several other services are much more widely available, heavily used, and increasingly ubiquitous.

Whatever is wrong with American education, public broadcasting has not offered any remedies. The situation is similar at the college level, where, after years of having almost exclusive rights to the use of television in higher education, the universities have provided little off-campus, in-home instructional service. It is notable that during the past five years, the Mind Expansion University, developed by Jones Intercable almost completely outside of the conventional public system, has joined forces with a number of universities to provide over two dozen formal, telecourse degree programmes nationwide, clearly modelling itself on the BBC's own, much heralded, Open University.

Structural Confusion

Les Brown, a well respected observer of television, former editor of *Channels*, and former senior fellow at the Freedom Forum Media Studies Center has noted that, "There is very little produced domestically (by public television) that is distinguished. The really big stuff that everyone writes or talks about is imported from England" (Knoffo 1989). The reason, Brown suggests, is that the system is not a network but a distribution mechanism "for a set of local and jealously independent public television stations. WGBH wants to be the main producing station, KCET wants to be the main producing station, none of them can produce worth a damn anyway. Nothing they've done has been world class." There is, in fact, real confusion about the very idea of quality –expressed in rather frustrated tones (in personal communication) by someone familiar with the Twentieth Century Fund Task Force inquiry into the future of public broadcasting: "There is a muddle (there is no other word for it) in the minds of most Americans over the concepts of 'quality' and 'popularity.' That is precisely the problem with the Task Force. Not a single member of the Task Force appears to think the two ideas can be – or should be – compatible. Again and again they have proposed prescriptions for public TV that confine it to a ghetto – an educational ghetto, or a public service ghetto, or a cultural ghetto – but always a ghetto."

One could argue that the idea of "quality" and how to achieve it has proved elusive in even the most successful public broadcasting communities. One would, for example, search long and hard within historical discourse and documentation surrounding the BBC to find such a meaningful definition. The philosophy, there as elsewhere, has essentially been one of "we all generally know quality when we see it." One could also argue, in sympathy with the American system, that even if there is a cultural ghettoish tone to its output, in serving such tastes public television is contributing to the general diversity of American television culture. The difficulty with this argument is that it seeks to universalize narrow, somewhat class-based taste, to a population which, not unreasonably, is less than welcoming, and, at the same time, it leaves the provision of popular culture to providers who could care less about concepts of quality. A consequence of the implicit Reithian patricianism of American public television is the brute reality that, for most Americans, there is no felt need for public television and many other distractions.

The issue of production – quality or otherwise – is largely academic for the large part of the public broadcasting system. The Boston Consultancy Group, in a study commissioned by the CPB, reports that according to PBS statistics for 1991, of the 345 public television stations, with their 11,215 full-time employees, the bulk of programming was made available by just eleven stations. Three hundred stations contributed not a single programme.

The organizational structure of American public broadcasting is a bizarre combination of both the monolithically bureaucratic and the anarchically fragmented. There is an unwieldy combination of university, state, and local education authority stations serviced by a confusing array of state and regional organizations, all overlain by an indescribably complex national bureaucracy represented by the welter of organizations known as the Corporation for Public Broadcasting (CPB), the Public Broadcasting Service (PBS), the American Program Service (APS), National Public Radio (NPR), American Public Radio (APR), the National Association of Public Television Stations (APTS), the Children's Television Workshop (CTW), and myriad other federal, foundation, and corporate funding and programming agencies. It has been widely reported that this chaotic structure severely restricts the creation of significant services, by permitting a complex pattern of competing interests who spend more time arguing over respective turf than designing and producing programmes. As legend would have it, "public television is one long meeting occasionally interrupted by a programme."

From time to time, major adjustments that would reduce the confusion have been proposed. These would create a much more rationalized, efficient system of multiple, distinct national programme services and complementary local stations that might even compete successfully with the new commercial services. Yet the elements of the system are so regularly at loggerheads with one another that any intelligent plans along these lines are regularly watered down and reduced to only minor rearrangements of the chairs around the table. One member of the Twentieth Century Fund Task Force on the Future of Public Broadcasting observed that, "there is so much inertia built into American public broadcasting that my guess is there will be little change until people sense a real crisis" (personal communication).

The Myth of the Local Community

It could be argued that the justification for public broadcasting stands or falls on the extent to which it represents and serves its local communities. There is, as has already been suggested, little evidence that it does either.

While it is true that the number of public stations continues to proliferate – due in large part to the continued stimulus of a federal funding programme for new facilities – it is unclear what they add to each community. Public broadcasters justify the need for all these stations on the grounds of increasing coverage and the ability to give voice to the different licensee organizations. For some time now, however, public broadcasting coverage has been nearly universal, and the amount of local programming, especially in public television, is almost negligible. The overall primetime programming of a college station, a community corporation station, and a state authority station is almost identical, even if all are available in the same city. One need only scan the schedules of the three stations available in the Washington, D.C. area to understand this reality. Where is the differentiated local voice and diverse set of interests in all this? As an editorial in *Broadcasting* forcefully stated in 1988, "the principle of localism remains the enemy within." The same editorial noted that the core problem of public television was not the centralized decision-making function of CPB, but "rather the political squabbling and factionalism that impede that decision making. Considering the competition, particularly from cable, for public broadcasting's target audience, a home divided could ultimately become a house of cards." In effect, the funding of public broadcasting is feeding a body at war with itself.

This problem is compounded by the manner in which the United States has evolved sociologically. It is a simple fact of life – well recognized, for example, by advertisers – that the idea of 'the local community is *passé* and that the United States is defined by a vast array of different taste cultures. Since those taste cultures dot the whole nation, clearly only pan-national services are likely to be relevant. With its relentless local ideology, however, public broadcasting has set its face against such a manifestly nationally organized service. It thus ends up expressing a commitment to ways of life which were always more mythologized than real. The funding of public broadcasting, particularly television, is too often spent to nurture nostalgia.

A specific illustration of the localism problem came several years ago from a supporter of public broadcasting, who also happened to have previously been one of its major station officials. The late Michael Rice wrote that, "mostly the problem is with the delusion caused by the officially promulgated, long perpetuated ideal that local stations exist to do local programming ... [with the odd exception] local programming on public TV has not persuaded viewers of its indispensable value. However heretical, it is time to admit that apart from local news, genuinely local programs have been given their fair test. Except in rare instances, they are of marginal value and disproportionate expense" (Rice 1981: 17). Figures produced almost a decade after Rice made this observation support his contention. According to the Boston Consulting Group (BCG), the cost of producing programmes at the local level, in 1989, was $570 million – a figure that includes overhead, studio costs, and salaries at the local stations. This figure was 43 percent of all public television expenditures, but produced only 7 percent of total broadcast hours. Figures for 1990 amplify the observation that the structure of localism is fiscally inefficient to the point of irresponsibility. Perhaps, however, the most telling figures are comparative ones, for example the funding available to the CBC in Canada or the BBC. In 1990, the CBC had revenues of approximately $988.3 million, and the BBC $1.57 billion. In the same period, about $1.5 to $1.6 billion (no one really knows) flowed through the U.S. public broadcasting system. Clearly, the CBC and BBC – two highly developed national broadcasting organizations – are vastly more efficient, in programme terms, in using their funding. Consider that just one station, WNET in New York, had an operating budget of $120 million in 1990. CNN – operating three national and international networks, 24 hours a day, running 19 foreign bureaus – had a budget of only $312 million. There is also an increasing disparity between the amount of money which the cable industry spends on programmes and that which public television spends on its national schedules. In 1990, for example, The Disney Channel, The Discovery Channel, Arts and Entertainment, and CNN spent $358 million on programming; PBS spent $201 million on its national schedule. It is likely that cable services will continue to increase their spending; PBS will not (BCG 1990).

In light of this analysis, it is only fair to conclude that the structure of localism has failed and that it is culturally irrelevant and a major financial drain on the system. This situation is the single most important reason why in an institution whose total revenue for 1994 was $1.89 billion, only 10 percent was spent directly on programming.

The Public Broadcasting Audience

Public broadcasters like to claim that they reach 120 million Americans, or nearly half of the population, each week, although recently one public relations campaign boosted this figure to 200 million. Furthermore, they claim that this audience is a cross-section that "mirrors" the demographics of the total U.S. population. Unfortunately, this interpretation of the statistics is a rather selective reading of the data. For one thing, the so-called weekly "cume" – the total number of homes reached by public television – includes anyone who is reported to have viewed once for only 15 or 20 minutes. The actual audience for any given public television programme is, in fact, quite minuscule.

The average primetime rating for public television in all television households remained steady for many years at 2.6 - 2.8 percent. In the mid-1980s, the growth of cable and Pay-TV began to undermine even this small base. David LeRoy, the premier public broadcasting audience analyst, reports that by the fall of 1989 the average primetime rating had fallen to 2.1 percent (less than 2 million households) (LeRoy 1990).

Something else became apparent by the late-1980s. Nielsen reported that public broadcasting subscribers who pledged money demonstrated a "disturbing predilection" for the likes of cable channels such as Arts and Entertainment and Discovery. An anonymous observer was quoted in *Variety* (17 April 1988) as saying,"the very people who had fed us were now feeding the lions who would devour us."

Finally, the claim of representativeness in the cumulative audience is spurious. Among the primetime audience, where the vast majority of the regular viewing occurs, the demographics are skewed markedly toward higher socio-economic characteristics – the elites public broadcasting likes to deny, except when seeking "underwriting" (sponsorship) from corporate funders. The cumulative weekly audience, which, in fact, represents light-viewing attention and loyalty, is said to be more balanced only because the much smaller audiences of children's programming are folded in with the more regular primetime viewers. In a report to public television stations, in February 1992, LeRoy pointed out that the figure was now 2 percent and that the "cume" was the lowest since 1984.

Perhaps the most telling evidence of the lack of real impact and audience loyalty is in the figures associated with those who actually donate to public broadcasting. By its own admission, public broadcasting can count only 10 percent of its already small regular audience as paying members. Of course, the viewing desires of this particular audience are as legitimate as any other. The problems lie in the way in which the force of their fiscal presence is a significant factor in crippling the ability of American public television to reach out and touch other audiences.

The Impact of Competition

In spite of all these problems, the most profound reality that public broadcasting must face is presented not by the interior structural, definitional, and demographic problems of public broadcasting, but by the rise of the "third age" of television and radio. The broadcast situation has changed dramatically in recent years. Over 60 percent of American homes now subscribe to cable, even more have VCRs, and the large majority have more than one television set. The launch of the direct broadcast satellite services offering more than 100 channels will almost certainly have a heavy impact, especially in those homes which cable cannot economically reach. Those developments will be enhanced, in the short term, by the introduction of digital compression technology, which before the end of the decade may well make 500-channel cable homes the norm. In the medium term, new fibre optic cables, high-definition television, and increasingly interactive cable-data systems will only further decimate the already small public broadcasting audience, offering the educational, cultural, and informational programming which public broadcasting used to claim as its own.

The inevitable recognition by any government, of any political hue, of the strategic industrial and economic significance and necessity of the wiring of the nation – the information super-highway – is of primary importance and will make inevitable a role for the telephone companies – the Baby Bells – alongside cable, in the provision of all kinds of information and video services. Such involvement will serve only to enhance massively the trends described.

In response, cable interests will, indeed already do, work hard to provide the public service elements that were admittedly so lacking in the old network-dominated broadcasting system. It was that shortcoming within commercial broadcasting that led to the policy of federal support for public broadcasting after the mid-1960s. Now, however, with the technological advances of the "third age" and its proliferation of special audience cable programming of all kinds, the old rationale for public support of non-commercial alternatives is at the very least undermined.

Thus, the claims to fame of public broadcasting, for example that it offers programming that the commercial system does not, are losing plausibility and rhetorical force. The range of genres available from the new media equal – indeed, probably surpass – those of public television.

Conclusion

With a deliberate argumentativeness, one might conclude that no strategic interest of the United States is served by public broadcasting in the economic, cultural, or social fields, and, thus, there can be little justification for the continued spending of federal, or any other, dollars on it. There is an extraordinarily inefficient use of available resources, as well as a complete failure to address the needs of this society, broadly defined, as American public television has turned its back on the mainstreams of culture. It is, thus, nowhere near as good as it could be, in terms of the character and range of the programming it offers and the lives it could touch. Public television is not "local," but merely Balkanized, and therefore cannot provide a counterpoint to the centripetal forces that threaten American society. While it has little or no imaginative programming vision and, thus, no developed sense of excellence, it also has little or no capacity or courage to look at itself with a cold unblinking eye.

As a result, others have begun to do that for it. There is, of course, a high rhetorical element to these concluding observations, although they are closely tied to the kinds of questions which are being asked elsewhere. The layers of structure, institutions within institutions; the bureaucracies piled on bureaucracy; the tribalism of the local structure; the extraordinary siphoning off of funds into things other than programmes; and the apparent absence of energy and excitement and innovation – those tones of a culture in exile – all lead one to conclude that there is a powerful need for a searching public inquiry into the state and future of American public television.

The key to all successful public television is coherent thinking, coherent structure, and coherent, consistent, and untainted funding. Any public inquiry into the condition and future of public television will need to address these issues first. The answers to everything else flow from their resolution. Any such inquiry would, therefore, need to consider basic changes in the organization and funding of public television. Are these appropriate to a multimedia age? Or is there a need for a total restructuring of the organization of public television so that a proper and efficient national programming service can become a reality? Any such inquiry would need to look very closely at the forms of funding. In such a searching examination, nothing should be sacred. Inevitably, and this is highly contentious, consideration would need to be given to extending the logic of commercial sources of revenue – that is, to advertising. The problem with advertising is not its source but is the linking of advertising to ownership and control of the system. People get greedy. If the link is prevented, however, then advertising simply provides a means of funding programmes. If this were not the case, how would one explain the undoubted success of Independent Television or Channel 4, in Britain, both of which have been responsible for remarkable television over many years, and both of which are funded by advertising?

Any such inquiry would also need to address the central mythology of public broadcasting: that the stations serve the local community and the nation. What do they mean by community, and how do they know they are serving it? The examination of these structural questions would be a necessary and central part of any inquiry into the future of public television. Parallel to that inquiry, however, would have to be a consideration of the purpose of broadcasting. There is no point in having an institution if it has no proper or clear purpose, and the character of the programmes offered is ultimately the only testimony to such purpose. Everything else is house-keeping.

The preservation of the status quo may broadly serve the needs and interests of those inside, and that tiny portion of the American public which attends to its offerings. It does not, because it cannot, serve American society in any broader sense. However, this society desperately needs a competent television service based on quality, range, and broad-based engagement with the public, and only public television has within it the inherent potential to so serve.

Any study of public broadcasting is thus framed inevitably by a number of questions which flow from the political origins of public television and the new environment in which it finds itself. What is the place of "the public entity" in a world of "the private?" How does, or could, the public television community articulate its purpose in a context in which the dominant philosophical language provides little space for any sense of the legitimacy of a public culture carried by public institutions? Historically, it has been that concept of, and commitment to, a public culture which has provided such a powerful argument for the provision of programming through a public television system. In contemporary America, what is public interest, public good, or public culture?

References

Becton, Henry. 1993. Paper presented at the inaugural meeting of the Hartford Gunn Institute. Chicago, 30-31 August.

Boston Consulting Group (BCG). 1990. *Strategies for Public Television in a Multi-Channel Environment: March 1990 Report*. Boston: BCG.

Carnegie Commission on Educational Television. 1967. *Public Television*. New York: Harper and Row.

Dewey, John. 1927. *The Public and its Problems*. Chicago: Castaway Books.

Fellows, Jim. 1993. Paper presented at the inaugural meeting of the Hartford Gunn Institute. Chicago, 30-31 August.

Knoffo, Robert. 1989. Making PBS Worth Watching. *Connoisseur* (September).

LeRoy, David. 1990. Unpublished paper presented at the Annual Conference of the Pacific Mountain Network. Monterey, California.

Rice, Michael. 1981. *Public Television: Issues of Purpose and Governance*. New York: Wye Papers, Aspen Institute.

PART TWO

Emerging models for development and democracy

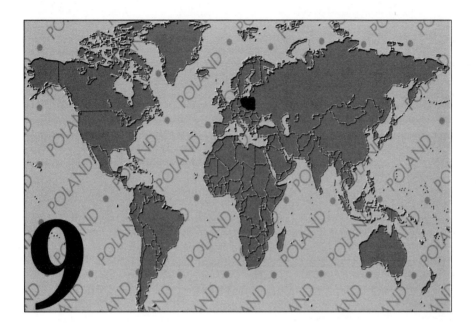

POLAND: PROSPECTS FOR PUBLIC AND CIVIC BROADCASTING

Karol Jakubowicz

Defining the Conceptual Framework

*A*mong the many drafts of the new Polish Broadcasting Act, the status of Polish Radio and Television was variously defined as "social," as "a state institution performing public functions," and as "national." This choice of words is significant, because each indicates a somewhat different definition of the former government broadcaster's proposed new position in the social sphere and vis-a-vis the authorities of the state. In a nation where the meaning of all concepts used in public discourse (especially those relating to social arrangements, politics, and power relations in society) was distorted, sometimes beyond recognition, by newspeak and official propaganda, the use of these concepts must also be seen as an attempt to restore or rediscover their true meaning.

"Party," "government," "state," and "social": in Communist-run Poland these adjectives could be placed in that order on a continuum of acceptability and approval, representing the way they were used in official terminology and by dissident circles.

In the totalitarian/authoritarian Party-State, it was an important (if largely symbolic) concession on the part of the political leaders – and a sign of liberalization – to acknowledge that some areas of activity were the province of the government and, therefore, distinct, at least theoretically, from the party. The legal status of an organization as a "state institution" was a rare and coveted one, enjoyed only by such august bodies as the Polish Academy of Sciences. As much as all "government" bodies and institutions, it was ultimately controlled by the party, but already twice removed from it. Everything that was "social" was disputed territory – a field of battle between the authorities and the dissidents. The authorities wanted to claim it for themselves and present themselves as the champions and true spokespersons for society. For the dissidents, to describe something as "social" was to recognize it as "ours"; that is, to give it the highest accolade. In the dichotomous "us and them" world of communism, "society" comprised millions of "us" against a handful of "them," who by definition were the sworn enemy. [1]

But what of "public"? The concept was not really used in the thinking on broadcasting reform in the first Solidarity period of 1980-81, except that reformers seeking a redefinition of the status of Polish Radio and Television sought ways of giving it the same status as was enjoyed by "public utilities" or "associations of higher public utility"; that is, separate from the state and devoted to serving some form of public service goals. What made such efforts difficult was that the concept of the public had been appropriated and distorted by the Communist system. In addition, "the public domain was enormously enlarged by the inclusion of the economy into it. It was also incorporated into the state and homogenized ideologically. In consequence, many of those who could potentially inhabit it were deprived of access to it, or marginalized" (Szacki 1994: 107). The original goal of the Communist strategy of remodelling social organization had, indeed, been to eliminate the private sphere and fill the void with the values and patterns of the official public sphere. As a result, for reformers, "the public space and its institutions were regarded as adversaries; they were mistrusted rather than trusted, and the same applied to groups and individuals beyond immediate affinity or friendship circles" (Korbonski 1994: 221; see also Marody 1992).

In addition, the Communist government's attempt to invade and control the private sphere proved unsuccessful and was rejected with such vehemence that one of the many concessions the system had to make was to respect the relative inviolability of a growing expanse of the private sphere: "Communist authorities became reconciled not only to the permanence of an uncontrollable private sphere, but also to the fact that it would be the domain of what they considered to be alien values. They insisted that these values were to be held and articulated in the private sphere alone ... while the public one was to remain purely 'socialist' in nature" (Szacki 1994: 108). Consequently, in the final stages of the system's existence, the Communist government was concerned solely with preserving its hold on the shrinking public sphere and protecting it from being invaded by the values of the private one.

Dissidents and, later, Solidarity naturally regarded mass communications as belonging primarily to the realm of the "social." "Socialization" of the media (described as a situation in which the media belong to, and serve, the whole society) became the officially proclaimed goal of Solidarity at its 1981 Congress. "Socialization" was seen as involving the following:

(1) creating mechanisms and structures of feedback, access, participation, and direct social management of the media by means of "socially representative" bodies overseeing the work of broadcasting organizations at all levels, or, for example, dividing Polish Radio and Television up so as to leave some channels in the hands of the state and turn over others to social forces; [2] and

(2) ensuring that all groups of society would enjoy equal opportunities to join the public discourse, preferably by means of their own media (though demands in this sphere were limited to liberalization of the print media).[3] These measures were part of a much larger project: that of developing civil society. [4]

The values surviving in the private sphere were to be built upon, but added to them would be an active "social resistance movement," based on the principle of "open, collective grassroots action" (Kuroń 1984), designed to "build up a pluralist structure in stages and gradually dismantle totalitarianism, step by step" (Kuroń 1981: 95). These ideas and plans proved to be a breeding ground for human rights movements, underground publishers and periodicals, independent educational and artistic institutions, religious and ecological movements, as well as fledgling political parties.

Andrew Arato (1981) correctly notes that this was a project of reconstituting civil society through the re-establishment of the rule of law, an independent public sphere, and freedom of association. He points out that an emancipated public sphere was more central in this nascent civil society than anywhere before (cf. Jakubowicz 1990). That was why civil society, as planned and projected in Poland under Communist rule (and later, in the first, idealistic, phase after it was overthrown), has quite aptly been called "a communication project" (Fedorowicz 1990).

While the Communist system was still in existence, therefore, the concept of public or public service broadcasting was not really in use in Poland. The plan was to turn "state" broadcasting into "social" broadcasting.

Staring Reality in the Face

As Poland, alongside other Central and Eastern European countries, embarked on remodelling its social and political system after the fall of communism, the question of what to do with the mass media was high on the agenda. Several schools of thought immediately became apparent. The first of these sought to put into effect earlier thinking on media reform and was motivated primarily by a desire to go beyond the classic negative definition of freedom of speech (as freedom from legal and administrative constraints). It sought to create a communication system based on the principle of justice and equality, by liberalizing and demonopolizing the media, but also, in part, by harnessing public policy and funds for the purpose of guaranteeing the satisfaction of the need and right to communicate (cf. Jakubowicz 1994). In addition to the legacy of dissident and opposition thinking on the nature of social communication (cf. Jakubowicz 1991), it was based on the belief, shared by many Central and Eastern European media reformers, that since democracy depends on the active participation and the free contribution of all members of society, new media policies should,

> in addition fully to satisfying the needs of the majority of passive participants in mass communication, provide ways and means of exercising of the right to communicate. Therefore, what is needed are new models, a positive, action-oriented policy of promoting democratic media policies and systems. The new media system should thus be truly open, giving access to the media to all who require it, and plural, i.e. marked by pluriformity (accommodating many media ownership patterns) and pluralism (providing a forum, within the law, for all ideologies, points of view and beliefs, as well as for general diversity of content). In other words, this requires a commitment to assisting the foundation and supporting or subsidizing in various ways the operation of newspapers, periodicals and broadcast media, etc. by minorities and groups incapable of doing so out of their own resources, in line with policies publicly defined and open to review. Also needed is a new definition of public service broadcasting as serving not only top-down, one-way, univocal communication, but also bottom-up, pluralistic communication (*In Search of a New Way* 1990).

In broadcasting, adoption of such policies in Poland was expected to lead to the emergence of three different sectors: (1) a financially secure system of public service broadcasting with a remit of supporting democratic communication, going beyond the traditional concept of public service; (2) commercial media; and (3) a civic sector, comprising non-profit oriented, socially motivated media, either privately or collectively owned and speaking on behalf of or to various groups, parties, organizations, movements, minorities, territorial groups, and communities. The emergence and existence of this sector was to be supported by public policies designed specifically for this purpose ('Główne założenia' 1991; Jakubowicz 1991).

By contrast with the 1980-81 period, after 1989 the concept of public service broadcasting was already being used. It had been borrowed from Western European practice and was seen as a way of defusing the battle for control of the state broadcasting system already raging between the various authorities of the new state. Another reason for its introduction was that the plan to "socialize" the country's broadcasting system had, meanwhile, lost support. For one thing, the idea that it should be run by a profusion of "socially representative governing bodies," such as programme councils, was now considered idealistic and impractical. For another, the new government, was, as we will see below, determined to retain control of Polish Radio and Television for as long as possible.

The idea of the civic sector was born out of a desire to design a media system serving primarily civil society.[5] Other perspectives regarding media reform included the following: fear and distrust of all forms of public regulation and intervention into social life, especially in an area so sensitive as mass communication; a free market orientation that regarded such intervention as unnecessary, since the market mechanism could be relied upon to regulate the media system; and government unwillingness to yield control of broadcast media.

The government's perspective was based on the "top-down" nature of the process of fundamental, systemic transformation in Poland, which was decreed and managed from above (Staniszkis 1994), with all the tensions that implied:

> Change is promoted in a top-down manner, without the assistance and sometimes even without the consent of social forces, while at the same time grassroots initiatives are blocked in a more or less overt fashion. [This] seems to be the worst way possible [as it] not only impedes the development of a required social infrastructure, and so provokes the tendency to adopt more and more undemocratic procedures on the part of the administration, but also generates a long-term conflict involving the state and its agencies (Frączak 1992: 36).

There were a number of reasons for this approach. The Solidarity-led government, which took over power in 1989, was the first non-Communist government in Central and Eastern Europe, surrounded by the entire Communist bloc, which looked as if it would continue to exist for quite a long time. The government (which included in key positions the people who had introduced martial law) co-habited with General Wojciech Jaruzelski (the last Communist leader of Poland), president of the country. It inherited from former times a civil service, army, and police, which, while they could be vetted so as to weed out people on whose loyalty the new government could not rely, had to remain largely unchanged (for lack of other, properly trained and qualified people who could replace them). Finally, it was preparing to administer shock therapy in the economy, which had to be very painful and provoke popular dissatisfaction.

Given these circumstances, it was perhaps inevitable that the government decided on that course of action. The same dissident and opposition leaders who had insisted that Communist regimes accept or reconcile themselves to the development of civil society [6] which "would populate the wilderness separating the individual from the [Communist] state" (Smolar 1991: 15) – after gaining power, "abandoned that language in favour of the classic concerns for the state and the market" (Smolar 1993: 40). They argued that the development of a full-fledged party system would be premature and that society should remain as united in facing the new challenges as it was in resisting the Communist system. Therefore, they hoped to maintain Solidarity as a mass social movement, providing a focus for popular backing for the process of transformation and delaying, as much as possible, the emergence of political parties, with all the political differentiation and power struggles that would bring in its wake. That policy involved effectively stifling some of the grassroots movements (such as the "civic committees" created to conduct the election campaign of spring 1989), which could have provided a foundation for the emergence of civil society (Frączak 1992).

The approach was less democratic than might have been hoped. It was also doomed to failure, insofar as the preservation of unity was concerned. While society had been united in the face of the common enemy, that unity could not be sustained once that enemy was gone (Synak 1992). The differences that were once artificially suppressed, both by the efforts of the Communist state to create an appearance of united support for the regime and by the special circumstances of resistance to it, now exploded into an infinite variety of political parties (about 250 in 1994). Their emergence was additionally spurred by the ideological confusion of Polish society and its search for an answer to the intractable problems of the transition period. As a result, what emerged was not civil society but "a political society" (Korbonski 1994).

It is in this general context that the media policy of the post-Communist governments has to be examined. They liberalized the print media immediately, but sought to hold on to state radio and television (Hankiss 1993, shows that this was true also in other Central and Eastern European countries) in order to control a powerful medium of communicating its ideas to an increasingly disgruntled and disenchanted society. They felt cut off from public opinion and unable to communicate their ideas to the public, so they can perhaps be forgiven for feeling that they needed support from at least some media. The need to re-regulate broadcasting was widely recognized, particularly in terms of creating procedures for granting licences to new private/commercial broadcasters, but the process of developing new law was politically contentious and, therefore, protracted. There were also genuine constitutional difficulties, in that the institutional arrangements for regulating and overseeing public and private broadcasting usually reflect a country's system of government; however, areas of competence and division of power between the various state authorities and branches of the government were still being agreed upon as the broadcasting law was under discussion.

Designing the System of Public Service Broadcasting in Poland

In the social and political circumstances of Poland described above, only one element of the proposed new tripartite system of broadcasting was not subject to dispute: that of the need to demonopolize broadcasting and create a commercial sector. Ironically, the need for both the public and civic sectors was open to question, and the effort to create them ran into serious difficulties.

From both a conceptual and political point of view, it is hard to postulate the creation of a public service sector of broadcasting in a highly politicized society with a fundamentally unstable political and party system, where politics and a power struggle invade and subordinate, to their ends, practically every aspect of public life. As for the civic sector, designed to empower various groups and segments of society through information and communication, its creation through the agency of public policy and public institutions would be even less likely, because any government would see its creation as giving a voice to real or potential political opponents. In any case, the spirit of participatory communication that once animated dissidents had, meanwhile, been redefined as participatory communication for government officials and politicians (Jakubowicz 1993).

Therefore, in Poland as elsewhere, the effort to create a civic sector never really got off the ground. The only remaining trace of this effort in the new Broadcasting Act (passed in December 1992, after numberless drafts and a stormy legislative history, including a presidential veto) is the provision that allows the fee broadcasters have to pay for receiving the broadcast licence to be varied, depending on the nature of the programme service provided.[7]

As for public service broadcasting, efforts to define its distinctive nature, while the broadcasting bill was still being discussed , proceeded on a number of levels: (1) its remit; (2) its legal and institutional form; and (3) the general system of broadcasting regulation, especially in terms of whether or not it would be designed to safeguard the autonomy of public service broadcasters.

Given that the Polish state and political system were still taking shape, and that Polish society was still redefining its identity, the real issue was where to situate public service broadcasting in social and public space. What made it really difficult was that all parts of the political system and practically all parts of Polish society lay claim to it. The shape of public service broadcasting reflects the way those claims and the conflicts they generated were resolved.

The Broadcasting Act defines the obligations of all broadcasters and those of public service broadcasters in quite different terms. For both public and commercial broadcasters in general, Article 1 of the act says that "the tasks of broadcasting shall be: to provide information; to provide access to culture and art; to facilitate access to education and science; to provide entertainment; to promote domestic audiovisual production." While all broadcasters are subject to regulations concerning domestic production quotas (and have to promote domestic audiovisual production), there is no expectation that commercial broadcasters will seek to achieve all the other programming goals listed in Article 1. They are free to pick and choose among them, though the licensing policy of the National Broadcasting Council may favour those offering balanced programming fare.

Also important, in terms of the programme obligations of all broadcasters, is Article 18: "(1) Programme items shall not propagate activities incompatible with the law or with the Polish *raison d'état*, or attitudes or convictions contrary to morality or the social good; (2) Programme items shall respect the religious feelings of the audience, and particularly the Christian system of values; (3) Programme items likely to impair the physical, mental or moral development of children shall not be transmitted between 6 a.m. and 11 p.m."

On the other hand, the remit of public service broadcasters is defined in Article 21 in a much more extensive way, involving a number of quite specific obligations:

1. The tasks of public radio and television shall include, in particular:

(1) production and transmission of national and regional radio and television programme services;
(2) construction and operation of radio and television transmitters and relay stations;
(3) transmission of text communications;
(4) conducting work on new technologies of production and transmission of radio and television programme services;
(5) conducting production, services and commercial activities involved in audiovisual production, including exports and imports;
(6) encouragement of artistic, literary, scientific and educational activity;
(7) production of educational programmes for people of Polish descent and Poles living abroad.

2. Programme services of public radio and television should:

(1) be guided by a sense of responsibility and the need to protect the good name and reputation of public broadcasting;
(2) provide reliable information about the whole diversity of devel opments and processes in Poland and abroad;
(3) promote the free formation of citizens' views and of public opinion;
(4) enable citizens and their organizations to take part in public life by expressing diversified views and orientations and exercising the right to supervision and social criticism;
(5) serve the development of culture, science and education, with special emphasis on Polish intellectual and artistic achievement;
(6) respect the Christian system of values, adopting as the basis the universal principles of ethics;
(7) serve the strengthening of the family;
(8) serve the combatting of social pathologies.

The provision concerning the obligation of public broadcasters "to respect the Christian system of values, adopting as the basis the universal principles of ethics," was highly controversial and was adopted under intense pressure from the Roman Catholic Church. It goes further than the obligation on all broadcasters to make sure that "programme items shall respect the religious feelings of the audience, and particularly the Christian system of values." However, item (6) gives preference to people of the Christian faith. While Christianity constitutes the largest practised faith in Poland, there are some religious minorities who might feel slighted by this language. The other obligations concerning especially politics and public life (items (1), (2), and (3) of para. 2) were adopted without great debate or controversy. They are complemented by two other articles, placing public broadcasters under an obligation to enable political parties and national trade union and employers' organizations to present their standpoints on major public issues (Article 23) and concerning an obligation to transmit electoral broadcasts (Article 24).

The provisions of Article 21 (especially items (2), (3), and (4) of para. 2) seek to situate public service broadcasting in the middle of, and at an equal distance from, all institutions of public life and all segments of society.

In general terms, however, the reason why the democratic remit of public service broadcasting, as defined by the Broadcasting Act, was accepted without great difficulty was that the real battle, concerning the shape of public service broadcasting and its relations with the authorities, was being fought elsewhere.

As for the legal and institutional form of public broadcasting organizations, the idea that Polish Radio should be separated from Polish Television was accepted quite early on, as a way of doing away with the one, monolithic broadcasting organization which for so long had dominated the Polish media system, serving as a propaganda arm of the Communist government. Then, however, the regional centres of Polish Television, acting through a group of friendly ministers of Parliament, submitted a broadcasting bill which called for additionally splitting Polish Television into a number of separate bodies. Channel 1 was to be a separate company, and the 11 regional centres were to be turned into independent companies, each operating in its own region and broadcasting a regional service. That added another, territorial, dimension to the repositioning of Polish Radio and Television in society, designed to keep it more in touch with the whole country. In addition, these new companies were to be given control of Channel 2, the second national service of Polish Television, forming a structure not unlike the German system's combination of national and regional services. In other words, that structure was designed, in theory, to reverse the one-way, top-down flow that had always been represented by government broadcasting, giving the population of various parts of the country a chance to communicate with one another and to the nation as a whole.[8] As a result, some Polish towns lobbied desperately to have the act specify that new regional stations of Polish Television be established in their territory.

The plan gained a lot of popularity among politicians from outside the capital, for reasons of a different nature. In addition to doing away with the centralized structure of Polish Television, the plan would enable the local political establishments to exert much more pressure on the new companies, if each was independent, than if they remained tied to, and managed by, Polish Television in Warsaw.

The debate over the shape of public service television raged on for two years. Ultimately, the parliamentary sub-committee working on the broadcasting bill decided to propose a different solution, which was accepted and written into the Broadcasting Act in its final form: to decentralize the former monocentric structure by separating the 17 regional stations of Polish Radio and turning them into independent regional public-service broadcasters. This solution was cheaper and easier to achieve, given that the regional stations of Polish Radio were already broadcasting full regional services, while the regional centres of Polish Television mostly opted out of the national network for half an hour a day. Meanwhile, Polish Television remained as one company with 11 regional subsidiaries. The act provided for each of those subsidiaries to be given a separate frequency to broadcast a regional service. It also empowered the National Broadcasting Company to set a minimum quota for their programmes to be broadcast on national services, so as to do away with the former top-down structure of Polish TV and the flow of programming within it.

Another problem legislators had to contend with was typical of post-Communist countries, where one of the thorniest questions was that of property, namely to whom ownership of previously state-owned institutions and organizations should be ascribed. Several possibilities for the status of the institution were discussed in this respect: as a foundation, a public corporation, a state enterprise, or a "one-person joint stock company of the State treasury."[9] The first two possibilities would have created a clear separation between public service broadcasters and the state. However, the legal form of a public corporation is not really well known in Polish law, and the forms of a foundation or a state enterprise were rejected in parliamentary debates (the latter because it was seen as leaving public service broadcasters too closely involved with the state). The decision was therefore made to create a wholly state-owned company, operating under both the Broadcasting Act and company law, but with several important modifications. First of all, the "owner," that is, the State Treasury represented by the minister of finance, has no legal right to interfere into programming matters. Second, the owner is not entitled to any dividend or any part of whatever profit the companies may have at the end of the year. Finally, the supervisory boards of nine members are almost wholly appointed by the regulatory body, the National Broadcasting Council, with only one member being appointed by the minister of finance as his representative on the board. It is the supervisory board which in turn appoints the board of management. In this way, public service broadcasters were to be insulated from political pressures and direct political interference. [10] Additionally, the Broadcasting Act provides for the creation within public broadcasters of Programme Councils, serving as consultative and advisory bodies whose members are to "represent parliamentary parties and social interests and expectations in regard of programming." The idea was to provide a forum for a debate on programming matters for, among others, representatives of political parties, in the hope of channelling any possible politically motivated controversies and pressures into those bodies, rather than to have the debates conducted in the public arena.[11]

As for the general system of broadcasting regulation, a National Broadcasting Council was created under the provisions of the Broadcasting Act. After the collapse of communism, the big question concerning Polish Radio and Television was whether it should continue to be subordinated to the government or be supervised directly by Parliament. The establishment of a broadcasting regulatory body was designed to address that question and to create a structure of broadcasting regulation and supervision similar to that of many Western countries. What still remained to be resolved, however, was the composition of the council and the manner of its appointment. Decisions in this area created another opportunity to test the relative importance and the nature of relationships among various authorities.

The structure that emerged after long consultations and controversies regarding proposals, which would have given various state authorities different degrees of influence on the council, was based on the appointment of four members of the council by the lower house of Parliament, two by the upper house, and three by the president of the country. They are appointed for six-year terms, with no possibility of serving a second term (with the terms staggered every two years). The president was also given the authority to appoint the council's chairman from among its members, while the deputy chairman is elected by the members themselves. Despite earlier proposals which called for some members to be appointed directly by the government, it was finally decided not to include them. The president's role was also reduced. It had originally been accepted that he should not only name three members and appoint the chairman but also exercise general supervision over the council's activities; however, that clause was eventually removed from the act.

Although it was first rejected as unconstitutional, the idea that the council should not be subordinate either to the legislature, to the president, or the government, and that its regulatory and administrative functions should cut across the traditional divisions between the legislature, the administration, and the judiciary, was subsequently retained. The council's autonomy, however, was reduced by means of an article in the act which obligates it to present an annual report to Parliament and the president. If the report is rejected by both houses of Parliament, and if the rejection is upheld by the president, the term of office of the current council ends, and a new council is appointed.

The council is described in the act as the "state organ competent in matters of broadcasting," whose duty is to "protect freedom of speech in broadcasting, the independence of broadcasters and the interests of receivers, and to safeguard the open and pluralistic nature of the broadcasting system." Its specific tasks are described in Article 6 as follows:

(1) to draw up, in consultation with the Prime Minister, directions of State policy in matters of broadcasting;
(2) to determine on the basis of authority granted under the present Act the legal conditions of broadcasting activity;
(3) to adopt resolutions, on the basis of authority granted under the present Act, concerning licences to transmit or retransmit programme services;
(4) to supervise the activity of broadcasters on the basis of authority granted under the present Act;
(5) to organize audience and content research in the field of broadcasting;

(6) to determine licence fees, fees for granting broadcasting licences and registration;
(7) to act in an advisory capacity in drafting legal acts and international agreements in the field of broadcasting;
(8) to initiate research and technical development and training in the field of broadcasting;
(9) to organize and initiate international cooperation in the field of broadcasting;
(10) to cooperate with appropriate organizations and bodies in protecting copyright and neighbouring rights, and the rights of producers and broadcasters.

As in all post-Communist countries, the council came under strong political pressure regarding its licensing policy. Because of spectrum scarcity, it was able, initially, to award only one national commercial television licence, which in the highly charged political situation in Poland naturally became a decision of considerable interest to various political authorities hoping for the licence to go to the company of their choice. It also received political pressure regarding its overseeing of public broadcasters, especially Polish Television, which in 1994 became the object of criticism from the ruling left-wing coalition. The president, displeased by the council's "excessive" independence and unwillingness to comply with his wishes,[12] acted a number of times to recall the chairman of the council and his other appointees and to replace them with other people. [13]

At the time of writing, a procedure to amend the Broadcasting Act is under way in Parliament. If, as originally proposed, it will introduce a system whereby the chairman of the council would be elected by its members, the amendment would serve to strengthen the council's independence. However, other ideas have also been mooted, which would restructure the council (to shift the balance in favour of people appointed by the lower house of Parliament, giving the ruling coalition the possibility of determining the orientation of the council) or would weaken the autonomy of public broadcasters.

There is no question that however the act is amended, political interests and pressures will long continue to threaten to undermine the very foundations upon which the new system of broadcasting – with an independent regulatory authority and public service broadcasters worthy of the name – are based.

Enter Public Service Broadcasters

Legally speaking, public service broadcasting appeared in Poland on 1 January 1994 – that is, almost five years after the fall of communism. It was then that Polish Radio and Television was liquidated as a "state organizational unit" and was transformed into 19 wholly state-owned companies: Polish Television Ltd., with its 11 subsidiaries; Polish Radio Ltd., as the company responsible for national public service channels; and 17 regional public service radio companies.

Polish Radio Ltd. broadcasts four national or sub-national services: a generalist channel, a cultural and classical music channel, a news and talk channel, and an educational channel. In addition, it operates Radio Polonia, the external service of Polish Radio. The regional public radio companies each broadcast a full-day regional service.

Polish Television broadcasts two national channels, TV Polonia (a satellite channel for viewers abroad), and 11 local services. These local services, which have only low-power transmitting capacity and restricted territorial coverage, are devoted to retransmitting TV Polonia programming for several hours a day. In addition, the regional stations opt out of the second national channel every day to broadcast on its frequency regional services of extensive territorial coverage. Its total air time thus amounts to over 80,000 hours a year, perhaps more than in any other public television in Europe.

Broadcasting monopoly was a thing of the past, and the private sector was already thriving, even before the passage of the Broadcasting Act, due to the emergence of a considerable number of pirate stations. According to available data, in June 1993, there were 55 pirate radio stations and 19 pirate television stations in the country, of which 12 formed "Polonia 1," a network of local stations, owned by Italian media entrepreneur Nicola Grauso. In addition, "Polsat," a satellite channel owned by a Polish company, but uplinked from Holland, was gaining in popularity among cable television subscribers.

In March 1994, "Polsat" received the only terrestrial national commercial television licence awarded in the first licensing process. Because of the political controversies disrupting the work of the National Broadcasting Council, the first round of licensing dragged on until the end of 1994. By that time, licences had been awarded to some 100 radio stations (including three national networks of which one is a non-commercial, Catholic organization) and to 14 television stations (of which two, Canal Plus and Telewizja Wisła are supra-regional networks). The great majority of these new stations were scheduled to start broadcasting in 1995. Meanwhile, "Polonia 1" had been shut down when its licence application was turned down, so the only existing serious competitor of Polish Television was eliminated.

At the time of writing, a new licensing process was due to begin soon, as new frequencies had been made available to the National Broadcasting Council by telecommunications authorities. While the number of frequencies is limited, another supra-regional television network may be licensed to complement those already in existence and to work gradually toward creating a second national commercial network, in addition to "Polsat," and boosting the competition faced by public-service television.

Half of Polish homes have VCRs. Around 16 percent of the population has access to cable television, while 14 percent have satellite dishes. While private stations have been quite successful in attracting an audience, Polish Television still has, by far, the largest audience share of all stations.

Both major public service broadcasting companies began developing comprehensive strategies for the future in terms of such things as programme services, financial and managerial systems, and technology. Polish Television has defined its remit in a statement entitled "The Mission of Polish Television as a Public-Service Broadcaster." The language of the Broadcasting Act is developed over several pages in order to set out, in more detail, the general nature of programming to be offered by Polish Television; its obligations vis-a-vis its viewers, the democratic process, culture, and education; its sources of financing; its desirable financial and managerial regime; and its policy vis-a-vis its staff. The mission statement is a distillation of familiar Western literature on the subject. Polish Radio was still, in mid-1995, working on such a mission statement.

Plans and strategies aside, however, both were quite late in starting a real process of reform. The reasons for this are quite interesting. Because of the political controversies surrounding the passage of the Broadcasting Act and the operation of the National Broadcasting Council, which disrupted demonopolization of broadcasting, the newly founded public broadcasters avoided immediately facing the full brunt of commercial competition. Meanwhile, the advertising market and advertising soared "mainly because Western consumer-goods companies want to influence shoppers [in Central and Eastern Europe] while their brand preferences are still forming" (*The Economist* 1994). According to some estimates, total advertising spending in Poland will grow from 391 million dollars in 1993 to 1,313 million dollars in 2000 (Rohwedder 1994) or from 300 million dollars (of which 177 million was spent on television advertising) in 1993 to 1,005 million (with 436 million going to television) in 2000 (*TV International* 1994).

So, while the private sector was growing very slowly and was unable to achieve national coverage, the state broadcaster and, later, the national public service channels were profiting from this unexpected windfall, which, especially in television, meant very high advertising revenues. Television attracted some 60 percent of total advertising spending, with state/public television accounting for 80-90 percent of the television advertising market. "Polonia 1" was quite popular and was beginning to win 25-30 percent of the audience in the towns in which its stations were broadcasting. Backed by the Berlusconi advertising agency, Publitalia, it was beginning to constitute a force to reckon with on the Polish advertising market, but its disappearance left a void which Polish Television was glad to fill. [14] While Polish Radio has strong competition from two national commercial networks, the regional public service radio stations are said to be cashing in on local advertising markets, where they have an established position.

The market situation has resulted in the following consequences:

(1) Public service broadcasters had no real incentive to streamline management, restructure their operations, and bring down costs and reduce employment; therefore, very little was done in this area in their first year of existence;

(2) These broadcasters – and especially Polish Television – embarked on a programme of costly expansion, which may leave them overexposed once advertising revenues begin to fall; and

(3) The share of advertising in their general revenue began to grow rapidly,[15] reaching, in the case of Polish Television, about 55 percent in 1994. That has had a clear impact on scheduling and programme policy.

Already in 1992-93, Polish Television started preparing to steal the thunder of commercial television, once it appeared. That tendency was continued in 1994, resulting in a clear move downmarket. The management of Polish Television believes (wrongly) that the company law under which it operates imposes on it an obligation to show a profit at the end of the year, and it operates accordingly.

Equally controversial were Polish Television's relationships with the authorities. It was charged with seeking to provide in its programming a right-wing counterbalance to the governing left-wing coalition. Whatever the truth behind that accusation, Polish Television soon came under strong political pressure and quite vicious attacks. That, together with the low professionalism of its news and current affairs departments, prevented it from fully and objectively covering developments in public life, provoking many conflicts. While the staff verbally accepts the principle of public service broadcasting, it defines it very narrowly to mean autonomy and independence from political pressures and from the need to pursue a political line imposed from above. In general, it has little understanding of, and patience for, the concept of public service or the public interest.

Altogether then, the first year of the existence of public service broadcasting in Poland was not very successful in terms of fully defining its underlying philosophy and obligations, implementing them in practice and winning general understanding and acceptance for them. Among all the post-Communist countries, the new Polish broadcasting system comes closest in terms of legal and institutional arrangements to what is traditionally understood as public service broadcasting, and goes furthest in protecting the National Broadcasting Council and public service broadcasters against direct government or political interference.

However, public service broadcasting is more than a sum of legal provisions and institutional structures. Certain prerequisites for its emergence and survival must exist before it can be created. These include a mature and stable democracy; the existence of a civil society and an independent public sphere; an accepted notion of the public interest; trust in, and acceptance of, public regulation of broadcasting to serve the public interest; and the emergence of journalistic professionalism based on a notion of public service.

Not one of these conditions has been met in Poland, or, indeed, in other post-Communist countries, and it will take a very long time before they are (Jakubowicz, forthcoming). An autonomous, impartial broadcasting system dedicated to public service is hardly conceivable in such circumstances. In a demoralized, deeply suspicious and sceptical society, where there is no accepted definition of the public interest, no ideal of public service, no trust in public regulation of social life and in the institutions called upon to develop and enforce such regulation, and where there is ample evidence that fine-sounding ideas and ideals serve primarily as a smokescreen for political or business interests, the conditions for the emergence of public service broadcasting can hardly be said to exist. Experience has shown that nowhere have broadcasting regulatory authorities and state/public broadcasting organizations escaped heavy political pressures which prevent their evolution toward autonomy, impartiality, and professionalism. These may be teething problems on the path of slow and tortuous evolution toward public service broadcasting. However, the combination of external and internal obstacles to this may constitute structural barriers which will be hard to overcome, leading either to the commercialization or the "Italianization" of the media (Splichal 1994b); that is, strong ties between the media and the political elite and lack of a clear concept of professionalism and ethics among the journalists. Poised between the lure of playing the political game or finding a place for themselves in the corridors of power and the fatal attraction of the market, incipient public service broadcasters in Poland and elsewhere have a long way to go before they truly start performing a public service.

As for the civic sector, the appearance of a considerable number of Catholic Church-sponsored radio stations has achieved limited progress in creating conditions for the sector's emergence. As already noted, the National Broadcasting Council has been able to win approval for lowering broadcasters' licensing fees when the station is non-commercial in nature (to 20 percent when the broadcaster runs no advertising and to 50 percent when the broadcaster undertakes to devote no more than 2 percent of air time to advertising). The Roman Catholic Church has actually suggested that a new category of "civic stations" be introduced, to cover private non-commercial stations dedicated to public service goals. It is doubtful, however, that the law will be changed to accommodate this proposal any time soon. In general, it is hard to see any realistic prospects for public policy designed to assist its emergence and survival to be adopted within the foreseeable future. In one way or another, the sector will make its appearance, but most probably in the familiar form of alternative, community radio and television (Jankowski, Prehn and Stappers 1992), existing on the fringes of the big media system.

Rychard (1993) argues that the paradigm of "transition to market and democracy," often applied to the process of transformation in Central and Eastern Europe, can at best be regarded as its ideological rationalization rather than an accurate description of the direction the process is taking. Transformation, he says, is determined by the way society reacts to changing circumstances rather than conforming to any predetermined pattern. Accordingly, its actual orientation is often far removed from that normative state of "transition to market and democracy." The same is true of the transition toward public service broadcasting in Central and Eastern Europe, with broadcasting systems changing by fits and starts in sometimes unpredictable directions.

Notes

1. Szacki (1991: 12) notes the tendency of any society undergoing a revolution to "idealize itself" and to create a utopian vision in which "the prerevolutionary society appears as a seeming unity, composed of society proper and the authorities which are like a millstone round its neck: there is the Nation, and there are, to its great misfortune, 'They'.

2. It has to be remembered that those ideas were formulated at a time when dissident and opposition organizations expected the Communist system to continue for a long time yet. So, since there did not seem to be any hope of abolishing state monopoly of broadcasting, these proposals were aimed at gaining some degree of participation in, and control of, the state broadcasting organization.

3. Solidarity was aware that the authorities would never give up control, and monopoly, of broadcasting, so here socialization meant reclaiming broadcasting as much as possible from government hands and positioning it half-way between the authorities and society (Jakubowicz, 1990).

4. Ogrodziński (1991) notes the existence of four models of civil society in the process of Poland's transformation: the original, classical model as developed in Western social thought; the "defective model" constituted by the private sphere, resisting the encroachments of the totalitarian public sphere; the "ethical model" developed by the anti-Communist opposition and perceived mostly in abstract, moral terms as an expression of the unity of "society"; and the "transformative model," a fairly confused set of ideas which combines features of the idealistic ethical model remaining after the collapse of the dream when faced with the realities of post-Communist transformation with those of the classical model, once also idealized by dissident thinkers.

5. Similar ideas were formulated in other countries, including for example Germany (Boyle, 1992) and Hungary (Price, forthcoming; see also Splichal, 1994a, 1994b). This concept is one of a whole range of solutions practised or proposed in many countries in order to "combine collectivist and market approaches in a synthesis that incorporates the strengths of both" (Curran, 1991: 48).

6. Opinion is divided on whether dissident and opposition movements in Central and Eastern European countries did or did not amount to full-fledged civil societies. At the time, the "utopia of civil society" was certainly widely prevalent, due to the idealism and what could be described as the romanticism of the opposition movement (Szacki, 1991). Today, many authors agree that Poland, for example, may at best have had a proto-civil society (Korbonski, 1994; see also Arato, 1994).

7. However, efforts to introduce this principle into practice were at first blocked by the ministry of finance, which was not pleased by the prospect that state revenues might be reduced thereby, on however small a scale. It

was only the development of non-commercial radio stations, owned by the Roman Catholic Church, which persuaded the ministry of finance to back down and allow the introduction of requisite regulations varying the fee for different categories of broadcasters.

8. An additional, and not unimportant, consideration was of a financial nature: the regional centres were hoping to gain a major new source of financing (apart from licence fees) by controlling a national network and being able to divide its advertising revenue among themselves.

9. This legal form was designed for previously state-owned industries designated for privatization. It is meant to be a temporary status allowing their "commercialization" (i.e. transformation into company operating under commercial law, managed by a board of management and a supervisory board, but wholly state-owned and accommodating to normal business practice before actual privatization).

10. Additional guarantees of the autonomy of broadcasters are provided by provisions of Article 13 of the Broadcasting Act, which says that "the broadcaster shall enjoy full independence in determining the content of programming" and of Article 14, which says that "the broadcaster may be put under an obligation to broadcast or not broadcast a particular programme item or message only subject to the provisions of this Act".

11. This has not really worked, and Polish Television, especially, is the object of a heated debate that continues to rage in Parliament, among politicians, and in the media.

12. That concerned primarily the Council's refusal to award the national television licence to Polonia 1, a pirate television network of 12 local stations created in Poland by Nicola Grauso, an Italian media entrepreneur. The network had made advances to the president, whose term of office ended in 1994. However, because of irregularities in the company's capital structure (Grauso had much more than the 33 percent of the stock which foreign interests are allowed, under the Broadcasting Act, to have in Polish broadcasting undertakings), the Council was unable to consider his application for the licence.

13. In all cases, his actions were later found by the Constitutional Court as being without legal foundation (the Broadcasting Act clearly specifies the very few cases when Council members can be recalled). However, the only recourse against his actions would have been to take the matter to the Tribunal of State, which the left-wing government and ruling coalition were unwilling to do, since that would have served the President well in his election campaign that he was again being persecuted by "Communists.

14. A few months later, the Polish Television's advertising department said in an interview that he received more advertising than he had air time for.

15. The Broadcasting Act allows both public and private broadcasters to devote up to 15 percent of air time to advertising. However, at the time of

writing, draft amendments to the act would empower the National Broadcasting Council not only to lower the overall share of broadcasting in the air time of public broadcasters (which it can do under the present act, but has not yet elected to use this competence), but also to ban advertising from their schedules at certain times of day or on particular days of the week. That would enable it, if need be, to divide the advertising pie more equally between public and private broadcasters.

References

Arato, A. 1981. Civil Society vs. the State: Poland 1980-81. *Telos* 47 (Spring).

Arato, A. 1994. The Rise, Decline and Reconstruction of the Concept of Civil Society, and Directions for Future Research. In *Civil Society, Political Society, Democracy*, edited by A. Bibic and G. Graziano. Ljubljana: Slovenian Political Science.

Curran, J. 1991. Rethinking the Media as a Public Sphere. In *Communication and Citizenship: Journalism and the Public Sphere in the New Media Age*, edited by P. Dahlgren and C. Sparks. London: Routledge.

The Economist. 1994. Off-beam, 17 December.

The European Institute for the Media (EIM). East-West Relations Commitee. 1990. *In Search of a New Way. National Media Policies: Transition From Centralized Command Systems to Open and Plural Ones*. Manchester: EIM.

Fedorowicz, H. 1990. Civil Society as a Communication Project: The Polish Laboratory for Democratization in East Central Europe. In *Democratization and the Media: An East-West Dialogue*, edited by S. Splichal, J. Hochheimer and K. Jakubowicz. Ljubljana: Communication and Culture Colloquia.

Frączak, P. 1992. Społeczeństwo obywatelskie: zmarnowany potencja. *Przegląd społeczny* 2: 28-36.

Główne założenia reformy radiofonii i telewizji. 1991. *Przekazy i 'Opinie* 1: 7-61.

Hankiss, E. 1933. *The Hungarian Media's War of Independence*. Budapest: Analysis. Center for Social Studies.

Jakubowicz, K. 1990. "Solidarity" and Media Reform in Poland. *European Journal of Communication* 5(2/3): 333-354.

Jakubowicz, K. 1991. The Case for Decisive Regulation of Broadcasting in Post-communist Countries: A Polish Case Study. *Parliamentary Responsibility for the Democratic Reform of Broadcasting*. Strasbourg: Parliamentary Assembly, Council of Europe.

Jakubowicz, K. 1993. Freedom vs. Equality. *Eastern European Constitutional Review* 2(2): 42-68.

Jakubowicz, K. 1994. Equality for the Downtrodden, Freedom for the Free: Changing Perspectives on Social Communication in Central and Eastern Europe. *Media, Culture and Society* 16(2): 271-292.

Jakubowicz, K. Forthcoming. Evolution Towards Free and Democratic Media in Central Europe: How Long to Go Before It Is Completed? In *L'autre Europe: les medias dans les transitions et les crises à 'l'Est*, edited by J. Semelin. Paris: L'Age d'Homme.

Jankowski, N., O. Prehn and J. Stappers, eds. 1992. *The People's Voice: Local Radio and Television in Europe*. London: John Libbey.

Korbonski, A. 1994. Civil Society and Democracy in Poland: Problems and Prospects. In *Civil Society, Political Society, Democracy*, edited by A. Bibic and G. Graziano. Ljubljana: Slovenian Political Science.

Kuroń, J. 1984. Myślio programie działania. In *Polityka i odpowiedzialność*. London: Aneks.

Lamentowicz, W. 1994. Perspektywy społeczeństwa obywatelskiego w Europie środkowej. U żródeł pesymizmu politycznego. In *Kontynuacjaczy przełom? Dylematy transformacji ustrojowej*, edited by W. Jakóbik. Warszawa: Instytut Studiów Politycznych PAN, Friedrich Ebert Stiftung.

Marody, M. 1992. Państwo a społeczeństwo. In *Społeczeństwo polskie. Dylematy okresu transformacji systemowej*, edited by B. Synak. Gdynia: Wydawnictwo "Victoria".

Ogrodzińaki, P. 1991. *Pięc tekstów o społeczeństwie obywatelskim*. Warsaw: Instytut Studiów Politycznych PAN.

Price, M. Forthcoming. Comparing Broadcast Structures: Transnational Perspectives and Post-Communist Examples. *Cardoso Arts and Entemainment Law Journal*.

Rohwedder, C. 1994. Rynek reklam telewizyjnych na Wschodzie przyciaga zachodnich inwestorow. *The Wall Street Journal Europe*, supplement to *Gazeta Wyborcza*, 10 October.

Rychard, A. 1993. Społeczeństwo w transformacji: koncepcja i próba syntezy. In *Społeczeństwo w transformacji. Ekspertyzy i studia*, edited by A. Rychard, M. Federowicz. Warszawa: Instytut Filozofii i Socjologii PAN.

Smolar, A. 1991. Dylematy "drugiej Europy". *Res Publica* 1: 12-22.

Smolar, A.1993. Polityka po końcu świata. *Res Publica Nowa* 9: 40.

Splichal, S. 1994a. *Media Beyond Socialism: Theory and Practice in East-Central Europe*. Boulder: Westview Press.

Splichal, S. 1994b. Civil Society and Media Democratization in Central and Eastern Europe. *The Mass Media in Central and Eastern Europe: Democratization and European Integration*. Warsaw: The National Broadcasting Council.

Staniszkis, J. 1994. Czy rewolucja odgórna jest możliwa? In *Kontynuacja czy przełom? Dylematy transformacji ustrojowej*, edited by W. Jakóbik. Warszawa: Instytut Studiów Politycznych PAN, Friedrich Ebert Stiftung.

Synak, B. 1992. Od pozornej jednorodności do wzmożonejróżnorodności społeczeństwo polskiego. In *Społeczeństwo polskie. Dylematy okresu transformacji systemowej*, edited by B. Synak. Gdynia: Wydawnictwo "Victoria".

Szacki, J. 1991. Inny kraj. *Res Publica* 5: 10-17.

Szacki, J. 1994. *Liberalizm po komunizmie*. Warszawa: Społeczny Instytut Wydawniczy Znak, Fundacja im. Stefana Batorego.

TV International. 1994. Vol. 2, no. 18, 20 September.

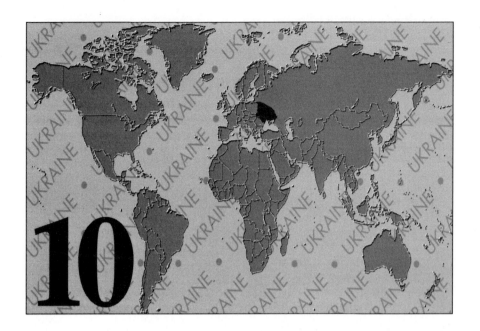

UKRAINE: PUBLIC BROADCASTING BETWEEN STATE AND MARKET

Olga V. Zernetskaya

History and Background

U kraine's proclamation of independence on 1 December 1991 is closely connected to the emergence of the Ukrainian national broadcasting system. Of course, there was broadcasting before that: radio broadcasting began on 16 September 1924, in Kharkiv, and in 1925 in major Ukrainian cities; and the first television broadcast took place on 10 April 1939 in Kiev. This period of broadcasting lasted until 22 June 1941, when Kiev was bombed by the Nazis. The outbreak of World War II and its consequences delayed the further development of state broadcasting in Ukraine up to November 1951. By that time, a new broadcasting centre had been built in Kiev, which was the focus of the second, very short, period when Ukrainian broadcasting produced and transmitted its own programmes for a restricted audience in the Kiev region. Soon after that, the Ukrainian Soviet Socialist Republic (SSR) began to receive Moscow programmes, which led to further expansion of the Soviet All-Union Gosteleradio (State Television and Radio Committee).

Over the next four decades, Ukrainian state broadcasting evolved gradually. Fourteen regional state broadcasting stations were opened in the Ukrainian

SSR. During that period, broadcasting was under the strong centralized, ideo-logical, political, and financial control of Moscow, as was the broadcasting of the other 14 Soviet Socialist Republics.

Over-centralization was clearly manifested in every aspect of the former Ukrainian republic's broadcasting. Legal and regulatory bases were derived from the ideology represented in the resolutions of the congresses and plenums of the Communist Party of the Soviet Union (CPSU). Moscow decid-ed what programmes from Central Television had to be shown on Ukrainian Television, and centralization was strengthened by the party and government control, as well as censorship at the republic level. Ukrainian broadcasting depended on the centre for technical reasons, because equipment was bought and distributed from there. Financing of Central Television and broadcasting from the republics, as well as the distribution of that financial support, was wholly a matter of the state budget, which was determined from Moscow. Of course, Central Television was much better equipped and financed than any republican station, which caused a constant flow of the most talented and creative personalities away from the republics and to Central Television, resulting in a considerably weakened republican broadcasting.

With the beginning of Perestroika and the *glasnost* period in the USSR, it became possible to speak about such notions as freedom of speech; the right to seek, obtain, and impart information; the right to communicate; and the related role of the media. Public debate about these issues had been lively throughout the Soviet Union. One of the fresh ideas of that time was the establishing of new forms of "alternative television." Many publications in the central and regional press discussed the "meaning of such important con-cepts as 'independent,' 'public,' 'people's,' 'non-state,' 'second,' 'other,' as well as 'parallel television" (Kachkaeva and Richter 1992: 512). These trends became more and more prevalent in 1988-89, which led to a heated debate, not only in professional and academic circles but in the corridors of power.

The first official response came from President Gorbachev, who signed a decree, On Democratization and the Development of Television and Radio Broadcasting in the USSR (15 July 1990). This decree, along with rather traditional social and political phrases about the important role of Soviet broadcasting in objective and complete coverage of social processes for the first time in its history, allowed public organizations, parties, and local Soviet Councils of Peoples' Deputies to found television centres and studios, using their own financing.

Soon after that, the council of ministers of the USSR issued a decree, On Regulation of Television and Radio Organizations in the USSR (20 July 1990). This decree established a regulatory basis for television centres and studios of non-state origin, requiring them to get licences from Gosteleradio in order to begin their broadcasting activity. The need for such regulatory measures was apparent: by that time some non-state television stations, centres, and studios had already started to broadcast.

The TONIS conglomerate was among the first. It was organized in 1989, in Mikolajiv (Ukraine), and very soon had stations in Moscow, Novosibirsk, and

Kiev (Bakhareva 1994). In 1989, there were about 32 TONIS stations in different regions of the USSR. TONIS's experience is of special interest, because it shows that the ideas around the emergence of non-state broadcasting were not only debated but successfully turned into practice in Ukraine.[1] Other television stations and companies were founded in different cities of Ukraine after the two all-union decrees mentioned above had been issued. Still, non-state broadcasting at that time was more an exception than a tendency. It became possible to speak about non-state broadcasting in Ukraine as a tendency only after Ukraine was proclaimed an independent and sovereign state and the subsequent disintegration of the Soviet Union.

A National Broadcasting Policy

The starting point of national broadcasting in Ukraine coincides with its independence. That does not only mean that the former republican broadcasting turned national and broke free from the dictate of Moscow. It means that, for the first time in its history, Ukraine had to work out its own communication policy. Ukrainian communication policy is still in the early stages of formation. Ukraine was the first among the former republics of the Soviet Union to adopt an Information Law, which presupposes the formation of a common legal basis to safeguard freedom of expression and the public's right to access of information about all spheres of Ukrainian social and state life. At the end of 1992, the Parliament of Ukraine accepted a second law in the field of communication: On Print Media (On Press). Additionally, certain aspects of the mass media's activities are regulated by Ukraine's Criminal Code.

It took much more time to pass the Law on Television and Radio. As one observer noted, "In all former socialist countries, changes in media laws have been initiated, but they are caught in a slow and controversial legislative process" (Splichal 1993: 100). It took more than two years from the proposal of the law by Parliament (May 1991) to its proclamation on 21 December 1993. Moreover, it was published in government newspapers only two months later (February 1994). The law was adopted after two readings in Parliament and many battles in the "corridors of power"(Zernetskaya 1994b: 5).

The Ukrainian cabinet was designated the official author of the law. It commissioned three high officials from the main state broadcasting organization, Derzhavna Teleradiomovna Kompania Ukrainy (Derzhteleradio State Broadcasting Company of Ukraine), to elaborate the law. They were the general director of the company, the head of the main directorate of television and radio, and the head of the legal department of the company. They started to work in May 1991 and sent a draft Law on Television and Radio to the cabinet on 20 August 1991. However, events in Moscow that led to a plot against President Gorbachev greatly hampered its completion, and the first hearing on the law was not until 27 December 1992 (Novosvitnij 1994).

About 40 members of Parliament took part in the debates around the law. The most active were members of the Parliamentary Commission on Glasnost and Means of Mass Information. Other members of Parliament who were interested in these debates were members of such parliamentary commissions as On Market Reforms, On Human Health, On Foreign Affairs, On Development of Basic Industries, On Veterans, and On Revival of the Country. It seems somehow strange that such parliamentary commissions as the Commission on Education, the Commission on the Issues of Legislature and Legality, the Commission on the Issues of State Sovereignty, and the Commission on Youth Affairs were rather indifferent to the discussion of the law, even though there were some articles in the law that concerned them.

In general, members of Parliament, as well as the public at that time, were unaware of the significance of the Law on Television and Radio. There was almost no discussion about the forthcoming law in the Ukrainian mass media. The Ukrainian public was not prepared to acknowledge the fact that the issue of national broadcasting was a vital one, being closely connected to their human rights to be informed, to acquire information, and to communicate. For the Ukrainian people, these issues were traditionally more connected to the press, because, even before Glasnost, there had been such a semblance of free press in *Samizdat*. Later on, in the Perestroika period, the fresh winds of freedom were first of all associated with an abundance of critical materials in newspapers and magazines and the unprecedented emergence of new editions. Broadcasting was always regarded as strictly an instrument of the state, through which party and governmental policy was promulgated and partly implemented. Bearing in mind that the authors of the first draft of the law were representatives of state broadcasting, it is understandable that there was a bias toward preservation of the status quo of Derzhteleradio. In Article 7, "Antimonopoly Restrictions," it was stated, "One television or radio company broadcasting on the territory of state, republic, oblast [province], city, or other region which is indicated in its licence shall not use more than two channels for television and three channels for radio" (Porivnjalna Tablitsja 1993: 21). Although two members of Parliament brought in a bill saying that "one tele-radio-organization has no right to broadcast on more than one channel for television and two channels for radio," their amendment was voted down. Parliament voted for the existing practice, in which the state broadcasting company preserved all the channels (two for television and three for radio) it had before.

Further discussion concentrated around Article 8, "Protection of Interests of National Television and Radio Production." Mixed opinions were expressed on it. From one side, there were two almost similar propositions to enlarge the percentage of programmes (films) produced by the given company from 50 to 75 percent and even 80 percent of the general amount of broadcasting. From the other side, it was stated that, on the contrary, this percentage should be much less – about 25 percent. The desire to protect national culture is quite understandable, but the realities of the disintegration of the Soviet Union automatically made "foreign" all Soviet films, as well as recorded and live television programmes, except those that were Ukrainian, which would have made the process of programming without violation of the law very difficult. Ukraine does not have a sufficient amount of its own film and television productions; moreover, in the years since independence, the

Ukrainian film industry has been in decline, leaving little hope for the expansion of film production in the near future. For those reasons, both propositions were declined by Parliament.

It was generally agreed that "the structure of television and radio broadcasting in Ukraine would consist of state television and radio broadcasting and non-state television and radio broadcasting" (Porivnjalna Tablitsja 1993: 27). That decision consolidated the *de facto* existing situation in the national broadcasting of Ukraine.

The most heated debates unfolded around Article 5, "The National Council for Television and Radio Broadcasting," which drew a lot of attention because all members of Parliament realized the significance that this body would have. In reality, the National Council for Television and Radio Broadcasting allows for a more intelligent direction of national broadcasting in Ukraine. So, the main question under discussion was who would have a decisive influence on the council, the president or Parliament?

One of the key issues was the principle of appointing members to the council, the number of them, and the term of their activity. Some speakers suggested that the council be composed of an equal number of members from the ruling party and the opposition; others suggested that the members be appointed by the president and Parliament instead. The latter proposition was accepted, creating an eight-member council, even though one member of Parliament urged that there should be no such body at all. Difference of opinions may be explained by the variety of parliamentarians' attitudes concerning the great power this body would have. During the first hearing, little was clarified about the functions of the council. The authority of the council was appointed for the term of work of the current Parliament.

The second hearing widely discussed this issue and pointed out the main functions of the council: licensing of television and radio companies; distribution of broadcasting frequencies among them; and control over the fulfilment of the legislation on television and radio broadcasting. At the same time, it was stressed in the final version of the law that there would be separate legislation governing the National Council.

The first draft of the Law on Television and Radio had considerable drawbacks. One of its weak points was indetermination of the main terms in the law.[2] That led, for example, to constant confusion and, as a result, to misuse of such terms as "network," "channel," "programme," "programming," and "broadcast." The second drawback of this draft was the desire of its authors to consolidate the *status quo* of state television even in details that might change over the course of time. The third factor that hampered a constructive and effective elaboration of the legislation was absence of broadcasting law specialists and insufficient understanding of the role of this law as an instrument of power.

These reasons partly explain the fact that the second reading of the law in Parliament was delayed to 21 December 1993, when it was finally adopted.

By that time, the awareness of the important role of broadcasting had been growing, not only in the minds of the members of Parliament but in public consciousness as well: "Television in Ukraine has been acquiring enormous power that is increasing daily at a time when so many newspapers are disappearing or reducing their circulation because of the extreme shortage of paper"(Zernetskaya 1994a: 32). The forthcoming parliamentary and presidential elections (1994) made the question of influence on television of prime importance. The opinion polls during the election campaign confirmed this. According to the results of four polls conducted during the 1994 campaign, 62 percent of the respondents obtained all needed information from television (Polls 1994: 28); 54 percent named television as a source from which they got election information[3] (Polls 1994: 36); and 42 percent happened to see the television programme in which the candidates for Parliament in their election district had represented their campaign platforms (Polls 1994: 36).

With the approach of the elections, the need for the National Council for Television and Radio became more and more evident. The state remained without a regulatory and legislative body for broadcasting for another half a year. That meant that there was no authority to supervise violations of the law during the 1994 parliamentary and presidential elections. That also meant that legal and regulatory processes in Ukrainian broadcasting were deliberately impeded.

The long-awaited decree signed by the first president of Ukraine, Leonid Kravchuk, On the National Council for Television and Radio Broadcasting, appeared on 25 April 1994 (Ukaz 1994a). It was issued in the midst of the parliamentary elections, after the first round had been completed. Still, there were no governmental documents regulating the work of the council and appointing its members. President Kravchuk signed the second decree, On Provisional Regulations on Television and Radio Broadcasting, on 3 June 1994 (Ukaz 1994b), when the old Parliament had already been dissolved and a new one had not yet begun its work. The president appointed all members of the council himself, which led to a situation that violated Article 5 of The Law on Television and Radio, according to which the president had the right to appoint only four members of the council and the other four members had to be nominated by Parliament. One should bear in mind that the second decree was issued in the crucial period of the elections – during the second round. Only two candidates for president, Kravchuk and Kuchma, were left out of the nine candidates in the first round. The struggle for the presidency was rather fierce, which might have urged President Kravchuk to issue the decree that he assumed might have helped him in his election campaign.

The provisional National Council for Television and Radio Broadcasting appointed by Kravchuk existed for only one month, but even during that short time it created a precedent which partly caused its dissolution. To understand the essence of the precedent, some details of the 1994 presidential elections are important. Kravchuk was strongly supported by state television, while Kuchma was backed by non-state (private) television of Ukraine and Russian state channels. Gravis was among the private broadcasting companies on which Kuchma appeared during the election campaign. Not long after the first round of the campaign (on 30 June 1994), Gravis' broadcasting licence was suspended by order of the National Council. It "decided to suspend Gravis' operations because they were using more hours of air time than was permitted by their old licence. Vladimir Popov, the commercial director of Gravis, said that the punishment was overly harsh, and that due procedure had not been followed."[4] Popov explained the action taken against Gravis in the following terms: "I think Gravis was closed because we support Kuchma, who used our company to claim that there were irregularities during the first round of the Presidential elections. After this broadcast, we offered Kravchuk the chance to give us an interview, but he did not respond." Kravchuk himself publicly claimed to have no knowledge of the Gravis case (European Institute for the Media, 1994).

One of the first decrees signed by President Kuchma after his election on 4 August 1994 overturned Kravchuk's decree of 25 April 1994, which had created the National Council for Television and Radio Broadcasting. He also overturned the provisional regulation on broadcasting that was found to be in conflict with Article 5 of the Law on Television and Radio and decreed that the decisions of the National Council were not valid and that the council would be liquidated (Ukaz 1994c).

Once again, Ukrainian broadcasting was left without a governing authority. On 15 December 1994, the Supreme Rada (Parliament) of Ukraine issued a decree, On Draft Regulation on the National Council of Ukraine for Television and Radio Broadcasting, which mandated the parliamentary Commission on Legal Protection of Freedom of Speech and Means of Mass Communication to draft the promised law creating the National Council (Postanova 1995). The same day, Parliament approved composition of the National Council for Television and Radio Broadcasting. The authority is composed of eight members (four appointed by the president and four by Parliament), four of which are recruited from among academic circles, three from the state television structure, and one from the president's press service (Kalendarni Podij 1994). An analysis of its composition indicates that the council is not as independent as it should be from governmental influence, given that four members are directly connected either with the state television structure or with the office of the president. Such a balance of forces makes it rather difficult to maintain the principle of impartiality in the decision-making process.

Nevertheless, the positive aspect of the appointment of the council is that it has already started its work. On 19 December 1994, it passed a resolution with four key points: (1) The council insists that all broadcasting companies, regardless of their forms of property, shall adhere to the *Law on Television and Radio*; (2) Broadcasting companies that have already had permission to broadcast shall be allowed to do so up to the beginning of licensing; (3) The council shall carry out necessary work to investigate the condition of broadcasting in different regions of Ukraine, to be prepared to license and enforce the rules of competition; and (4) Broadcasting companies shall inform the council of their intention to apply for a licence (Mastenko 1995).

In addition, the council is to appoint several working groups, one of which will gather and summarize proposals of broadcasting companies and citizens concerning changes to the Law on Television and Radio.

According to the provisional regulations regarding the National Council, it is constituted to maintain realization and control of the state legislature in the sphere of television and radio broadcasting; to safeguard freedom of expression; to defend the rights of consumers, subscribers, manufacturers, and disseminators of broadcasting information; and to supervise the use of frequencies. The main functions of the council are the following: to promote state policy in the sphere of television and radio broadcasting; to ensure legislation is enforced in this sphere; to issue and withdraw licences for television and radio broadcasting; to control usage of television and radio broadcasting during election campaigns; and to control advertising (Timchasove Polozhennja 1995). Understandably, at present there are no mechanisms and regulations to implement all functions of the council. The authority is in the process of organizing its activity, including its budget, personnel, and the creation of its departments.

The Structure of Broadcasting in Ukraine

Parallel to the development of the legislative process is the development of everyday practice in broadcasting. According to the Law on Television and Radio, the structure of television and radio broadcasting in Ukraine consists of state television and radio broadcasting and non-state television and radio companies which are founded by legal entities and individuals in accordance with the effective legislation. The basis of national television and radio broadcasting in Ukraine is found in Derzhavna Teleradiomovna Kompania Ukrainy (Derzhteleradio). In 1991, it was financed mainly by the state budget. In 1994, however, it received only 41 percent of its budget from the state. The question arose as to where to get the rest of the financing, and it was suggested by the vice-president of the state company that the company should earn it itself (Panasjeva 1994). Derzhteleradio is a national company involved in the production of television and radio programmes, which are broadcast for the whole territory of Ukraine and for a foreign audience. It has branches in different regions, oblasts, and cities of Ukraine and the republic of Crimea. All of them are subordinated to Derzhteleradio.

State television and radio broadcasting has the priority right to use state television and radio networks of the ministry of communication. Derzhteleradio rents two channels from this ministry, and, for that reason, the communication sector still may be regarded as almost entirely under strong governmental control. The reason given for political control of television is the limited number of airwaves, which restricts the number of channels available. One channel is occupied by UT-1 (Ukrainian Television 1); the other Derzhteleradio channel is occupied by UT-2 and UT-3, together with Television Rossia, a Russian Federation company. Ostankino, a third channel, is the unified channel of the Commonwealth of Independent States (CIS). All these channels are Ukrainian and Russian state television channels.

As previously mentioned, the current state of broadcasting in Ukraine has its roots in the structure and history of broadcasting in the former USSR. There is strong external competition in the television sector, and the majority of the population of Ukraine watches Russian channels. The most popular among them is Ostankino. Its ratings may have fallen, but it still maintains an impressive market share. Sociological surveys have indicated that 91 percent of Ukrainian viewers watch programmes on Ostankino, while 63 and 43 percent watch the programmes of UT-1 and UT-2, respectively. "Initiatives to restrain broadcasting of Russian channels by technical means (such as use of the same frequencies but with stronger signals) meet with little enthusiasm from the general Ukrainian public (and not only in the Russian-speaking East and North-East of the country). Despite the great popularity of certain programmes broadcast by Russian television, the regional Ukrainian Derzhteleradio studios were still granted the right partially to overlap with the Russian programmes. The only inviolable Russian broadcast is that of the American soap-opera *Santa Barbara*"[5] (Ukrainian 1994).

Programming

The main trend in the communication policies of Ukrainian state television is to develop the Ukrainian people's sense of national identity and awareness. As stated in the Law on Television and Radio, "the purpose of state television and radio broadcasting companies are the following: (1) efficient informing of its audience about social and political events in Ukraine and abroad, distribution of official information, explanation of the decisions of legislative and executive bodies; (2) producing and distributing economic, publicist, cultural, educational, entertainment, sports programmes as well as programmes for children and youth; and (3) strengthening international relations between Ukraine and other countries, its authority in the world community." Generally speaking, the influence of the state on the electronic media is more significant than on the print media, since there is no competition to the state company, Derzhteleradio, at a national level. The president and the vice-presidents are appointed by decrees of the president of Ukraine.

The state company is being sharply criticized for many of its drawbacks. Its programmes are considered inferior to those of its competitors, Ostankino and Rossia, because of the lack of high professional and cultural standards. Viewers are not satisfied with the work of some reporters, political journalists, and commentators. This lack of professionalism became extremely obvious during the 1994 election campaigns, when commentators and reporters more often than not looked helpless and clumsy in the debates. The use of the Ukrainian language by a number of journalists and presenters sometimes is far from perfect, and they do not know how to communicate with the audience. The programming, as a whole, lacks originality.

Very often, programmes of Ukrainian state television look like unsuccessful remakes of Russian state channel programmes, even though the standards of Russian state channels have been noticeably lowered. There are several reasons for the decrease in quality:

The political and economic chaos [that] has engulfed Russian broadcasting since August 1991 is clearly reflected in the content of television. The lack of any regulatory structure, and the shortage of state funds, means that "state television," as we have seen, [has] become, *de facto*, commercial television. All the state channels frequently interrupt their programmes with advertising, and permit formal and informal sponsorship. We refer above to [the] "mafia-like" nature of many of the sponsorship arrangements, and the fact that much advertising is "hidden," but even the visible forms – commercials for chocolate bars, ice cream, Mercedes, and soap powders – occupy a larger portion of air time than is found even in highly commercialized broadcasting systems such as those of Australia or the United States. As to their content, advertisements for foreign goods, such as "Snickers" and "Coke," display high production values, although they increasingly employ Russian crews and locations. As one would expect, ads produced by indigenous companies such as banks, currency exchange firms and import-export agencies, are more primitive in their techniques" (McNair 1994:18). It should be added that the Russian state channels constantly air alcohol and tobacco advertising.

Ukrainian viewers have to watch all commercials shown on the Russian state channels, even though alcohol and tobacco advertising are prohibited in Ukraine, according to Article 31, "Prohibition and Restriction of Advertising," of the Law on Television and Radio. It is a general tendency in Europe to ban tobacco advertising. Some countries have complete bans on tobacco advertising and others are considering such bans. "The European Commission has taken a determined stand on the issue of tobacco advertising, and the Broadcasting Directive, for example, banned all tobacco advertising on television throughout the European Community" (Stanbrook 1993). In addition, the Ukrainian audience has to consume commercials from the Russian state channels as well as "a good portion" of commercials shown on the Ukrainian state channels. Advertising on UT-1, UT-2, and UT-3 is not as prolific as it is on Russian state channels, but that situation could change with increased cutting of Derzhteleradio's budget by the state.

The Economy and Non-state Broadcasting

The economic problems of Derzhteleradio are those of the Ukrainian economy as a whole. Ukraine is now in a deep economic crisis. It is difficult to quantify the extent of this crisis, if only because the inflation rate renders figures out of date so quickly. Perhaps one example is sufficient: in June 1994, one dollar bought 45,000 karbovanets, and in January 1995, one dollar bought 156,000 karbovanets. At the national level, the Ukrainian budget deficit was 20 percent of the gross national product (GNP) in December 1994.

The virtual collapse of the national economy led to the unprecedented situation in financial and social spheres, generating beliefs that the economy was in a critical or even catastrophic state. According to the results of national public opinion polls, two-thirds of the respondents believe that power is still in the hands of those who held it in the pre-independence period (*Political Portrait* 1994: 3). The majority of the Ukrainian population believes that the economic policy of the government is without any direction (52 percent) or incorrect (31 percent). Most of the respondents (84 percent) blame the present government bodies for the economic crisis (*Political Portrait*1994: 4).

The deepening crisis of the economy in Ukraine leaves no hope for state television to have 100 percent state funding, and therefore broadcasters have been allowed to undertake commercial activities or to have sponsors for certain programmes. It is believed that such actions will make up the deficiencies of state funding. Different departments of Derzhteleradio are now trying to attract sponsors, but for the majority of them, it is a difficult task, since programmes need to be popular to attract sponsors. There are only a few popular programmes on Derzhteleradio: some quiz-shows, pop-music programmes for youth, and live sports events (like football and volleyball matches).

The current economic, financial, and, thus, creative situation in Derzhteleradio may be defined as a period of stagnation. Its popularity is not high at all and has been challenged by non-state television.

Regulatory and legislative changes opened the way for establishing non-state radio and television companies, stations, and studios. They are created, for the most part, on a commercial basis as private enterprises, joint ventures with Ukrainian and foreign capital, or in cooperation with Derzhteleradio or regional state administrations. However, the majority of them are not fully independent of the government. They not only rent airwaves and broadcasting time from the ministry of communication (RTT), but in some cases they are business partners with the ministry.[6] The approximate number of non-state television and radio stations, studios, and companies is difficult to determine. According to one source, it is about 100 (Bestalannaya 1994). Another reliable source gives a figure of about 500 (counting all small television and radio stations, computer graphics and other studios, and other facilities). The number of radio stations among them is 20. Some of them are registered but do not function. "Every new poll shows that independent stations cover more and more territory of Ukraine. But their influence is preserved only on [the] local level" (Kogutjak 1994: 2). Indeed, it is evident that, as previously stated, many small business ventures and television companies had been waiting for the *Law on Television and Radio* to be adopted in Ukraine (Zernetskaya 1994: 33).

Ukraine surpasses Russia in the number and quantity of non-state television stations in the major cities. For example, it is somewhat of a surprise for Muscovites when they visit Kiev to discover that there are more television channels in the capital of Ukraine than in Moscow. There are currently ten television channels in Kiev, and seven of them are non-state: Tet-a-Tet, UTAR, ICTV, Channel 7, Gravis, Tonis, and Channel 35. They are competing successfully with the Ukrainian and Russian state channels mentioned above.

According to the results of an October 1994 poll, conducted by Socis-Gallup, an independent polling firm in Kiev, the popularity of the Ukrainian state and non-state channels among Kievites looks as follows: the most popular is Tet-a-Tet, then come TONIS, UTAR, Channel 7 and Gravis, and the least popular are UT-2, ICTV, UT-3, and UT-1 (Kogutjak 1994). Besides broadcasting companies that have separate channels, there are several television companies and studios that rent air time or produce programmes and sell them to other broadcasting companies, both state and non-state. The situation in Kiev concerning the number of non-state television stations and studios is not unique. There are six television stations and studios in Kharkiv (some of them are private, others are joint ventures), five in Mikolajiv, and three each in Lugansk, Zhitomir, Simpheropol, Poltava, and Ternopil.

All the commercial channels are predominantly entertainment-oriented. When they began their broadcasting (in 1991-92), their programmes consisted of a parade of video clips, animated cartoons, and feature films (usually from the United States, rarely from France, Italy, Britain, Mexico, Japan, or China). Not all of them were of high aesthetic quality, and many of them were pirated copies. According to a journalistic investigation, "about 700 pirated films are shown per month on television screens of Kiev only. Ukraine has already promulgated the Law on Copyright (1994) but nobody seems to adhere to it" (Sec 1994).

Video piracy is discouraged, to some extent, by the existence of The Association of Non-State Television and Radio Stations, UNIKA-TV. This association, founded in March 1993 uniting more than 20 television and radio stations as its members, has at its disposal The Exchange Video Library, making available approximately 850 hours of licensed national and foreign video productions (Obednannja 1994: 7).

The most ambitious and far-sighted of commercial companies have realized that their programmes need to be more varied to be competitive. They are working hard now to develop their "menu," including economic programmes, local news, programmes for children and youth, and religious programmes. Religious programmes are a completely new phenomenon on Ukrainian state and non-state television.

Another new tendency in non-state television is the creation of serious information programmes. Among the first information programmes on commercial television were *Novini UNIAR* (UNIAR News), on UTAR, and *Shotiznnja* (Every Week), a programme about economic reforms in Ukraine, on UT-3, jointly produced by UNIKA-TV and Price Waterhouse. This tendency appears in regional commercial stations as well, for example in Lviv, Ternopil, Sumy, Rivne, Kharkiv, Donetsk, and Dnipropetrovsk. New information programmes produced and distributed at the International Media Centre – Internews – have appeared recently[7]: "*Paragraf*" (Paragraph), a weekly programme of economic analysis; "*Rehiony*," (Regions) a bi-monthly magazine comprising materials from local non-governmental television stations; "*Vikna*" (Windows), a weekly half-hour news magazine, which is firmly established as the credible alternative to state television news; and

"Vikna Top News," a five minute news programme produced weekdays to supplement Monday night "Vikna." The last two programmes are aired nationally on UT-3. Here again is a break in tradition: a state broadcaster, UT-3, airs information programmes which have the reputation for being informative alternatives to government-controlled shows.

Broadcasting and the Democratic Process

The developments mentioned above reflect a general tendency in Ukrainian broadcasting: liberalization and democratization. These processes are developing rather slowly, alongside political and economic reforms, and illustrate "the extent to which the politics of broadcasting constitute a microcosm of political life itself" (Raboy 1993). For the first time in the history of Ukrainian broadcasting, citizens of Ukraine have the possibility to acquire information about Ukraine and the world from different sources and thus to make their own choices among different points of view.

The first point of view is the official one (the carriers of it are UT-1, UT-2, UT-3). The second point of view is presented by Moscow (Ostankino, TV Rossia), and, more often than not, it gives counter-information about Ukraine. The third one may be called international (translated into Ukrainian or original versions of the information programmes of CNN, BBC, ITN, Window to America, etc.). The fourth is that of independent commercial companies (Zernetskaya 1994a; 33-34). Of course these commercial companies may be called "independent" only to a certain extent. Many of them have political, economic, and financial dependencies and alliances with specific interest groups, since they were founded with the help of regional, local, or municipal authorities, or since they are joint ventures with domestic or foreign firms, who invested money in Ukrainian television companies, as business partners . In addition, many foreign foundations, such as the International Renaissance Foundation (Soros Foundation), have mass media programmes that proclaim their goals "to help non-governmental mass media institutions increase their competitiveness and develop alternative information sources that provide a diversity of high-quality information" (IRF's 1994: 13). Among the other foreign foundations are the Canadian Bureau of Technical Assistance, Foundation Eurasia, private U.S. foundations The American House, Freedom Forum, and IREX, as well as a company, Price Waterhouse (Washington).

A special role in fostering development of democratic processes in the Ukrainian mass media belongs to the European Institute for the Media, which has a branch in Kiev. This institute implemented a project of monitoring the Ukrainian mass media during the 1994 parliamentary and presidential elections. The project was financed by the programme Technical Assistance to the New Independent States (TACIS) on Democracy of European Community. The institute held seminars in Kiev, where the question about the necessity of public service broadcasting was raised before representatives of commercial media and members of the Parliamentary Commission on Legal Protection of Freedom of Speech and Means of Mass Communication.

The idea of public service broadcasting cannot be regarded as a wholly imported one. There is a growing understanding among broadcasting professionals and academics in Ukraine of the necessity of public service broadcasting. It is not only debated during international seminars and round tables, but is stressed in the Declaration of the Council of the Ukrainian Television Association[8] (March 1994) and was a topic of discussion among cabinet ministers, members of Parliament, and academics (Zvernennja 1994) in debates that took place in the autumn of 1994 (with no positive results).

A new situation has arisen with President Kuchma's decree, On Improvement of the System of Management of the State Television and Radio of Ukraine, which was issued on 3 January 1995. According to the decree, a new State Committee on Television and Radio Broadcasting (*Derzhavnij Komitet Telebachennja i Radiomovlenja* [Derzhteleradio Ukrainy]) shall be organized, replacing Derzhteleradio. Its main tasks are these: to ensure realization of state information policy by television and radio broadcasting; to organize enforcement of broadcasting legislation and decisions of the National Council for Television and Radio Broadcasting; to ensure access to national television and radio; and to organize television and radio broadcasts to foreign audiences. The cabinet is required to liquidate the old Derzhteleradio and subordinate the following companies to Derzhteleradio Ukrainy: (1) Natsionalna Television Kompany Ukrainy (The National Television Company of Ukraine); (2) Natsionalna Radiokompania Ukrainy (The State Radio Company of Ukraine); (3) Derzhavna Teleradiocompany "Crym" (The State Television and Radio Company "Crimea"); (4) Kievska, Sevastopolska Derzhavni Regionalni Telradiokompanij (Kiev and Sevastopol State Regional Companies); and (5) Oblasni Derzhavni Teleradiokompanij (Oblast State Television and Radio Companies). These changes are intended to strengthen the role of the state in Ukrainian national broadcasting.

The future of Ukrainian national broadcasting is interrelated and closely connected with the pace of economic reforms and with the process of further political and social structuring of Ukrainian society. In the framework of these processes, television is, and will be for a long time, in the hands of the state structures of power. Therefore, one of the central problems for the Ukrainian broadcasting system is "how to ensure that the political power of the state, as a structuring authority of vast social systems, is put into service of civil society and not self-interested projects of its dominant elites" (Raboy 1990: 34). The study of transformations and reforms of national broadcasting leaves open the question of how soon public service broadcasting will emerge in Ukraine.

Notes

1. Private corporations such as TONIS are not obliged to disclose their founders, and, thus, information on who owns them is not available. Now TONIS is represented by several private television companies in Ukraine, including TONIS-Centre (Kharkiv), TONIS-South (Mikolajiv), and TONIS - 25

Channel (Kiev). TONIS initiated and organized the international festival of television programmes "Barkhatnij sezon" (A Velvet Season) in 1994 in Ukraine. Since April 1994, TONIS's authorities have been working on an ambitious project, "Slavjanskij Kanal" (A Slav's Channel) – a long-term project for a station to be transmitted by EUTELSAT. It is projected to be an independent satellite channel in the European territory, which will strengthen the links with the Ukrainian Diaspora and be a source of objective information about Ukraine.

2. The author of this chapter was invited by the Parliamentary Commission on Glasnost and Means of Mass Information, in May 1993, to provide more precise definitions during the development of the law.

3. Other sources included meetings with the candidates (16 percent); leaflets with the candidates' platforms (43 percent); radio (33 percent); newspapers (30 percent); and conversations with other people (21 percent) (Polls 1994: 36).

4. According to Vladimir Popov, "there had been no official or juridical order, but only a telegram informing them of the council's decision. He outlined the proper procedure, whereby the council had first to issue a warning and then to apply economic sanctions before it was legally able to suspend a station's activities if it persisted in transgressing." Popov did not acknowledge the legitimacy of the council, since its composition had not been confirmed by the Parliament (Ukrainian 1994).

5. Imported soap operas are extremely popular among a large proportion of Ukrainian viewers. To some extent, almost paradoxically, they even help to activate the audience and to make them understand their rights as viewers. For example, after it was announced in December 1994 that the situation with fuel and electric power was critical in Ukraine, "The vice-president stressed that among the measures that should be taken from December 27, 1994 all television channels would sharply reduce time of broadcasting their programmes: from 7 to 11 o'clock p.m." (Kokhanets 1994). The president of Derzhteleradio, Savenko, said that "television had become a hostage of [the] general economical situation in Ukraine "(Na Dumku 1994). Numerous letters and telephone calls of infuriated viewers to Derzhteleradio, the cabinet, the prime-minister, and the president urged the president to abolish the decree, since it violated the Law on Television and Radio.

6. For example, the founders of International Commercial Teleradio Company (ICTY) are Concern RTT (Ukraine) and Story First Communications (USA). It was founded on 4 June 1992.

7. International Media Centre – Internews (funded privately in 1992 and since July 1993 by U.S. Agency for International Development) – also has an information and press centre. Its computer information services, library, and reference publications were used to gather information for this chapter.

8. The Ukrainian Television Association was founded in November 1991 as a social organization (about 5,000 members) of the non-state television stations of Ukraine.

References

Bakhareva, T. 1994. `Slavjanskij Kanal´ – Ne Tolko dlja Slavjan. *Vseukrainskie Vedomosti*, 9 December, Kiev.

Bestalannaya, O. 1994. Pochti Sto Teleradiolitsenzij. *Kievskie Vedomosti*, 16 December.

The European Institute for the Media. 1994. The Ukrainian Parliamentary and Presidential Elections in the Ukrainian Media. Monitoring of the Election Coverage in the Ukrainian Mass Media. Unpublished Report.

IRF's Mass Media Program is Approved. 1994. *Renaissance, International Renaissance Foundation Bulletin* 4-5: 13-14.

Kabinet Ministriv Ukrainy. 1993. *Porivnjalna Tablitsja Proektu Zakonu Ukrainy pro Telebachennia i Radiomovlennja*. Verkhovna Rada Ukrainy, Kiev, 27 May.

Kachkaeva, A. G. and A. G. Richter. 1992. The Emergence of Non-State TV in the Ukraine. *Canadian Journal of Communication* 17: 511-523.

Kalendarni, Podij. 1994. *Ukrainskij Media Bulletin* 3: 12.

Kogutjak, Y. 1994. Issledovanija SMI Ukrainy. *Socis/Gallup International*, Kiev.

Kokhanets, L. 1994. Budut Trudnosti z Teplom i Svitlom. Timchasovi. Skilki Tiej Zimy....*Golos Ukrainy*, 27 December.

The Law of Ukraine on Television and Radio. 1994.*Golos Ukrainy*, 22 February.

Mastenko, I. 1995. U Natsionalnij Radi z Pitan Telebachennja i Radiomovlennja: Khronika, Dokumenti, Materiali. *Govorit I Pokazue Ukraina*, 1 January.

McNair, B. 1994. Television in post-Soviet Russia: From Monolith to Mafia. Paper presented to Turbulent Europe: Conflict, Identity and Culture, EFTSC, London.

Na Dumku Prezidenta Derzhteleradiocompanij Ukrainy Oleksandra Savenka. 1994. *UNIAN-Noviny*, 27 December.

Novosvitnij, V. 1994. Telebachennja v Zakoni. *Khrestjatik*, 25 January, Kiev.

Obednannja Teleradiostantsij Ukrainy. 1994. *Ukrainskij Media Buleten* 1.

Panasieva, T. 1994. Viktor Leshik: `Pora Platit za Gosudarstvennoe TV'.*Kievskie Vedomosti*, 25 November.

A Political Portrait of Ukraine. 1994. *Dateline: Ukraine. An Informational and Analytical Bulletin, Elections 94/5*.

Polls. 1994. The Results of Four Polls Conducted During the 1994 Election Campaign in Ukraine. *A Political Portrait of Ukraine* 4: 1-65, Kiev.

Postanova Verkhovnoi Rady Ukrainy. 1995. Pro Proekt Polozhennja pro Natsionalnu Radu Ukrainy z Pitan Telebachennja i Radiomvlennja. *Golos Ukrainy*, 15 January.

Raboy, M. 1990. From Cultural Diversity to Social Equality: The Democratic Trials of Canadian Broadcasting.*Studies of Broadcasting* 26: 7-41.

Raboy, M. 1993. The Public Service Basis of Canadian Broadcasting. In *Public Service Broadcasting in a Multichannel Environment*, edited by R. K. Avery. New York and London: Longman.

Sec, A. 1994. Komertsijne Telebachennja jak Dzerkalo Nashogo Zittja. Piratstvo jak Zasib Isnuvannja.*Ukrajina Moloda*, 11 November.

Splichal, S. 1993.The Civil Society Paradox' and the Media in Central and Eastern Europe. *Research on Democracy and Society* (1).

Stanbrook, L. 1993. Tobacco Advertising.*Executive Briefs*. London: The Advertising Association, 6 May.

Television Series Produced and Distributed at the IMC. 1994. *IMC Bulletin*, Fall.

Timchasove Polozhennia pro Natsionalnu Radu Ukrainy z Pitan Telebachennja i Radiomovlennja. 1995. *Golos Ukrainy*, 13 January.

Ukaz Prezidenta Ukrajiny. 1994a. Pro Natsionalnu Radu z Pitan Telebachennja i Radiomovlennja. *Urijadovij Kurier*, 25 April.

Ukaz Prezidenta Ukrajiny. 1994b. Pro Timchasove Polozhennia pro Natsionalnu Padu z Pitan Telebachennja i Radiomovlennja. *Urijadovij Kurier*, 3 June.

Ukaz Prezidenta Ukrajiny. 1994c. Pro Ukazi Prezidenta Ukrainy vid 2 5 kvitnja 1994 roku No 186 ta vid 3 chervnja 1994 roku No 280.*Uriadovij Kurier*, 4 August.

Zernetskaya, O. V. 1994a. Broadcasting Reform in Ukraine.*Media Development* 41: 32-34.

Zernetskaya, O. V. 1994b. Television and Democracy in Ukraine. Paper presented to Turbulent Europe: Conflict, Identity and Culture, EFTSC, London.

Zvernennia Rady Ukrainskoj Televizijnoj Spilki. 1994. *Kijivskij Visnuk*, 1 March.

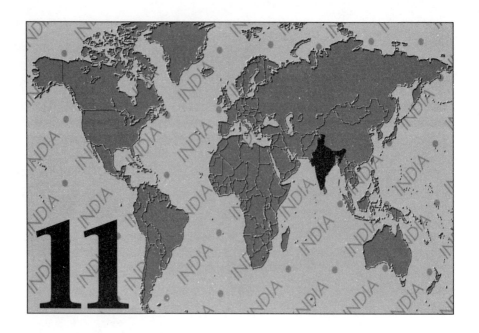

India: Television and National Politics

Nikhil Sinha

Introduction

On 9 February 1995, the Indian Supreme Court delivered a decision that, in effect, set aside the legal basis for the government's monopoly over radio and television broadcasting. The decision capped three years of revolutionary change in India's television environment, a period that saw one of the most closed and controlled television industries in the world transformed into an open, multichannel competitive television market. The advent of international satellite television services, the beginning of Indian satellite-based services, and the response of the government-owned and -controlled television network, Doordarshan, to these developments have dramatically changed the country's television environment. The objective of broadcasting in the public interest, always under strain from the exigencies of political expediency, are now under even greater pressure from commercialism. In this era of increasing struggles between states and markets, between domestic and international capital, and between global and national cultures, Indian television may provide an important example of the struggle to establish and preserve, if not public broadcasting, at least broadcasting in the public interest.

Historical Context

Broadcasting began in India with the formation of a private radio service in Madras, in 1924. In the same year, the British colonial government granted a licence to a private company, the Indian Broadcasting Company, to open radio stations in Bombay and Calcutta (Desai 1977). The company went bankrupt in 1930, but the colonial government took over the two transmitters and the department of labour and industries started operating them as the Indian State Broadcasting Corporation (Mehta 1992). In 1936, the corporation was renamed All India Radio (AIR) and placed under the department of communications. In the meantime, the government had also licensed the princely states of Baroda, Hyderabad, Jodhpur, Mysore, and Travancore to set up their own radio stations (Chatterji 1991). At independence, in 1947, AIR was made a separate department under the ministry of information and broadcasting, and the various independent radio stations were folded into it.

The history of the early development of radio broadcasting in independent India is important, because that period set the parameters for the subsequent role of television in the country. At independence, the Congress government under Jawaharlal Nehru had three major goals: to achieve political integration, economic development, and social modernization. Broadcasting was expected to play an important role in all three areas.

Broadcasting and National Integration

The most important challenge the government faced at independence was that of forging a nation out of the diverse political, religious, geographic, and linguistic entities that composed independent India. In addition to the territories ruled directly by the British, over five hundred "independent" princely states had joined the new nation, some quite reluctantly. The country immediately found itself at war with Pakistan over one of those states, Kashmir. The trauma of partition and the communal violence between Hindus and Muslims had further weakened the political stability of the country. Parts of the north-east were not fully integrated into the new nation-state, and there were princely states, like Hyderabad, which had no wish to be part of the union. These immediate problems overlay the considerable traditional lingual and cultural diversity within the country.

It seemed only natural, therefore, that broadcasting be harnessed for the task of political nation building. National integration and the development of a "national consciousness" were among the early objectives of AIR. It also seemed natural that broadcasting be organized as the sole preserve of the chief architect of the process of political integration: the state. Nandy (1989: 3) argues that the Indian state emerged as a compromise between two political impulses: the traditional Indian notion of the state as a *post facto* justification of a slowly emerging political order built on existing political practices ... [and] a projection of, and a means of dealing with, a chaotic political reality." That is, the Indian state became an overarching construction that retrospectively coped with the heterogeneity and contradictions of the Indian political process. In addition, there was the relatively new idea of an Indian state to be modeled along the lines of the modern European nation states. To the early architects of the Indian state, Nehru, Vallabhai Patel, and Babasaheb Ambedkar, the compromise was to be temporary, and in time, as the country's chaotic political diversity and heterogeneity disappeared, India would develop into a modern nation state. This expectation was not only part of the formal ideology of the new Indian state, but it was also written into the institutions of political socialization that evolved in the post-independence era (Nandy 1989). Broadcasting was prominent among those institutions.

Broadcasting's task, therefore, was to help in overcoming the immediate crisis of political instability that followed independence and to foster the long-term process of political modernization and nation building that was the dominant ideology of the newly formed state. Neither a commercial nor a private system of broadcasting could be relied upon to take on this role, and, therefore, radio was organized as a government-owned and –controlled monopoly. The expectation was that, in time, a modern broadcasting system would emerge that would mirror the development of the modern state. In 1948, Nehru told the Constituent Assembly that was writing India's Constitution, "my own view of the set-up for broadcasting is that we should approximate as far as possible to the British model, the BBC; that is to say, it would be better if we had a semi-autonomous corporation. Now I think that is not immediately feasible" (quoted in Chatterji 1991: 182).

Broadcasting and Economic Development

Along with political development, broadcasting was also charged with the task of aiding in the process of economic development. The Indian Constitution, adopted in 1950, mandated a strong role for the Indian state in the economic development of the country. Alongside a Bill of Rights, it lays down a set of principles directing the Indian state to actively engage in the process of economic development. The impetus for the "developmental" state came from a number of different sources. Many of the leaders of the independence movement, particularly Nehru, were considerably impressed by the Soviet Union's economic performance. While they were by no means Communists or against private ownership of property, they believed that the state could play an important role in economic development through the planning process. The setting up of the Planning Commission and the adoption of a five-year planning mechanism institutionalized the government's control over the economy.

There was also a growing belief that the problems of underdevelopment in India, and elsewhere in the developing world, required an activist state and could not be left to the markets to solve. Hirschman (1981: 10-11) argues that the problem of late industrialization that developing countries faced seemed to call for state planning to overcome the related disadvantages, through "a deliberate, intensive, guided effort .... with new rationales for protection, planning, and industrialization itself" – in short, an economically active state.

This thinking was closely linked to the distrust of the market system as extolled by neoclassical economics. Development economists argued that neoclassical economics did not apply well to underdeveloped countries. As Sen (1984) points out, this contention was not surprising, since neoclassical economics did not appear to apply very well anywhere else either. However, the role of the state and the need for planning and deliberate public action seemed stronger in underdeveloped countries, and in India it took on a strong socialist flavour. The use of broadcasting to further the development process was a natural corollary to this state-led developmental philosophy. Since the leading role in the process of economic development was to be played by the state, and since a major objective of broadcasting was to aid the process of development, it seemed natural that broadcasting be part of the governmental sector.

Broadcasting and Social Modernization

Broadcasting was especially expected to contribute to the process of social modernization, which was considered an important prerequisite of economic development. The dominant philosophy of the time identified the problems of development as primarily internal to developing countries. These endogenous causes, to which communication solutions were considered to exist, included traditional value systems, lack of innovativeness, lack of entrepreneurial ability, and lack of a national consciousness. In short, the problem was one of old ideas hindering the process of social change and modernization (Sinha 1994).

Consequently, the role of communication in development was to provide an inlet for the flow of ideas, and what better way to do this than to utilize the relatively modern technology of broadcasting. The role of broadcasting was perceived at two levels. At the individual or community level, it served to introduce new ideas so as to overcome traditional normative and psychological barriers and to introduce innovations that could change traditional modes of economic activity. At the societal level, broadcasting was thought to aid in the process of national integration and was considered an important instrument of social change.

Given the high levels of illiteracy, radio was an obvious vehicle for the introduction of information on a wide variety of social issues ranging from agricultural information to messages on health and family planning and from promoting an interest in sports and games to highlighting the special problems of women and children in society. Here again, the primary task for social modernization was undertaken by the state and its organizations, such as AIR.

The Introduction of Television

It was in the context of this dominant thinking about the role of broadcasting in India that television was introduced in 1959. The government, particularly Nehru, had been reluctant to invest in television until then, because he felt that a poor country like India could not afford the medium. Television had to prove its role in the development process before it could gain a foothold in the country. The idea to start a television service in India was first put forward at the 1956 General Conference of UNESCO, held in New Delhi. UNESCO and AIR agreed to launch an experimental service to assess the value of educational television programmes for community development through the production and broadcast of programmes aimed at improving adult education, health education, and general urban and rural conditions (Desai 1977).

Broadcasts started from a single station in Delhi, in September 1959. Programmes were broadcast twice a week for an hour each day on such topics as community health, citizens' duties and rights, traffic and road sense, and the danger to public health posed by the adulteration of food products by unscrupulous merchants. In 1961, the broadcasts were expanded to include a school educational television project. The schools project involved 250 schools in the Delhi area for in-school teaching of science and English. After a series of evaluations of the experimental programmes, regular daily black and white television services began broadcast from the Delhi station in August 1965. Programmes were broadcast for only about two to three hours a day and consisted mainly of educational, agricultural, and social development programmes, as well as a short news bulletin. In time, Indian films and programmes consisting of a compilation of musicals from Indian films joined the programme line-up as the first entertainment programmes. A limited number of old U. S. and British programmes were also telecast sporadically.

The first phase of the expansion of television in India began in 1972, when a second television station was opened in Bombay, followed by stations in Srinagar and Amritsar the following year, and Calcutta, Madras, and Lucknow in 1975. Relay stations were also set up in a number of cities to extend the coverage of the regional stations. In 1975, the government carried out the first test of the possibilities of satellite-based television through a programme known as SITE (Satellite Instructional Television Experiment). SITE was designed to test whether satellite-based television services could play a role in socio-economic development. Using a U.S. satellite and uplink centres at Ahmedabad and Delhi, television broadcasts were beamed down for about four hours a day to about 2,400 villages in six states. The programmes dealt mainly with in- and out-of-school education, agricultural issues, family welfare and planned parenthood, and national cohesion and integration. The SITE programme was fairly successful in demonstrating the effectiveness of satellite-based television in India, and the lessons learned from it were used by the government in designing and utilizing the domestic satellite service, INSAT, launched in 1982.

The early history of television in India, then, reflects the emphasis on economic development and social modernization that underpinned the role of broadcasting in the country. Television was considered a facilitator of the development process, and its introduction was justified by the role it was asked to play in social and economic development. It also reflected the confidence that Indian planners had in a state-led development process. Since the primary role of television was to aid in economic and social development, and since the primary task of development was being carried out by the government, it was natural that television be institutionalized as an arm of the government. There was little need to consider the establishment of television independent of the governmental system. In fact, in these early years, television broadcasting was considered merely a natural extension of AIR and was set up as a separate wing of the corporation.

By 1976, however, the government found itself running a television network of eight stations, covering a population of 45 million over 75,000 square kilometres. Administratively, it was no longer possible to manage television as part of AIR, and the government constituted Doordarshan, the national television network, as a separate department under the ministry of information and broadcasting, in 1976. Though the administrative structure changed, broadcasting was still a government monopoly, and Doordarshan was tightly controlled by the ministry. The establishment of Doordarshan also marked the government's recognition of its political importance, which shall be discussed in the next section.

The year 1976 marked another significant event in the history of Indian television: the advent of advertising. Until that time, television had been funded through a combination of television licences and allocations from the annual budget (licences were later abolished as advertising revenues began to increase substantially). Advertising began in a very small way with under 1 percent of Doordarshan's budget coming from advertising revenues in 1976-77. In 1980, Doordarshan permitted advertisers to sponsor entire programmes in addition to buying 15 and 30 second spots. However, in 1982, television began to attain national coverage and to develop as the government's pre-eminent media organization. Two events triggered the rapid growth of television that year. INSAT-1A, the first of the country's domestic communications satellites, became operational and made possible the networking of all of Doordarshan's regional stations. For the first time, Doordarshan originated a nationwide feed, dubbed the "National Programme," which was fed from Delhi to the other stations. In November of 1982, the country hosted the Asian Games, and the government introduced colour broadcasts for coverage of the events. In 1984, Doordarshan launched a second channel in Delhi, which was quickly followed by second channels in Bombay, Calcutta, and Madras.

The introduction of colour and the development of a national network through INSAT-1A and its successor, INSAT-1B, changed the face of Indian television. To increase television's reach, the government launched a crash programme to set up low- and high-power transmitters that would pick-up the satellite distributed signals and retransmit them to surrounding areas. In 1983, television signals were available to only 28 percent of the population, but this had doubled by the end of 1985, and by 1990 over 90 percent of the population had access to television signals. The possibility of reaching a nationwide audience made television increasingly attractive to advertisers. In turn, Doordarshan began to shift the balance of its programming from educational and informational programmes to entertainment programmes. The commercialization of Doordarshan brought the development of soap operas, situation comedies, dramas, musical programmes, quiz shows, and other similar programmes. By 1990, Doordarshan's revenues from advertising were about $300 million, meeting about 70 percent of its annual expenditure.

By 1991, Doordarshan's earlier mandate to aid in the process of social and economic development had clearly been diluted. Entertainment and commercial programmes had begun to take centre stage in the organization's programming strategies, and advertising had come to be Doordarshan's main source of funding. However, television was still a modest enterprise, with most parts of the country being able to receive only one channel, except in the major cities, where two channels were received. However, in 1991, the government launched a major economic liberalization campaign, and international satellite broadcasting began in India. These events combined to change the country's television environment dramatically.

International satellite television was introduced in India by CNN through its coverage of the Persian Gulf War in 1991. Three months later, Hong Kong based Star-TV started broadcasting five channels into India using ASIASAT-1. By early 1992, nearly half a million Indian households were receiving Star-TV telecasts. A year later, the figure was close to 2 million, and, by the end of 1994, an estimated 12 million households (a little less than one-fourth of all television households) were receiving satellite channels, making India the largest market for Star-TV. A number of Indian satellite-based television services were also launched between 1991 and 1994 – prominent among them were Zee-TV and an all-Hindi service now partly owned by Rupert Murdoch's News Corporation. By the end of 1994, there were 12 satellite-based channels available in India, all of them using a handful of different satellites. The number is expected to double in 1995, with a number of Indian would-be programmers lining up for transponder space in the 11 satellites expected to be launched that year, as well as international media companies like Turner Broadcasting, Time-Warner, ESPN, CANAL 5, and Pearsons PLC seriously considering the introduction of new satellite television services for India.

The nearly 60,000 small cable operators now providing cable services in India are largely responsible for this rapid spread of satellite television. The cost of a satellite reception dish is just high enough to make it too expensive for individual households to install, but just low enough to make retransmission services like cable very profitable. In short order, cable systems have proliferated in the neighbourhoods and alleyways of Bombay, Delhi, Calcutta, and Madras and are now spreading across the rest of the country at an estimated 5,000 new cable homes every day. Cable operators typically offer most of the satellite-distributed channels and all of Doordarshan's channels, which they are now required to do by law.

The advent of satellite-based television shook Doordarshan out of its complacency. It responded to competition on two fronts: by increasing the number of channels and by changing the nature of its programming. In 1993, Doordarshan merged the four second channels that were being programmed by the Delhi, Bombay, Calcutta, and Madras regional stations and networked them into a single national channel, dubbed the Metro Channel or DD2. Programming for the new channel was taken over by Doordarshan's national programming staff. Later that year, the reach of the Metro channel was further extended to cover 18 cities, and Doordarshan revealed a plan to offer four additional satellite channels, DD3 through DD6. Early in 1995, Doordarshan launched a satellite-based Development Channel and, in March of that year, an International Channel to beam programmes to West and South Asia.

The new channels reveal Doordarshan's changed programming strategy. DD2 has been organized as purely an entertainment channel, and now offers a variety of programmes, including soap operas, sit-coms, game shows, film-based programmes, and music video shows. Unable to buy or commission enough programmes to fill time, Doordarshan has started to lease portions of the channel to private programmers, with the programmes requiring prior approval from Doordarshan. Perhaps the most visible icon of the changing nature of Doordarshan's programming is MTV (to many Indians the symbol of Western cultural values), which in 1994 moved from Star-TV to DD2. Such a programme would have been out of the question as recently as 1993, when Information and Broadcasting Minister K. P. Singh Deo announced a "befitting response" to the "cultural invasion" by satellite television, suggesting that Doordarshan would respond with an indigenous programming strategy. However, commercial competition has threatened Doordarshan's audiences, and self-preservation has spawned a new ideology in Doordarshan, which is in the process of reinventing itself, co-opting Western television to recapture viewers and advertising rupees lost to Zee-TV and Star-TV.

Of the remaining four channels, DD3, DD4, DD5, and DD6, the last three are regional language services catering to different parts of the country. In Doordarshan's original plan, DD3 was to have been an up-market programme channel carrying "serious" programming in the fields of dance, drama, music, and current affairs. The revamping of the current affairs programming was aimed at building credibility and competitive advantage for its news service, by taking advantage of Doordarshan's monopoly over live broadcasting from India. But the tension between the new commercial competitiveness and traditional political exigencies became manifest when Prime Minister P. V. Narasimha Rao scrapped DD3 just days before its debut in October 1994. The prime minister balked at the inclusion of live, privately produced current-affairs programmes, even though this development would have lent Doordarshan the news credibility it is perceived to lack. The suspension of the channel denied Doordarshan that credibility and the chance to build on a marketing advantage: live programming. Elections in several key states in November and December made DD3 too risky for the Congress government, which had suffered significant electoral defeats in two key southern states earlier that year. DD3 is expected to be launched sometime in 1995, without live current-affairs programmes. The struggle over DD3 reveals the conflict between the new ideology of commercialism and the traditional political commitment expected of Doordarshan. In this conflict, what is at stake is the extent of Doordarshan's commitment to broadcasting in the public interest and democratic values. As one producer who used to work for Doordarshan put it: "TV exposes the lie of our democracy."

Television and Democratic Politics: The Indian Experience

The relationship between politics and television in India has been dominated by two major issues. The first is the question of what the nature of government control over the medium should be, and the second is what the role of television should be in the political process. The two questions are, of course, closely related, with the nature of governmental control over television and the rationale that governments have given to maintain that control often being justified on the basis of the television's expected role in the political process.

Doordarshan: Organizational Structure and the Politics of Government Control

Doordarshan is a corporate entity attached to the ministry of information and broadcasting; it is essentially half-way between a public corporation and a government department. It is not directly a part of the ministry's administrative structure, as a department would be, nor does it enjoy the financial and administrative independence of a public corporation. In practice, however, Doordarshan operates much like a government department, at least as far as critical issues of policy planning and financial decision making are concerned. It is headed by a director general, who is appointed by the ministry. The ministry itself, and sometimes the office of the director general as well, is staffed by members of India's civil service.

In principle, Doordarshan is answerable to Parliament. Parliament lays down the guidelines that Doordarshan is expected to adhere to in its programming, and its budget is debated and approved by Parliament. However, the nature of parliamentary democracy ensures that, ultimately, Parliament can do nothing more than rubber stamp the decisions made by the executive. The guidelines established by Parliament to ensure Doordarshan's objectivity are largely ignored, and in the face of the brute majority that ruling parties have held in Parliament, Doordarshan has been subject more to the will of the government than to the supervision of Parliament. In effect, therefore, Doordarshan is an arm of the government, a department of the ministry of information and broadcasting, and subject to the same political and bureaucratic controls that any other department of the government is subject to.

Until recently, Doordarshan's budget came out of the government's consolidated revenue fund. Under the government budgetary rules, all revenues collected by a government department are credited to the fund and are not retained by the department itself. Thus, Doordarshan's advertising revenues went into the government's general coffers, even though, as a "commercial" department, it did maintain a profit and loss account. Doordarshan's budget is part of the ministry's budget, which is, in turn, part of the government's overall annual budget as approved by Parliament. In 1977, the government introduced a separate fund into which Doordarshan's commercial revenues would be paid, but it continued to specify the activities for which the money from the fund could be used.

The tight control over Doordarshan's finances has been one of the instruments through which the government has controlled the growth and development of television in India. However, with Doordarshan's commercial revenues growing, with increased competition from satellite services, and with the government in the midst of a major economic restructuring programme, the issue of Doordarshan's control over its finances has become increasingly important. In 1994, the government ordered Doordarshan to raise its own revenues for future expansion. This new commercial mandate has gradually begun to change the broadcaster's perception of its primary constituents –from politicians to advertisers.

The first serious attempt to determine an organizational structure for television in India was made in 1964, when Indira Gandhi took over as information and broadcasting minister. The committee she appointed, which has become known as the Chanda Committee (after its chair, A.K. Chanda, a former auditor general of India), made two major recommendations with respect to television: first, that television be separated from AIR and given a 20 year development plan; and, second, that broadcasting be structured along the lines of a corporation like the BBC.

The committee submitted its report in 1966, but the government took four years to fully evaluate it. Even though the government accepted the committee's premise that television needed to be expanded, it rejected the two main recommendations of separating radio and television and of setting up a body like the BBC. The government contended that the time was not yet ripe for such autonomy. Part of the rationale of keeping broadcasting under the direct control of the government was on the grounds that broadcasting in India should contribute to the process of economic and social development that was being spearheaded by the government. But even more important, the Congress Party (led by Indira Gandhi, who had become prime minister in 1966) had by then harnessed broadcasting to the task of meeting its emerging political challenges.

In 1967, the Congress party suffered serious electoral losses both in elections to Parliament and in the states. The leadership crisis within the party, which began in 1967, came to a head in 1969, when Gandhi nationalized banks and abolished the special privileges enjoyed by the rulers of the erstwhile princely states. She went on to engineer the defeat of the party's official candidate for president and split the Congress party in the process. By the time the elections were held in 1971, radio and the nascent television service had become major vehicles for popularizing the adoption of the party's socialistic measures, including its *Garibi Hatao* (Eradicate Poverty) programme. The Congress faction, led by Gandhi, won a clear victory in the parliamentary elections, and the boundary between broadcasting to support national development and broadcasting to support the government in power was permanently blurred.

It was with Gandhi's declaration of the national emergency, in June 1975, that the politicization of broadcasting, and television in particular, became institutionalized. Using the powers granted to it through the emergency provisions of the Constitution, the government instituted stringent censorship rules for radio, television, and the press. Recognizing the important political role that television would play during this period, the government separated Doordarshan from AIR (ten years after the Chanda Committee Report) and made it a separate department of the information and broadcasting ministry.

With few journalistic traditions to fall back upon, Doordarshan became nothing more than the mouthpiece of the government during the emergency. A white paper, issued by the united opposition (Janata party) government after it came to power in 1977, noted that, while Doordarshan "was subjected to same pressures as AIR, perhaps it succumbed more readily" (Government of India 1977: 75). However, while the government could exercise extraordinary control over television under the emergency provisions, the government's interference and control over Doordarshan went far beyond that during the 19 months of the emergency. The white paper cited 35 instances of misuse of Doordarshan by the Congress government that violated even the powers granted to it under the emergency provisions. Even more important than the direct manipulation of news and coverage was the government's redefinition of the role of television in the political process – a redrawing of the relationship between the government and Doordarshan.

Beginning with a meeting of top bureaucrats the day after the emergency was announced, Gandhi held a number of meetings in which the role of government media was discussed. In September 1975, she told senior officials of the information and broadcasting ministry that, "While anybody is in Government service they are bound to obey the orders of the Government. If they feel that the Government policy is not right, they are unable to obey, they have some other views which they want to express, nobody is stopping them from resigning and joining any organization where they will have that freedom" (Government of India 1977: 9). Taking their cue from the prime minister, the officials issued a formal letter to the heads of the government media saying, "There cannot be any difference of view or opinion once orders have been passed or instructions given by an officer superior in hierarchy, and it could also be treated as loose talk if there is an expression of opinion, oral or written, contrary to decisions once taken by a higher authority" (Government of India 1977: 9). The lasting legacy of the emergency was a television system in which the identification of the ruling party with the state was almost complete.

The politicization of television and its misuse during the emergency became major election issues when the Janata party confronted the Congress party in the 1977 general election. A major plank of the Janata party's election manifesto was autonomy for Doordarshan and AIR. After winning the election, the Janata party set up a working group (also known as the Verghese Committee after its chair, George Verghese) to construct the modalities of autonomy for both organizations. The group submitted its report in 1978. It recommended the establishment of an independent National Broadcast Trust, named Akash Bharati, to run both AIR and Doordarshan. The trust would be a constitutional body, thus ensuring its autonomy from the government. The group also recommended the decentralization of decision making and the right of educational institutions to run "franchise" stations.

After considerable public debate, the Janata party government introduced the Akash Bharati Bill in Parliament to restructure broadcasting in India. However, the bill did not include the two main recommendations of the working group: the setting up of the trust and the provision of constitutional safeguards to ensure its autonomy; and the decentralization of decision making. Responding to the emasculated bill, the members of the working group issued a statement noting that, "the reason why the people want an independent Corporation is because the executive, abetted by a captive Parliament, shamelessly misused broadcasting during the Emergency, that is what has to be prevented for all time. Democracy is not something based on the pillar of one institution, such as Parliament or the judiciary, however important it may be. It is a tapestry woven out of many institutions, of which a free, responsible and creative broadcasting system is one of the most significant" (quoted in Chatterji 1991: 168).

After almost two years in power, ridden with internal dissension and faced with a resurgent Congress party, the Janata government felt it could not afford to relinquish control over what it had come to recognize as an increasingly important political instrument. The rhetoric of democratic functioning had floundered on the *realpolitik* of power. Ironically, the Akash Bharati Bill turned out to be a futile effort. In 1979, the Janata party imploded into its constituent factions which then proceeded to lose the ensuing elections to the Congress party. By 1980, Gandhi was back as prime minister, and the issue of autonomy for Doordarshan was set aside for over a decade.

What Gandhi's government did do, in 1982, was to set up another working group, chaired by P.C. Joshi, with the narrowly defined mandate to evaluate and make suggestions for programming on Doordarshan. It took 12 months for the Joshi Committee to complete its report and another 18 for the government to present it to Parliament. The committee sought to introduce a significant public service component into Doordarshan's programming, to strengthen public participation in programming decisions, to foster the development of local and decentralized programming, to reintroduce developmental objectives into Doordarshan's programming agenda, and to ensure that the country's diversity was represented in its programmes. It severely criticized Doordarshan's "non-participatory, top-downward style" that showed "so little orientation towards the common people" (Joshi 1984: 16). The committee realized that decentralization, localism, and the development of public interest programming could not be achieved under Doordarshan's prevailing organizational structure. Therefore, even though the committee had not been asked to make suggestions on organizational changes for Doordarshan, it felt compelled to do so. While stopping short of advocating complete independence, the committee advocated "functional autonomy" for Doordarshan.

Although the Joshi Committee's report was presented to Parliament, the government initiated no parliamentary or public debate on it, nor did it implement any of the report's recommendations. In fact, the report was never widely disseminated. Once again, political realities and the growing political role of television vitiated any attempt to democratize the medium. Even as the committee was in the midst of its work, the government launched its special programme to extend the reach of television through relay transmitters. Instead of decentralizing programming, the plan set out the development of the "National Programme," which expanded the reach of centralized Delhi-based programming across the country (Chatterji 1992).

More important, the committee's report was submitted and considered during a period of severe political crisis. Through 1983 and the first half of 1984, the Sikh secessionist movement in Punjab had been gathering steam. In April, Gandhi ordered Operation Bluestar, the Indian Army's assault on the Golden Temple, the Sikh holy shrine in Amritsar, where the secessionists were holed up. Operation Bluestar triggered a wave of extremism and terrorism in Punjab, which was put under virtual military rule. It was one of the most serious threats to the territorial integrity of the country in recent years and led to the assassination of Gandhi in October 1984.

The government used television to try to mould public opinion in Punjab against the secessionists and to garner support for its Punjab policy in the rest of the country. Television was used to frame news events dealing with the Punjab situation, and the government tightly monitored the reporting of events from Punjab. An informal censorship mechanism was established, whereby news stories on Punjab were vetted by the prime minster's office and the home ministry. In this political environment, the government was completely unprepared to relinquish any control over Doordarshan or decentralize either its organization or its programming.

Until the Supreme Court's 1995 decision, referred to at the beginning of this chapter, the government drew its right to operate the country's broadcasting services from the Indian Telegraph Act of 1885, which empowers the government with the exclusive right to "establish, maintain and work" wireless services. In addition, the Constitution lists broadcasting as the sole domain of Parliament, effectively shutting out the states from making any laws with regard to television. Within the ambit of these provisions, it was assumed that media autonomy or liberalization in any form was the prerogative of the government to grant. Since the mid-1980s, however, a number of legal and media scholars have been arguing that broadcasting should be subject to the same freedoms as the press, be recognized as a fundamental right, and that the government's monopoly should be challenged in the courts (Chatterji 1991).

This is precisely what the Board for Cricket Control of India and Transworld International (TWI), a foreign sports television service, did when the ministry of information and broadcasting and Doordarshan forbade them to first telecast and then initiate a satellite uplink to a cricket tournament in Calcutta. In 1993, the board signed a contract with TWI, giving it the right to telecast the Six Nation Hero Cup cricket tournament. The contract was signed after TWI put in the highest bid in a global tender that included Doordarshan. Doordarshan initiated a series of measures aimed first at preventing TWI from telecasting the tournament at all, and, when that failed, from preventing it from uplinking live to its satellite-based platform. In the course of this process, Doordarshan accused TWI of violating the country's foreign exchange rules and had its equipment seized by customs officials. It also accused the country's cricket administrators of having sold the country's honour by accepting the 170 million rupees offer of TWI over the 10 million offered by Doordarshan.

In its judgment upholding the right of TWI to telecast the tournament live, the Supreme Court held that Article 19 (1) (a) of the Indian Constitution, states that "the fundamental right to freedom of speech and expression includes the right to communicate effectively and to as large a population not only in this country but also abroad, as is feasible" and that "there are no geographical barriers to communication. Hence every citizen has a right to use the best means available for the purpose" and "at present, electronic media, that is, TV and radio, is the most effective means available for the purpose" (quoted in *The Hindu*, 20 February 1995). While the decision recognized that airways are public property and that the government has the right to regulate broadcasting in the public interest by including broadcasting as part of the fundamental right to freedom of speech and expression, the court held that the Constitution forbids monopoly of any media by either individuals or the government. It concluded that "air waves and frequencies were public property and hence in the public interest they should be protected from monopoly" (quoted in *The Telegraph*, 20 February 1995). The court directed the government to establish an independent public authority (rather than a government or private agency) for "controlling and regulating" the use of airwaves for radio and television. It said the public authority should be formed with representatives of various social interests but left it to the government to work out the constitution of the authority and its method of functioning. The court's decision holds the promise of significant structural changes in Indian broadcasting and the possibility that television may finally free itself from governmental control.

Television And The Political Process

Underlying the problem of government control over television in India has been the larger issue of the role that television has been expected to play in the country's political processes. Three sets of relationships have defined the role of television in Indian politics: television and the dissemination of government information; television and party politics; and television and centre-state relations.

The leading role that the Indian state has played in the development process has been the leverage that successive governments have used to force the dissemination and support of government policies by AIR and Doordarshan. As early as 1951, when the country's first Five Year Plan was developed, the plan document stipulated the following: "A widespread understanding of the Plan is an essential stage in its fulfilment. An understanding of the priorities of the Plan will enable each person to relate his or her role to the larger purposes of the nation as a whole. All available methods of communication have to be developed and the people approached ... through radio, film, song and drama" (Planning Commission 1951). Over the years, the dissemination of news and information by Doordarshan has been conditioned by the mandate that television's role is to aid in the process of dissemination, promotion, and support of the policies and plans devised by the government for economic and social development.

The increasing politicization of Doordarshan has meant, however, that, in practice, the dissemination of news and information has been more conditioned by the political exigencies of the party in power than any policy or developmental objective. In its report, the Joshi Committee observed that Doordarshan's newscasts and current affairs programmes were dominated by the activities and statements of ministers, with no attempt to distinguish between policy and public relations. Even more problematic has been the use of the mandate to block out the coverage of reports that are critical of government policies or plans. As the Joshi Committee observed, Doordarshan plays down "if not altogether blacks out negative news such as anti-government demonstrations" (Joshi 1984: 17).

Part of the problem with the pro-government bias in Doordarshan is, of course, structural. As a government department, subject to the same rules and regulations as other departments, the freedom permitted to the bureaucrats and professionals who work in Doordarshan is extremely limited. But the problem goes beyond those restrictions. The protections provided to Doordarshan, under the guidelines approved by Parliament, offer considerable leeway within the restrictions of departmental functioning. However, Doordarshan has seldom used those guidelines to develop an objective, balanced, or credible news and information service. Direct interference from the party in power and veiled and blatant threats of bureaucratic retribution have served to keep checks on Doordarshan and AIR.

The politicization of Doordarshan is acutely felt when the time and attention devoted to the ruling party is compared to the time and attention devoted to the opposition. The opposition is routinely sidelined in Doordarshan's coverage of political events, in terms of both the amount and the nature of the coverage. Doordarshan's charge under the guidelines set by Parliament that the "dissemination of information, news and comment should be done in a fair, objective and balanced manner" and that "contrasting points of view on events and developments should be presented" is regularly breached by the organization. All parties have been guilty of misusing Doordarshan's information and news channels. In response to allegations of government bias, the Joshi Committee noted that similar complaints were made against both the

Congress and Janata parties when each were in power. The problem has been that "a firm line has yet to emerge between the ruling party and the government" (Joshi 1984: 23). Under the garb of disseminating government information, ruling parties have routinely used Doordarshan as a vehicle for political advantage over the opposition.

Ironically, the politicization of Doordarshan has worsened, not improved, with the coming of different parties to power in the centre and the states. Chatterji (1991) makes the point that because the Congress party was in power both at the centre and in all the states until 1967, differences between the central government and any of the state governments were ironed out within the ruling party. Since 1967, however, with the formation of central and state governments of different parties, the tensions between the various ruling parties has spilled over into Doordarshan. While state governments have had some say in Doordarshan's policies in the regional stations, the central government has sought to strengthen its control over the organization and to use it as an instrument in its political battles with state governments belonging to other parties. At times, this practice has been carried to the extent of using Doordarshan to undermine the image of constitutionally elected governments in the states and to justify the central government's interference in state politics.

The problem of access to Doordarshan becomes particularly contentious during national and state elections. Election broadcasts by political parties are regulated by the Election Commission, which also monitors the coverage of both Doordarshan and AIR to ensure that the two organizations are not biased in favour of any party. However, the commission cannot stop Doordarshan's routine coverage of the government, thereby allowing it to serve as an instrument by which the ruling party uses governmental action as part of its election campaign. Nor are there any regular political party broadcasts between election periods. Without any specified right-to-reply or other form of access to television, the ruling party can use Doordarshan to enormous political advantage both during and between elections.

Between States and Markets: Television and the Public Interest

From its formative years, the role of television in India's democratic process has been conditioned and constrained by the overwhelming role of the state in the country's economic, social, and political development. Nandy has argued that the most prominent feature of modern India has been the emergence of the state as the principle "hegemonic actor in the public realm" (Nandy 1987: 1). The Indian state has taken upon itself the task of setting the ideological agenda of the nation, rather than implementing the will of its citizens. As long as the state was identified as the only viable mechanism for ensuring political stability, economic growth, and social modernization, it was relatively easy to identify the development of the state with development in general. The emergence of state-led development within a socialist agenda provided the early rationale for the control over television and the development of television to serve the state's social and economic agenda. However, as the dividing line between state and government and between government and party progressively blurred, television, or, more specifically, the Doordarshan organization, was increasingly subverted to fulfilling the political agenda of the party in power.

It took the economic crisis of 1991 to force the state to recede from the commanding position it had come to occupy in Indian society. Toward the end of that year, the Congress government, led by Narasimha Rao, announced a new economic policy that began the process of rolling back the control of the state over the economy. Under the liberalization programme, patterned along the lines of the International Monetary Fund's structural adjustment policy, the government did away with industrial licensing, revamped the country's trade regulations, began selling off public sector enterprises, and threw open the economy to private domestic and international capital. With greater economic openness has come a change in the orientation of the government toward the media. Doordarshan has been ordered to generate its own revenues for further expansion, forcing it to become, if not in principle then at least in practice, a commercial television service.

Though the state has not easily relinquished control over television (particularly with respect to news and current affairs, as the DD3 episode shows), it has, for all purposes, relinquished almost all of television's early commitment to the development process. According to Rajagopal (1993), while television grew in India as an instrument of state expansion, the state's attempt to retain control over it failed, because of its inability to develop programming that could retain audiences in the face of external competition. Sponsorship of private programmes through Doordarshan has become the mechanism through which the state has attempted to retain control over the viewer-citizen. The result, according to Rajagopal, is that from a "completely state-dominated medium ... television became a carrier of commercially sponsored, privately produced programmes" (Rajagopal 1993: 93).

Over time, the state's control over television will continue to diminish. Already, there is talk of, if not privatizing it, constituting Doordarshan's commercial channels as a separate network run by a public sector corporation. As its revenue structure begins to change and Doordarshan begins to respond to increasing commercial pressures, the character of its programming will increasingly reflect the demands and pressures of the market place. Caught between the state and the market, the public interest finds itself increasingly squeezed out of the country's television agenda. However, the Supreme Court's recent decision ordering the government to establish an independent broadcasting authority to regulate television in the public interest holds the promise of allowing Indian television to escape both the stifling political control of the state and the commercial pressures of the market. There are a number of other constituencies, such as educational institutions, non-governmental organizations, and social service agencies, who can develop and maintain an alternative broadcast system. The original goals of educational and developmental television need not be lost in the state-market conflict. The Supreme Court has provided an opportunity to develop a "public" alternative. How the country responds to this opportunity in the next few years will determine the future of public broadcasting in India in the next century.

References

Chatterji, P. C. 1991. *Broadcasting in India*. New Delhi: Sage Publications.

Desai, M. V. 1977. *Communication Policies in India*. UNESCO: Paris.

Hirschman, A. 1981. The Rise and Decline of Development Economics. In *Essays in Trespassing: Economics to Politics and Beyond*. Cambridge: Cambridge University Press.

India. Planning Commission. 1951. *First Five Year Plan Document*. New Delhi: Government of India Press.

India. 1977. *White Paper on Misuse of Mass Media During the Internal Emergency*. New Delhi: Government of India Press.

Joshi, P. C. 1984. An Indian Personality for Television: Report of the Working Group on Software for Doordarshan. *Mainstream*: 15-30.

Mehta, D. S. 1992. *Mass Communication and Journalism in India*. New Delhi: Allied Publishers.

Nandy, A. 1989. The Political Culture of the Indian State. *Daedalus* 118(4): 1-26.

Rajagopal, A. 1993. The Rise of National Programming: the Case of Indian Television. *Media, Culture and Society* 15: 91-111.

Sen, A. 1984. *Resources, Values and Development*. Cambridge: Harvard University Press.

Sinha, N. 1994. Telecommunications, Capabilities and Development: Towards an Integrated Framework for Development Communications. *Pacific Telecommunications Review* (March): 10-20.

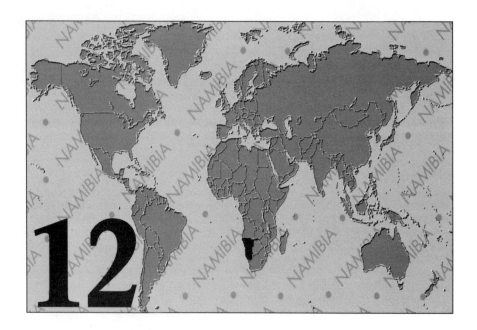

NAMIBIA: BROADCASTING AND DEMOCRATIZATION

Nahum Gorelick[1]

Introduction

With the arrival of independence in 1990, the new Namibian Broadcasting Corporation (NBC) was thrust into the role of being the first noteworthy broadcaster in southern Africa to undergo fundamental restructuring in order to become a democratic, efficient public service organization. It was challenged by, first, the transformation from the South West Africa Broadcasting Corporation (SWABC) and everything it stood for, and, second, by being the first public, rather than state, broadcaster in the region.

Dismantling the SWABC was not a simple task, since, for one, it had been part of a media that had enhanced South African propaganda and, at the same time, tried to block information critical of the ruling government. Draconian laws and regulations relating to the dissemination of information were only one component of the apartheid system under which it functioned.

The NBC's unique task in trying to combine ideals and realities in order to create a completely democratic broadcaster is mainly hampered by two things: a small population spread over a vast area, making a technical infra-structure for broadcasting expensive, and the cultural, ideological, and language diversities prevalent in Namibia. These are especially difficult, given that democratization in Namibia is still very much a learning process. While the NBC is meant to be the forerunner in democratizing the Namibian population, it stands very much on its own in that regard.

Nonetheless, the NBC has accepted its role in advancing unity in diversity, which is a powerful catalyst for development of national culture and which is one of the key areas that is being developed over the NBC airwaves. Furthermore, NBC programmes attempt to reflect a "transformation process and development taking place presently within Namibia, [which] support the creation of its civil society and aim at strengthening the democratic culture and principles, structures and procedures" (Gorelick 1993). The notion of development, as interpreted by the NBC, is to enable and enhance all Namibians to overcome the serious gap created through the historical apartheid regime which resulted in a very small group of the population con-trolling all formal sectors of activity in the country, including development in areas of economic, social, political, cultural, and educational activities.

Background

The first local radio news bulletin in Namibia was broadcast in November 1956, as a result of the appointment of news representatives in South West Africa, the territory known today as Namibia. The planning policies and legis-lation in this territory were dependent on the system imposed by South Africa, and, thus, the South African Broadcasting Corporation (SABC) was responsible for the regional news bulletin, broadcast on shortwave, in both English and Afrikaans. As demand increased and the need for more dissemi-nation of information was felt, FM transmissions were implemented in Windhoek, in April 1969, by the first regional manager of the SABC, who was appointed to an office in the capital. In December 1969, three radio stations started broadcasting in the territory as part of the SABC Bantu component. In 1974, the SABC broadcast directly from Johannesburg, with listeners in the Caprivi region able to receive their programme in the Lozi language. Although a television news team was dispatched to Windhoek in 1975, it was only in 1981 that a relay television system was established.

In July 1978, a fundamental change in broadcasting took place in the territo-ry. As part of the activities of the transitional government in South West Africa/Namibia, a broadcasting board was appointed and established to take over the assets and equipment of the SABC, resulting in the establishment of the South West Africa Broadcasting Corporation (SWABC). Under the authori-ty of the administrator general of the territory, nine ethnic radio stations, including the national service, were formed. The national service, however, was broadcast only in English and Afrikaans, while the remaining stations had English, Afrikaans, German, Owambo, Herero, Lozi, Tswana, and Damara/Nama services.

Although television contained mostly relayed material from the SABC, local news bulletins were pre-recorded and broadcast in the evening. This service continued under the strict control of the director general, who was also chair of the SWABC board and who reported directly to the administrator general in the territory. With legislation similar to that in South Africa, the SWABC was, in fact, a state broadcasting organization with very strict controls as to the nature of programming and how it could be disseminated. Being a state broadcasting instrument during a war, all information relating to the local environment had to be cleared by the security police and the military, thus restricting the freedom of journalists and programme producers to move about as they would have liked.

In March 1990, shortly before Namibia's independence from South Africa, the corporation changed its name to the Namibian Broadcasting Corporation (NBC). Shortly after independence, a new board and director general were appointed by the president of Namibia through the information and broadcasting minister. It was the task of the director general and the board to transform the organization into a public broadcaster from a state broadcasting organization. Their first action was the introduction of a policy code that gave a new direction to the organization. The board of the NBC adopted this new policy code for programmes and news services at its second meeting in Windhoek on 27 June 1990. The tenets of the code are as follows:

- The corporation's programmes and news services will act in the best interests of the country and its people, with particular emphasis on nation building and development.

- Publicly supported broadcasting is primarily for disseminating information and reflecting newsworthy events. As a parastatal organization [partially funded by the state], run autonomously by an independent board, according to the Constitution which guarantees freedom of the media, the corporation endeavours to propagate and strengthen the ideals of public interest among its staff members.

- The corporation will encourage responsible and professional reporting, free from government or outside interference.

- In addition to news programmes, the corporation will encourage the broadest possible access to broadcast dissemination for public organizations and associations that wish to inform and educate the public.

- The corporation's function is to inform, entertain, and contribute to the education of the people through its radio and television programme services. These services will cover Namibian events both national and local – as well as African and international news.

- Particular emphasis will be placed on reporting to the Namibian people about the internal functioning of all three branches of the government.

- News reports and news commentary will be presented on a factual and balanced basis. The corporation will provide a forum for active and investigative journalism. Debate, critical analysis, and discussion on current affairs will facilitate the free flow of information but are free from censorship or manipulation.

• The content of information broadcast is subject to the Constitution and the laws of Namibia. This content shall, at all times, remain sensitive to the values of the people and uphold the principles of the Bill of Fundamental Human Rights as enshrined in the Constitution.

• The Republic of Namibia is a secular state and the corporation will, therefore, encourage tolerance and respect for all religious persuasions in terms of the Constitution (NBC Policy Code 1990: 1).

The next phase in the transformation of the NBC involved restructuring the organization. One of the biggest problems encountered was the filtering of information through a very top-heavy structure to the executive of the organization. The structure, at that stage, consisted of a support-dominated environment, in which services such as technical, financial, administrative, and human resources were under the administration of a deputy director general, who reported to the chief executive. Programmes and news comprised another department, also reporting to the director general through a deputy director general. In an effort to change this filtering of information, a major restructuring of the organization took place at the end of 1990 and was implemented in 1991.[2]

The new structure consisted of the director general as chief executive and representative on the board. Below him was a less-complex division of two programme departments – one radio and television and the other news and current affairs, both headed by senior controllers. The support departments were headed by the controller of the administration department. In essence, the restructuring flattened the top structure and reduced top managerial posts from 26 to 11. The total number of staff at the NBC was 720. This reduction substantially improved the communication channels and information flow vertically, resulting in a much smoother functioning organization. In addition to this change in structure, the NBC was faced with the challenge of changing the attitude of the staff from being "civil service" oriented, as it was in the state broadcasting environment, to one of professional producers and journalists, in order for the true essence of public broadcasting to develop.

According to the Namibian Broadcast Act of 1991, the minister appoints the board who, in turn, appoints the chief executive and delegates authority in order to run the national broadcaster. Although the act does not make any reference to the autonomy of the organization, the board stipulates that the organization be run autonomously, in terms of editorial standards. However, because 68 percent of the organization's financing comes from the state, the NBC is dependent on state funding for most of its operation and cannot be run autonomously in the true sense of the word.

The Broadcasting Act of 1991 contains four key objectives that the NBC, as public broadcaster, must fulfil. The corporation must carry on a broadcasting service in order, "(a) [to] inform and entertain the public of Namibia; (b) to contribute to the education and unity of the nation and to peace in Namibia;(c) to provide and disseminate information relevant to the socio-economic development of Namibia; and (d) to promote the use and understanding of the English language." In light of these objectives, the following programme priorities have been listed as part of the NBC programme policy.

Programme Priorities

First and foremost, programmes broadcast on the NBC must be relevant within the Namibian multicultural societal context. This involves taking into account, among other things, the cultural wealth and diversity of the Namibian people, as well as equality and respect for fellow Namibians. Advancing unity in diversity is a powerful catalyst for development of a national culture, which is one of the key areas that must be developed over the NBC airwaves. Furthermore, NBC programmes must reflect the transformation process and development currently taking place in Namibia, support the creation of a civil society, and aim at strengthening the democratic culture, principles, structures, and procedures. A special effort must be made to encourage development through local and foreign programmes.

Second, programmes must be relevant within the wider African setting. Namibia must be reflected in the roots of the African culture and advance its culture from within this continental environment.

Third, Namibia's link to and membership in the international community at large should be established and maintained through foreign programmes. The programmes should encourage and foster understanding, respect, and learning from the diversity and achievements of other nations as expressed in a variety of economic, social, cultural, and spiritual activities.

Finally, the content of information broadcast is subject to the Constitution and the laws of Namibia. This content should, at all times, remain sensitive to the values of the people and uphold the principle of the Bill of Fundamental Human Rights enshrined in the Namibian Constitution.

In order to enforce these priorities, the organization has developed the following mission statement: The mission of the NBC, as the national public broadcasting service, is to effectively inform, educate, and entertain the people of Namibia in order to promote peace, national unity, and development.

The main issues concerning the organization, since independence, revolve around the NBC's autonomy. With regard to financial dependency on and regulation by the government, the debate centres on how the NBC can maintain its editorial freedom. The board advocates the organization's editorial autonomy and supports the principle of maintaining it. With regard to financing, the issues are two fold: (a) reduced financing from government, due to the autonomous stand the organization has taken; and (b) the extent to which a public broadcaster can accept external revenue from commercial and sponsor sources and still maintain a public broadcasting profile. The debate on these issues is ongoing and is being investigated on a regional level through the Southern African Broadcasting Association (SABA), which was founded at the end of 1993.

With regard to regulation and political control, the Broadcast Act of 1991 is explicit as to the lines of communication – that is, the board reports to the minister through the annual report. A Namibian communication commission has been set up through legislation, but it deals primarily with the licensing of private broadcasters and the regulation thereof. It does not affect the NBC in any way.

The organizational changes that took place within the SWABC, which allowed it to emerge, in 1990, as the NBC, were some of the most fundamental changes within any large Namibian corporation. The SWABC had been seen as one of the "instruments of colonial power, and lost credibility as the political, cultural, economic and social aspirations of the people changed" (Gorelick 1992: 29). The organization, therefore, had to change into a parastatal corporation catering to all the people in Namibia through nine language services on radio in a democratic fashion, as opposed to a strictly controlled propagandistic state broadcaster. According to the Namibian minister of information and broadcasting, "The programme policy should give first priority to education and news. Mobilizing for national reconciliation and unity should have second priority" (Dyvi 1993: 3).

The Namibian Broadcasting Act was to set the rules for this change in 1991. The new act did not merely modify the SWABC Act, but repealed it entirely. Constitutional guidelines relating to freedom of speech and other fundamental rights are obvious in the act, and J.D. G. Maritz notes the following in his concluding comments to a legal opinion on the act:

> The mechanism created for the NBC to form and incorporate or establish, and to manage and control a company for the purpose of a broadcasting service is of substantial importance. It was probably inspired by Article 98 (2)(c) of the Namibian Constitution and intended to give the NBC greater flexibility and allow private participation by members of the public in such a company (Maritz 1991:32).

One aspect in the new act, however, differs substantially from the SWABC Act – that of the powers vested in the minister. Maritz comments:

> It must, however, be borne in mind that such company would in effect be state controlled and will probably not be an attractive alternative for a broadcasting company which intends to operate in competition with the NBC (Maritz 1991: 35).

While caution is certainly appropriate, since the minister has the final say over appointments, as well as programme content, direct interference by the minister has been minimal to date.

Another substantial change is the implementation of affirmative action, which lay mainly in the hands of the board. As yet, the NBC has no clear policy on affirmative action, but it developed some guidelines during a top management meeting in August 1991. Without any legislation pertaining to the issue, it is commonly accepted that the implementation of affirmative action is practised; however, due to a lack of guidelines, the practice is not always fair or consistent. Staff at the NBC went through some changes, notably strict control on foreign staff, resulting in the retrenchment of mainly white South Africans and a traumatic large retrenchment action in 1992 due to drastic budget reductions from the state.

Party-political tensions, as well as ideological differences, are also experienced on all levels. Since the NBC is pioneering changes to become a democratic, efficient public broadcaster, it is very much on its own, with affirmative action only one of its new frontiers. Political versus social issues play a constant role in the determination of the NBC's responsibilities. While the Namibian Constitution contains some of the most democratic clauses relating to the freedom of speech, both the legislation and the Constitution are currently being tested in court, laying ground rules vital to the success or failure of a democratic Namibia. The NBC has gone through numerous court cases, most significantly one which tests the Constitution against legislation.

A case in point is the State versus NBC, which involves a criminal charge against the NBC in terms of a new Namibian law, the Racial Discrimination Prohibition Act of 1991. The case involves a NBC news report that reflected the views of a community leader on a particular incident involving the Namibian police. The NBC is challenging the charge constitutionally in an attempt to establish the right of freedom of expression. This case has been pending for over three years, and it was hoped that it would be finalized by mid-1995.

The changes currently taking place at the South African Broadcasting Corporation are on a much bigger scale than those at the NBC. Changes at the NBC were preceded by a period of frustration and, after independence, "golden handshakes" got rid of many bureaucrats, while professional staff were left largely in place. Changes at the SABC, however, are more widespread, but also handled in a much more transparent way. The board of the SABC was chosen in a very public and social manner, while the NBC's board was appointed by the minister. Although retrenchments have also been necessary at the SABC, staff seem to have fewer problems concerning idealistic differences.

The NBC is still hampered by bureaucratic and political thinking and acting, inherited from five decades of South African control. This tendency is evident throughout the country. In comparison to its neighbour, South Africa, although the ruling parties in both countries have fought for freedom in the region side by side, Namibia possesses a much more party-conscious population, with the result that ideologically motivated leaders are generally not aware of the wants, needs, and demands of the people. Amongst staff that came over from the SWABC, a tendency to resist change has been noted, while some new staff members are often criticised for serving their political party rather than their people.

However, as indicated in the introduction to this chapter, the bureaucratic and political issues must be seen in the broader socio-historical context of the SWABC's role in the government of South Africa's dissemination of propaganda. Many of those entering the NBC after independence came from the black majority of Namibians and were sympathetic toward the new government. Used to a censored media, both sides practised self-censorship – some for idealistic reasons, others for fear of criticism from superiors or government officials. A lack of training and inability by staff and managers to successfully implement guidelines concerning a democratic approach to programming and news further aggravated the situation. A loss of technical quality in the more innovative production techniques, again due to a lack of trained personnel, could also be noted soon after independence, and both aspects still need attention today. However, despite problems experienced in programme content, the new, more global and national approach sought by the NBC is clearly evident. Training has also been extensive during the last five years, and the quality of both radio and television has improved considerably. Previously ethnic-based structures have been removed, and the emphasis on nationally relevant and unitary information is evident in the broadcasts.

The NBC must still, however, address the issues of the diversity of Namibia's relatively small population. The national service, which is broadcast in English, is transmitted nationwide, but only 4 percent of its listeners define English as their mother tongue, while 73 percent describe themselves as being able to speak and understand the language, and 16 percent understand basic English but cannot speak it. Furthermore, 7 percent of the listeners neither understand nor speak English (NBC 1994: 60). The nine language services in radio broadcasting, for example, are each currently limited to geographic areas in which the language is spoken, that is, catering to the traditional language listeners in each area. This situation still, however, enforces ethnicity and reaffirms ethnic thinking rather than national unity. Despite the NBC's efforts to introduce cross-information from all other Namibian language and cultural groups, language service presenters still give greater importance to events in their own cultural communities.

All of the information received on these stations is broadcast from Windhoek, except for the three regional stations in the north. Two additional offices contribute news but do not broadcast. This centralization creates a serious problem regarding the dissemination of information to a predominantly rural population in Namibia. Regionalization will enable the NBC, through a parallel network of regional as well as national radio, to achieve specific information dissemination at all levels, in a more effective manner than is currently in place.

The dilemma of combining a Third World infrastructure with First World media systems is further enhanced when it comes to television. While radio can be made accessible through a relatively affordable structure, television, in an African state, is still a luxury, for both the broadcaster and the audience. It requires a costly infrastructure, qualified professionals in both the technical and programming fields, and, for the audience, a substantial initial outlay for the receiver. The NBC's television infrastructure used to rely on a limited terrestrial network, but changed to satellite broadcasting in 1994, which enables it to broadcast to virtually all corners of Namibia, reaching 65 percent of the population through television. However, it is important to avoid equating accessibility with investing in an infrastructure which would exclude many radio listeners if there were a movement away from radio toward television. This move would especially affect content related to development information. Radio, with its popular success, confers on itself the dual role of not only informing but also educating at a grassroots level.

NBC television broadcasting is, thus, at this stage, a service involuntarily catering to a more urban, affluent, and educated audience, creating a dilemma with respect to programme content. The clash of two worlds – rural and urban, developed and developing – which television provides, is felt strongly in Namibia. The traditional cultural way of life in the rural areas is based in a very different set of values from what is expected and demanded in the urban environment. Urban violence, as portrayed on television, is unacceptable in the rural context, where moral values tend to be much more conservative and the negative reaction much stronger. The solution is to be extremely selective and to encourage people to be tolerant of each other.

The costs involved in television production force public broadcasters, such as the NBC, to incorporate principles of, on one hand, using television to accelerate the basic education process for illiterate youth and adults, and, on the other hand, to import programmes with different value structures and social behaviour. This predicament is experienced throughout Africa, where most countries import between 50 and 80 percent of their programmes. While the NBC is in the same situation, importing 80 percent of its programmes, the programme policy has set a target of reducing that to 50 percent by the end of 1995. In effect, Namibian audiences, like most African audiences, are subjected to values and lifestyles alien and often in conflict with their own sets of values and circumstances. However, good African products are expensive, erratic, and difficult to find, and large local productions lack funding and expertise.

The challenge that the NBC faced after independence, of being the first public rather than state broadcaster in the region, was significant, since government-controlled broadcasters are the norm in Africa, and the SWABC was no exception. While the NBC has the legislation and even a certain degree of government goodwill behind it, its audience lags behind in the process of change, since democracy in Namibia is still a developing concept. Not perceived as a priority by the government, the NBC has mostly been left alone, perhaps to its advantage. The printed media, especially the "opposition media" is, however, keeping a close watch on the corporation's development.

In its task to open the broadcaster to all Namibians, the NBC immediately introduced programmes such as the "National Chat Show" and "Open Line," both radio programmes that give listeners the opportunity to phone in and air their views. It is especially in these programmes where the need for democratization is most evident. Issues such as the death penalty, land reform, and the role and duty of government officials are discussed, among other things. However, these programmes show a certain reluctance on the part of the Namibian population to promote unity and separate the government from the NBC. Being divisive in nature, these programmes are often the source of criticism that the NBC fosters divisiveness rather than unity, one of the many dilemmas of state versus public broadcasting. Being used to a government dictating them, and now under a government they chose, Namibians are inclined to accept the NBC as a state broadcaster rather than a public one. This puts the NBC in the difficult position of guarding its independence against government clamp-downs, but doing so on its own, without the necessary support from the people. While government has not yet interfered with the NBC, the corporation would stand very much on its own should the government ever decide to do so. The perceptions and ideologies of untrained staff contribute to the general perception of the NBC as a state broadcaster rather than a public one.

Namibia is a highly politicized country. This state of politicization emerged at the start of the struggle for independence and continues to operate on a high level, reflected in the public's contributions to political issues. The type of programming that is being developed and broadcast must attempt to maintain this framework and to add to it by making Namibian people more aware of the socio-economic and cultural issues that are essential for nation building, which can only be achieved through participation by all agencies in Namibia, not only the government (Gorelick 1993).

While, as previously mentioned, government interference has not occurred at the NBC during the last five years, neither has there been strong support for the corporation's role in nation building. Public personalities have fallen into the trap of giving more importance to television coverage than radio, in effect depriving the majority of people of the information they want to have broadcast.

During 1993 and 1994, the first two commercial radio stations were awarded licences under the Namibia Communications Act of 1992. They fulfil the role of much needed entertainment stations and, thus, provide healthy and needed competition. Both have limited reception areas and aim at a specific audience that can be described as mainly white, middle-class, and interested in entertainment rather than educational and informative broadcasting. However, a February 1995 NBC survey showed that more than 90 percent of the audiences of both commercial stations also listen to the NBC, while 21 percent of their listeners believe the stations are part of the NBC.

Like the commercial television station broadcast from South Africa, M-net, these commercial broadcasters fulfil a role within the Namibian society that the NBC, as a public broadcaster, is forced to neglect: that of providing pure entertainment. In that sense, the competition is healthy, bridging a gap in broadcasting in Namibia. In M-net's case, the initial outlay for the decoder, as well as the monthly rental fees, make the station available only to an elite. However, since the same audience watches NBC television and M-net, during the same time slots, the NBC is losing some viewership, especially between from 5:00 to 7:00 p.m. Research has shown however, that M-net's viewers will switch between channels, with NBC news at 8:00 p.m. regaining virtually all television viewers, once again emphasising the demand for local information, on the one hand, and light entertainment on the other.

The NBC has been warned by the government to do its utmost to come up with its own funding and not be dependent on government support to the extent that it has been. While a marked improvement has been achieved, reducing state funding from more than 80 percent to 68 percent currently, the pressure is still strong. Television advertising is expensive, and there is only a very small market in urban areas that is of interest to advertisers, who want to target a market that has the economic power to buy their products. This market is represented more by privately owned broadcasters than the NBC, which concentrates on the previously disadvantaged majority of the population. Therefore, while competition in terms of programming is minimal, competition for the already small and exhausted advertising market is certainly pressuring the NBC. Since television has become the entertainment medium of our age, viewers expect it to please and satisfy them, whatever their demands. Consequently, the NBC finds itself needing to create funding through advertising, on one hand, while also adhering to public service guidelines, on the other. This situation often means not being able to meet either advertisers' or audiences' expectations, and, hence, losing potential advertisers. The situation is not as problematic for radio, since advertising on radio is cheaper and advertising in the different languages is used especially by a significant business sector in the north of the country, one which is not as yet reached by any of the commercial broadcasters.

In short, commercial competition is forcing the NBC to look into more commercial ventures and into commercializing some of its own broadcasting in order to generate funding. However, as a public broadcaster, it cannot start targeting audiences for commercial gain, but could find a reasonable balance between its role as educator and informer for all Namibians and its needs for financially profitable ventures targeted at specific audiences.

Conclusion

> Freedom of conscience, of education, of speech, of assembly are among the very fundamentals of democracy and all of them would be nullified should freedom of the press ever be successfully challenged (F.D. Roosevelt, *Letter to W.N. Hardy*, September 18, 1940).

The Namibian constitution has guaranteed its people these freedoms, the basics of democratic ruling. The NBC has taken its responsibilities to heart, namely ensuring these rights through societal access to the public broadcaster. However, in a highly politicized society, such as Namibia, changes in people's perceptions are slow. Never exposed to an open democratic society, Namibians have a tendency to perceive their government as the ultimate rulers. This is not uncommon in Africa, but is in direct conflict with any democratic notions.

After the need for democracy, economies of scale are the second largest problem in African countries. Broadcasting is the most expensive form of media, and local productions on a large scale are virtually impossible on an ongoing basis in most countries. It is with this background that the Southern African Broadcasting Association (SABA) was formed in order to establish an exchange system of African produced programmes. During its second general assembly, in December 1994, the members of SABA accepted a resolution which states that the strength of public broadcasting lies in truly reflecting the interests and concerns of the citizens to whom it needs to be accessible and accountable. This sense of place and identity with its audience gives public broadcasting the edge over any existing or upcoming competitors, be they locally owned commercial enterprises or foreign/international satellite services. In the final analysis the most forceful supporter of public broadcasting will always be the public itself (SABA 1994).

The formation of SABA is also part of a southern African attempt to ensure that public broadcasters are independent of government interference, giving people the chance to communicate through a free media. This learning process also has to occur within the NBC in order to make its staff acutely aware of its responsibilities. However, changes like these do not come overnight and certainly not without opposition, as we saw concerning audience participation in the daily "National Chatshow." Training and education can be identified as the keywords for a successful transition in this regard. Despite its problems, the NBC is well on the way to providing the training needed. Having been taken out of its vacuum through the formation of SABA, the NBC's exchange of ideas and programmes with other broadcasters in the region should only strengthen its quest to become a true forerunner in public broadcasting in southern Africa.

Notes

1. The author would like to acknowledge, with thanks and appreciation, the kind assistance given by Katjia Berker, whose dedication, time, and help made this chapter possible.

2. The restructuring was carried out with the assistance of the Thomson Foundation.

References

Dyvi, Ellen Beate. 1993. *Radio and National Identity in Namibia*. Oslo: University of Oslo.

Gorelick, Nahum. 1992. *Sash* 35 (2): 29.

Gorelick, Nahum. 1993. The Role of the Electronic Media in Nation Building. Speech prepared for the Prime Minister's Consultative Meeting with the Media, November.

Maritz, J. D. G. 1991. Memorandum Of Opinion. *Namibian Broadcasting Act.*

Namibia Broadcasting Association. 1994. *Television and Radio Research in Namibia*. Windhoek: NBC.

Southern African Broadcasting Association (SABA). 1994. Record of Proceedings of the Second General Assembly.

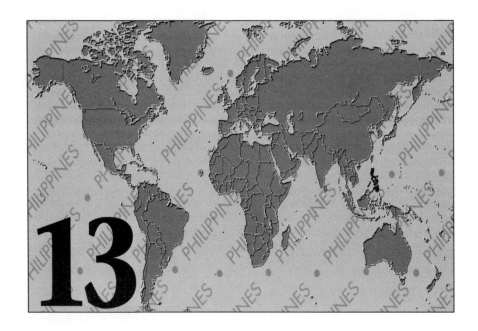

PHILIPPINES: TOWARD AN ALTERNATIVE BROADCASTING SYSTEM

Florangel Rosario-Braid (with Ramon R. Tuazon)

Introduction

*T*he emergence of East Asia as the world's newest and most dynamic centre of economic power has generated global interest and attention. Policy makers everywhere, including those in developed countries, are in search of lessons from the so-called East Asian Miracle. Most governments from these "tiger" economies argue that democracy is a Western concept alien to Asian culture. They also assert that economic development often conflicts with political development, and that the latter should, therefore, give way until growth is achieved.

The politico-economic system of a society provides the context essential to the search for alternatives in the communication sector. Useful units of analysis are, therefore, found in patterns of ownership, control, and public access, as well as in existing policies, whether explicit or implicit. These patterns are manifest in perceptions and decision making around how the media are utilized.

The Philippines presents a unique case study in the region. While it aims to duplicate the economic miracle of its neighbours, it has also chosen to remain faithful to its democratic tradition, which has just been restored. Within this vision, what role should mass media play? The Western press, to which the Philippine press has been moulded, is described as enjoying unbridled freedom, thriving on conflict, sensationalism, and excessive commercialism. On the other hand, its Asian neighbours envision a "free press that is committed to societal ideals" (Ibrahim 1994). Just as they are searching for an "Asian" model of democracy, political leaders in the region are now in search of an Asian model for the press.

In the Philippine context, the challenge is how to develop an alternative to the existing independent and free enterprise media system. A public broadcasting system (PBS) is one such alternative. This model may not, however, apply in the other Asian countries, where broadcasting is primarily government-owned and -controlled. The concept of a PBS is also perceived as technologically obsolete, since specialized programming, the main feature of public broadcasting, is now provided by the unlimited channels made possible by the communication technology revolution. In addition, as the Philippine case may prove, a PBS may find it hard to compete and survive in a "market" where commercial broadcasting has become entrenched.

Community-based broadcasting (CBS) is another option. CBS empowers local communities to plan and produce their own programmes using available channels, sometimes cooperatively owned or managed by members of the community. This model blends well with the "communitarian" values of most Asian societies.

Finally, the examination of current global trends provides the critical base for proactive planning. One such trend is the emergence of a global economy, with the approval of the Uruguay Round of the General Agreement on Tariffs and Trade (GATT). Since the agreement would lead to the "freer" flow of images and messages, concerns have been raised about the potential for cultural convergence, involving the homogenization of values and lifestyles, and cultural domination by those who control technology. In this regard, what socio-cultural safety nets can we suggest? What role can community broadcast stations play? Will this global communication order revive the need for a public broadcasting system?

A Historical Overview

Philippine broadcasting started in June 1922, when an American businessman in Manila opened three 50-watt radio stations, not for commercial broadcasting but as a demonstration channel for his electrical supply business. Two years later, the first commercial radio stations went on the air: station KZKZ, owned by the Radio Corporation of the Philippines, and KZRQ, owned by Far Eastern Radio, Inc. The provinces first experienced this medium in 1929, when station KCRC was set up in Cebu City. Subsequently, radio stations established during this period were primarily advertising channels set up by American businessmen.

Radio programming from the pre-war to the early post-war period was primarily entertainment-oriented and, as expected, "flavoured with colonial productions," including even canned American serials. News and public affairs, including government programmes, were unheard of until two years before the end of World War II.

In the 1950s, farm programming started over some radio stations. Its early years were difficult, since many station managers and advertisers were doubtful of the effectiveness of radio as a medium for information and education. The introduction of television in 1953 was accompanied by political intrigue, as the first television station was owned by the brother of the incumbent Philippine president, who was set to run for re-election the following year. This television station was later bought by one of the leading newspapers in the country, *The Manila Chronicle* which subsequently added a second station. By 1960, a third station was in operation, and, by 1966, there were 16 privately owned television stations around Manila. The first provincial television stations were established in 1968 in Cebu, Bacolod, and Dagupan.

Economic constraint during these early years of television forced a dependence on imported programmes from three U.S. networks – ABC, CBS, and NBC. It was cheaper to import programmes than to produce them locally. In addition, canned programmes appeared to be more popular among local audiences, even though initiatives were made in educational programming.

The earliest initiative to use local television for education was through a programme called "Education on TV," aired three times a week in 1961 and hosted by a Jesuit educator. In the same year, the National Science Development Board aired a college course, "Physics in the Atomic Age." The government television station was inaugurated for educational broadcasting, but it was disenfranchised a year later.

In 1963, the Metropolitan Educational Television Association (META), in coordination with the closed-circuit TV project of the Ateneo de Manila University, produced and aired over two stations 30-minute kinescopes (taped video presentations) on physics, Filipino, and social studies, which were used for classroom instruction in selected secondary schools in Manila and its environs. Other experiments include the following: the Distance Study System (1976) of the Department of Education, Culture, and Sports (DECS); "Lingap ng Pangulo sa Barangay" (1977), focusing on integrated rural development; "Tulong-Aral" (1982), launched by DECS using radio and television for teacher in-service training; and Philippine "Sesame Street" (1983), which evolved into the current popular children's programme, "Batibot."

A clear pattern evident in these experiments using broadcast media for education is that most of the projects were unable to go beyond the pilot stage, and most had a life span of three to five years. Evaluation was not emphasized, and, therefore, subsequent projects failed to learn from experiences of the past.

The commercial thrust of Philippine broadcasting has made it unique among other East Asian countries, where the electronic media are controlled and operated by the government. While this free enterprise environment made local broadcasting globally competitive, the same environment made it difficult to produce and broadcast public service and "development" oriented programmes. It engendered a "that's entertainment" mentality in both the advertisers and the general public.

The Broadcast Industry Today

Radio is now acknowledged as the primary source of news and the most pervasive, persuasive, and credible medium. It reaches 85 to 90 percent of the population with 25 million radio sets nationwide. Industry estimates suggest that the average listening time is two to three hours a day.

In 1994, there were 250 AM and 178 FM radio stations; 83 VHF, 6 UHF, and 25 cable television stations. About 92 percent of both radio and television stations are commercial. The non-commercial stations are owned by either the government or by educational and religious groups. The government radio stations are organized under the Philippine Broadcasting System, which operates 22 AM and FM stations nationwide. The Departments of National Defense (DND), Science and Technology (DOST), and state colleges and universities – all government agencies – also own and operate broadcast stations.

Satellite and cable technologies have made virtually universal access to broadcast media possible. For example, ABS-CBN Radio has an estimated coverage of 90 percent of the archipelago, while its television affiliate reaches approximately 88 percent. The network is linked with the Pan American Satellite (PANAMSAT), which provides its programmes to all cable operators and direct-to-home markets within the satellite's footprint. Through a cable television system, it can reach Filipino communities in the San Francisco Bay Area of the United States. Similarly, GMA Radio Television Arts Network reaches the entire country through its 30 stations nationwide. Filipinos in Southeast Asia, Hawaii, Guam, Saipan, Canada, and the United States can tune in to GMA-7, either through the Palapa B2P satellite or cable television systems.

Until recently, UHF television broadcasting was unheard of. Only those who could get access to the Far East Network of the U.S. Armed Forces Radio and Television Service, beamed to the U.S. bases in Clark Air Base and Subic Naval Base, were familiar with the bandwidth. Southern Broadcasting Network (SBN Channel 21) and Molave Broadcasting Network (Channel 23) were the first commercial stations to broadcast on the UHF band in mid-1992. SBN 21 features "global-oriented" programmes from World TV, a local VHF channel, while Channel 23 carries MTV programming as received via satellite from Hong Kong's Star TV. After the initial success of these stations, others followed: Byers Communication's Channel 68 became the first Pay-TV channel; Rajah Broadcasting TV 29 was the first home shopping channel; and

Radio Mindanao Network Channel 31 was the first all-movie channel. The two UHF stations are in Baguio City and Cebu City. More UHF stations are expected to go on the air as the economy continues to pick up.

The most phenomenal growth, however, has been in cable television. The growth of early cable television, introduced in 1969, was stunted during the Marcos regime, because of a decree granting exclusive franchise to a business ally of the former president to install and operate cable TV nationwide. This decree was abolished by President Aquino in 1987. The introduction of satellite programming by TV networks ABS-CBN and GMA Channel 7 in 1991 spurred interest in cable television. Provincial community antenna TV (CATV) systems have been set up to receive broadcast signals from stations originating in Manila. Metro Manila is now one of the most advanced urban centres in Asia with respect to cable TV, where two major cable systems, Skycable and Prime Cable, offer 40 channels or more.

The Philippines also plans to launch its satellite system by 1996. With support from several private telecommunication companies, it has applied to the International Telecommunications Union for four orbital slots.

Hollywood Programming and Related Concerns

The history of broadcasting in the Philippines closely follows related developments in the United States. Advertising is broadcasting's lifeblood, which makes stations dependent on ratings for survival. This commercial orientation of television is evident in its content, where over 50 percent of total programming consists of musical variety shows, soap operas, and situation comedies. There is a larger percentage of domestic over imported programmes, although the theme and format of most local productions are modelled on Western programmes.

Television programming is oriented toward urban interests, and most provincial stations function merely as replay or relay stations. A few produce their own local programmes, but this is constrained by prohibitive production costs. Even the strengthening of TV signals has not reduced the one-way traffic of images from the urban to the rural areas. The consequences, in terms of homogenization of urban values and lifestyles and the erosion of traditional values in the countryside, are bewailed by social critics who blame the media as one of the forces contributing to social violence.

The prevailing emphasis on trivia and entertainment takes away airtime that could be allocated to development issues. Equally serious is the little support given to the concerns of marginalized sectors – women, youth, cultural communities, rural and urban poor, peasants, and others. These sectors are given prime time treatment if they are subjects of sensational reports focusing on them as victims of violence and calamities. Otherwise, their voices on critical national and local issues are seldom heard.

The Self-Regulatory Framework

The broadcast industry operates under the principle of self-regulation. The *Kapisanan ng mga Brodkaster sa Pilipinas*, or KBP, organized in 1973, provides the framework for self-regulation through its radio and television codes. The Department of Transportation and Communication (DOTC) and the National Telecommunications Commission (NTC) of the government recognize the self-regulatory principle of the KBP "to police its members on matters relating to the enforcement of broadcast rules and regulations" (Escaner 1994).

Self-regulation involves a consultative process in which broadcasters partici-pate in drafting rules and regulations. Likewise, the formulation of govern-ment policies and programmes related to the broadcast industry involves continuing dialogue and consultation with the KBP. An accreditation programme, based on written examinations and performance evaluation given to radio personalities, has been instituted by KBP.

The KBP Television Code sets programme standards for news, public affairs and commentaries, political broadcasts, children's and religious program-ming, and television advertising. It also sets guidelines on the coverage of sex, obscenity, and violence. The code promotes social and economic enhance-ment for the people, and it encourages broadcast stations to promote nation-alism and to produce, schedule, and air, preferably during primetime, their own developmental messages. A similar code was adopted for radio station members. Both codes are regularly reviewed and updated.

The two codes of ethics that govern the advertising industry – the Philippine Association of National Advertisers (PANA) Code and the Advertising Board of the Philippines, Inc. (Adboard) Code – provide guidelines on presentation, comparison advertising, specific claims, slogans and terms, testimonials, scientific claims, suggestive brand names, and appropriate messages for children, among other issues. Appropriate guidelines are imposed for violation of the codes. However, the codes have failed to deter malpractice and corruption, due to lack of monitoring mechanisms. Public apathy, which may be due to ignorance, is a contributing factor. The public has not been adequately informed of the codes and procedures for complaints or for the redress of grievances.

Existing codes emphasize sanctions (don'ts) rather than encourage the devel-opment of an atmosphere conducive to the upgrading of media standards. The few incentives for quality programming include annual awards by organi-zations for exemplary performance.

Democratization, Deregulation, and Public Access

The government of Philippine President Fidel V. Ramos has demonstrated strong political will in pursuing the constitutional mandate to democratize mass media and telecommunication in ownership, control, and public access. Telecommunication has been liberalized through a series of presidential edicts, which resulted in the following: the breakup of the Philippine Long Distance Telephone Company's monopoly; compulsory inter-connection to the international gateway by telecommunication companies; and the provision or improvement of local exchange carriers. Telecommunication companies have more liberal entry into the market, and there is now fear that the market cannot afford competition among the new service providers. In addition, the National Telecommunications Commission's (NTC) executive order prohibiting cross-ownership in mass media is now enforced, thus leading to divestment of ownership of certain media enterprises.

In 1991, ABS-CBN pioneered in opening ownership to the public through the stock market. Several broadcast networks are now considering following this scheme, not only to "democratize" ownership and ensure public access, but also to provide the networks with a source of funds for expansion.

One divisive issue related to deregulation is the granting of franchises. The power to grant a franchise was vested in Congress by the 1987 Constitution. The same provision, however, does not inhibit Congress from delegating that power to a specialized body, such as the NTC. In fact, a bill providing for such has been filed in Congress, giving the following as reasons: (1) issuance of a franchise should be considered essentially an executive function; (2) a centralized issuance of franchises by a quasi-judicial body would ensure the issuance of a certificate of public convenience and necessity; (3) the provision would minimize if not eliminate the unauthorized sale of franchise to a third party; and (4) Congress could be relieved of some of its load.

The NTC is in a better position to renew franchises, because it monitors performance of the broadcast stations. One criterion for evaluation is the track record of the station in terms of balanced programming. As in the case of the U.S. Federal Communications Commission (FCC), stations should be made accountable for the quality and diversity of their programming.

A real threat posed by deregulation is that it may lead to excessive commercialism, due to stiff competition. Programming will be determined more by "what sells," with little regard to social responsibility and cultural sensitivity. The problem becomes even more complicated when one considers the current trend toward globalization of the world economy.

It is true that over-regulation can lead to curtailment of press freedom. On the other hand, unfettered deregulation can put the public at the mercy of broadcast networks. If there is one concept that could guide our policy framework, it is *balance*– through which participating structures would promote a "win-win" outcome. Business would earn reasonable profits, and the public, particularly the marginalized sectors, would be enabled to have adequate access to basic broadcasting and telecommunication services. A pluralist society, such as in the Philippines, requires a policy structure in telecommunications and broadcasting that would balance both self-regulation and deregulation as well as freedom and social responsibility.

In the recent past, several multisectoral policy fora have been convened to develop a comprehensive communication policy. Aside from representatives from government, mass media, and telecommunications, stakeholders from non-government organizations (NGOs), such as peasants', labour, women's, religious, and business groups, also participated. The series of fora resulted in a consensus on what values are necessary in defining a policy framework: common good, democratization, access and participation, cultural diversity, and national identity and integration.

Still, Congress, which is mandated by the Constitution to evolve a comprehensive communication policy, has not come up with such. Several reasons have been cited. One dilemma raised by legislators is that, with a comprehensive bill, Congress would run the risk of too many discussions: how comprehensive and how much detail? Others argue that communication is too vast and that each sector or industry should have its own legislation.

An Alternative Broadcasting System?

Immediately after the 1986 People Power Revolution, one of the intended areas for structural change in the government was the freeing of the television network, Maharlika Broadcasting System, from what was, at that time, complete government control, by converting it into a public broadcasting system. The continual inability of the media system to present a plurality of views on global, national, and local issues, as well as access to the marginalized sectors, was the popular argument used to rationalize the existing media structure.

In spite of the expansion of media freedom as an aftermath of the People Power Revolution, media still continue to reflect the views of the elite and vested interest groups. The maintenance of the status quo can be attributed to the fact that the revolution resulted merely in cosmetic political change and did not bring a more radical structural reform. The capital-intensive nature of media is another reason for the continuing control of media by the business elite. The dominant business ideology – free enterprise – has been reflected in conservative programme philosophy and content.

On the other hand, the agendas of almost every NGO have continually expressed key concerns: the need for an impartial channel for information on development issues, which supports the public's right to pluralistic information; and the need for a regular outlet for development programmes to educate people in livelihood, health and nutrition, science and technology, and culture and responsible citizenship.

The urgency to set up an alternative broadcasting system can also be underscored by a glimpse at the impact of television on our value system. As former U.S. State Secretary Zbigniew Brzezinski noted, "there is nothing comparable, either in the era of enforced religious orthodoxy or even at the high point of totalitarian indoctrination, to the cultural and philosophical conditioning that television exercises on the viewers" (Brzezinski 1993: 70). Of major concern are the values that Western programmes propagate even to developing countries, which are often on the receiving end. According to Brzezinski, these programmes "extol self gratification, normalize intense violence and brutality, encourage promiscuity ... and pander to the worst public instincts."

Even our national vision of a newly industrializing country, or "Philippines 2000," will be affected by how much functional information the mass media can provide which will enable people to be productive, quality conscious, and globally competitive. Paul Kennedy, in *Preparation for the Twenty-First Century* identified access to information as one of the major preconditions for survival in the new millenium.

A PBS could be a channel for the production and dissemination of creative and high quality programmes, which existing broadcast networks have failed to produce due to the ratings game. This programming thrust would complement the traditional programme orientation of commercial stations. A PBS is also perceived by many as the necessary structure to rectify the one-way flow of programming. It could also provide the mechanism that would encourage provincial stations to produce programmes relevant to the cultural and economic realities of their communities. A PBS can also provide NGOs with technical assistance for production of their specific advocacy programmes.

Commercial broadcast stations welcome the entry of public broadcasting, as they perceive the existing government network as a competitor for a piece of the limited advertising pie. What is needed, according to the KBP, is a network which provides complementary programming.

The 1987 Philippine Constitution has provided for a policy environment conducive to setting up a PBS. The Constitution provides that the State "recognizes the vital role of communication and information in nation building" (Article II. sec. 24), and the "emergence of communication structures suitable to the needs and aspirations of the nation and the balanced flow of information into, out of and across the country" (Article XVI. sec.10). These provisions were integrated into the fundamental law of the land to correct the urban bias of media, concentration of media resources in the centre, and the one-way flow of information from the urban to the rural areas.

The Contours of the Proposed Public Broadcasting System

When the Philippine Congress reconvened in 1988, a number of bills were filed in both houses of Congress proposing the creation of a PBS. Some of the features of the bills included the following: PBS was proposed either as an attached agency to the office of the president or as a public corporation, but its independence and autonomy was to be assured. Its board of directors would have a pluralistic composition whose members would be appointed by the president according to equal representation from government, academic, labour, and viewer/consumer sectors. The directors would come from among the nominees of the organizations or sectors they represented.

The proposed PBS affirmed the principle that communication and information are a national resource to be harnessed for nation building and the common good. Senate Bill 1193, for example, drew up practical guidelines by which the state might carry out its responsibility to provide the favourable communication environment for wider public participation and access, relevant and balanced programming, and harmonious accommodation of the nation's socio-culturally diverse population.

As the composition of the PBS governing board would be democratized, so would the programming be designed in accordance with the system's educational and public service bias. A normal day's broadcast would be devoted to non-formal education, cultural presentations, news and public affairs, as well as special programs on farming, livelihood, women, children, and youth. An essential role of PBS is to inform the public of government initiatives in promoting the public welfare; thus, substantial coverage of the executive and legislative branches of government would be a regular feature of the programming.

To balance the private networks' heavy use of Western cultural products, a majority of the PBS programs would be locally produced, and a majority of the songs played over the air should be original Filipino music. Heavy dependence on advertising was to be avoided if the PBS was to be anything different from the private networks. Commercial content would be limited to no more than 11 minutes per hour, though slight variations below that maximum limit would be allowed between foreign-produced and locally produced programs and between Metro Manila and provincial stations.

PBS would be funded largely from the regular government budgetary allocation and partly through priority rights to broadcast production services for public corporations and government agencies. These public agencies would appropriate at most 2 percent of their total budgets for such a purpose. In addition, PBS would be allowed to accept paid announcements, advertising, and blocktime arrangements (in which independent producers buy airtime on specific time slots). It could also accept donations and gifts for the improvement of the technical quality of broadcast programs. Additional revenues would come from tax on all television and radio sets sold in the Philippines. At the same time, PBS would provide incentives to local broadcasting companies or firms that show over-all artistic excellence and project true Filipino values by giving them grants which would be taken from 10 percent of the total PBS budget.

An Issue of Timing and Political Will

Despite initial legislative support for a PBS, the bills seeking its creation did not get congressional approval. Instead, People's Television 4 (PTV 4) was converted into a full government corporation, now known as People's Television Network, Inc. (PTNI). Several reasons have been cited for the legislative decision in favour of a government corporation over a PBS. First was the need for a strong government communication and information machinery, which was recognized after a series of coup attempts against the Aquino government. A television network would undoubtedly enhance the capability of the government not only to communicate to the public and gain its support but also to counter the anti-government propaganda being initiated by groups representing diverse ideological and political stances. As the Republic Act 7306 notes, supporters of this move contend, "if a government has such functional arms as administration, production, marketing and finance, there should be also a communication arm."

Some PBS advocates, however, believe that the real reason for failure of the bills is the lack of political will to create the PBS. There is reluctance among politicians to let go of the network, knowing fully well its power as a propaganda machinery. This attitude is reflected in the long-delayed privatization of sequestered broadcast networks – Radio Philippines Network and Banahaw Broadcasting Corporation – nine years after their sequestration by the government (for being part of the so-called ill-gotten wealth of the Marcoses or their cronies).

Another reason is the fear that a PBS may not be financially viable in the long run. It will be noted that many of the public broadcasting systems in other countries had to depend on funding agencies, subscriptions, and institutional advertising. These funding strategies may not be sustainable in most developing societies.

Finally, sustained public lobbying appears to be lacking, as the concept of a PBS is relatively vague to traditional lobbyists of NGOs. The issues involved in the need for a PBS are not clear; only a small percentage of professional communicators and academicians have displayed sustained interest in pursuing the plan to establish a PBS.

The People's Television Network, Inc.

Republic Act 7306, otherwise known as the charter creating People's Television Network, Inc., was signed by then President Corazon C. Aquino on 26 March 1992. The PTNI has the following functions:

(1) to serve as an effective medium for national unity and political stability by reaching as much of the Filipino population as possible through the effective use of modern broadcasting technology;

(2) to serve as a vehicle for bringing the Government closer to the people in order to enhance their awareness of the programmes, policies, thrusts, and directions of the government;

(3) to ensure that the programmes broadcast by the network maintain a high general standard in all respects and, particularly, in respect to their content, quality, and proper balance of educational, news, public affairs, entertainment, and sports programmes; and

(4) to serve as an effective outlet for alternative programming.

In accordance with its role as an "alternative" to commercial stations, PTNI puts emphasis on education, cultural, news/public affairs, and sports programmes. In 1993, these programmes took up two-thirds of 88 total broadcast hours per week, while news and public affairs took up one-fourth of total broadcast time. To generate advertising revenue, entertainment programmes occupy the primetime evening slots.

As the primary agency for broadcast information on government programmes, PTNI in Metro Manila provided continuing coverage of the Senate and the House of Representatives, as well as the line agencies and the judiciary. Continuing news and information support was provided to the five priority programmes of government and "Philippines 2000," the President's vision for development. These priority areas are economic recovery, attainment of national stability, energy/power development, environmental protection, and streamlining of the bureaucracy.

As a future direction for news and public affairs, PTNI is considering a 24-hour news operation, the establishment of specialized news desks, augmented assignments to major beats, and the inclusion of an Association of Southeast Asian Nations (ASEAN) news segment in the regular newscast. Linkages with major regional and international news agencies and foreign television organizations will be strengthened.

As for educational broadcasts, a pre-school children's programme and youth programme are on the drawing boards. In addition, a distance education project for elementary and high-school teachers will be launched in cooperation with the Department of Education, the U.P. Institute for Science and Math Education Development, the Philippine Normal University, and the Department of Science and Technology.

In the spirit of earlier legislative proposals, the governing board was democratized, with three members coming from the private sector and two from government. PTNI was provided equity funding, but no funding from the General Appropriations Act for operations. This restriction has hampered the network's ability to produce quality programmes.

To improve the technical quality of its programmes and widen its reach, PTNI upgraded its network facilities, set up new provincial stations, and increased the power of existing stations. State-of-the-art digital equipment was installed to provide improved presentation and immediate live coverage of news-breaking events. Twelve new provincial stations were added to the original eight stations. In the major urban centres of Cebu in the Visayas, and Zamboanga and Davao in Mindanao, the power of the stations was increased from 100 watts to 10 kilowatts. Most of the newly opened stations will operate on one kilowatt. These developments have considerably improved PTNI's potential and ability to promote community-based broadcasting. PTNI is embarking on a gradual upgrading plan for news coverage and production facilities for the provincial stations. The upgrading will improve the capability for news gathering and transmission, programme production, and development of materials that will meet the needs of provincial audiences as well as provide avenues for discussions on issues directly affecting the locality.

The next challenge is to develop the network's human resources and acquire regular funding for operations, so that the provincial stations may not be limited only to serving as relay for broadcasts originating from Manila, but may develop their own quality programmes to answer the needs of local audiences.

Government But Not Public

Since PTNI is a government corporation, the public, especially the marginalized sectors, is not ensured of sustained access and participation in programme planning and production as envisioned in the PBS concept. In addition, autonomy from political and other pressure groups has not been ensured. The television network is, of course, expected to present government viewpoints on global, national, and local issues. A question often asked is: Can NGOs and other sectors of society also use the channel to air views divergent from those of the government? While the Board of Directors has been "broadened," it has not been diversified enough to include multisectoral representation, especially from the non-elite sectors – cultural communities, grassroots organizations, consumers, labour, peasantry, and others.

One of the greatest stumbling blocks in the creation (and operation) of a PBS is the establishment of regular funding sources. Dependence on one source makes the network vulnerable to infringement on its editorial independence. PTNI is a unique case, because while its charter recognizes it as part of the government information system, it merely provides for equity funding and stipulates that no funds from the General Appropriations Act (annual national budget) will be provided for its operations. Government appropriations are only for building infrastructures. PTNI has to raise its own resources through advertisements, blocktimers, and other sources. In this sense, PTNI is still "commercial." The lack of financial resources has affected PTNI's effort to provide real alternative programming. To ensure adequate revenue, it has entered into a contract with a commercial enterprise in connection with regular coverage of the professional Philippine Basketball Association (PBA) games. This agreement has provided the network's primary source of income for some time. As a result, PTNI's public image is as a sports television station. About 38 percent of its total programming hours is devoted to sports, which is dominated by live coverage of the PBA games.

The network's educational and cultural programmes (which comprised about 24 percent of total broadcasting hours in 1993) are produced mostly by the network, with little or no linkage with appropriate sectors that could provide support, particularly in terms of content. For example, cultural programmes, which represented only 6.4 percent of total broadcast hours in 1993, can be further enriched by co-producing with such agencies as the National Commission on Culture and Arts (NCCA), the Cultural Centre of the Philippines, and the Department of Tourism. The use of the network for formal and non-formal education through open learning or distance education is still on the drawing board. Other topics that need specific attention are science and technology, the environment, health and nutrition, women and gender issues, children (especially early childhood), entrepreneurship and livelihood, functional literacy, and ethnic issues.

According to its mission statement, PTNI shall embark on niche (specialized) programming. It will define its target audiences more pointedly and programme for them accordingly. There will be "more attention given to the viewing needs of the public as well as greater sensitivity and responsiveness to issues and concerns that affect them" (PTNI 1993: 4).

Commercial Television and Developmental Programming

While broadcast codes state that stations should include public affairs and other developmental formats, current programming focuses primarily on "hard" stories, highlighting power plays, competition, and violence. Over the past few years, the broadcast industry has displayed sensitivity to growing public criticism for its lopsided programming, and there has been a discernible increase in public affairs programming (other than news programmes), which has recently gained public following.

These programmes in various formats – straight talk shows, news magazines, documentaries – are, however, packaged for limited viewership, because they use the English language. In general, Filipino, the national language, is used in entertainment programmes, giving rise to perceptions that Filipino cannot be a language for intellectual discourse.

Public service programmes are still quite popular. Some video and television programmes show the needy being given medical and other forms of social assistance. Opportunities for the public to seek redress for grievances through television is now available, although still on a limited basis. These programmes are now among the popular programmes aired during evening primetime.

Instructional programmes, such as ABS-CBN's Sine Skwela, a 30-minute daily programme on science for elementary pupils, are now helping to improve instruction in science and technology. Soon to go on the air is the Continuing Education Program for Science Teachers Via Television (Constel), which will broadcast three telecourses for teachers – elementary science, chemistry, and physics. Constel is an inter-agency project of the DECS, University of the Philippines Institute of Science and Mathematics Education Development, the Department of Science and Technology Philippine Normal University, and PTNI.

For pre-school children, the internationally award-winning "Batibot" has been on the air for over a decade. Like other developmental programmes, "Batibot" suffers from lack of advertising support.

Educational broadcasting obtained a needed boost with the launching of Educational Television Channel 36. In addition, since 1990, the Asian Institute of Journalism and Communication (AIJC) and the UNESCO National Commission of the Philippines have conducted annual workshops on the National Distance Learning Program (NDLP), which involve networking 15 universities – private and state-owned – and NGOs involved in distance education for neo-literate women and out-of-school youth.

However, specialized programmes for specific interest groups, such as women, cultural or ethnic groups, or consumers, have not gone beyond tokenism. Although there are 120 ethnic groups in the country, little is known about their culture. Media have been remiss in providing adequate coverage of issues affecting cultural communities. The limited coverage emphasizes primarily conflict situations, while the more visible groups are projected in stereotyped images.

Ecology and related stories get sufficient coverage only because the worldwide environmental movement is felt here and because of the sustained advocacy of local environmental groups. Other less controversial issues, like children's rights, human rights, consumerism, and health and nutrition, get fleeting attention from the media.

The series of natural and man-made disasters over the past decade has underscored the importance of disaster communication. An Emergency Broadcasting System, activated by the NTC, the KBP, and private telecommunications companies, has established a disaster preparedness and management system. Public Calling Offices (PCOs) have been installed in central Luzon towns frequently affected by mudflow from Mt. Pinatubo Volcano.

Television networks have exerted considerable effort to diversify and provide balanced and creative programming. This effort is attributed to factors such as an increasing sense of social responsibility among network owners; KBP's effort to improve professionalism and standards in broadcasting; sensitivity to public advocacy for improved programming; and competition not only among television networks or stations but also with emerging cable television stations.

Public Broadcasting in the Information Age: A Question of Relevance

Is the concept of public broadcasting still relevant in this age of information super-highways and multimedia? This question has been raised in the light of the experiences of public broadcasting in Europe and the United States over the past five years. A special report on television in *The Economist* (12 February 1994) noted that the cable boom and satellite televiewing has already reduced considerably both the audiences and revenues (from advertisements) of public channels such as Italy's RAI, Spain's RTVE, Germany's ARD and ZDF, and the United Kingdom's BBC. Historically, public broadcasting and state television were justified by "spectrum scarcity." The airwaves were limited and precious resources required state stewardship to ensure that the common good was served. The limited frequencies could not be given to just any institution that would utilize them only to perpetuate commercialism. An alternative broadcast system, either government- or public-owned, was therefore deemed necessary.

However, satellites, cable, fibre optics, digitization, and compression of signals have made the argument of "spectrum scarcity" obsolete. The new information super-highway has made channel explosion a reality. The prospect of 500 television channels is no longer far-fetched. With channel explosion comes niche programming, which means that programming is becoming more specialized as viewing markets are segmented according to such categories as interest, ethnic background, political affiliation, and religion. In particular, cable television has introduced specialty channels featuring news, music, sports, public affairs, environment issues, and education.

The use of television and radio as alternative delivery channels for social development in areas of education, health care, nutrition, and livelihood, will become more widespread. Some channels may even focus on delivering one theme, as in the case of educational television. Televiewing will be further revolutionized by the integration of computer processes. It will become interactive, allowing viewers to watch what they want when they want. It will provide options that even the public broadcasting system was unable to provide: viewer control, unlimited choices, and participation in production.

Commercial television networks are severely affected by satellite and cable television. Noting that the top three U.S. network's audience share fell from 90 to 62 percent from 1970 to 1993, *The Economist* contended that "broadcast networks (perhaps public broadcast systems included) are a creature of a time when TV was a medium of scarcity, oligopoly and mass consumption. Today, TV is a medium of abundance, competition and personalization."

Satellite televiewing has been shown to affect the relevance of public broadcasting. With about 300 satellite television stations worldwide, and 70 satellites to be launched between now and 1997, satellite televiewing is expected to explode. Satellite television has further opened programming access and choices in the global arena. To illustrate, CNN and BBC's World Service Television are involved in aggressive expansion and marketing campaigns to have "total global coverage."

With the Philippines in the mainstream of the technological revolution, developments are expected to become more advanced, especially in the light of adoption by government of more liberal policies in telecommunications, trade, and investment.

The Emergence of the Global Market

The ratification and subsequent implementation of the Uruguay Round of GATT will have considerable impact on global and national broadcasting, particularly with respect to the Trade Related Aspects of Intellectual Property Rights (TRIPS) and to the General Agreement on Trade in Services (GATS). On the positive side, the agreement will provide tougher rules to protect, among others, the following: copyrights, trademarks, and patent (20 years for broadcast signals); market access, by lifting entry restrictions on service providers; and universal coverage of services. Already, critics warn of homogenization of tastes, wants, needs, and lifestyles as trade becomes more liberalized. Since it is the broadcast companies in the developed world which own and control media production and distribution, both images and messages will naturally reflect their economic interests and cultural biases.

As early as 1980, the UNESCO-sponsored MacBride Commission Report noted negative effects of the media explosion. According to the report, "the rapid increase in the volume of information and entertainment has brought about homogenization of different societies ... and people become more cut off from the society in which they live." At the extreme, the report added, "modern media have trampled on traditions and distorted centuries-old socioeconomic patterns" (MacBride 1980: 160).

The MacBride Report's warning was recently re-echoed in an early draft of the World Report on Culture and Development (February 1994), prepared by the World Commission on Culture and Development (WCCD) chaired by former UN secretary general Javier Perez De Cuellar. The draft report noted that "individual identity is increasingly being determined by worldwide fads and fashions and transient material possessions of great diversity rather than cultural heritage." The report added that "products are designed for the world market, with cultural differences largely dealt with through marketing."

An alternative (public) broadcasting system (ABS) can be seen as a socio-cultural safety net for the threats of cultural domination due to the unrestricted flow of images from the technological superpowers. ABS programming could put greater thrust on cultural programmes, which would enhance national identity and cultural integrity. An ABS could also provide a mechanism to balance global and local programming. While a global perspective is now necessary with the emerging global economy, community interests should also be projected. The GATT Agreement would force national broadcast networks and related industries (e.g., the music industry) to be more globally competitive and, at the same time, increase their volume of production, without sacrificing quality, to be able to survive in the global economy.

Finally, sectors of society that may be adversely affected by the GATT Agreement could expect information support from an ABS. For example, farmers, to be able to compete globally, should have access to (global) information on new innovations and technology, credit, market prices, and post-harvest facilities. This information, however, is not readily available in the current (commercial) media fare. Thus, an alternative media could serve as the information conduit for farmers and other affected sectors.

Options for Alternative Public Broadcasting

Both the opportunities and challenges brought about by the technological revolution and the global economy force us to re-examine our broadcast policies and priorities. Should we pursue our goal of setting up a PBS? If yes, what role should such a system play, given the impact of ongoing technological revolution? What structure should it adopt?

The concept behind PTNI, which is really a quasi-public service station, is to provide support to development programmes and projects. For example, the Philippines Medium-Term Development Plan must be communicated in order for it to gain continuing public support. Thus, despite government control, PTNI could still provide these public service functions. Its limitation, however, would be felt by active NGOs committed to priority development concerns such as overseas workers, street children, women, environment, foreign debt, and sovereignty issues. Often, NGO perspectives on these issues differ from the official position. Their search for a voice in policy decisions and the government's support for pluralism and cultural diversity may be factors that could lead to stronger support for alternative media, whether community-based or a national PBS.

Given that the state chose to establish a government channel as an alternative to commercial broadcasting, community-based broadcasting (CBS) seems to be the viable alternative. Its major limitation is its inadequate reach and, consequently, its limited impact at the national level. A PBS similar to the BBC or Germany's *Deutsche Welle* and the two channels, ARD and ZDF, may not be realizable in the immediate future for the reasons mentioned. Even in Germany, public broadcasting is undergoing a crisis due to competition from private companies. One way to guarantee its continued existence is legislation, which would increase subscriber fees and the market share. In the Philippines, a strong political will and a more robust economy in the future, which would improve purchasing power, including willingness to pay subscriber fees, may revive the vision of a PBS. The popularity of cable television, the recognition of the importance of distance education via broadcasting, and the growing information requirements of a country entering the global economy are reasons to justify the need for a PBS. In the meantime, creative energies may be channelled toward the strengthening of existing community broadcast stations, many of which support grassroots development initiatives, as well as educational broadcast stations which cater to the requirements of distance education.

One example of a CBS is radio DZJO in Infanta, Quezon, a marginalized community. Owned and operated by the Catholic Church, the station works in partnership with the local government and non-government organizations to create a true model of a people's radio station. DZJO engages the community in participating and planning the content and format of its programming to make it relevant to its listeners. In addition to the fact that its board of directors includes representatives from the church, community leaders, cooperatives and other sectoral organizations, and the broadcast station, the station has also provided mechanisms that enable the people of the community to actively participate. For example, a broadcaster visits the community regularly to generate the topics and themes for the programme, and the station acts as a broker between the community and local government and non-government leaders in discussion of community issues and subsequent problem-solving.

A similar innovation in community-based media is the Radyo Tacunan in Davao City, which consists of improvised radio facilities and is run by farmers for farmers. The equipment is rudimentary, but the programming is imaginative. Using a simple karaoke system – two microphones and an amplifier with a 500-watt power capacity – twenty-seven farmer broadcasters take daily turns at the announcer's booth at the end of the working day to pass on information about cooperatives, farm inputs, and health services to their listeners. The radio also serves as a forum for discussion of community issues. Similar set-ups are operating in communities in Zamboanga City, Isabela, Laguna, and Iloilo.

UNESCO, in cooperation with the Danish International Development Agency (DANIDA), implements the project Tambuli, designed to serve local small communities. Its main channel is a low-powered (solar powered) FM station. The long-term objective of the project is to integrate about 12 isolated communities into the mainstream of national development through community media.

Community-based programming can also be organized around communities of interest groups – workers, farmers, women, professionals, or ethnic groups, among others. In the Philippines, a labour radio station, DYLA, based in Cebu City, pioneered such an undertaking. The station was supported by a labour union and, thus, ensured a voice for the workers in the preparation of a national agenda for and discussion of critical issues. NGOs and people's organizations must be provided with access to technical assistance which would enhance their media production capabilities. Community broadcasting is able to combine the salient features of a PBS plus more. The big city mentality of centralized media has contributed to "Manila-centric" programming, which focuses on viewpoints of urbanized and elite groups. A decentralized, more autonomous broadcasting system can tackle alternative issues such as education, health care, social justice, and the peace process. Community-based stations need not operate from a parochial point of view. New technologies now allow "small" media to be linked with each other and to national media. The flow of images and messages should be two-way and should facilitate the integration of local issues with those on the national and global agenda.

One of the advantages of the current communication technology revolution is the declining cost of setting up media establishments (as in the case of the low-powered radio stations and desktop community newspapers). This development has encouraged individuals and groups to form and operate media cooperatives. A "demassified" media can better address the needs of its members and, at the same time, promote democratization of media ownership. This option will require strengthening of the capability of various sectors in media planning and production.

Another option is to link a PBS with academic institutions. More and more institutions, including those in developing countries, are now establishing open learning and distance education through multimedia. Many universities have set up their own educational television stations (using a cable channel). Broadcast hours could be enriched and diversified further if other educational programmes are integrated. A "partial" PBS, based on a university campus, could benefit from a multidisciplinary approach to programming and could maximize use of available academic research. In addition, communication programmes would be assured a "laboratory," and the students would be provided exposure to more socially oriented programming.

The concept of a regional Multimedia Resource Centre (MRC) as an alternative to a PBS must be examined. The proposed centres would be created in regional centres, and their mandate would include production of prototype developmental programmes using various formats; technical assistance to local government agencies, non-government organizations, and civic clubs in the production of their multimedia materials; and training in media planning and production.

Alternative broadcasting need not be limited to a PBS. Political developments (such as deregulation) and the technology revolution (particularly the channel explosion and satellite television) have made an alternative possible. Alternative media, being more independent and non-partisan, are more effective channels for articulating people's views. In line with the global trend of decentralization, community-based broadcasting appears to be the most viable and attractive option in the Philippines.

Summary and Conclusions

Historically, Philippine mass media are commercial and entertainment-oriented. Early experiments in alternative programming, in the late 1950s for radio and early 1960s for television, have not succeeded in introducing distinct changes in programming. Even the government-owned broadcast stations had to conform to popular appeals through commercial packaging, in order to attract audiences. Because of this, mass media, particularly broadcasting, are perceived as entertainment channels for the 64 million Filipinos. Media have always been given a significant place in the political landscape of the country, due to close linkages among media owners, the business elite, and political leaders. Thus, media play a critical role in defining the nation's political agenda. Their "halo effect" is demonstrated by their having successfully created political and public celebrities from media practitioners. Related to this is media's ability to magnify issues and personalities. Obscure individuals have been made national celebrities "overnight," through constant media exposure. Conversely, popular personalities have been unmade by adverse media publicity. This power of media has made it a very potent political tool. Political leaders have found it difficult to insulate government-owned media from partisan politics. While the concept of a PBS, in the traditional sense, may be popular, it is not politically feasible. The Philippine media system is regarded as "one of the freest in the world," when highlighted by the fact that media in most Asian countries are used to supporting existing political regimes. But the autonomy and independence of major Philippine media have become a double-edged sword. Media are being criticized for being rambunctious, floundering in sensationalism, acrimony, and mudslinging. Their dependence on advertising has developed a consumer society predisposed to Western tastes and standards.

Meanwhile, technological developments and global economic trends (such as the emergence of a global economy after the adoption of GATT) have hastened the advent of the global village. Satellite and cable systems are transforming people into global televiewers whose choices of channels and programmes are virtually unlimited. Technology has empowered the media user, as he now controls programming (through specialized channels), schedules, and costs. Amidst the technological revolution, however, lies the real threat of cultural domination by those who control technology. The interactive and two-way features of modern technology should be harnessed to the fullest by national governments, to ensure cultural harmony, integrity, and identity. An alternative broadcasting system is envisioned as a socio-cultural safety net for sectors of society likely to be adversely affected by the enforcement of GATT and other international agreements that promote open and free trade.

Ethnic conflict has replaced ideological conflict, which is currently being played out in all parts of the world, from Eastern Europe to South Asia and Africa. Again, media can play a vital role not only as a watchdog against human rights abuses but, more important, by providing a venue for cultural understanding and social integration and by promoting a culture of peace.

An alternative broadcasting system may yet emerge, not merely as a complement to existing commercial or government-owned stations but, more important, as a natural consequence of the global trends discussed earlier. For example, cable television has ensured niche programming, while desktop publishing has encouraged community ownership and control of media.

The concept of a public broadcasting system is now being redefined. From the traditional BBC-type structure, it may also include demassified or community-based media systems which empower local people to plan, manage, and produce their own programmes that reflect their needs and visions. A favourable trend is the growth of the NGO sector, which hopefully will contribute to a strong civil society. With the modest contribution offered by community broadcasting as a catalyst for development initiatives, there may still come a time when a national PBS will be perceived as feasible.

In the meantime, government's role is essential in mediating their entry into a global economy, by ensuring that existing communication technology is utilized to inform, educate, and mobilize society toward a smooth transition into the future.

References

Asian Institute of Journalism (AIJ) 1985. *Needs and Resources for Development Broadcasting: The State of Internship Programs in the Philippines*. Sta. Mesa, Manila: AIJ.

Asian Institute of Journalism (AIJ). 1991. *Follow-on Study on Philippine Media Needs Assessment*. Sta. Mesa, Manila: AIJ.

Braid, Florangel Rosario, ed. 1981. *Urban Community Media in the Philippines*. Sta. Mesa, Manila: AIJ.

Braid, Florangel Rosario, ed. 1991. *Communication and Society: The Philippine Context*. Metro Manila: Cacho Publishing House.

Braid, Florangel Rosario, ed. 1991. *Public Access: Multisectoral Consultations on Communication Issues*(Towards a National Communication Policy Framework). Sta. Mesa, Manila : AIJ.

Braid, Florangel Rosario, ed. 1994. *Telecommunications in the Philippines: Some Policy Challenges* (Policy Review). Philippines: Senate Policy Studies Group.

Brzezinski, Zbignew. 1993. *Out of Control : Global Turmoil on the Eve of the Twenty-First Century*. New York : Collier Books Macmillan.

Congress of the Philippines. 1988. *Republic Act No. 7306*. 5th. reg.sess.

The Economist. 1994. Television Survey, 12 February.

Escaner, Jose, Jr. 1994. *The Future of the Philippine Broadcasting Industry*. Manila: Kapisanan ng mga Brodkaster sa Pilipinas.

Ibrahim, A. 1994. *Towards a New Journalism Model*. Paper presented at the Forum on Press, Politics and Development, convened by the Center for Media Freedom and Responsibility.

Kapisanan ng mga Brodkaster sa Pilipinas. 1993. *The 1993 KBP Media Factbook*. Makati, Metro Manila: Kapisanan ng mga Brodkaster sa Pilipinas.

Kapisanan ng mga Brodkaster sa Pilipinas. 1989. *Radio Code of the Kapisanan ng mga Brodkaster sa Pilipinas*. Rev. ed.

Kapisanan ng mga Brodkaster sa Pilipinas. 1990. *Television Code of the Kapisanan ng mga Brodkaster sa Pilipinas*. Rev. ed.

Kennedy, Paul. 1993. *Preparing for the Twenty-First Century*. New York : Vintage Books.

MacBride, Sean. 1980. *Many Voices, One World*. London: UNESCO.

Maslog, Crispin C. 1990. *Philippine Mass Communication: A Mini History*. Quezon City: New Day Publishing.

People's Television Network. 1986. *Brief: People's Television Network* (PTV4). Philippines: [s.n.].

People's Television Network. 1993. *The People's Television Network, Inc.: 1993 Annual Report*. Quezon City: PTV 4 (The Flag Station).

Naisbitt, John. 1994. *Global Paradox : The Bigger the World Economy, The More Powerful Its Smallest Players*. New York : William Morrow and Co.

San Suu Kyi, Aung. 1994. Empowerment for a Culture of Peace and Development. Paper delivered during the Regional Consultation for Asia and the Pacific of the World Commission on Culture and Development, Manila, Philippines.

Senate of the Philippines. 1988. *Senate Bill No. 906*. 2d. reg. sess.

UNESCO. 1994. *Draft Preliminary Outline of the World Report on Culture and Development*. San José, Costa Rica : UNESCO.

EQUATORIAL AFRICA: BROADCASTING AND DEVELOPMENT

Charles Okigbo

Introduction

O riginally seen as an instrument for promoting central government interests throughout the region, broadcasting in equatorial Africa has assumed new roles following changes in the political structures and policies of individual countries. The equatorial region of Africa contains countries that are so diverse that the only common denominator might appear to be their colonial experience. But even this colonial history varied from one country to another, as a result of the 1844 Berlin conference at which European powers carved up their spheres of influence. In West Africa, the French claimed Senegal, Côte d'Ivoire, Benin, Togo, Mali, Guinea, Burkina Faso, and Niger, while the British took Nigeria, Ghana, Sierra Leone, and Gambia. Cameroon had the unique experience of having been controlled by two colonial powers (Germany and France), while Liberia, the resettlement for ex-slaves, was never actually colonized. In other sub-regions of equatorial Africa, the colonial period brought about such significant changes that the marks appear to be indelible. To a large extent, some of the prevailing problems of political and social development in the sub-regions can be attributed to the arbitrariness that characterized many colonial policies.

An illustrative case is the common demarcation of national boundaries. The colonialists showed little respect for the natural collectivities that ought to constitute individual countries. The arbitrary grouping of peoples to constitute nations, without any serious or sustained effort to promote national unity, has led to some of the political crises in the region. Not surprisingly, some countries have been trying to form unions between two or among more neighbours, with varying results. Senegambia (the union of Senegal and Gambia) was not as successful as Tanganyika (the unification of Tanzania and Zanzibar). It is doubtful whether the three East African countries of Kenya, Tanzania, and Uganda will ever coalesce into one country as some East African leaders have hoped.

Equatorial Africa was pilloried by slave trade, ravaged by colonial exploitation, and, in more recent times, plagued by waves of military *coups d'état*. These drastic experiences have contributed immensely to the persistent underdevelopment of the region. The low level of development in the region is experienced even in the communication sector. Though every African country now has some kind of news media system, the continent is still the least endowed with both print and broadcast media. According to Hachten (1973: 7) "nowhere in the world are the barriers to the development of news media more formidable than in Africa as a whole."

Fortunately, these barriers are not insurmountable, and so all across the continent, especially the equatorial region, individual countries have been engaged in serious attempts to bring about vigorous development in communication. The developments in broadcasting are some of the most enduring. Broadcasting has a mission in the Third World, including equatorial Africa. This mission has been given different interpretations from one country or period to another. One thing that is clear from the various interpretations is the expectation that broadcasting should play a key role in promoting responsible and sustainable development in Africa.

Historical Background

The uneasy manner of acquiring territories in Africa during the colonial era necessitated the use of persuasive (and sometimes intimidating) communication to get the cooperation of the natives. Vast territories had to be administered from head offices that were not more than mere trading posts. A modicum of peaceful coexistence was achieved through capitalization on common commercial interests, and later the redemptive faith that was the hallmark of the missionaries. Such peace was, however, tenuous and sometimes short-lived.

First, the print and, later, the broadcast media had to be employed to promote the various interests of the early formal governments in the region. In each of the four sub-regions of equatorial Africa (East, Central, West, and Sahelian), the development of radio and television followed a pattern that reflected the geopolitical and economic interests of the early governments.

In West Africa, radio was initiated by the personal interest of Sir Arnold Hodson, who established a radio distribution service in Sierra Leone in 1934. His transfer to Ghana led to the subsequent establishment of a wired radio distribution system in Accra in July 1935. In the same year, the Colonial Office in Nigeria introduced the British Broadcasting Corporation (BBC) Empire Service, which developed into a Radio Distribution Service (RDS) to service the principal towns in Nigeria. Thus, across British West Africa, radio was instituted through a redistribution service, which later developed into public service broadcasting stations.

Ghana's first radio station was established in 1939, when a small 1.3 kilowatt transmitter was installed in Accra on an experimental basis. As part of World War II propaganda, a bigger 5 kilowatt station was established in 1940. In Nigeria, the transformation from rediffusion to full broadcasting was achieved in 1951, when the Nigerian Broadcasting Service (NBS) was established as an arm of the Federal Ministry of Information "merely for the purpose of disseminating government information and providing some form of entertainment" (Osuntokun 1989: 345). In 1961, Ghana launched its External Service Broadcasting in English, French, Hausa, Swahili, Arabic, and Portuguese as part of President Nkrumah's vision for a United States of Africa. Four years later (1965), television was introduced after extensive planning and training processes that took about six years (Ansah 1985).

Consonant with Nkrumah's conviction of the media's role in education, he had directed thus:

> Ghana's television will be used to supplement our educational programme and foster a lively interest in the world around us. It will not cater for cheap entertainment nor commercialism. Its paramount object will be education in the broadest and purest sense. Television must assist in the socialist transformation of Ghana (Nkrumah 1965: 3).

Television in Nigeria was initiated through a regional government which pre-empted the federal government. Following a protest walk-out of Parliament, in 1956, staged by a party leader and his supporters, the governor general used the National Radio Broadcasting Service to criticize what he called "the perfidy of the Action Group." When the party leader, Chief Awolowo, requested access to the same radio station to reply, he was denied, and, as a result, his party went ahead to establish not only a radio station, but also a television station, WNTV, which started transmission on 31 October 1959. It was joined in quick succession by three public stations, each owned by three different governments: Eastern Nigeria Television, 1960; Nigerian Television Service, 1962; and north-based Radio Kaduna Television, 1962.

South African Broadcasting had a curious beginning. As early as 1910, experimental and amateur broadcasting took place in some settler communities, but it was not until 1924 that three stations were established, by private operators. In 1927, the government stepped in and ceded the licences of these operators to the African Broadcasting Company, a private enterprise. Public radio broadcasting came on 1 August 1936, when the state-owned South African Broadcasting Corporation began operations.

In Kenya, radio broadcasting arrived in phases, beginning in 1927 when a private company, the British East African Company, was given the contract to establish the first regular service on behalf of the Kenya Broadcasting Service (KBS). The KBS underwent transformations, becoming the Kenya Broadcasting Corporation in 1960 and, later, Voice of Kenya in 1964. In 1989, it changed back to the Kenya Broadcasting Corporation, which it remains today.

The character of broadcasting in francophone African countries was markedly different. Because France's former colonies stretched in a contiguous nature southwards from Morocco to Gabon, it was attractive to set up an entire series of radio relay stations that transmitted centrally produced programmes. These stations came under the authority of La Société de Radiodiffusion de la France d'Outre-mer (SORAFOM), which was established in 1956 and was supervised by the French minister for overseas territories in Paris. The stations were located in these places: Dakar, Niamey, Yaounde, Bamako, Fort-Lamy, Conakry, Doula, St. Louis, and Brazzaville. Though this arrangement terminated when the individual countries gained independence, the influence has persisted for a long time:

> Francophone Africa is as dependent today on French programmes as it has ever been. These programmes are still broadcast from Paris (where they are made)to Africa, and are intended to be recorded and then retransmitted when convenient. Not only are such programmes in French, but they are mainly about France and French culture (Nyamnjoh 1988: 88).

France's strong influence in radio broadcasting in her former territories became even more dominant with the establishment of the pan-regional super-station Africa Number One, in February 1981. Though the station is a joint venture between France and Gabon, it broadcasts only in French and relays programmes intended for Africa from the French public station, Radio France International (RFI).

The recent establishment of private radio stations is more pervasive in the francophone countries of equatorial Africa. Senegal has two private radio stations: Radio Dunyaa and Sud FM. Côte d'Ivoire has licensed two private stations, in addition to the Catholic Church's operations through three FM stations. Togo, Benin, and Gabon have at least one private radio station each, while Mali has more than 15 private stations. The stations in anglophone countries include Ray Power FM in Lagos, Nigeria, and Sanyo Radio and Capital FM in Kampala.

Because of cost implications, private television stations are coming more slowly. Though public television was introduced in equatorial Africa early in the 1960s, private television is still a rarity. The former French territories are serviced by France's Canal Horizon, which is only a relay station with heavy emphasis on sports, films, and entertainment. The few existing private television stations are overloaded with foreign programmes.

The character of broadcasting in East Africa is markedly different from that in West Africa, because what colonialists considered "inhospitable natives and ubiquitous mosquitoes" by the coast discouraged European settlements. By 1927, some white settlers in Kenya already owned wireless sets with which they could monitor world news. About the same time, the first transmitting station was established by the British East African Cable and Wireless Company, which was then contracted by the colonial government to monitor and relay BBC broadcasts. Though radio broadcasting started in Tanzania in 1951, it was not until 1993 that the first television station was established on this mainland part of Tanzania.

All across the region, there is a persistent call from multiparty enthusiasts and Western diplomats for the licensing of more private radio and television stations to provide greater access to the people. Kenya has licensed three private television stations, of which only one is operational. Similarly, Nigeria has licensed six private television stations and 11 cable/satellite retransmission operations.

Key Current Issues

The expectation that broadcasting should play a key role in promoting responsible and sustainable development in Africa pervades all the current main issues surrounding contemporary broadcasting. Specifically, the five key areas are these: (1) purpose; (2) financing; (3) regulation; (4) political control; and (5) new technology.

Purpose

Broadcasting in equatorial Africa does not have one universal purpose. Rather, a particular setting determines the unique mission or purpose which it is expected to serve. Such a purpose also changes over time, and it is clear that politics has a strong influence on broadcasting and the purposes to which it is put. For instance, in the case of Ghana, although broadcasting has been used to promote political transformation, the colonial government had introduced radio redistribution for the information needs of the settlers, colonial administrators, the handful of Africans who worked with the colonialists, and students in school.

The purpose is not always wholesome. Sir Arnold Hodson thought that radio should also be a narcotizing time-filler to keep educated Africans occupied:

> [E]ducated Africans ... for the want of better subjects, turn all too frequently to agitation and anti-governmental, not to say communistic activities. Broadcasting, however, provides a valuable and cheap antidote to these proclivities; music, talks, lectures, plays fill the minds of the listeners to the exclusion of more mischievous papulum (Ansah 1985: 4).

The airwaves are neutral and ready to serve the purposes of the broadcast managers. Thus, broadcasting has often been employed as a mechanism for propaganda and public opinion. This function was not lost on the colonial governor of the Gold Coast, who told the Legislative Assembly in January 1939 that broadcasting would "prove of great value as a means of conveying information or urgent propaganda to an intelligent and level-headed section of the community which is capable of exercising a strong influence for good on public opinion" (Ansah 1985: 10).

Broadcasting is a strong ideological tool, although it is a neutral actor that must be directed to its tasks. Thus, whereas Governor Hodson of the Gold Coast was using broadcasting for promoting British colonial interests, the first president of Ghana employed the same channels toward the attainment of a "socialist transformation of Ghana, for the education and edification, the enjoyment and entertainment of our people" (Nkrumah 1965: 3).

Financing

The airwaves may be free, but broadcasting is a very expensive enterprise. Thus, the issue of financing has always been one of the perennial problems that both governments and, lately, private entrepreneurs have to contend with. In equatorial Africa the earliest tradition of broadcasting was one of government ownership, which did not allow commercials. It was generally felt that accepting advertisements would compromise the public service principles that informed the establishment of the stations.

In Ghana, it was not until 1967 that the Ghana Broadcasting Corporation revoked an earlier policy of not accepting advertisements. In Nigeria, whereas the federal station did not accept advertisements at inception, the rival state station (WNTV) was clearly designed as a commercial station.

Because early broadcasting in much of equatorial Africa was a public service that was controlled, in most cases, by the various governments, advertising revenue was not an important issue. The assured regular supply of government subsidy meant that the creativity and aggressive drive that characterize private broadcasting were not always evident.

The recent arrival of private broadcasting stations in the sub-regions has ushered in a new philosophy of financing. This philosophy has implications for social responsibility, serving the public, and regulations by governments.

Regulations

The limited availability of channels and the potential for mass information through broadcasting have made it mandatory that governments carefully monitor what broadcasters are doing. Thus, not surprisingly, many of the countries in the region have regulatory statutes, agencies, and codes to ensure that the tremendous power of broadcasting is not abused.

Until the recent liberalization of both the politics and the economy in many African countries, the state was the sole regulator of broadcasting. In some countries now, journalists and similar communication professionals are get-

269

ting the opportunity to have more say in how stations are to be run. The National Broadcasting Commission of Nigeria not only licenses broadcast stations, but also controls the quality of programming. Kenya's Media Commission is currently designing a blueprint for regulating all significant media activities, including approvals for new broadcasting licences.

Most countries in equatorial Africa have completed studies and public hearings on electronic media privatization, while many of them have already licensed private stations. In each country, the legislation that allows private broadcasting seems to favour the ruling party or central government. The World Association of Community Broadcasters (AMARC) was told at its Sixth World Conference in Dakar (February 1995) that one of the biggest handicaps to private broadcasting is the fact that the state broadcasting authority, in some countries, is also responsible for licensing private stations. Some countries have entrusted this responsibility to independent commissions. In practice, however, these commissions are less independent than they appear, as they are still subject to some subtle political control.

Political Control

The earliest radio and television stations in equatorial Africa were obviously political tools established to serve the colonial administration and, later, the independent governments that inherited the reins at the demise of colonialism. Any changes these independent governments introduced in their management of broadcasting were mostly cosmetic. These changes were designed to favour the ruling regimes, rather than elevate the listenership or viewership.

The political control of broadcasting is most evident in the use of the electronic media to support the policies of the ruling regime, or, in cases of *coups d'état*, to announce the overthrow of a regime. Recent changes in Africa have led to a de-emphasis on broadcasting politics. The emergence of more private stations now makes it easier to have more variety, though the strong influence of the government is unmistakably present.

The political control of broadcasting has both local and international flavours. Whereas, locally, individual countries try to control the establishment and operations of individual stations, internationally, France, Britain, the United States, and Germany exercise political influence over broadcasting facilities in respective African countries that are of interest to them. Such influences are often disguised under cultural agreements, aid for media development, international programme sales, and foreign station or cable operations. The practice of U.S. producers channelling their programmes for Africa through the French, for example, is motivated by political more than economic considerations (Cantor and Cantor 1986).

New Technology

The debate about new communication technology touches one of the most important issues of contemporary broadcasting. Among the newest developments are satellite broadcasting and the information super-highway. The magic of satellite broadcasting now makes it possible for every part of the globe to be covered instantly with broadcast signals. The promise of the new technologies in contemporary Western society is well known already. In much of Africa, which is yet to be technologized, we expect that the new technologies will make more and more people active participants in the information age, rather than have them be further displaced or alienated by it.

The new information super-highway has serious implications for broadcasting in Africa. African stations – whether public or private – appear to capitalize on their entertainment functions, while the super-stations emanating from Britain, France, Germany, or the United States (such as the BBC, Radio France International, Radio Deutche Welle, and VOA) are mostly propaganda outfits. This development has not yet attracted the attention of African policy makers. Just as the arrival of the new communication technologies in Europe led to a call for "a new kind of media politics," which focuses not only on "content" but also on "structures" of communication systems (McQuail and Siune 1986), the present massive invasion of Africa by foreign broadcasters requires a new kind of response. The nature of that response will depend on how the various key actors in African broadcasting understand their roles.

Key Actors

Broadcasting in equatorial Africa today addresses a range of "publics," but the three key actors are governments, private broadcasters, and community operators. Public broadcasting generally means state-owned and -controlled broadcasting, with stations being wholly-owned by the governments, which exercise varying levels of control.

Governments

Because broadcasting is such a sensitive medium in Africa, it has usually attracted the attention of national governments, many of which are unwilling to relinquish the ownership of stations they inherited from pre-independence regimes. As Berwanger noted of the practice of the colonial governments in bequeathing radio or television stations to the newly independent states in Africa, "[for] most of the colonies in Africa, [on] becoming independent, quite often a television station found its way into the colonial power's 'farewell gifts'" (Berwanger 1987: 33).

Even today, radio and television stations are perceived as high priority institutions by African governments. Nigeria presents an interesting case: In 1967, there were three political regions, each of which had individual radio and television stations. Subsequent creation of additional states by successive governments led to the establishment of new radio and television stations by each of the new states. Today, each of the 30 states in Nigeria has at least one radio and/or one television station, some of which are owned by the state governments, while others are owned by the federal government. In addition, there are 27 television stations and eight radio stations which are owned and controlled by the federal government. This situation of plural outlets does not necessarily imply diversity.

The history of broadcasting in equatorial Africa is intimately related to government ownership and control, making public broadcasting the most dominant form, from pre-colonial times to the present. From the introduction of radio in South Africa in 1924, and Kenya in 1927, the government has been the chief architect. It is not surprising that "all broadcasting in the colonial territories was initiated and administered by the colonial governments ... the burgeoning African political parties had no voice in radio until after independence" (Mytton 1983: 53).

Private Broadcasters

Independent African states continued the colonial tradition of government ownership and control of broadcasting. Even two decades after the independence era in Africa, the *World Radio TV Handbook* (1982) reported that there were only three privately owned commercial radio stations on the entire continent – with three other stations operated by church organizations, and four relay stations used by U.S. and European external services stations.

The situation has just started to change with the current wave of privatization and/or commercialization of public companies in many African countries. Private and independent African entrepreneurs who are now venturing into broadcasting will have a significant impact on the uses of radio and television in Africa. The deregulation of broadcasting is one of the most significant media developments in Africa; however, in some African countries, it cannot be expected to be the panacea for its appalling contribution, so far, to development in the continent. Based on his analysis of the telecommunications industry in the United States, Mosco has argued against "an uncritical acceptance of deregulation as a model for public policy" (Mosco 1990:36). Time will tell how well the private stations meet the challenges of deregulation.

Community Operators

A third group of actors is the growing number of community activists who are now beginning to establish radio stations that are neither government-owned and -controlled, nor driven by the commercial interests of private entrepreneurs. The establishment of community radio stations in Africa has benefitted from the interests of many Western donors and international development agencies, who are eager to use these unique stations to achieve their objectives of participatory communication development. For now, these community stations appear to be more popular in southern than in equatorial Africa, with the most successful examples being those of Zimbabwe and South Africa.

It is uncertain how long community radio stations will last in Africa. They may go the way of community viewing centres for television, which were introduced in a few countries ten years ago, but have long since been discontinued because of the high costs of maintaining the equipment. In Nigeria, for instance, TV viewing centres penetrated the hinterland, but are now decrepit. Many people seem to have a preference for video (rather than television) viewing centres, and, thus, in Nigeria, Ghana, Kenya, and other countries, "video parlours," which are sometimes called "video cinema rooms," are becoming more prevalent. The expectation is that community radio stations will survive better, because in addition to their community listenership, they are community-owned and -operated. Thus, they make for greater involvement by the people, who make a significant input in the programming and other operations. Community radio stations are closer to public broadcasting in the sense that they are driven by utilitarian principles of public service. Though private radio operators argue that they too are driven by the principles of the greatest service to the greatest audience, we know that this is the case mostly where advertising revenue can be maximized.

The Christian churches in Africa also sponsor broadcasting activities which function in a similar way to community broadcasters, in terms of independence and public service principles, but these face some resistance. In the past, the Christian churches brought not only Western education, but also the print media to Africa. Many of the earliest newspapers and periodicals in Africa had a distinct religious character, because they were founded by Christian missionaries. In the broadcasting sector, the churches established less than ten stations in all because of the unwillingness of the governments to grant them licences.

The era of church-owned and -operated stations appears to have passed, although the various denominations are ever eager to use existing radio stations for their evangelism campaigns. In the African countries where private ownership of radio and television stations is now being promoted, the Churches are not favoured applicants. The enabling law in Nigeria prohibits religiously affiliated broadcasting stations. The Catholic Church in Uganda has not been favoured with an approval, even though it was one of the earliest applicants.

Private entrepreneurs and community interest groups are the two latest actors on the broadcasting scene in equatorial Africa. The example of private broadcasting in the United States is very appealing to Africans. Nevertheless, there are many problems that accompany the establishment of private stations in a social situation that is characterized by strong ethnic or factional interests.

Community radio operators in Africa hold great promise for the full utilization of radio in development programming. The usually decentralized structure of programme planning and production makes the operations amenable to greater participation by the local public. Whereas public broadcasting and private-enterprise broadcasting are usually plagued by problems associated with government propaganda and the profit motive, community broadcasting is often characterized by a high sense of social responsibility, with appropriate attention directed to the elevation of the social conditions of the community.

Though community radio has been described as being "in the best position to satisfy needs for multiple access and control" and is known to take "many provocative forms around the world," it is worth noting, however, that, even in the developed West, "adequate funding is a problem, as is the difficulty of sustaining interest and commitment by largely non-salaried staff" (McCain and Lowe 1990: 98).

With reference to the key actors in broadcasting in equatorial Africa today, the governments, which have always been identified as the main promoters of public broadcasting, are the major protagonists. Because of the fear that broadcasters can control the minds of the public, and the consequent unwillingness of African politicians to completely relinquish ownership and control of radio and television stations, public broadcasting will be a feature of life in Africa for a very long time.

Problems

Broadcasting in Africa is plagued by a myriad of serious problems, many of which have been redressed, but some of which have proved intractable. Among some of the most serious problems are these: ethnicity, local versus foreign input, development, and personnel.

Ethnicity

Ethnicity is an inescapable fact of life in Africa, and it underscores the political and economic reality that allegiance and patronage are often defined primarily in terms of ethnic groups. The fear that broadcasting can serve dangerous political purposes is located in the suspicion of opposition ethnic groups or political parties, who, it is suspected, would use radio and television to appeal to the primordial ethnic instincts and feelings of their people.

Existing public broadcasting stations in Africa have, so far, managed not to lead to a feared ethnic debacle. Rather, they have succeeded, to a large extent, in maintaining a strong audience following, irrespective of their ethnic affiliations. This has been achieved through employment and programming arrangements that portray a national, rather than sectional, character. Because public broadcasting stations usually provide wide geographical coverage, they have tended to produce programmes for all sections of the populace. As for the emerging private stations, we have to contend with the fact that they have limited geographical coverage (sometimes only five miles radius) and may need more specific targeting and segmenting of their markets. Especially in the urban areas, they may exacerbate feelings of ethnic loyalty if they are perceived as promoting or catering to identifiable ethnic interests.

Although ethnicity is a problem in broadcasting in Africa, it also presents both policy makers and broadcast station operators with unique opportunities to promote harmony among people of diverse ethnic backgrounds. The ethnic-oriented massacre in Rwanda in 1994 was said to have been fuelled by a divisive radio broadcast that called on Hutus to avenge the alleged assassination of President Habyarimana. In the ensuing melee, radio was again employed to manage the vitriolic ethnic tension and encourage more responsible behaviour among the ethnic groups.

Local Versus Foreign Input

The problem of balancing local and foreign input is a perennial concern among policy makers, broadcasters, and media critics. The problem is more serious in television than in radio, because of the high costs associated with the former. In many African countries, the percentage of local input is so low that some of these broadcasting stations are basically diffusing or distributing foreign programmes to local audiences. The Kenya Television Network (KTN), which prides itself on being the only alternative to the public television services provided by the Kenya Broadcasting Corporation (KBC), relays CNN all day, until 4:00 p.m., when it starts to screen old American movies, discontinued British comedies, and the Australian soap opera, "Neighbours." This programming decision is based on cost factors. An episode of "Neighbours" costs about $100, while a locally produced documentary of the same length might cost more than $10,000. Most of the local input in African television relates to sports coverage, discussion programmes, and quiz shows, which are easy and cheap to produce.

Public broadcasting stations have a better record than the emerging private stations in providing coverage of local issues and affairs. So far, private radio has been little more than a music box that provides round-the-clock entertainment. What is even more disturbing is the obvious over-emphasis on foreign music.

It is bad enough that there are very few development-oriented programmes on these private radio stations; however, it is inexcusable to have mostly foreign music. If the broadcast media are to live up to any expectations with respect to the development of Africa, they must address the problems of local versus foreign input, and they must involve the people more than they have done so far.

Development

When the broadcast media first came to equatorial Africa, the colonial governments did not intend that they be used for development. In East Africa, they were used mostly by the settler communities, and, in British West Africa, they were meant to promote the interests of Her Majesty's government. French stations were ideological and cultural tools to facilitate assimilation policies. With independence, the mandate for broadcasting was expanded, and development became the key function. However, this was development as defined by the political leaders.

Traditional paradigms of development and communication propose that the media can play critical roles in bringing about development. Even when these paradigms have been revised to make the development process more participatory and the use of communication more people-oriented, there are specific tasks for the mass media.

Development communication, as "the use of the principles and practices of the exchange of ideas to achieve development objectives" (Moemeka 1994: 2), will be incomplete in Africa without the involvement of broadcasting. African stations have not lived up to expectations as channels for development communication. The record of the public stations is better than the private stations. The emerging community stations hold more promise and will hopefully fill the gap left by the existing public and private stations. Resolving the problem of using broadcasting for development has proved difficult, partly because of different approaches. An equally important reason is that radio and television audiences see these media more as tools for entertainment rather than for purposive learning for development.

Personnel

The public broadcast media in Africa are plagued by the scarcity of trained personnel. Because the print media can compete better with other industries in the private sector, they tend to attract and retain more qualified personnel than the public electronic media. The personnel policies of public broadcasting stations are usually affected by the surrounding politics. The inherent inflexibility of such policies and their slowness in rewarding talents make public broadcasting stations less attractive to qualified personnel.

Public broadcasting is usually supervised by the ministry of information, which, like other arms of government, often suffers from frequent and unnecessary cabinet reshuffles. Such frequent changes lead to instability in broadcast station administration and policies. The emerging private stations are spared this unfortunate personnel situation, though they are afflicted by such malaise as the private sector's over-emphasis on profits and cash-based criteria for performance.

The personnel problems of public broadcasting have not made it easy to have appropriately trained staff that can help realize the development-oriented objectives of these stations. The civil service mentality which pervades public broadcasting is not conducive to an expanded employment of the media to address the problems of development on the continent. Colonial-era broadcasting stations made do with untrained broadcasters, while the immediate post-independence stations have had generalist information officers, usually seconded from the ministry of information. In this era of advances in information technology and public campaign management, both public and private stations need properly trained personnel.

Strategic Alternatives

Political Development

Recent economic and political changes in Africa have set the stage for subsequent developments in broadcasting on the continent. World Bank structural adjustment policies brought about greater liberalization in the economic sphere, while the demise of the cold war, along with international expectations of more open political structures, have resulted in a new African politics of multiparty democracy. There are only a few pockets of autocratic military rule, and even fewer cases of sit-tight political despots. These changes have proved very difficult for public broadcasting to manage.

Being creations of the various governments, African public broadcasting stations have had to dance to the tune of their masters' music – sometimes more vigorously than expected. Even when multipartyism has been achieved, some state broadcasting stations still see themselves as mouthpieces of the government, contrary to the expectation that they serve public interest. The media in Africa are usually closely identified with demands for political freedom and responsible governance. The tendency for some public broadcast media to identify more with the government of the day and the ruling party may prove detrimental to the interests of the general public. Such unwholesome tendencies have led to retributive maltreatment of some media and journalists when a ruling party loses an election.

The emerging private stations in Africa are set up with the blessings of the governments, and, thus, are not strongly in opposition. Because the governments still reserve the right to grant broadcasting licences to private operators, these operators have tended to be neutral or pro-government.

This is not to say that there is no room for objective and critical political coverage. The further advancement of the unfolding political democracy in Africa will benefit immensely from the objective and critical coverage of political affairs from the perspective of public education and mobilization. The indication so far, however, is that the private operators care more about profit than public service.

African Broadcasting

The question of whether a uniquely African broadcasting is possible and what it would be is currently a contentious issue in African communication practice and scholarship. The technology of broadcasting is the same universally, but, within each culture, broadcasting communication is produced and consumed in the context of the people's norms and practices. To the extent of creatively producing and consuming communication, we can argue that African broadcasters must use broadcasting technology in a unique way, to address their peculiar problems of development.

There are already many instances of such creativity, for example in Cameroon, where radio is used for sending personal messages to relatives in the hinterland; and in Nigeria where television is used extensively, especially on Thursdays, to announce deaths and funerals. For symbolic and functional reasons, radio and television stations are also the theatre for military coups, and, not surprisingly, some of them have more military hardware than some military barracks. For broadcasting to be a more useful tool of social development in Africa, African broadcasting operators must create more unique applications of the technology and create authentic African broadcasting. The seeming failure of broadcasting in African development is attributable to the low incidence of authentic African forms in contemporary African broadcasting.

Both a "new development" and a "new broadcasting" are needed in Africa, if the magic of the airwaves is to be expected to touch people's lives in a significant manner. Many Africans have mistakenly thought of development in modernizing terms, exemplified by electricity, pipe-borne water, hospitals, tarred roads, brick walls, and zinc roofs.

Radio and television have also been misunderstood to be "talking boxes" for relaxation and entertainment. Africa is in need of a redefinition of development to show that it fosters the elevation of the people, not necessarily in material terms, but in the context of what makes living and life better. Broadcasting must be Africanized further to position it as an "information machine" which is relevant in traditional communication contexts. In addition to its use in sending interpersonal and "private" messages in Cameroon, and announcing deaths in Nigeria, new uses relating to traditional rites, rituals, ceremonies, and similar occasions must be found and popularized for African broadcasting. These are the alternative strategies to wholesale adoption of Western broadcasting by African peoples.

Recent examples of the incorporation of aboriginal cultural communication elements in Australian broadcasting show clearly that the broadcast media can be indigenized to make them more relevant. Among the adaptable traditional forms are brief stories, poetry, and music. Radio and television should be used as cultural tools that reflect the social milieu (Browne 1990).

Marketing Approaches

Broadcasting in equatorial Africa has suffered from a myopic interpretation of marketing approaches. In the tradition of government subventions, African public stations relied solely on government budgetary allocations and, in fact, were not allowed to take advertisements. Increasing operational costs, declining subventions, and the new policies on privatization or commercialization of public enterprises have now led to a belated introduction of marketing approaches to public broadcasting. Many years of reliance on government handouts have made many public station operators lazy and unimaginative.

The new private stations, on the other hand, seem to be too eager to make profits, at any cost. The danger is that both the survival instinct and profit motive will make them less attentive to the demands of social responsibility, public service, and responsible development. Being licensed by government, many of them are less public-spirited than pro-government in their coverage of public affairs. In the marketing arena, they seem to be propelled by maximal advertising motives.

Both public and private broadcasting need to adopt an expanded view of marketing approaches, with the ultimate aim of serving the public interest. Since the airwaves are public property, the public interest should be dominant in all considerations of broadcasting practices and programmes. It is the failure of the existing public and private broadcasting operators that is responsible for criticisms levelled against the former for being blind to government impudence and the latter for being too commercially oriented.

Marketing approaches could affect the public service idea through increased attention to sustainability, profitability, and meeting advertisers' needs; however, traditional African communication is neither pro-establishment all the time, nor is it driven by the profit motive. Rather, it is a true example of public service aimed at engendering responsible development.

The Future of Broadcasting

The fact that developments in Africa are largely unpredictable is indisputable. Not many political scientists could foresee the way that colonialism ended in many African countries between the 1950s and 1960s. Nor could they have predicted the domino-style removal of the sit-tight despots who had made themselves "life presidents." In Malawi, the former life president was not only defeated in the national election, but he is facing trial for murder.

In broadcasting, there is a revolution in the ongoing liberalization and privatization of the electronic media which had been monopolized by the state. Though one cannot predict with certainty how this revolution will play out, it is obvious that its implications for politics, civil society, and social development will be momentous. The recent introduction of private radio and television, coupled with the popularization of satellite dishes and cable in some countries, are already producing significant reverberations.

Politics

The recent changes in media ownership, which have led to increasing private participation in broadcasting in Africa, have come about as a result of the increasing tempo of demands for political democracy. The political developments also benefitted from the new media structures, suggesting that two phenomena of media and politics fed each other. However, as was the case in the transformation of media and politics in East Germany, where Willnat (1991: 206) found the "the journalistic changes followed the political changes, and not vice versa," the opening up of the airwaves to private broadcasters came from the opening up of the politics.

The sustenance of open and democratic politics in Africa will benefit from a continued practice of open broadcasting that provides variety not only in station establishments, but also in programme content – with the important task of supporting democracy through greater access and participation always kept in view. As Klee (1993: 61) has argued about broadcasting and African democracy,"participative democracy cannot succeed without wide-ranging information being made available to the broad population about the nature of democracy, its pre-conditions, and the way it works." He is quick to caution that "western models should not be pressed upon African societies." African broadcasting stations of the future will, in all likelihood, have to demonstrate their commitment to the ideas, goals, and objectives of their societies with respect to social development. They should be more than marketing tools for consumer goods if they are to be alive to their responsibilities.

Trado-Broadcasting

Though broadcasting can hardly be said to be part of traditional African communication, it must be incorporated into the full repertoire of contemporary communication in Africa, which must appreciate African cultural values. Western models of broadcasting should not be foisted on African societies. The successful African stations of the future will have to be "African," and not relay or rediffusion boxes for Western broadcasters. The easiest approach so far has been for the broadcasters to imitate the typical Western models as if these are the only options. But as Blake (1993: 10) has argued,

> information and communication technologies are not antithetical to traditional norms and traditional media systems ... In fact, the new technologies create the possibility of incorporating indigenous knowledge into the fund of knowledge generated from outside so that it can usefully be applied in contexts other than those in which such knowledge was generated.

So far, African broadcasters have been slow in applying traditional norms to make broadcasting more relevant to the majority of the people. Neither the old public broadcasters nor their new private counterparts can be exonerated from the neglect of traditional forms in African broadcasting. Trado-broadcasting is the incorporation of traditional forms and not the perverse use of broadcasting on rural peoples in the name of community media. The examples of Mali and Burkina Faso, where rural radio is designed by the respective governments as a means of decentralization and accessibility to the local people without their involvement, do not illustrate trado-broadcasting. Trado-broadcasting, being traditional media, requires people's involvement. The movement against the misdirected rural radio stations of Mali and Burkina Faso has "led to the growth of popular radio fuelled by masses who want to have their own voice" (Mwangi 1994: 2).

Afro-Development

African broadcasting today does not have much to say or show on the controversial issue of development. The little it presents often seems to suggest that development must be conceived in terms of European and American standards – tarred roads, piped water, and classroom education, among others. The rich cultural heritage, the creative management of the traditional environment, and other indicators of achievement have not attracted adequate attention from African broadcasters. African media will have to champion the cause for a redefinition of development to direct the focal attention on relevant African values. Some community broadcasters are already doing this through the structure and content of their operations.

A philosophy of Afro-development in broadcasting will obviate the compulsive adoption of the dominant Western paradigms of development. African community media operators are more suited to the necessary utilization of the broadcast media (especially radio) to champion the African definition of development and exemplify the same in their daily operations. In the spirit of the 1993 Bamako (Mali) Declaration on Radio Pluralism in Africa, broadcasting should provide the public with a tool that facilitates greater freedom of expression in the context of responsible development. Such development must be in the terms that are reflective of and consistent with traditional African values.

Unlike the print media in Africa, which have failed to serve Afro-development purposes, the electronic media, with their adaptable nature, can more easily accommodate the voices of the people and allow them to determine their own parameters for development.

Though the experience of some African countries with liberalized broadcasting suggests that the norm is imported music and commercial trappings designed with mass audiences and advertisers in mind, African broadcasting in future will be a serious tool for mobilization, advocacy, and the promotion of Afro-development. There will be differences in levels of attaining these objectives among the various countries and even among stations within any particular country.

Conclusion

Public broadcasting has a long history in equatorial Africa and was used at various times as a tool for propagation of public support for colonial regimes, independent states, and, more recently, multiparty democracy. Following recent changes now culminating in Africa, we are witnessing the licensing of private radio and television stations to compete with and supplement the existing public stations.

Public broadcasting in Africa has often been castigated for various reasons. According to Thiombiano (1994: 36), who is a pioneer entrepreneur of private radio in Ouagadougou,

> For thirty years, since most African states achieved independence, the predominance of political slogans on the radio over the free exchange of information and culture has slowed down development and done a great deal of damage to the minds and ways of thinking of the African people.

Many critics are quick to note the failures of public broadcasting, and only few observers and researchers have acknowledged the achievements. The advent of private stations in Africa has not led to significantly greater choice or even better programmes. However, currently, all across equatorial Africa, the establishment of independent stations is in vogue and bound to continue until every country in the region introduces private broadcasting.

Public and private stations, as well as the emerging community broadcasters in Africa, are expected to promote authentic African culture and values. The broadcast media in Africa have a bright future that rests on their becoming more relevant in the lives of African peoples and, thereby, contributing to the responsible and sustainable development of the continent. Despite competition from private and community stations, public broadcasting will always be part of the electronic media landscape in equatorial Africa.

References

Ansah, P. A. V. 1985. *Ghana Broadcasting Corporation: Golden Jubilee Lectures*. Tema: Tema Press.

Berwanger, Dietch. 1987. *Television in the Third World*. Bonn: FES.

Blake, Cecil. 1993. Development Communication Revisited: An End to Eurocentric Visions. *Development* 3.

Browne, Donald R. 1990. Aboriginal Radio in Australia: From Dreamtime to Prime Time. *Journal of Communication* 40(1).

Cantor, M. G. and J. M. Cantor. 1986. American Television in the International Marketplace. *Communication Research* 13(3).

Hachten, William. 1973. *Muffled Drums*. Ames: Iowa University Press.

Klee, Hans Dieter. 1993. The Mass Media and Democratization of Africa. *Development*.

McCain, Thomas A. and G. Ferral Lowe. 1990. Localism in Western European Radio Broadcasting: Untangling the Wireless. *Journal of Communication* 40(1).

McQuail, D. and K. Siune. 1986. Media Policy in Transition. In *New Media Politics: Comparative Perspectives in Western Europe*, edited by D. McQuail and K. Siune. London: Sage.

Moemeka, Andrew. 1994. *Communicating for Development*. Albany: SUNY Press.

Mosco, Vincent. 1990. The Mythology of Telecommunications Deregulation. *Journal of Communication* 40(1).

Mwangi, Wangu. 1995. Freeing the Voices. *Econews Africa* 4(3).

Mytton, Graham. 1983. *Mass Communication in Africa*. London: Edward Arnold.

Nkrumah, Kwame. 1965. Speech by Osagyefo President Kwame Nkrumah on the inauguration of Ghana Television, 31 July. Tema: State Publishing.

Nyamnjoh, Francis. 1988/89. Broadcasting in Francophone Africa: Crusading for French Culture. *Gazette* 43 (2).

Osuntokun, Akinjide. 1989. National Communication Policy and Foreign Policy in Nigeria. In *Philosophy and Dimensions of National Communication Policy*, edited by Tony Nnaemeka, Egerton Urighara and Didi Uyo. Lagos: CBAAC.

Thiombiano, Moustapha. 1994. Radio Horizon - FM. *Topic* 203. Washington: United States Information Service.

CAMBODIA: BROADCASTING AND THE HURDLE OF POVERTY

Gareth Price

Introduction

*T*he Cambodian people –who for successive generations
have lived under god kings, military dictators, fanatical
Marxists and communists – have been left to conclude
that liberty is anarchy (Jonathan Miller, *Financial Times*, London, 1
November 1994).

Cambodia was not the only post-Communist country to come to the conclusion above at the end of 1994. The same sentiment could have been
expressed by most eastern European and Commonwealth of Independent
States nations regarding their struggles as emerging democracies in the 1990s.
The difference in Cambodia is that it is one of the poorest countries in the
world, suffering even now from a resurgence of guerilla warfare by the Khmer
Rouge. In such a climate, it is difficult for democracy to flourish and even
more difficult to develop the idea of an independent and pluralistic media.

Politics Without Ideology

This study of the Cambodian media began when the government in Phnom Penh asked UNESCO, in February 1994, for consultancy advice on "a broadcasting model based on the BBC." It would be difficult to adapt the British Broadcasting Corporation's (BBC) model to any emerging democracy, despite the fact that, in the past, its structure has been copied all over the British Commonwealth. For example, the man who founded the BBC, John Reith, also designed the South African Broadcasting Corporation (SABC), and an old-fashioned BBC structure is still visible not only in Johannesburg, but also in many countries around the world. But today's state and public broadcasters work within parameters very different from those facing the BBC, and they are forced to fight with their commercial competitors for advertising revenue. Most of those broadcasting organizations exist in countries with democratic limitations and fragile economies. Furthermore, there is a severe limit to which one can use relatively wealthy broadcasters in stable democracies such as Australia, Canada, or the European Union as role models for others. The strength of television in the United Kingdom, for example, lies in the equilibrium achieved since the mid-1950s by two strong organizations – the BBC and Independent Television (ITV) – providing competition in programming, while avoiding competition for funding. Even today, only four terrestrial channels dominate the market – two complementary channels run by the BBC, one competitive channel run by ITV, and one alternative and minority channel, Channel 4. All organizations have a strong public broadcasting ethos in which the "national" broadcaster has set the programming tone for its commercial competitors.

Emerging democracies in a post-Communist society have a totally different starting point. Most state broadcasting organizations were nothing less than propaganda machines for their respective governments and, now, in the mid-1990s, have great difficulty in adjusting to the idea of independent news reporting. When one government falls in an election, it is replaced by another which usually proceeds to change its broadcasting chiefs. The change is politically motivated and based on the politics of personality and friendship rather than on any ideology or sense of professionalism. It follows that most broadcasting chiefs will, with varying degrees of subtlety, influence news programming in the direction of the political masters who appointed them and who often do not expect to survive them. The commitment is to the political mentor and not the professional broadcaster.

In addition, there is the constant confusion between the terms "state" and "public" broadcasting. In most new democracies, the terms are often regarded as synonymous. Thus, the BBC, for example, is often regarded in such countries as a state broadcasting organization. There is little understanding of the need for a separation of powers between government and media in order to develop the credibility of a broadcast news service, given that the same government appointees are likely to be in charge of the organization, whether it takes the form of a ministry or a free-standing corporation.

Under these circumstances, the development of public broadcasting requires the emergence of private or commercial competition, which often leads to greater independence in news programming and forces state broadcasters and their masters to rethink not only the quality of their output, admittedly over a long period of time, but also how to develop a credible image for their channels. Competition is necessary, but not sufficient, in developing credibility. There is also the need for competition to be regulated. Too much competition, for example through allowing everybody a licence to broadcast, as in Romania, merely leads to the law of the jungle in weak economies of new countries.

Living with the Khmer Rouge

How much more difficult, then, to solve such problems in Cambodia, a country effectively in the grip of civil war, where the draft Press Law is being constantly revised, where there is no broadcasting law, and where the rule of law is difficult to enforce. Indeed, one of the basic questions being asked in many emerging democracies is whether it is desirable to live with a weak law rather than no law. Even a "good" media law allows government the opportunity for censorship when there is a threat to the security of the state. In Phnom Penh today, that security is fragile – and for good historical reasons.

Modern-day Cambodia is still suffering from the effects of some 20 years of continuous war, including four years of genocide by the Khmer Rouge, who killed at least one million people and conducted a deliberate campaign to smash Cambodia's pre-revolutionary culture between 1975 and 1979. Most families lost many loved ones, and, in addition, highly educated and skilled people were particularly targeted for execution. It is the only country that has evacuated its own capital, a horror story brilliantly captured in the film *The Killing Fields*. Today, it is a society that is still in the slow process of rebuilding itself, both in terms of the lives of the people and the face of the countryside. The massive mine-awareness campaign, run by the ministry of information through the media, highlights the care required in spotting possible mined areas and minimising risk to the community. It can only limit loss of limbs in a rich agricultural countryside whose full potential for a return to normalcy must await the quelling of the dissidents and their disruptive effect on much of Cambodian life. Currently, foreign tourists are advised to stay away because of the potential threat of kidnapping and murder by the Khmer Rouge.

The Broadcasting Background

A 1991 UNESCO mission report states that only four radio broadcasting engineers and a few print journalists or newspaper technical personnel are believed to have survived the conflict of the 1975-79 period. The report also documents the state of the broadcasting resources in the country. The fact that much of the equipment (in technical communications) still operates is testament to the commitment of Cambodia's technicians and engineers, who have shown dedication and skill in ensuring that equipment remains in service. The outmoded studio equipment at the national radio station is in pristine condition, albeit lacking spare parts, despite much of it being more than 30 years old. Radio and television broadcasters face both a lack of equipment and an unreliable electricity supply, thereby curbing their plans for expansion. Everywhere there is a shortage of writers, journalists, broadcast and print technicians, programme production personnel, and experienced senior management.

Cambodia's written and audio-visual heritage has all but gone. The entire gramophone and tape collection of the national radio station in Phnom Penh was destroyed by the weather, after being discarded outside. Countless thousands of still photographs and 15 years of Cambodia's film history have gone for ever. As a means of retrieving the fragments of a former society, radio VOK has broadcast a particularly popular programme that concerns the search by people for friends and relatives missing from the 1975-79 period. Names and contact points are broadcast in the hope that reunions can result (UNESCO 1991).

After 1991 and during the build-up to the mid-1993 elections, the United Nations Transitional Authority in Cambodia (UNTAC) installed a completely new radio station, as an additional channel to the state radio system, to impart advice and encouragement to a young democracy's forthcoming election. The journalist William Shawcross described it as follows:

> UNTAC sowed the seeds for a free press. It compelled the government to provide the opposition parties with radio and television time. It insisted that the SOC [State of Cambodia party in government] allow FUNCINPEC [the leading opposition party] to start a radio and television station. Most important, it established Radio UNTAC, which played a vital role in educating the population about the election. Together with other branches of UNTAC's Information-Education Division and of the Electoral Component, Radio UNTAC convinced people that their vote really would be secret, a considerable achievement in a country where such a concept was previously unknown (Shawcross 1994).

This enterprise was on the air for only six weeks and was custom-built for the elections at an enormous cost. Estimates of US$4 million have been reported in the building of three AM transmitters, the six "state-of-the-art" studios, and editing facilities of Radio UNTAC, all of which now lie totally idle in the former hotel building owned by a businessman who was reported to have received US$14,000 per month as rent. This facility was handed over to the Cambodian government, which could not even afford to run the air-conditioning system, let alone pay the rent. The existing national radio station will benefit from some of the equipment, but it would have been far better to have moved the national radio station to the UNTAC Studios. When the three AM transmitters were built, the fuel costs alone were so prohibitive that it would have been impossible for the ministry of information to use them. Furthermore, in February 1994, all the technical equipment from the AM transmitter in Siem Reap was stolen or destroyed. Only the mast remains.

The Broadcasting Inheritance

The Cambodian infrastructure is still not conducive to good communications. The telephone network is so bad that the few who can afford it rely instead on expensive mobile telephone systems. There are only three mobile telephones in the state television broadcasting building. The land lines are silent. The road between the two most populous conurbations is in an appalling condition, but it is the only method of sending tapes between the relevant broadcast stations. The basic problem facing the government of Cambodia is an obvious lack of finances in an economy still staggering under the strain of civil war. Under these circumstances, the media do not have a high priority.

Since so many records were destroyed during the genocidal Pol Pot era, information is difficult to ascertain, even on numbers of personnel, a situation emphasized by new senior civil servants struggling to find out the facts for themselves. The limited funds for programming and capital equipment could be boosted by retrenchment and rationalization, but it would take at least two years to give a proper appraisal of the quality of personnel, assuming that government employment policy would change sufficiently to confront the problem. The suffering of the nation over the past 20 years precludes proper debate about overstaffing at this time, since it would lead to further trials through job losses for a government with an unclear social policy.

Income levels in broadcasting and most other industries are so bad – approximately US$20 per month – that most people have one other job. It is rumoured that the director-general of the state television system, TVK, is paid US$40 per month. The state coffers are low due to the lack of an efficient tax system, and, currently, there is heavy dependence on donor aid, particularly for equipment. Meanwhile, the state broadcasting organizations are facing intense competition from unregulated commercial radio and television broadcasters who are better paid and who have superior technology and coverage. The state broadcasters themselves blame the lack of modern technology for their problems. Unquestionably, the lack of a financial system which allows for flexibility between capital and operating expenditure, or between staff salaries and programme budgets, constitutes a serious problem. Furthermore, the ministry of finance, in its struggle to achieve control of the economy as a whole, has not yet devolved financial control to ministries such as information. The result is that even a request for a mobile telephone has to be referred to the ministry of finance. Overall, there is a lack of leadership, because the concept of management is unknown. Experience and skills are at a premium at all levels, because training is in its infancy.

A public broadcaster must seek to be independent of its government, even though much of its income is derived from that government. It follows that government funding should be provided indirectly and that a broadcasting structure be created which allows the public broadcaster to operate at arm's length from government. This is easier said than done. Politicians the world over are notorious for their desire to keep control of the media. It was, therefore, most encouraging to hear from the highest political levels in Cambodia, in February 1994, that support for public broadcasting is an essential element in an emerging democracy. Subsequent events, however, do not bode well for the immediate future of independent journalism. Prince Narodom Sirivudh, the minister for foreign affairs, has repeatedly said that the media "belong to the nation and the people and the government treats them as its watch-dogs," but there have been increasing signs that some ministers are increasingly irritated by any press criticism. There have been warnings about showing dead bodies on television; issues of one paper were seized following criticisms of King Sihanouk; and, in June 1994, the editor-in-chief of *Intervention* was mysteriously murdered, an incident which has attracted international concern.

There are also disagreements over a Press Law. One new draft, prepared by a young American lawyer, has been compared with a reactionary 1992 Press Law declared void by UNTAC. Meanwhile, King Sihanouk, in a liberal mode, has been quoted as saying, "I don't think we need to draft regulations or laws for Khmer and foreign journalists" (Shawcross 1994). No broadcasting law exists, and the minister of information has been advised to await the fate of the Press Law before debating the dilemma of radio and television.

News By Morse Code

In a country that still suffers from civil war, news programming obviously has a top priority, despite the security clamp-downs on many activities relating to the Khmer Rouge. Broadcast news in Cambodia is characterized by too many newsrooms offering too little news. Commercial television has two active companies, the most important of which is unquestionably the Thai-owned IBC, which started in May 1993. The other commercial operator, CTV9, was started by FUNCINPEC and claims to have changed from a political party channel to a straight commercial channel. The state radio and television stations in Phnom Penh – National Radio of Cambodia (NRC) and Television Kampuchea (TVK) – each have their own newsroom, relying heavily on the National News Agency (AKP). Only AKP has a regional presence, although reporters from all organizations follow government ministers on regional visits. The waste of resources is obvious. Three reporters might cover a ministerial tour, while leaving events in the rest of the country, outside Phnom Penh, unreported. In Phnom Penh itself, all the newsrooms have too few resources, and a rationalization of the news collecting and distribution system is overdue.

In the NRC, there are at least 40 radio journalists preparing only five live bulletins a day. The early morning bulletin is recorded the previous night. The first live news bulletin of the day is transmitted long after listeners have gone to work, and there is a gap of seven hours between daytime news bulletins. The newsroom has no telephones that work, and it relies on the AKP news agency for much of its information, supplemented by recordings from international news services such as the BBC World Service and Radio Australia.

In TVK's news department, there are 38 journalists, but about a dozen of these are printers recently removed from the government newspaper and totally unsuited to journalism. Five ENG cameras and a variety of editing machines are dedicated to news coverage, which is held in greater esteem than that of its main commercial rival. A straw poll of ordinary viewers and experienced print journalists indicated that TVK went into greater depth than the two commercial television channels. The small staff of journalists has its information supplemented by the state news agency, AKP, which does not feed the commercial stations. TVK journalists claim that the Thai-owned television station, IBC, will run a whole ministerial speech on its news bulletins, and they accuse them of keeping on the "right side" of the politicians. For example, the Thai owners were suspected of obtaining permission to open the station on the understanding that they would support the State of Cambodia government party in the run-up to the elections. Even the five cameras are considered insufficient to cater to ministers' expectations of consistent coverage. The deputy director of TVK news reported that he did not have enough cameras to cover prime ministers and ministers, let alone other events worthy of attention. The newsroom does not have a feed from AP, Reuters, or UPI, since only one contract is made with one Cambodian organization – namely AKP, which also provides all the regional stories through its local reporters.

AKP has a staff of about 400 people, housed in a large block in the extensive compound of the ministry of information. One intelligent insider says of AKP that, "the work could be done by 100 people. Of the 400 staff, some come to work and don't work. Some don't come to work." The workload consists of a daily press bulletin printed in Khmer, English, and French. A study of the publication for 19 January 1994 showed that it consisted of nine stories: four international, one regional, and four government stories, all having an international link.

Such publications are widely used by radio and television, but are not adequate to serve the voracious appetites of a modern broadcasting service. Despite having 400 staff in Phnom Penh, there are relatively few correspondents in the provinces, and they have declined in number. In Battambang, there are four AKP reporters, in Siem Reap only one – despite the fact that it is an active area for the military and is the heart of the world-famous Angkor Wat tourist industry. Direct communication from such centres is only possible by Morse code, and equipment is limited. The pay of the Siem Reap correspondent is approximately US$12 or 30,000 Riels per month, plus free accommodation. The low pay is the main reason for the decline in personnel in the last few years, although the management in Phnom Penh has declared that budgetary problems forced them to require only one multi-skilled man to be reporter, photographer, and Morse code operator, instead of the three men in previous times.

There is obviously a need to overhaul the news-gathering operation in Phnom Penh. The over-dependence of the broadcasters on the state news agency, the overstaffing of the agency in Phnom Penh, and the lack of information from the provinces create a situation that requires total revision. The first solution is to split the ministry's personnel into two sections in order to separate the Government Information Service from the agency's news-gathering operation. The agency would, hopefully, take on the most talented people and develop a credible news service from the provinces, supported by technical equipment more in keeping with modern times.

Radio

Radio is by far the most effective means of communication in Cambodia, since the circulation of newspapers is relatively small, rural literacy rates are low, and distribution is difficult, while reception of television from Phnom Penh and the two provincial stations is limited by low transmission power. Approximately 550 staff are employed at one national radio channel, NRC, although that large a workforce is not always apparent. Echoing the AKP situation, one senior official in the ministry said, "There may be up to 600 staff, but only 100 are actually working."

Despite a large staff and seven studios, there were large gaps of up to four hours between the afternoon transmissions. Although an excuse for the lack of programming has been the poorly equipped studios, there has obviously been no will in the past to address the problem of how to make the best use of available resources, and the station's image suffers in comparison with its commercial competitors. No consideration had been given to the design of a sound studio to facilitate self-operating methods of work. Music programmes are being recorded in the most laborious way, each link and disc recorded separately. As with all broadcasting departments, there are problems in getting small-scale equipment, such as tape recorders for reporters, as well as proper transport and travel budgets. The company's resources are outmoded, inflexible, and inadequate.

On the other hand, FM 90 is a tiny commercial radio station that transmits 17.5 hours a day with a staff of only 20 people – a startling contrast to NRC. It operates from a tiny studio with a small FM transmitter on top of a suburban house. Its format is simple – popular music with occasional links, but very little news coverage. FM 90 began as Funcinpec Radio – a political party radio station that started up in February 1992. It is already making a profit and pays salaries of US$110 per month to the ten experienced or skilled staff – dramatically different from NRC's US$20 per month. FM 90 works out of what must rate as the smallest and most inadequate broom cupboard in the world. They need more studio space and are working toward obtaining a larger transmitter. They plan further relay stations in order to increase their current radius of 40 kilometres, and they would like to transmit using digital technology. They have a strategy. Above all, they have a large but unquantified audience, which forces the state broadcasters to think about filling their schedules.

But is it public broadcasting? It is often argued that commercial radio in the developing world relies almost entirely on background wall-to-wall popular music. At its best, a private station can offer immediate local news coverage, as well as other information, and as the economy grows there will be the gradual emergence of more sophisticated targeting of a variety of different audiences, offering greater listener choice and an obvious alternative to the state radio services. At its worst, it can rely on the popularity of its services to neglect news. It is too early to say in which direction the radio services of Cambodia are going. At the moment, private radio has the right professional attitudes, while the state service (NRC) seems to be waiting for an injection of new leadership.

Two Tales of Television

Cambodian television is a story of extremes – an extremely poverty-stricken state television service competing with two commercial television stations that are much better endowed in equipment and have a much better paid staff. The contrast is at its greatest when comparing the state channel, TVK, with its biggest challenger, IBC.

TVK has a relatively small staff of approximately 150, who work under very difficult conditions. Advertising income is small, unknown in quantity, and disappears into government coffers. The only studio is located in a large house, which is totally inadequate for modern broadcasting purposes and consists of a large room with two old tubeless cameras and a third, even older, camera that is used for captions. The station's one transmitter has a strength of only one kilowatt and is at a severe disadvantage to IBC, which broadcasts on a ten kilowatt transmitter and claims to reach up to 85 percent of the Cambodian population. However, the majority of the population does not have access to a television monitor, and substantial areas of the country only receive satellite television for the handful who can afford it. Nevertheless, there can be no question of the station's popularity within the existing viewing audience.

The programme schedule of TVK as a whole is restricted to some five hours per evening. It offers a basic output of children's programmes, music, and documentary programmes, but the company cannot afford to buy substantial numbers of good imported programmes for dubbing or subtitling, and its own productions are limited because portable cameras are mainly dedicated to news. Nor can it afford to buy many programmes from an independent market that is increasing its input to IBC.

TVK does well with limited resources; however, it is the only area of the ministry's media that could benefit from more, rather than fewer staff members –providing they were selected for professional reasons and properly trained. In a country where development and educational programming in so many areas is going to be a critical element in future economic growth, it is essential that the various ministries – education, health, and agriculture – contribute the relevant programmes to educate the people of Cambodia at all levels, both formally and informally. To do that, however, they need additional resources.

At TVK there is no concept of modern financial or personnel management. There is no capital or operating budget and no knowledge of total costing.

But there is a will to learn and a growing professional attitude among top management. TVK needs a substantial increase in capital investment for up-to-date, compatible, and interactive equipment; however, with severely limited government finances, such investment relies heavily on donor aid. The French government has provided substantial amounts of equipment, as well as a promise of further funding dependent on broadcasters buying equipment from France.

IBC has 150 staff members, only eight of whom are Thai, most of them in managerial positions. The station claims an advertising revenue of US$10,000 per month and an operating expenditure of US$15,000 per month. In the absence of any regulatory law for commercial media, IBC was approved by the National Investment Committee. Its parent company is the regional media giant, Shinawatra, which has substantial investments in Thailand and, at the time of writing, was about to launch the TAICOM satellite with a footprint covering Thailand, Cambodia, Laos, Vietnam, and the South China Sea Region. The satellite broadcast will include 45 minutes a week in the Khmer language.

IBC itself plans a relay station in Battambang, the second largest conurbation in Cambodia, but all its staff are located in the capital for reasons of security. The company also claims 35 percent local production in the Khmer language and some 50 percent of material dubbed from Thai, including music programmes, which are particularly popular. Nevertheless, their news programmes are not regarded as highly as one would expect in a nation where freedom of expression in the state media is limited – in some emerging democracies, for example in the Caribbean, Poland, or Kazakhstan, commercial television has been known to push back the frontiers of news publishing, albeit on a limited scale. Its news staff is small in number, and the newsroom is badly equipped compared to the obvious capital investment in its technical facilities in a large new studio complex. The marketing of IBC is very good, and the company obviously has substantial backing. It pays a small tax on revenue and has a five-year contract, as agreed to by the National Investment Committee, ending in 1998. The company fears, however, an attempt to change the contract in the event of a change of government. It is expected to make an operating profit in 1995.

The other commercial operator, CTV9, transmits every evening for about five hours from a well-equipped studio with modern technology not available to TVK. There are five portable single cameras, two studio cameras, and one overworked VHS editing suite. About 80 people are employed at the station, which transmits on a 100 watt transmitter that is not strong enough to cover all of Phnom Penh; therefore, it is at a disadvantage compared with both IBC and TVK. CTV9's next financial priority is to obtain a ten kilowatt transmitter.

In programme terms, CTV9 has a reasonable news output, which, as with both the other channels, is widely viewed by the audience able to receive it. No reliable viewing figures are available. It transmits a high proportion of Chinese films compared to the others. There is a general shortage of Khmer language programmes, and each Khmer programme is aired many times.

When it started, it was as well, if not better, regarded by the audience than TVK, but that is no longer the case. The changeover to a commercial channel fighting for advertising revenue in a limited market is taking its toll. Like TVK, it charges only US$50 per minute for advertising, compared to IBC's US$300 per minute. It needs a stronger transmitter and a new injection of investment in order to maintain its early promise. Such a channel suffers strong commercial competition from both IBC and TVK, but the Phnom Penh economy is probably too weak as yet to sustain three terrestrial channels.

The Vacuum of Regional Broadcasting

Regional radio and television in Cambodia are in their infancy, whether in supplying the networks in Phnom Penh or in offering broadcasting services on a regional or local level. There is a critical need for more regional and local broadcasting. It is interesting to note that the important military and tourist area of Siem Reap, which has no local radio or television, no Cambodian television, and often suffers from bad reception of Phnom Penh's national radio service, can, nevertheless, receive very clearly the services of Star-TV from Hong Kong. Many of these programmes, such as international rugby, have little relevance to a community that has been left well behind in an age of satellite communications. The governor of the province feels strongly about the need for regional broadcasting to promote psychological warfare against the Khmer Rouge, while admitting that the local economy could not support commercial broadcasting. The problems of Battambang's radio station are an indication of why regional broadcasting is limited in scope. A staff of 31 people broadcast three hours a day from one studio on a 20 kilowatt medium-wave transmitter, which, in 1994, was operating on reduced power of 14 kilowatts and was in bad condition. The biggest problem for the station is the cost of fuel. Some 3 million Riel, out of the total expenditure of approximately 5 million Riel per month, is spent on fuel, and this in itself limits the number of hours it is possible to broadcast. During the mid-1993 pre-election period, the station was transmitting programmes during the early morning, lunch time, and evening hours for up to seven hours a day, but this effort exhausted available provincial budgets.

Power cuts effectively curtail the scheduling of both radio and television to the same hours each evening, from 6:30 until 9:30 p.m. Radio Battambang has one primitive studio, but it is no worse than the FM 90 premises in Phnom Penh. As with NRC in Phnom Penh, there is little understanding of modern broadcasting techniques.

Most of the tapes on TV Battambang are first transmitted on TVK and then sent by car from TVK in Phnom Penh. The station relies heavily on these programmes, as well as on the pirating of BBC and French television, but the staff of 27 produces 20 minutes of news each evening, again in a fairly primitive setting.

Radio and television in the provinces are in the process of being placed under the control of Phnom Penh. The advantage of this change is that the ministry is able, for the first time, to take a strategic view of Cambodian broadcasting as a whole, and it must take into account the fact that, currently, broadcasting outside the capital is severely limited in range. That strategic view must encompass local and regional radio and television. A community like Siem Reap should be able to talk to itself. It is very far from the capital, and its concerns are different. Phnom Penh should provide for the whole nation, and its other leading cities should attempt to cater to the people living in its diverse regions, particularly through the less expensive medium of radio.

Toward a Public Broadcasting Ethos

It is easy to bemoan the broadcasting situation in Cambodia in the current climate, but one has to plan for a hopefully peaceful future and the renewed probability of prosperity in a region of increased economic activity. If democracy and the rule of law strengthen their hold, it is possible to build a broadcasting structure in Cambodia that gradually distances itself from government and develops an ethos with important public broadcasting elements within it.

That ethos does not merely relate to the old BBC adage, "to inform, to educate, to entertain," but, in countries like Cambodia, it will have to be based on the need for national reconciliation and development programming. The requirement of national unity is obvious, following an era of national tragedy unsurpassed anywhere in the world since World War II. Working toward quality programming is going to be more difficult, because of the lack of production expertise. Yet that oldest form of communication, storytelling, is all the more potent when the stories are compelling listening and viewing. There is no shortage of stories to tell in Cambodia, whether transmitted in the form of news, drama, or documentary.

Public broadcasting in a democracy requires addressing the needs of the audience. The first priority is an information programming policy that the audience can trust. It follows that the spine of a broadcasting service, whether radio or television, should take the form of a news service independent of government, while resisting commercial influences, so that the public is fully informed, with due attention to accuracy and fairness, and subject only to limitations regarding national security, libel, privacy, taste, and decency. Failure to provide such a service, in an age of satellites when comparisons can be made and information stifled only with great difficulty, leads to the lack of the one thing essential to public broadcasting: credibility.

The second priority is education of a whole nation, and its importance to Cambodia is obvious. Development programming usually takes the form of advice on basic requirements in health, hygiene, and agriculture. In Cambodia, there is the overriding need to continue the campaign of mine-awareness. It is the only way to rescue its rich agricultural potential and limit the loss of human limbs. In addition, educational and women's programming is a high priority, given that so many intellectuals were killed under Pol Pot and that the population's majority is female.

Finally, the total programme schedule should embrace information, education, and entertainment programmes in order to provide a balanced diet, with programmes made as visual and as professional as possible. The one advantage of a nation's television service, whether provided by the state or private broadcasters, is that it can reflect the mosaic of its own communities to that nation in a way that is impossible for the global television services to do. Broadcasting, at its best, is often the reflection of the universal through the particular, and nothing is more relevant than the production of programmes about one's own people in one's own land – what the chairman of the European Broadcasting Union's programme committee, Geraint Stanley Jones, calls "a sense of place." That sense increases the more one has a policy of regional and community programming.

A public broadcasting ethos embracing these principles can only be established in Cambodia by constructing a broadcasting structure that takes maximum advantage of limited resources – financial, human, and technical. The economy is weak, human skills are at a premium, and the capital investment for modern technology is heavily dependent on donor aid. As always, the key is financing, and the broadcasting structure will eventually have to deal with this particular problem if there are to be real improvements in viewers' choice from the broadcasters of Phnom Penh. The creation of a quality public broadcasting schedule requires a higher level of expenditure on programming than an average commercial channel, since information and educational programmes are expensive to make. There are other extraordinary costs. One of the early tasks of the restructured management teams must be to prepare a set of personnel policies covering key areas such as recruitment, discipline, employee relations, performance appraisal, pay policy, and training. These need to be designed to attract, motivate, and retain employees who possess the ability, knowledge, energy, and commitment to carry out the tasks assigned to them. There is also a need for training at all levels of the media in Cambodia – management, journalism, general production, and technical training to supplement the almost heroic efforts of the newly established Cambodia Communications Institute, led by a lone Australian woman and backed by Danish and French investment.

Increased investment in public broadcasting can only be made available from three sources: maximizing advertising revenue, taxing the viewers, and/or taxing the commercial broadcasters – all well-known methods in established democracies. In Cambodia, taxing the viewer or listener through a licence fee is out of the question, because there is little hope of an efficient method of collection. A public broadcaster with a defined programme strategy, using the other two financial methods to sustain that strategy, has to have independence from government in order to establish its credibility. This is usually achieved through a board of governors, a commission, or authority established by Parliament or the government.

In a report to UNESCO in February 1994, recommendations were made to create an authority in Phnom Penh, which would be of particular relevance to the future of Cambodia. The recommendations entail the creation of an independent broadcasting commission, a board with the power to redistribute a proportion of private sector profits to the national broadcaster in order to develop competition and, therefore, the potential for increasing viewers' choice in a properly regulated environment (Price 1994).

It follows that the commission would regulate that environment by being held responsible for the future of the whole radio and television industry in Cambodia, allowing the current state broadcasting organizations to be separated from the ministry. It would also regulate the number of private stations in relation to what the market will bear. Conceivably, it could provide, in one stroke, both a political and economic solution to the structural problems facing the media. While it would be naive to expect any independent broadcasting commission to change the attitudes of politicians or broadcasters overnight, it could well represent a first stage in the creation of an independent and pluralistic media in Cambodia.

There are precedents for this method elsewhere. In the United Kingdom, the most recent example was the creation of Channel 4 in the early 1980s. The British government, reluctant to invest in a new channel, solved the problem by transferring the levy or taxes it was already raising from the commercial companies in the existing commercial branch of the system to the new Channel 4, which was devised as an alternative channel with a definite public broadcasting remit. It is public broadcasting subsidized by commercial broadcasting through an indirect diversion of institutional taxable income.

Although it is true that the state broadcaster competes with the commercial competitor for advertising income, in Cambodia, as in most other countries in the world, the state broadcaster is usually at a disadvantage, because the entrepreneurial motive is absent. Companies in the private sector are able to pay more to marketing staff, because all staff in the public sector are poorly paid civil servants. It can also attract more advertising revenue, because it can afford to buy foreign feature films with high production values at peak times. The public sector has little money for purchasing programmes. The fight over a limited advertising revenue in a poor economy is one which inhibits the growth of income for the Cambodian state broadcaster. In the absence of overseas donor aid in the area of operating expenditure, it is inevitable that maximizing revenue for public broadcasting can only be increased substantially in the longer run by taxing the private sector when it becomes profitable. The need for a strong private sector can, therefore, relate to competition in credibility, programme quality, and economics in a country searching for stability and economic growth. Ultimately, however, true public broadcasting will emerge only if the political will exists to make it work. In Cambodia, it will have to wait for civil peace.

References

Price, Gareth. 1994. *A New Beginning for Broadcasting*. Report on the Cambodia Media. UNESCO.

Shawcross, William. 1994. *Cambodia's New Deal*. Carnegie Endowment Publication, June.

UNESCO. 1991. *Communication and Information*. Report of the Inter-sectoral Basic Needs Assessment Mission, by Martin Hadlow. Doc. 19, chap. 5.

Latin America: Community Broadcasting as Public Broadcasting

Rafael Roncagliolo

Introduction

L atin America, unlike Europe, Africa, and Asia, is unfamiliar with the idea
of public service broadcasting. The countries in this region adopted radio
and television only a century after independence and release from
colonial domination. For that reason, they did not imitate European models
but looked to the commercial system of broadcasting in the United States. In
spite of this lack of a public tradition, a series of community radio and television stations have generated a different but genuine public broadcasting.
Therein lies the region's unique communication feature and its contribution
to a rethinking of public broadcasting.

A Unique Region

Latin America is a non-typical, perhaps exotic, region in terms of its radio and
television systems, for three reasons. First, because of the way its broadcasting

services were organized, non-commercial channels account for less than 10 percent of the transmissions and audiences. All of the region's countries have public radio stations, but some – like Ecuador and Paraguay – have no public television, even though in most of them radio and television broadcasting were introduced by the ministries of education.

Second, the transmission infrastructure and levels of consumption of radio and television messages are such that there is a wealth, rather than a paucity, of programmes. For example, Latin American countries averaged 500,000 hours of television transmission in 1988 – 444 percent more than European countries in the same year (Roncagliolo 1989). In addition, Venezuela, Colombia, and Panama have a higher ratio of VCRs to television sets than either Belgium or Italy. Bolivia has one of the world's highest ratios in television stations (75) to television sets (10,000) – a clear indication that the number of transmissions is not tied in with the degree of economic development. In Argentina, two out of every three families have cable television linkups, and there are more than 2,000 companies offering this service in the country.

Finally, the rapid growth of social movements and networks that utilize broadcasting media distinguish this region.

Community Radio and Television

Community radio broadcasting dates back to the 1940s, when Radio Sutatenza was created in Colombia, laying the groundwork for Accion Cultural Popular, the first systematic effort to use radio for education. This movement spread and was later consolidated through the Latin American Educational Radio-broadcasting Association (ALER). This interlinkage of radio and education is central to the idea of public service, and the ALER marked the birth of community media in Latin America.

During the same period, Bolivia's 1952 revolution spawned the birth of stations operated by miners, farmers, and the Catholic Church, inaugurating Latin America's tradition of community radio stations (Beltran 1994). It is important to recall that these pioneering radio stations emerged in association with social organizations and movements, thus making them an early and genuine expression of civil society.

During the 1960s, and above all in the 1970s and 1980s, the community radio and television movement spread, spearheaded by community and university stations. The formal emergence of non-governmental organizations made it possible to set up radio broadcasting stations that compete heavily for audience preference, as is currently the case with the Peruvian stations of Radio Cutivalu in Piura, Onda Azul in Puno, and Yaravi in Arequipa.

Community radio stations can be small and informal, consisting of networks of loudspeakers, or they can be fairly large, with even an urban or metropolitan coverage. Their distinguishing feature in all cases is their attitude toward, and aptitude for, furthering education and development.

These communication instruments were first organized into national and regional networks like ALER and, more recently, have been linked up in the World Association of Community Radio Broadcasters (AMARC), with members in all countries of the region.

Community groups quickly took advantage of video's appearance on the scene. So-called people's video groups successively undertook (1) video listing; (2) group videos; (3) video shows; (4) counter-information videos in countries under dictatorship; and (5) mass broadcasting videos (Roncagliolo 1991), thus ushering in community television stations that are taking hold throughout the entire region.

The Notion of Public Service

In Europe there has always been a clear-cut distinction between the economic profitability governing commercial ventures and the socio-cultural profitability motive behind public service undertakings. This dichotomy has never existed in Latin America, where state owned radio and television have, above all, been political instruments rather than oriented toward public service, and they have failed to have any effective socio-cultural impact.

Based on Latin America's experience, three different operational motives for broadcasting can be distinguished:

(1) The economic profitability motive, distinctive of commercial enterprises, in which communication is financed through advertising and the primary recipient market is subordinated to the secondary market of announcers who buy audiences;

(2) The political profitability motive, characteristic of government or party apparatuses that use broadcasting as an instrument of domination, manipulation, and imposition – in short, of power. This is the reasoning of authoritarian systems, and it is the hallmark of Latin America's state-owned media; and

(3) The socio-cultural profitability motive, the European ideal of public service, which in Latin America has been developed not by the state but by non-governmental organizations without commercial ends, through which civil society is organized and expresses itself.

Community radio and television are accordingly defined by the socio-cultural motive, which corresponds to the idea of service, and by the aims of strengthening democracy and achieving self-sustained development. This definition makes it possible to clarify the nature of this type of broadcasting. Community radio and television are not defined by legal status but by an operational motive. They can be registered as either public or private (university, regional, and municipal) enterprises. What is important is that they be non-profit enterprises without partisan aims.

Their size or coverage are not important. Their community nature does not mean necessarily that they are small or informal. In fact, the existing stations are striving to upgrade their technical standards, and those that are being set up, such as Radio Trinidad FM in Paraguay, seek to do so with proper equipment. Community ownership is also not equated with aesthetic poverty, bad quality, or boring programming. The discourse and denunciations that undoubtedly characterize these stations in their early stages of development rapidly give way to entertaining and playful communication that touches upon all aspects of human life.

The Achievement of Legal Status

Since 1993, the existence of these community media has begun to engender a series of legislative measures aimed at their legalization. Chile already has a law for radio stations with a minimum coverage, which authorizes a maximum FM wattage of one; it does, however, forbid the sale of advertising, which still constitutes a discriminatory measure. In Colombia, on the other hand, where a highly advanced democracy is upheld by its constitution, up to 500 watts are authorized, and advertising is permitted, but not for political propaganda. In Ecuador, community radio stations have legal status, with a maximum permitted wattage of 150 for FM and 250 for AM broadcasting. Paraguay also safeguards the rights of community radio stations, while in Brazil and Bolivia the Uniao de Redes Radiofonicas and Educacion Radiofonica, respectively, have reached advanced stages of negotiation for this purpose. In Mexico, a proposal has been put forward to create "citizen radio and television" stations.

In this way, the coexistence of private, public, and community stations, corresponding to each of the three sectors into which contemporary democracy is organized, is advancing on the radio and television broadcasting front in the region.

Community media have clearly gained their legitimacy, as was seen at a UNESCO conference on media and democracy held in Santiago, Chile, in May 1994. It is pertinent, in conclusion, to cite the first chapter of the "Plan of Action" adopted at the Santiago meeting:

1. Promotion of community media in rural, indigenous and marginal urban areas

A. Taking into account the increasing importance of community media in the democratic process in the region, to request the United Nations Educational, Scientific and Cultural Organization (UNESCO), with the assistance of professional organizations and research institutions, to survey the current situation of community media concerning legislation, frequencies, power limitations and advertising restrictions, with a view to making recommendations for the consideration of the governments concerned.

B. To request the International Programme for the Development of Communication (IPDC) of UNESCO and donor agencies to support projects for the creation of new community media, both print and broadcast, and projects aimed at strengthening existing community media in accordance with international norms, especially those media serving women, youth indigenous populations and minorities.

C. To call upon professional organizations and the regional and national representatives of international organizations involved in community development issues to encourage community media to exchange information among themselves and with other media. In so doing, they will contribute to the development of communication networks.

References

Beltran, Luis Ramiro. 1994. Neoliberalismo y communicación democrática en Latinoamérica: Plataformas y banderas para el tercer milenio. In *Nuevos Rostros para una Comunicación Solidaria*. Quito: OCIC-AL, UCLAP, UNDA-AL.

Registro Oficial. 1995. Organo del Gobierno del Ecuador, Ano III, no. 691, May.

Republica de Colombia. Ministerio de Comunicaciones. 1994. *Decreto Número 1695*.

Richeri, Giuseppe. 1988. *La televisión entre servicio público y negocios*. Barcelona: Gili.

Roncagliolo, Rafael. 1989. Adiós a las dicotomías. *Corto Circuito* 4 (May).

Roncagliolo, Rafael. 1991. The Growth of the Audio-visual Imagescape in Latin America. In *Video the Changing World*, edited by Nancy Thede and Alain Ambrosi. Montreal: Black Rose Books.

UNESCO. 1994. *Report*. Seminar on Media Development and Democracy in Latin America and The Caribbean, 2-6 May, Santiago, Chile.

CONTRIBUTORS

Marcus Breen is a consultant on multimedia and broadband services to the Department of Business and Employment, Victoria, Australia, and former Research Fellow at the Centre for International Research on Communication and Information Technologies, Melbourne.

Jean-Claude Burgelman is Professor of Media Policy and Director of the Centre for the Study of New Media, Information and Telecommunication at the Free University of Brussels, Belgium.

Nahum Gorelick is Director General of the Namibian Broadcasting Corporation.

Wolfgang Hoffmann-Riem is Director of the Hans-Bredow-Institute on Radio and Television Broadcasting, Hamburg, Germany.

Olof Hultén is the Head of Strategic Analysis in the Unit of Corporate Development at Sveriges Television, Stockholm, Sweden, and teaches in the Department of Journalism and Mass Communication at the University of Goteborg.

Karol Jakubowicz is Deputy Chairman of the Board of Directors of Polish Television in Warsaw, Poland.

Pierre Juneau is Chairman of the World Radio and Television Council and former President of the Canadian Broadcasting Corporation.

Charles Okigbo is Executive Coordinator of the African Council for Communication Education, based in Nairobi, Kenya.

Peter Perceval is a doctoral candidate and former researcher at the Centre for the Study of New Media, Information and Telecommunication at the Free University of Brussels, Belgium.

Gareth Price is Director of The Thomson Foundation, the international media training and consultancy organization based in Cardiff, UK, and formerly Controller of BBC Wales.

Marc Raboy is Full Professor and Director of the Communication Policy Research Laboratory in the Department of Communication, University of Montreal, Canada.

Rafael Roncagliolo is Director of the Instituto Para América Latina (IPAL) in Lima, Peru, and President of the World Association of Community Radio Broadcasters (AMARC).

Florangel Rosario-Braid is President and Dean of the Asian Institute of Journalism and Communication and Chair of Communication of the Philippines Commission for UNESCO.

Paddy Scannell is Reader in Media Studies in the Centre for Communication and Information Studies, University of Westminster, London, England, and an editor of *Media, Culture & Society*.

Shinichi Shimizu is the auditor of the Hoso-Bunka Foundation, Tokyo, Japan, and former Director of International Cooperation of the Japan Broadcasting Corporation (NHK).

Nikhil Sinha is Assistant Professor, Department of Radio-TV-Film at the University of Texas at Austin, USA.

Michael Tracey is Professor and Director of the Centre for Mass Media Research at the University of Colorado at Boulder, USA.

Olga V. Zernetskaya is Senior Scientific Researcher for the Institute of the World Economy and International Affairs, National Academy of Sciences of Ukraine, Kiev.